ORIGINS OF INTELLIGENCE

Infancy and
Early Childhood

Contributors

DORIS ALLEN, Department of Psychology, Einstein College of Medicine, Bronx, New York

BEVERLY BIRNS, Department of Education, State University of New York, Stony Brook, New York

MARION BLANK, Department of Psychology, Einstein College of Medicine, Bronx, New York

JEANNE BROOKS, Institute for Research in Human Development, Educational Testing Service, Princeton, New Jersey

PATRICIA A. DANIEL, Department of Psychology, Boston University, Boston, Massachusetts

MARK GOLDEN, Department of Education, State University of New York, Stony Brook, New York

JEANNETTE HAVILAND, Institute for Research in Human Development, Educational Testing Service, Princeton, New Jersey

MARJORIE P. HONZIK, Institute of Human Development, University of California, Berkeley, California

JANE V. HUNT, Institute of Human Development, University of California, Berkeley, California

MICHAEL LEWIS, Institute for Research in Human Development, Educational Testing Service, Princeton, New Jersey

ROBERT B. McCALL, The Fels Research Institute, Yellow Springs, Ohio

FRANK A. PEDERSEN, Social and Behavioral Sciences Branch, National Institute of Child Health and Human Development, Bethesda, Maryland

FREDA REBELSKY, Department of Psychology, Boston University, Boston, Massachusetts

SANDRA SCARR-SALAPATEK, Institute of Child Development, University of Minnesota, Minneapolis, Minnesota

INA C. UZGIRIS, Department of Psychology, Clark University, Worcester, Massachusetts

LEON YARROW, National Institute of Child Health and Human Development, National Institutes of Health, Bethesda, Maryland

JOHN WATSON, Department of Psychology, University of California, Berkeley, California

MARSHA WEINRAUB, Department of Psychology, Virginia Polytechnic Institute and State University, Blacksburg, Virginia

ORIGINS OF INTELLIGENCE

Infancy and Early Childhood

Edited by
Michael Lewis

The Infant Laboratory
Institute for Research in Human Development
Educational Testing Service
Princeton, New Jersey

PLENUM PRESS · NEW YORK AND LONDON

Library of Congress Cataloging in Publication Data

Main entry under title:

Origins of intelligence.

Includes bibliographies and index.
1. Intellect. 2. Developmental psychology. I. Lewis, Michael,
Jan. 10, 1937-   [DNLM: 1. Intelligence tests—In infancy and
childhood. BF431 069]
BF431.067   155.4'13   75-31530
ISBN 0-306-30867-3

First Printing - January 1976
Second Printing - July 1977

© 1976 Plenum Press, New York
A Division of Plenum Publishing Corporation
227 West 17th Street, New York, N.Y. 10011

United Kingdom edition published by Plenum Press, London
A Division of Plenum Publishing Company, Ltd.
Davis House (4th Floor), 8 Scrubs Lane, Harlesden, London, NW10 6SE, England

Printed in the United States of America

Preface

A preface is an excellent opportunity for an editor to speak directly to the reader and share with him the goals, hopes, struggles, and production of a volume such as this. It seems to me that I have an important obligation to tell you the origins of this volume. This is no idle chatter, but rather an integral part of scientific inquiry. It is important before delving into content, theory, and methodology to talk about motivation, values, and goals. Indeed, it is always necessary to explicate from the very beginning of any intellectual and scientific inquiry the implicit assumptions governing that exercise. Failure to do so is not only an ethical but a scientific failure. We learn, albeit all too slowly, that science is a moral enterprise and that values must be explicitly stated, removing from the shadows those implicit beliefs that often motivate and determine our results. No better or more relevant example can be found than in the review of the implicit assumptions of the early IQ psychometricians in this country (see Kamin's book, *The Science and Politics of IQ*, 1975). What might have been the result had we known their biases? What might have been the result had we known from the very beginning that their scientific quest was not one in which their values were removed, but in fact their hypotheses and their values were highly integrated? The comments that are to follow are an attempt to elucidate the reason for this volume.

The thought of this book occurred nearly fourteen years ago when I first became interested in the subject of infant mental activity. In the early 1960's there was relatively little work on the subject of infancy. When Jerome Kagan and I first set out to look at infant behavior, we had in mind the idea of studying infant mental abilities. The major question that we confronted was, "What do we mean by mental abilities?" Was there such a thing or things, and how might they be measured? We have both struggled with these questions.

Although I knew relatively little about infant intelligence tests, the notion of intelligence testing, specifically infant intelligence testing, was never one that particularly interested me. I chose instead to study particular cognitive functions of the infant and sought through this means to come to an understanding of mental activity. Specifically I chose to explore infants' attentional behavior with the hope of understanding through the infant's transactions with the environment what might be the structure and processes guiding some mental activities. From the outside, an important guiding premise has been to study the infant's changing behaviors as a function of demand characteristics of a situation in which he might find himself. The specific model that I chose was the attention paradigm. I chose to look at the organism's attending behavior—defined in a variety of ways—through the presentation of redundant information. From the results of these studies and others, one finds that the infant's attentive behavior declines as it interacts with redundant information. Moreover, when that information is altered, attentive behavior recovers. I saw in that paradigm and in the organism's changing transaction with its environment the basic feature of intelligence behavior, namely, the adaptation of the organism to its environment. Having undertaken these studies, it appeared important to determine the relationship between attending behavior and other measures of infant intellectual capacity. Supported by the National Science Foundation I undertook a longitudinal study in which attentive behavior, object permanence as measured on the Corman–Escalona Sensorimotor Scales, infant intelligence tests as represented by the Bayley, and language capacity as represented by the Peabody Picture Vocabulary Test, were all administered to groups of children in the first two years of life. The aim, quite frankly, was to show that attentive behavior to redundant and changing information was related to other measures of infant intelligence. To my surprise, several results emerged and it was in the emergence of these findings and their significance that the seeds of this volume were sown.

First, to my dismay, I found that the infant's attentive behavior bore no relationship to the infant's performance on the other intellectual tasks. However, when I looked carefully at the infant's performance on the Bayley, Object Permanence test, and language test, I found: (1) Within the first two years of life these tests were not highly correlated with one another. Thus a notion of a unitary concept of intelligence which could be tapped over a variety of different tasks was seriously questioned. (2) Within any particular task there was little individual stability over the first two years of life. Thus a child who performed well on object permanence at three months was not necessarily the child at 18 months or 24 months who likewise performed well. The same was true for the Bayley Mental Development Index. Parenthetically, the infant's attending task did show more individual stability than did either of these two other infant tasks.

These results confused and then shocked me. What did I mean by infant intelligence? What in fact did others mean by infant intelligence? The reviews of the literature on infant intelligence quickly revealed that our findings were not unique and in fact Bayley herself had written:

> The findings of these early studies of mental growth of infants have been repeated sufficiently often so that it is now well established that test scores earned in the first year or two have relatively little predictive validity.

With this rather late but startling insight, I began to explore the issue of infant intelligence. This exploration has led to the present volume.

The creation of this volume is motivated by the desire to come to understand what people think and study about when they think and study about infant intelligence and intelligence scores. What I wanted to do was a volume which would look at infant intelligence from a wide variety of perspectives—a biological perspective, a social perspective, a cognitive and affective perspective. By viewing infant intelligence from a multi-perspective in this way, the end result should be the emergence of a picture of a construct which could not possibly be obtained by its examination from any particular single perspective. Thus it seemed absolutely essential from the very beginning that a multi-dimensional perspective be given, because it was only through this perspective that one could come to view clearly this conceptualization. Simply stated, I wished to get the best people there were—in terms of their effort, interest, and knowledge—to examine the concept from the perspective they were most comfortable with. In that way, each perspective would have an advocate. There is no summary statement to be found in this volume. No one will do the work for the reader—it must be the reader himself interacting with each of these perspectives (and their sum) that will enable the emergence, successful or otherwise, of the concept that is being grappled with here. Thus in some sense it is a truly interactive process between the perspectives of the various authors and the mind of the reader.

As the contents of this volume make clear, the perspective is broad—the views personal and educated. Thus it is left to the interaction between the reader and this volume; the hope is for a clearer understanding of the concept of infant intelligence.

Finally, to Rhoda, Benjamin, and Felicia, who molded reason with love and who altered knowledge with experience, I dedicate this volume.

Princeton, New Jersey   MICHAEL LEWIS

Contents

1

*What Do We Mean When We Say "Infant Intelligence Scores"? A
      Sociopolitical Question* ----------------------------------- 1
MICHAEL LEWIS

2

A History of Infant Intelligence Testing ----------------------- 19
JEANNE BROOKS AND MARSHA WEINRAUB

3

Value and Limitations of Infant Tests: An Overview -------------- 59
MARJORIE P. HONZIK

4

*Toward an Epigenetic Conception of Mental Development in the
      First Three Years of Life* ------------------------------- 97
ROBERT B. MCCALL

5

Organization of Sensorimotor Intelligence ---------------------- 123
INA C. UZGIRIS

6

*An Evolutionary Perspective on Infant Intelligence: Species Patterns
      and Individual Variations* ------------------------------- 165
SANDRA SCARR-SALAPATEK

7

Early Learning and Intelligence -------------------------------- 199
JOHN S. WATSON

8

*Environmental Risk in Fetal and Neonatal Life and Measured
        Infant Intelligence* -- 223
JANE V. HUNT

9

Understanding "Why": Its Significance in Early Intelligence -------- 259
MARION BLANK AND DORIS A. ALLEN

10

Cross-Cultural Studies of Infant Intelligence --------------------- 279
FREDA REBELSKY AND PATRICIA A. DANIEL

11

Social Class and Infant Intelligence ------------------------------ 299
MARK GOLDEN AND BEVERLY BIRNS

12

*Looking Smart: The Relationship between Affect and Intelligence
        in Infancy* -- 353
JEANNETTE HAVILAND

13

The Interplay between Cognition and Motivation in Infancy -------- 379
LEON J. YARROW AND FRANK A. PEDERSEN

Author Index -- 401
Subject Index --- 409

1 What Do We Mean When We Say "Infant Intelligence Scores"? A Sociopolitical Question

MICHAEL LEWIS

The concept of intelligence—the belief that it is relatively easy to measure and that, as a monolithic construct, it is a useful predictor of subsequent human behavior—is firmly entrenched in the mind of Western man.

In any discussion of the construct it is necessary to define as precisely as possible what we mean when we say *intelligence*. This essay will attempt to do this. As a consequence of the discussion we will discover that this construct is rather frail. It lacks the strength usually associated with it in theory and therefore fails to support the elaborate superstructure based on the premise of its existence. Such a discussion must lead the reader into a serious consideration of the uses and misuses of the IQ score in a technological society.

THE CONCEPT OF INTELLIGENCE

In common with many others Burt *et al.* (1934) expressed a view of intelligence that is a good starting point for our discussion. Burt *et al.* viewed intelligence as a finite potential with which the individual is endowed at conception and that is subject neither to qualitative change nor to environmental influence. Finally, they believed intelligence is easily measured. This definition possesses a wide assortment of features

MICHAEL LEWIS · Educational Testing Service.

that must be carefully explicated. These features are specified:

1. There is a *single* factor called *g* that subsumes all mental activity.
2. *All* performance in mental activity can be predicted by this factor.
3. It is an easily measured factor.
4. This factor can be measured by the measurement of a subset of behavior.
5. This factor is innate.

Since we are interested here in a rapidly developing organism, we must consider a final feature derived from Burt's view:

6. Intelligence is not subject to qualitative change.

While these features can be discussed for organisms at any age, we will restrict our discussion here to the opening years of life, as our subject is infant intelligence.

A Single Factor

Probably no one feature is more central to the construct of intelligence than that it is a single potential, a single factor—often referred to as the *g* factor. Intelligence, therefore, is not like cognitive activity, since cognitive activity never has been considered a single capacity but rather a wide and varied set of skills.

Is there any basis in fact for this single-factor view of intelligence, especially in infancy? First, in order to understand the multifaceted nature of this question, it is necessary to consider how tests of intelligence are constructed. One central feature in test construction is the production of items and subtests that are related to one another and to the score on the test as a whole. Items are so constructed and eliminated that this may be the case. Thus if there are 10 test items, 9 of which are highly related to one another and to the total test score, the tenth item will be eliminated. It is no wonder that these tests have high interitem agreement as well as high split-half reliability (consistency); they are designed that way! Thus test construction perpetuates the notion of a single factor by the manipulation of items designed to produce just such an outcome.

More direct evidence comes from studies of infant performance on standardized tests of infant IQ. McCall *et al.* (1972) took great pains to find individual or factor item stability across tests and age; nevertheless they were forced to conclude that even with this type of analysis and the use of a variety of other multivariate techniques, the correlational relationship between different ages "remains modest and of minimal practical utility." In conclusion, they rejected the simple conceptualization of a g factor in infancy:

> The search for correlational stability across vastly different ages implies a faith in a developmentally constant, general conception of intelligence that presumably governs an enormous variety of mental activities. Under that assumption, the nature of the behavioral manifestations of g would change from age to age, but g itself is presumed constant, and this mental precocity at one age should predict mental precocity at another. Confronted with the evidence reviewed above, this g model of mental development must be questioned. (p. 736)

Perhaps if we turn from the standardized kinds of tests, such as the Bayley or the Gesell, to the more recent approaches suggested by the Genevan school, we can find a single factor of infant mental ability. It may be necessary to utilize Piagetian theory and explore tasks more closely related to sensorimotor development to find this factor. King and Seegmiller (1971) applied the Uzgiris and Hunt sensorimotor scales (1966) to 14-, 18-, and 24-month-old infants. The consistency of scores on these seven scales was compared across three ages, as was the relationship at 14 months across the different scales. Not only did the authors find relatively little consistency in terms of the correlations of scores (only 4 out of 24 possible correlations were significant) but they also found relatively little consistency across the various scales at a single age. Uzgiris (1973), in trying to understand the patterns of sensorimotor intelligence, measured a limited number of subjects' performance on seven subscales of the Uzgiris and Hunt (1966) sensorimotor intelligence scale. The most parsimonious explanation of her results was that there was almost no agreement between performance on one scale and performance on the others. Thus, even when we consider the nonstandard intelligence tests and look at sensorimotor development, at least as measured by the Uzgiris and Hunt scales, we find no evidence for a g factor.

Lewis and McGurk (1972) obtained and related three different types of infant intelligence tests. Infants were seen longitudinally from 3 to 24 months, at which time they received the Bayley Scales of Infant Development (1969) and the object permanence scale from the Corman and

Escalona sensorimotor scales (1969). In addition, at 24 months the children received a modified Peabody Picture Vocabulary Test in which both comprehension and production language scores were obtained. For the Bayley scales and the object permanence scales, the interage correlations proved to be relatively weak. Lewis and McGurk also observed the correlation between the Bayley and the object permanence scales at each age and between language development at 24 months and the Bayley and the object permanence scores at each age. In general the results failed to indicate any consistent pattern across the tests that might be likened to a g factor.

There is little consistency across different measures of intellectual functioning, for example, between the Bayley scales and the sensorimotor scales, and little consistency within the sensorimotor scales or across different factors such as those found by McCall *et al.* (1972) for the Gesell scales. The data, therefore, offer little support for the notion of a single g factor in infant intelligence.

The Predictability of Behavior

An important source of the glamour of intelligence scores is the belief that by knowing an organism's IQ score we also know a great deal about the organism's potential performance in all activities. IQ scores might not be important for some activities, but which ones? Presumably those activities not involving intellectual capacity. Here we encounter a difficulty: We believe, on the one hand, that IQ is an underlying general capacity predicting performance in some activities, but on the other hand we have no good theory to tell us which activities. Thus, if we believe carpentry involves intellectual activity, we must conclude that IQ scores will predict carpentry ability. On the other hand, if we do not think carpentry has intellectual components, then one's IQ should not predict his performance as a carpenter. Thus, to a large extent, what we believe falls within the domain of intellectual activity will determine how broadly our IQ can predict behavior.

Historically the IQ test was designed around school performance (see Chapter 2 by Brooks and Weinraub). Thus the high relationship between IQ and school performance is not a measure of the validity of the IQ construct but rather only an example of how a test can be constructed to predict performance in a particular type of activity. If we choose not to consider carpentry or hockey playing intellectual activity, there is no reason for IQ and performance in these skills to be related.

For the first time in this discussion it becomes apparent that we must choose specific criteria to define *intellectual activity* (a choice not based on any apparent scientific theory). These criteria should be as explicit as possible. Toward such a goal we might ask why school performance has been and continues to be the intellectual activity most related to IQ scores. That this is a reasonable relationship should be questioned.

Our doubts about the predictability of behavior from IQ scores are further reinforced by our knowledge that intelligence has not been shown to be a unitary factor. If this is indeed the case, by what logic could IQ test performance be related to all intellectual activity (given that we could logically define the domain)? It could well be that we have tapped only a certain portion of that intellectual domain by our test and at the same time related it to an activity within the domain but not within that portion tapped by the test. In such a case, there would be no relationship between IQ score and performance. Our everyday experience lends at least some face validity to the belief that this is indeed the case.

In terms of infant behavior the relationship between IQ performance and alternative intellectual behavior has received almost no attention. In a recent study Lewis and Lee-Painter (1974) related the Bayley intelligence performance scores of 100 twelve-week-old infants from a wide variety of socioeconomic backgrounds to their behavior in interaction with their mothers in a naturalistic home situation. The results showed that there were no significant relationships between performance on the Bayley intelligence scores and the infant behaviors as measured by the infant–mother interaction. Moreover, although infant IQ performance has been related to infant trauma (see Chapter 8 by Hunt), there is no evidence that infant IQ test performance is related to other infant intellectual activities. Finally, we have already discussed the findings indicating a lack of relationship between performance on a variety of different tests, all reporting to measure intellectual activity.

It is necessary to discuss one further set of findings having to do with infant IQ performance, namely, the relationship of test performance over age within infancy and test performance in infancy as related to older ages. Bayley (1970) has concluded, "The findings of these early studies of mental growth of infants have been repeated sufficiently often so that it is now well established that test scores earned in the first year or two have relatively little predictive validity" (p. 1174). Stott and Ball (1965), Thomas (1970), and McCall *et al.* (1972) have all reported relatively little predictive validity between the early scores of infant IQ and later measures of intelligence. One might argue that intelligence is stable but the behaviors in its service may vary in an ontogenetic fashion. Thus there may be no reason to predict consistency from epoch to epoch. McCall *et al.* (1972), in their structural consideration, give little support to such a view. Finally, it has been amply demonstrated that even within an epoch—within the first two years of infancy—there is little consistency in IQ performance (Lewis, 1973).

From logical as well as from empirical considerations we have reason to question the feature of intelligence that allows us to predict performance in activities from scores on IQ tests, even when the activities in question are themselves labeled as IQ tests. Our difficulties are only compounded when we consider activities not directly related to school performance. That school performance has been singled out as the criterion measure of intelligence is a historical accident with sociopolitical implications. Since, in our culture, success is so interwoven with school performance, it is no wonder that IQ seems to be predictive of a wide range of human activity. Unfortunately we have not seriously considered the relationship of intellectual activity to activities in general. This being the case, we cannot possibly review the predictability of IQ performance in terms of human activity. Until we are able to develop a taxonomy of human activity and are able to see the functional significance, intellectual or otherwise, of the activities organisms perform at each age, it will not be possible for us to talk about how accurately IQ scores predict performance in other activities involving intellectual capacity. Until our theory has caught up with our bias, it may still be necessary to select a carpenter for his carpentry skills rather than his IQ scores, as it may be important to select a teacher for his teaching performance rather than his IQ scores.

Measurement of IQ

The measurement of IQ is based upon a series of assumptions that must be reviewed. First, the criterion measure of intellectual behavior is

school performance. Thus the tasks and materials are designed around
the tasks and materials used in school. This design would be of little
concern if all that we were interested in was, in fact, school performance. Unfortunately we have not stopped at this point, but we have
chosen instead to generalize test performance to all mental activity, not
just school performance. As has already been discussed, we recognize
that we have not yet been able to define what we mean by *mental activity*.
This logical slippage is rather interesting, and it is necessary to question
its origin. While we have no answers to this problem, it is important to
determine historically why a test used as a measure of school performance became a test of general mental ability. Clearly the association
between school performance and mental ability is tenuous. The question
of what constitutes mental activity is by no means easy; perhaps this
explains the ready acceptance of school performance. If so, our scientific
inquiry has again given way to a nonscientific assumption.

This problem, difficult to solve for both adults and children, is made
more so when we consider infant mental activity. Simply put, how do
we measure infant mental ability? Reaching for a red ring hardly seems
to qualify as a mental activity, yet a careful survey of infant tests reveals
a wide variety of such items. As Yarrow and Pedersen (see Chapter 13)
and Haviland (see Chapter 12) have suggested, one might consider
many of the items in infant tests of mental activity to be motivational or
affectional in nature rather than mental. Moreover, test items have been
freely borrowed from test constructor to test constructor, giving these
items a high reliability, if no validity. Again our theory and empirical
evidence of what constitutes mental activity lag behind our test construction. A notable exception is Piaget, who has tried to explicate
mental activity. Unfortunately he has constructed a model that both
ignores and utilizes behaviors that he chooses to call nonmental. Thus
Haviland (see Chapter 12) quite rightly calls attention to the fact that
Piaget uses affectional responses to infer mental activities. It is interesting to note that with the growing influence of Darwin and ethology,
there is a renewed attempt to observe a wide variety of the young
organism's activities and responses. Such a methodology may well give
rise to a taxonomy of mental activity in the very young. This taxonomy
(since school performance cannot be used as its criterion) must be more
encompassing than the one constituted for school-age children. Thus for
the very young it may be possible to free ourselves from the constraint of
a school performance criterion of mental activity. As a result, however,

test items for infant mental activity may take on a rather strange appearance, such as nose-directed behavior in mirrors (see Lewis and Brooks, 1975) or surprise effects in a new social situation (see Lewis and Rosenblum, 1974).

It is clear that school performance cannot be the sole measure of intelligence. As we are able to rid ourselves of this bias, we will be able to include a wider range of test items. Historically the measurement of mental activity went from sensory capacities to activities related to school performance. It is now necessary that school performance give way to a large set of activities only just beginning to be considered. Thus we must explore the sociopolitical influences that dictate our scientific requirements (item selection) at any one point in time and use them to broaden our understanding. It may be that an authoritarian ideology requires tasks of rote memory, while an ideology of personal freedom requires tasks of creativity. This connection between ideology and the nature of tests of IQ must be explored.

Nature, Nurture, and Social Needs

The literature on the role of innate factors versus environmental influences is elaborate. We will not go into detail on this issue, since it has already received more space than it requires. It is our strong belief that the nature–nurture argument is an across-paradigm discussion resting on quite different views of the nature of man. We will follow Overton (1973) and argue that across-paradigm discussions do not lend themselves to easy solution and that the evidence for one paradigm does not negate the evidence for the other. More to the point, we will argue that the nature–nurture controversy on the nature of man is more a sociopolitical issue than a scientific one.

The nature–nurture controversy now centers on the issue of heritability coefficients. The index of heritability coefficients for performance on an IQ test has been estimated, at least for whites, to be as high as 0.80. Since we have spent a great deal of time arguing that IQ scores may have relatively little to do with the domain of mental activity, it would be foolish to argue that IQ scores, even if they are solely determined by heredity, would in fact mean that mental activity in general is so determined.

Scarr-Salapatek (1971) has presented ample evidence that a 0.80 heritability index for whites tells us little about the index for nonwhites and that it is not possible to talk of white–nonwhite differences as a function of heritability. However, the nature of this position still supports the heritability argument; the position merely argues that we do not have enough information to comment on individual or group differences. Implicit in the argument is that if we did know the heritability index of nonwhites, we could in fact speak to the IQ score differences as a function of race (or genetic pool, if we wish to be scientifically accurate). This heritability discussion has led us to believe that IQ performance as well as mental activity is possessed in the genes and that individual differences are also so determined. Let us quote from a recent article by Lee Cronbach (1975):

> The evidence is that differences among American or British whites in the past generation have been due in part to genetic differences. The precise proportion, but not the principle, of hereditary influence can be debated. If the statistic is an index of social-cultural conditions, not a biological inevitability, change the distribution of nutrition, home experience, and schooling in the next generation, and the heritability index will change. Findings on heritability within white populations tell us nothing whatsoever about how white and black groups would compare if their environments had been equalized. (p. 2)

Thus we are talking about sociocultural and political conditions, not issues of biology. In case this is not clear, let us continue the quotation:

> Note also that a high degree of heritability does not imply that in truth environment can have no effect. Even if the heritability index is as high as .80, two children with the same genotype may differ by as much as 25 IQ points if one is reared in a superior environment and the other in an unstimulating one. (p. 2)

Thus, given heritability coefficients and given an index as high as 0.80, two children can differ by 25 points on a standard test of IQ. Simply put, a person with an IQ of 95 (just average) and a 120-point child (a college graduate) may have the same genetic potential. It would seem, then, that IQ differences as differential measures of mental activity are as often as not a function of sociopolitical and cultural issues. Thus, to argue for heritability differences between individuals and groups (given an index of 0.80) and to base social policy on these indexes is to deny that differences can be accounted for by cultural as well as biological factors. Thus a heritability index or difference indexes still have nothing to tell us about the performance differences between two people or two groups. Why then our interest in heritability? The sociopolitical consequences of heritability appear to be more important than its scientific value, since to know a heritability index (even one as high as 0.80) is not to know the phenotypic outcome.

The Issue of Intervention

It has been argued that the success or failure of intervention programs in early childhood and infancy is an indicator of the effect of environment on the intellectual growth and capacity of the child. If a variety of intervention programs are shown to be ineffective, then intervention or environment *per se* is ineffective in altering the intellectual performance capability of the infant. If, on the other hand, the intervention procedures are effective, then changes in environment are a useful tool in altering intellectual performance. The use of intervention becomes highly relevant to the issue of infant intelligence and its ability or inability to change with time or situation. Indeed one might argue that this is the one important method for getting at the effect of environment on the infant's intellectual capacity.

We have already discussed some problems of measuring the effect of intervention by pointing out that infant intelligence cannot be considered a unitary construct measured by a single instrument. Moreover, it is necessary to match the evaluation of the intervention with the appropriate instrument. Thus, if one were affecting the object permanence capability in the young infant by such interventions as a peek-a-boo game and showing the child how to find hidden objects, then the type of measurement should not be a Peabody Picture Vocabulary Test or some other verbal task but rather a specific measure of sensorimotor capacity. Thus, if we are to use intervention programs as a means of assessing whether the infant's intellectual ability is fixed and unalterable by environment, we must match the nature of the intervention procedure to the criteria of effectiveness. This, unfortunately, is rarely done.

Of even more importance is the notion that all children can benefit from the same type of intervention procedure. This is a naïve view, yet, unfortunately, it is also widely held. Under this model every infant in an intervention procedure must receive the same treatment, for the sake of either "scientific objectivity" or technical simplicity. Thus every child is to watch a particular TV program or be instructed about a particular concept using a particular set of instructional materials. The popularity of this method is surprising since both the educational experience in the classroom and more recently the educational psychology literature have increasingly shown that children need different types of intervention programs to arrive at the same goal. Both children and infants, after all, come into the intervention procedure with different kinds of experience. The educational literature refers to the aptitude–treatment interaction or the subject–treatment interaction in discussing this issue. In order to reach the same goals it is often necessary to apply different kinds of intervention (have various curricula), dependent upon the characteristics of the child. In a review of this subject Berliner and Cahen (1973) make a strong argument for this position in educational programs and more importantly in the evaluation of their effectiveness. The evaluation of environmental effectiveness is one important way to consider the innate quality of infant intellectual capacity.

Let us look at an example of how we create difficulty by not considering the subject–treatment interaction and by not evaluating the effect of the child's experience on intervention programs. Assume that we have 100 children in intervention program A and that 10% of these children show increases in some measure of the effectiveness of intervention A. On the other hand, 90% show no effect or even show some negative effect of intervention A. When we look at the data of the experimental group averaged over all 100 children, we must conclude that intervention A was not a success. If we have 10 different intervention programs, each of them helping a different 10% of the experimental group, we would conclude that each of these programs failed to affect the measured capacity of these 100 children. Thus intervention *per se* seems ineffective in influencing the child's intellectual capacity. In fact, this is not the case. All 10 intervention programs succeeded in affecting the children's intellectual capacity but did not do so for the group as a whole. Thus across all 10 programs the intellectual capacity of all 100 children, at least of those that were supposed to be affected by the intervention procedures, did show improvement. However, when we look at mean data, we cannot locate any significant positive effect. This example argues most powerfully for a subject–treatment interaction design, both in terms of the nature of the program to be used and in terms of the evaluations of the effectiveness of that program. It becomes, then, the function of the experimenter, the curriculum developer, the evaluator, and the theoretician to find what conditions each individual child needs to optimize his intellectual capacity. Until such programs are initiated, it is not far wrong to conclude that intervention *per se* is ineffective or, further, that intellectual capacity cannot be altered by environmental change. This discussion makes it obvious that the methods of evaluation and the methods of intervention have not yet reached such a sophistication that they can be used as tests of the effect of the environment on infant intellectual capacity.

A final issue has to do with the nature and effort of our infant intervention programs. Remember that the hypothesis underlying intervention is that IQ can be affected by environmental factors. How is this general hypothesis tested? We wish to argue from the outset that those supporting an environmental position do so within conditions that restrict the opportunity for a significant effect. If intervention is, in fact, the test of the malleability of infant intelligence, why then are infant intervention programs so limited in their scope? It would seem that in order fully to test the hypothesis under discussion, large amounts of time, energy, and money per child should be invested in the intervention program. Thus a child and his family should receive as much money as necessary to change their total life style—for example, the housing, medical care, nutrition, and educational experiences for all the family. In other words, a complete and total program of environmental change. Instead, what is normally undertaken? Several hours a day, at the most, of a limited type of intervention program are provided, usually just for the infant. How can one argue for the hypothesis of malleability of IQ through environmental influence when the total environment is hardly affected—at least in terms of what we could think of doing? What underlies this limited strategy is the question of how IQ can be affected for the least amount of money. That is a sociopolitical issue and should not influence the test of the hypothesis. The first order of inquiry must be to test the general hypothesis; to do so, we must expend great quantities of time, effort, and money. Once it has been demonstrated that with the expenditure of unlimited resources and with a complete change of environment it is possible to alter intellectual capacity, the next question—and a sociopolitical one, at that—must be the cost of this change and the test of practicality for the society. However, to ask such questions prior to the test of the general hypothesis is both to interfere with the test of the hypothesis and to insert sociopolitical factors into the discussion of environmental influences on intellectual capacity.

Recapitulation: A Concept of Intelligence

Recall that at the outset we outlined several features that needed to be reviewed when the concept of intelligence is being considered. In our discussion of these features, we have tried to indicate that none of them is free from sociopolitical considerations. This is not surprising, for it would be naïve to believe that science in general and certainly psychology in particular is devoid of moral considerations. Science, although it may try, is not valueless but rather is value-laden. The task of the scientist is to expose the values so that their consequences will be apparent. When we fail to recognize the values in our scientific effort, we fall prey to blind ignorance. Kamin's (1975) exposé of the values of many of the scientists responsible for the current views and data on IQ should make this point all too clear. If it is true that the features inherent in the concept of IQ all have sociopolitical aspects, it may not be too strong to suggest that the IQ score is more a sociopolitical than a scientific construct. In the section to follow we explore the function of the IQ score.

The Use and Function of Infant IQ Scores

A review of the empirical research on infant intelligence tests supports the notion there is no consistency across or within age in a wide variety of tests purported to measure infant mental functioning. Therefore, the concept of a developmentally constant, general, unitary concept of intelligence is not very tenable. What do these conclusions imply for the notion that intelligence is "inherent or at least innate, not due to teaching or training and remains uninfluenced by industry or zeal" (Burt et al., 1934)? Such a model of human capacity must clearly be dealt a severe blow by a review of the infancy literature. And yet such a conception of man remains and tests continue to be sold and taken. While these intelligence scales have been acknowledged to have limited function, they still are widely used in clinical settings in the belief that, although lacking in predictive validity, they provide a valuable aid in assessing the overall health and developmental status of babies at the particular time of testing (see Chapter 8 by Hunt). This procedure is justified only if the scores are regarded solely as measures of present performance, not as indicators of future potential. What this "present performance" may mean is questionable, since superior performance may be followed by poor performance. For example, Bayley (1955) shows a negative correlation of 0.30 between males' early test behavior and their IQ at 16–18 years. Just as infant scales are quite invalid as measures of future potential, it is also unlikely that they properly assess a child's current performance *vis-à-vis* the other children, except when extreme samples of dysfunction are utilized.

Concurrently intelligence test scores are widely used as a criterion measure in the evaluation of infant intervention or enrichment programs. The experimental subjects are compared to the control subjects in terms of their performance on intelligence tests. If the scores of the experimental group are higher than those of the control group, the program is evaluated positively; if not, it is evaluated negatively. Implicitly assumed is that infant intelligence is a general, unitary capacity and that mental development can be enhanced as a result of an enrichment experience in a few specific areas. Similarly it is assumed that infant scales are adequate to reflect an improvement that occurs in competence as a consequence of a specific enrichment experience. However, as our previous discussion has made clear, infant intelligence—or intelligence at any age, for that matter—as a general unitary capacity is highly questionable. Moreover, that infant skills are adequate to reflect improvement from specific enrichment experiences must also be questioned, since a variety of infant skills tested shows relatively little interscale or intrascale consistency.

Thus the data on infant intelligence tests also cast doubt on whether the scores can be generalized beyond the particular set of abilities or factors sampled at the time of testing. An infant who showed dramatic gains in testing involving sensorimotor function would not necessarily manifest such gains in tests involving verbal skills. The implication of these conclusions for a wide variety of evaluation policies concerning infant intervention must be considered. For example, infant intelligence scales, no matter how measured, are quite unsuitable instruments for assessing the effects of specific intervention procedures, primarily because infant intelligence is not a general unitary trait but is rather a composite of skills and abilities that do not necessarily covary. Such a view of intelligence is by no means new (see for example, Guilford, 1959), but it is one that must be repeatedly stated in order to counteract the tendency to utilize simple and single measures of infant intelligence. An example can be used to clarify this issue.

Consider an intervention procedure that is designed primarily to influence sensorimotor intelligence—for example, the development of object permanence. An appropriate curriculum must involve training infants in a variety of peek-a-boo and hide-and-seek tasks. According to the data presented, a standard infant intelligence scale would be the wrong instrument to use in assessing the efficiency of such a program and is likely to lead to erroneous conclusions concerning the program's efficiency. Even more serious is the possibility that by using the wrong instrument of evaluation over a large number of programs, one would erroneously conclude that intervention in general is ineffective in improving intellectual ability, thus supporting the genetic bias that environment is ineffective in modifying intelligence. There are few who would suggest that schoolchildren should be administered a standard intelligence test after a course in geography. Yet such a procedure would be exactly analogous to using an intelligence test to measure the success of teaching the object permanence concept to the infant. The success of a geography course is best assessed by a test of geographical knowledge, and by the same token the success of a program stressing sensorimotor skills is best assessed by specific tests of sensorimotor ability. In both cases there may in some instances be improvement in intelligence test scores. But such improvement has to be regarded as fortuitous.

The general view that intelligence is a unitary construct and easily measured cannot be supported by the data. Why then should this view of intelligence hold such a dominant position in the thinking of contemporary scientists and public alike? The answer to such a question may be found in a consideration of the functional use of the IQ score in a technological society. The function of the IQ score is and has always been to help stratify society into a hierarchy. The purpose of this hierarchy is to create a division of labor within the culture—that is, to determine who will go to school in the first place, who will get into academic programs that lead to college, etc. These divisions, in turn, determine the nature of labor the child will perform as an adult and, in turn again, will determine the child's socioeconomic status and his social, economic, and political position in the society. This division of labor and, as a consequence, the division of goods and services available to those who succeed are a necessity in a complex society. This stratification is then justified by scores on a test designed to produce just such a stratification. If we cannot make the claim that IQ differences are genetically determined, then we must base them on differences in cultural learning. But these differences in cultural learning, for the sake of the division of labor, are exactly what the IQ tests are intended to produce. The hierarchy of labor is thereby maintained by the genetic myth. The hierarchy produces the test differences and the test differences are used to maintain the hierarchy. Thus IQ scores have come to replace the class systems or feudal systems that previously had the function of stratifying society and distributing the goods and wealth of that society. Whereas these earlier systems were supported by the invoking of constructs having to do with the Almighty, the present system invokes Mother Nature instead. In any social system in which stratification is necessary in order to distribute the wealth of that society in a disproportionate fashion, some sort of stratifying device is necessary. The 20th-century technological society's stratification device has become the intelligence test. As such the intelligence test rests more upon its function for distribution of wealth than on its scientific merit.

REFERENCES

BAYLEY, N., 1955, On the growth of intelligence, *American Psychologist, 10*: 805.

BAYLEY, N., 1965, Comparisons of mental and motor test scores for ages 1–15 months by sex, birth order, race, geographical location and education of parents, *Child Development, 36*: 379.

BAYLEY, N., 1969, "The Bayley Scales of Infant Development," Psychological Corporation, New York.

BAYLEY, N., 1970, Development of mental abilities, *in* "Carmichael's Manual of Child Psychology," Vol. 1, P. Mussen (ed.) Wiley, New York, p. 1163.

BERLINER, D. C., AND CAHEN, L. S., 1973, Trait-treatment interactions and learning, *in* "Review of Research in Education," Kerlinger (ed.), Peacock, Itasca.

BURT, C., JONES, E., MILLER, E., AND MOODIE, W., 1934, "How the Mind Works," Appleton-Century-Crofts, New York.

CORMAN, H. H., AND ESCALONA, S. K., 1969, Stages of sensorimotor development: A replication study, *Merrill-Palmer Quarterly, 15*: 351.

CRONBACH, L. J., 1971, Five decades of public controversy over mental testing, *American Psychology, 30*:1.

GUILFORD, J. P., 1959, Three faces of intellect, *American Psychologist, 14*:469.

HUNT, J. McV., AND UZGIRIS, I. C., 1966, Scales of perceptual cognitive development, unpublished manuscript, University of Illinois.

KAMIN, L. F., 1975, "The Science and Politics of IQ," Halsted Press Division of Wiley, New York.

KING, W., AND SEEGMILLER, B., 1971, Cognitive development from 14 to 22 months of age in black, male, first-born infants assessed by the Bayley and Hunt–Uzgiris scales, presented at the Society for Research in Child Development meetings, Minneapolis.

LEWIS, M., 1973, Infant intelligence tests: Their use and misuse, Human Development, 16:108.

LEWIS, M., AND BROOKS, J., 1975, in press, Infants' social perception: A constructivist view, in "Infant Perception: From Sensation to Cognition," L. Cohen and P. Salapatek (eds.), Academic Press, New York.

LEWIS, M., AND LEE-PAINTER, S., 1974, Mother–infant interaction and cognitive development, paper presented at the Eastern Psychological Association meetings, Philadelphia.

LEWIS, M., AND McGURK, H., 1972, The evaluation of infant intelligence: Infant intelligence scores—true or false? Science, 178(4066):1174.

LEWIS, M., AND ROSENBLUM, L. (eds.), 1974, "The Origins of Fear: The Origins of Behavior," Vol. 2, Wiley, New York.

McCALL, R. B., HOGARTY, P. S., AND HURLBURT, N., 1972, Transitions in infant sensorimotor development and the prediction of childhood IQ, American Psychologist, 27:728.

OVERTON, W., 1973, On the assumptive base of the nature–nurture controversy: Additive versus interactive conceptions, Human Development, 16:74.

SCARR-SALAPATEK, S., 1971, Race, social class and IQ, Science, 174:1285.

STOTT, L. H., AND BALL, R. S., 1965, Infant and preschool mental tests: Review and evaluation, Monographs of the Society for Research in Child Development, 30(Serial No. 101).

THOMAS, H., 1970, Psychological assessment instruments for use with human infants, Merrill–Palmer Quarterly, 16:179.

UZGIRIS, I. C., 1973, Patterns of cognitive development in infancy, Merrill–Palmer Quarterly, 19:181.

UZGIRIS, I. C., AND HUNT, J. McV., 1966, An instrument for assessing infant psychological development, unpublished manuscript, University of Illinois.

WECHSLER, D., 1949, "Wechsler Intelligence Scale for Children," Psychological Corporation, New York.

WECHSLER, D., 1955, "Wechsler Adult Intelligence Scale," Psychological Corporation, New York.

2   *A History of Infant Intelligence Testing*

JEANNE BROOKS
AND MARSHA WEINRAUB

The infant intelligence test, like all other psychological tests, has its roots in the intelligence testing movement of the late 19th and early 20th centuries. If we are to understand the rise of infant testing, it must first be put in the perspective of the testing movement itself. Infancy was never the focus of the early test developers and was only studied because *idiots*, the lowest classification of the mentally retarded, were thought to exhibit the mental abilities of a 2-year-old (Binet and Simon, 1905). However, infants were not entirely neglected, as the child study movement led by Darwin and Preyer resulted in an interest in the early development of the species. As the testing movement gained momentum and branched out into more areas in the 1920s, a series of investigators in America began intensive studies of infants and preschoolers. This study ultimately led to the development of normative scales and intelligence tests such as those developed at Yale, Minnesota, Berkeley, and Iowa. These tests, appearing in the late 1920s and early 1930s, gained widespread acceptance and they led to a series of studies on the stability of scores from month to month, the test–retest reliability from testing to testing, and the predictive validity from infancy to childhood.

The following discussion is an attempt to delineate the early developments in infant intelligence testing. The topics outlined in the preceding paragraph will be discussed in the belief that this knowledge will illuminate the infant testing movement of the 1970s and the issues raised in this volume.

JEANNE BROOKS · Educational Testing Service.
MARSHA WEINRAUB Virginia Polytechnic Institute and State University.

INTELLIGENCE TESTING IN THE NINETEENTH CENTURY: HISTORY AND ORIGINS

The fervor of the scientific community in Western Europe in the late 19th century made it an exciting time. Advances in medicine, the surge of interest in evolution, humane concern for the mentally deficient and the insane—all were widely discussed. The variety and richness of interests in the scientific community resulted in a favorable atmosphere for the growth of mental testing. At the outset different outlooks were characteristic of different countries as testing in Germany, France, England, and America sprung from different milieus. As cross-fertilization and adaptation occurred, the strong national flavor subsided, ideas converged, and the rapid acceptance of the Binet tests and the development of other tests occurred.

The French Interest in Mental Retardation and Diagnosis

That there are differences among persons with respect to intellect as well as physiognomy has long been recognized. Mythology abounds with references to such differences in beasts and man, and the Greeks were said to have destroyed so-called inferior individuals in infancy (Peterson, 1925). Physiognomy and especially phrenology were believed to be correlated with deficiencies, both intellectual and emotional. This belief has been held throughout the history of Western civilization.

Prior to the 1800s mental deficiency and insanity were not differentiated. The first attempt to differentiate them was made by Esquirol, a French doctor who, in his 1838 treatise on mental illness, stated that:

> Idiocy is not a disease but a condition in which the intellectual facilities are never manifested or have never been developed sufficiently to enable the idiot to acquire such amount of knowledge as persons of his own age reared in similar circumstances are capable of receiving.

Not only did Esquirol differentiate between mental retardation and insanity, but he anticipated several later developments in the study of mental retardation. First, he realized that there was a continuum from normalcy to idiocy and that retardation was not an all-or-none phenomenon. Second, in his attempt to classify mental retardates (and he was the first to do so), he used language capability as his classification criterion, not measurements of sensations or physiognomy. The use of speech as the best predictor of intelligence was not mentioned again until 1918, when Terman essentially reiterated Esquirol's statement about language (Goodenough, 1949; Terman et al., 1918).

At the same time that the French medical community was distinguishing between the mentally deficient and the insane, a controversy arose about the educability of the former. Esquirol himself did not believe that the retarded would benefit from training, which was the stance taken by most of the Paris medical community. Some 30 years before Esquirol's treatise appeared, Itard had published his accounts of the wild boy of Avergnon (1801, 1807, translated by Humphrey and Humphrey, 1938), whom he had spent five painstaking years trying to train. Although the boy improved dramatically, he was not able to function in society and Itard felt he had failed.

However, Itard's failure was not regarded as such by the entire French scientific community (Goodenough, 1949; Seguin, 1907 edition). In fact, Itard's student, Seguin, started a school for the mentally deficient in 1837 in the belief that training was possible. His program was a huge success, as his students did learn, albeit within certain limitations. Visitors came from all over the world and upon returning to their countries opened similar schools. By 1870 there were 80 schools for the mentally retarded throughout the Western world (Goodenough, 1949).

Although schools were being opened at a fast rate, there were no universal or empirically based criteria for the evaluation of mental deficiency. As a result, of course, admission procedures were quite arbitrary. As Binet said, upon surveying the admission criteria at a number of schools and institutions in France, "We have compared several hundreds of these certificates, and we think we may say without exaggeration that they looked as if they had been drawn by chance out of a sack" (Binet and Simon, 1907, translated by Drummond, 1914). Thus the need for a reliable and valid diagnostic procedure was recognized by the French medical and pedagogical community in the late 19th century. However, nothing was done until 1904, when the Minister of Public Instruction in Paris appointed a commission to study the question of special education.

Binet was part of this commission, which authorized the development of a mental test to be given to schoolchildren in Paris to identify those who would benefit from special education. Binet was not a clinician but an experimental psychologist, who had studied mental functioning in normal children for at least 10 years before the appearance of his now-famous test. However, Binet had always been interested in retardation and even wrote a book on the subject (Peterson, 1925), although he was not involved in retardation research until 1900. In 1900 Simon, under Binet's direction, gave anthropometric tests to both mentally retarded and normal boys, but these tests failed to distinguish between the two groups (Peterson, 1925; Simon, 1900).

The French concern about mental deficiency and diagnosis, of course, ultimately led to the Binet tests. Concern about individual differences in mental functioning was not limited to France, however.

Evolutionary Theory and the Testing Movement in England

In England, during this time, Charles Darwin was developing his revolutionary theory of evolution, which he presented in his influential *Origin of Species* (1859) and in the *Expression of the Emotions in Man and Animals* (1872). The idea that intra- as well as interspecies variation might be due to evolutionary forces and intimately tied to the biological makeup of individuals was the catalyst for the work of Galton. Galton, who happened to be a cousin of Darwin, noticed that eminence ran in families; this observation was easily related to the notion of evolution and human variation. Galton's book *Hereditary Genius*, published in 1869, traced the inheritance of genius in families. When Galton's interests in both intelligence and individual differences became coupled with a belief in the efficiency of quantitative measurement, he opened a testing laboratory in the South Kensington museum in 1882, where anyone could take a variety of anthropometric tests for a small fee. It was thought that such measurements might be related to mental functioning. Galton's contributions to the testing movement were enormous, as he pioneered work regarding the genetic inheritance of intelligence, individual differences in general, and the quantification of psychophysiological abilities.

In addition, the work of Darwin and Galton generated interest in the development of certain abilities and behaviors in children. It was thought that the origins of behavior might be elucidated by a study of ontogenetic development. One of Darwin's theses, of course, was that facial emotions were not learned but were biological in nature (1872). What better way to study this than to watch the development of emotions in young children! A number of scientists, including Darwin himself, did just that, and numerous diaries and records of infant development were published (e.g., Darwin, 1877; Preyer, 1882; Shinn, 1900; Stern, 1914). These studies clearly showed both that there were developmental behavior sequences and that at the same time there were individual differences in rates of development (Goodenough, 1949). These diaries were carefully read by the developers of infant intelligence tests in the 1930s and provided many ideas for test items (Buhler, 1930; Buhler and Hetzer, 1935; Shirley, 1933).

Germany and the Psychology of Sensation

The psychology of sensation and perception reached its greatest heights in Germany, making the German laboratories very different from those in France and England. Individual differences were seen as sources of errors, not a legitimate area of study. However, even in the most controlled conditions, individual differences still appeared. Cattell, while working under the direction of Wundt, became interested in this phenomenon. Although Wundt was said to disapprove (Peterson, 1925; Cattell and Farrand, 1896), Cattell did his dissertation on individual differences in college students.

The fact that the Germans could not eliminate individual differences had an important effect on the testing movement. As Goodenough (1949) stressed:

> . . . the work of the psychophysicists served to point out the need for a different kind of psychological research by their very failure to account for all the sources of variation in responses. (pp. 30–31)

Early Tests of Intelligence

Even though 19th-century German psychology was not conducive to the testing of individual differences, in the 1890s there was a flurry of test development in Germany as well as in the rest of Europe. Series of tests were developed in America and Germany both for school-age children (Boas, 1891, as cited in Peterson, 1925; Gilbert, 1894; Munsterberg, 1891) and for college students (Cattell, 1890; Kraepelin, 1895; Jastrow, 1892). It was Cattell (1890) who first introduced the term *mental tests* in his article "Mental Tests and Measurements." The tests developed at this time included a series of tasks that measured, among other things, sensory, anthropometric, and memory functions, as well as reaction times and imagery. An underlying assumption of the test developers in the 1890s was that intelligence was related to the simpler sensory and memory functions. Cattell spoke for many in the early testing movement when he said that the "measurements of the body and of the senses come as completely within our scope as the higher mental processes" (Cattell and Farrand, 1896).

There were critics of this view, the most vocal being Binet. In the first issues of L'Année Psychologique, a journal begun by Binet in 1895, Binet criticized the German and American tests as being too sensory in nature. Instead of the choice of the most simple functions as measures of intelligence, he argued that higher mental functions should be measured since they are more likely to differentiate between persons (Binet and Henri, 1895, 1896). Binet and Henri listed memory, attention, and comprehension as 3 of the 10 mental functions that they felt should be studied.

Binet's advice was not followed, however, and the testing movement lost its momentum. Peterson (1925) suggested that disillusionment in testing was in part due to the fact that two widely publicized studies found no relationship between the current mental tests and school performance (Wissler, 1901; Sharp, 1898–1899). Even though the failure in the Cornell laboratory was due to the homogeneity of the students tested (all were graduate students) and the failure at Columbia was probably due to the sensory nature of the tests, the American interest in testing temporarily subsided.

Binet and the Development of the 1905 Scale

Binet, however, continued his work on the development of mental tests. His studies, which were usually conducted with normal, school-age children, were published in the journal L'Année Psychologique. A study of the journal from its inception in 1895 to the early 1900s shows Binet gradually moving away from the measurement of "simple" tasks and toward the measurement of more complex mental tasks. This occurred because, in study after study, performance on the sensory and physical tasks did not increase systematically with age, and the tasks related neither to one another nor to school performance. Binet, in the

French tradition of practicality, found it easier to reject concepts that proved fruitless than did his German and American counterparts. His well-known definition of intelligence, for example, reflects his increasing interest in complex mental function: "To judge well, to comprehend well, to reason well, these are the essentials of intelligence. A person may be a moron or an imbecile if he lacks judgment; but with good judgment he could not be either" (Binet and Simon, 1905a, p. 196).

The 1905 scale, then, grew out of this earlier work, which had already discarded the sensory and physical tasks for the more complex mental tasks; it also de-emphasized frequency tests, introduced more pass/fail items, and included items increasing in difficulty. The 1905 scale was commissioned by the Paris committee to find the children in the Paris schools who were eligible for special education. It included 30 items that were suitable for children ranging from idiocy to normalcy in intellectual ability. The items were either passed or failed and, although not age normed, distinguished among the three classes of retardation and between retarded and normal intellectual ability. The first 6 items covered the competencies available to idiots and to normal infants up to 2 years of age. The first item was following a lighted match with the eyes and head, the fourth was making an appropriate choice between a piece of wood and a piece of chocolate, and the sixth was following simple orders and imitating gestures. Fifty normal children aged 3 to 11 and an unspecified number of retarded children in both schools and institutions were used in the standardization sample.

The 1905 scale was the first test of its kind and revolutionized the testing movement. Intelligence would no longer be conceptualized as reducible to simple sensory tests. With this test the concepts of mental-age levels and unitary test scores became firmly established, despite the fact that Binet himself was not totally enamored of the concept of a single score.

Intelligence Testing Following the 1905 Scale

After the introduction of the first Binet scale, there were a number of revisions made by both Binet and others. Binet's own revisions appeared in France in 1908 (Binet and Simon) and 1911, while Goddard translated the 1908 scale into English in 1910 and Kuhlmann modified the same scale for use in America in 1911.

Mental testing was quickly adopted by the educational community. The value of the Binet tests had been recognized immediately by those in special education. Goddard (1910a,b, 1911), at the Vineland Training School in New Jersey, had been searching for a diagnostic test when he discovered the 1908 Binet scale. He adopted it immediately and gave it to hundreds of children in his institution and in the public schools in Vineland. The interest in special education and the problem of diagnosis led to the widespread use of the Goddard version of the Binet test in diagnostic and educational settings. This test was widely used until the Stanford–Binet appeared and was adopted in 1916 as the result of Terman's research.

At the same time conditions in the educational system also led to a rapid acceptance of testing. At the turn of the century compulsory education up to the age of 13 or 14 was prevalent in many states. Although progressive in nature, these laws affected the slow learner adversely. The child with limited intellectual capacity was left in the lower grades for longer and longer periods of time as the compulsory age increased. The U.S. Bureau of Education reported in 1908 that the percentage of children who were more than three years below age grade level ranged from over 20% in Birmingham to 6–10% in Detroit, Philadelphia, and Los Angeles (Strayer, 1911, also quoted in Goodenough, 1949). These children certainly were not benefiting from more schooling. Concern with the conditions led to the establishment of special classes within the public school system, which, of course, raised the question of diagnosis.

Testing also had advocates in the scientific community, as the tests developed by Terman and Kuhlmann indicate. Much of the interest in the testing of children was generated at Clark University under G. Stanley Hall. Goddard, Terman, and Kuhlmann all studied with him, although it was said that Hall opposed the study of mental tests (Peterson, 1925).

Early Interest in Infant Testing

Testing of school-age children was firmly established in 1910, but what about testing of children under 3 years of age? Pedagogical demands were for diagnostic instruments for the school-age and not the preschool child. Thus there was little interest in testing the preschool child. Nevertheless there were some attempts to measure mental development in infancy.

Binet, for example, included items for children in the first years of life and for idiots in the 1905 scale, but he excluded them in the 1908 and 1911 revisions. Goddard's revision did not include items for young children, although Kuhlmann's did. The 1916 Stanford–Binet (Terman, 1916), which became the standard mental test, had no items for the preverbal child.

Even though no infant intelligence tests were developed in the early 1900s, there were indications that the testing of infants might be of interest. First, the diaries of men such as Darwin on early development suggest that infancy was seen as an important and valid topic of study. Second, the social welfare movement was also coming of age in the 20th century. As adoption of children increased, so did the need for early diagnostic instruments.

Lack of interest in infant testing is well illustrated by the relatively unknown work of a New Orleans medical doctor. In 1887 an article on the testing of children up to 3 years of age appeared in the *New Orleans Medical and Surgical Journal*. Chaille, the author of the article, had devised a test that predated Binet's by eight years on a number of important developments, such as the concept of mental age. This test never received any attention, probably because it was published in a local journal and was too advanced for its time (Goodenough, 1949).

The Development of Infant Intelligence Tests

Infant Testing in the 1920s

As the concept of intelligence was redefined and reexamined, so too were notions regarding the constancy of intelligence through the life span. According to Goodenough (1928b), it had been generally assumed that the IQs of preschool children were as stable over time as the IQs for school-age children. However, with the growing interest in the 1920s in the preschool child and the effects of nursery school, this assumption came into question. Tests were needed to investigate empirically the constancy of IQ from the preschool period through adulthood. Thus most of the new tests developed in the 1920s were further revisions and extensions of Binet's original test to provide for the measurement of the mental development of preschool children. Burt (1921) produced an English revision that measured intelligence from 3 years of age and older. The Yerkes, Bridges, and Hardwick Point Scale, originally introduced in 1915 for children 4 years and older, was revised and extended downward in 1923.

Because of difficulties of finding representative samples of infants, the limited behavioral repertoire of the infant, and the lesser practical importance of testing infants, infant testing received limited attention at this time. Only three infant tests were published in the 1920s.

In 1922 Trabue, an educator, and Stockbridge, an author and journalist, introduced the Mentimeter. The Mentimeter was a comprehensive system of tests calculated to measure inherited mental ability at all ages. It was to be used by parents, employers, and teachers, as well as anyone interested in self-knowledge and self-improvement. The tests were unusual in that they included tests for infants. There were three items each at the 3- and 6-month levels, three items at 1 year and six items at 3 and 4 years. These items tapped various aspects of muscular control, imitation, language production, and language comprehension. Administration was informal, the tests were not standardized, and reliability and validity were not assessed. These tests were not influential in the infant testing movement, probably because they were intended for a lay audience. Nevertheless their appearance demonstrated the great popular concern with testing at all levels, and they forecast the types that were eventually adopted in the area of infant testing.

The first serious professional attempt to measure mental development in infancy was Kuhlmann's (1922) second revision of the Binet–Simon scale. Kuhlmann both revised the scale and extended it downward to include five items for each of the following age groups: 2, 6, 12, 18, and 24 months. The new test included measures of coordination, imitation, recognition, and speech. As with other intelligence tests of the day, a mental age was calculated and IQs could also be obtained. According to Stott and Ball (1963), only a small sample of children were tested at the preschool and infant levels; these small samples were probably unrepresentative, judging from the high IQs that were obtained.

The Kuhlmann infant tests were never widely used. For example, in Goodenough's (1928a) validation study of the test, there were no children under 18 months included in the sample of nearly 500. Though Goodenough recognized that preschool testing was an important and a promising area of research, her conclusion that the currently available tests for preschool children were not "sufficiently refined to render them serviceable for use in the solution of problems for which a high degree of precision is necessary" (p. 127) may have been responsible for the relegation of the *entire* scale—infant as well as preschool measures—to obscurity. Other reasons the Kuhlmann–Binet scale may have been abandoned are incorrect placement of items (Goodenough, 1928a; Driscoll, 1933) and inadequate standardization of tests (Driscoll, 1933). In 1939 a new revision of the Kuhlmann Tests of Mental Development was introduced, but little data on the reliability and validity of the measure have been provided.

A third infant test appeared in 1928, when Linfert and Hierholzer produced the first well standardized scale of intelligence in infants. The test consisted of two series: 29 items for infants from 30 to 132 days old and 35 items for infants from 153 to 365 days old. The tests were standardized on 300 infants; 50 of the infants were seen longitudinally. Although this was the best infant test to date, it never received widespread attention.

Infant Testing in the 1930s: The Major Tests

By the end of the 1920s and the early 1930s, the infant testing movement had built up steam, so that many tests were developed. During this period several now well-known investigators—Gesell at the Yale Clinic of Child Development, Buhler in Vienna, Shirley at the University of Minnesota, Bayley in the Berkeley Growth Project, and Fillmore at the University of Iowa—began to publish reports of scales they and their colleagues had been working on for some time. Their work will be considered in turn.

Gesell's Developmental Schedules

The most extensive series of investigations of infants and preschool children were carried out at the Yale Clinic of Child Development under the direction of Arnold Gesell, a pediatrician. These investigations continued for nearly 40 years, refining methods of observation and collecting extensive normative data. The tests originated out of the need for normative data on behavioral development. Working in association with the pediatric and well-baby clinics of the New Haven Dispensary, doctors had been increasingly called upon to examine children psychologically as well as physically. Finally, in 1916, a project was undertaken to observe and record infant and preschool behavior at home and in the clinic in order to collect comprehensive norms of development.

In the preliminary investigation, 50 children were observed at each of 10 age levels—0, 4, 6, 9, 12, and 18 months, and 2, 3, 4, and 5 years. Data in several areas of development were collected. These areas included *motor development* (including posture and prehension), *language development* (including comprehension and imitation), *adaptive behavior* (including eye–hand coordinations, recovery of objects, alertness, and manipulation of objects), and *personal-social behavior* (including reactions to people, initiative, independence, and play behavior). Gesell and his colleagues were the first to develop the procedure of observing the child's natural responses in natural situations (Buhler and Hetzer, 1935).

The norms collected in this preliminary survey, which covered about 150 behavioral items, were codified into a "Developmental Schedule." Normative levels were referred to using the concept of "developmental age." It must be emphasized, however, that Gesell did not regard this schedule as an intelligence test in any way. In fact, Gesell's only references to the concept of intelligence were generally phrased in the negative. Interested in a more general concept of "mental growth," Gesell assumed that mental growth, like physical growth, followed an orderly pattern of maturation. Since growth was regarded as lawful, reliable diagnoses were viewed as possible so long as accurate and extensive observations could be made.

In 1927 a larger, more systematic normative program to investigate further "the wealth and variety of behavior patterns" (Gesell and Thompson, 1934, p. 4) of the infant and preschooler was initiated. A homogeneous group of 107 boys and girls from carefully selected white, middle-class families were seen longitudinally. From 26 to 49 children at each age were observed monthly throughout the first year, at 18 months, and at each birthday until 5 years. Protocols on each child included a home record, a medical history, a daily record, anthropometric measurements, maternal observations, detailed behavioral reports of the child's day at the clinic, a normative exam, and ratings in each developmental category.

Several years later, after they had examined hundreds of children, the work of Gesell and his colleagues culminated in the presentation of the Gesell Developmental Schedules (1940–1947). These schedules provided standardized procedures for observing and evaluating the child's behavioral development from ages 1 month through 6 years. The items were grouped into four subtests: *motor items,* including postural reactions, balance, sitting, and locomotion; *adaptive items,* which Gesell felt included "alertness, intelligence, and various forms of constructive exploration" (1954, p. 338); *language items,* including facial expressions, gestures, and vocalizations; and *personal-social items,* including feeding, dressing, toilet training, and play behavior. Age placements were determined by the percentage of subjects who passed each item. Gesell cautioned against the presentation of a composite score—an all-inclusive developmental quotient—and suggested instead that developmental quotients on each of the subtests and clinical judgments be used to evaluate each child's developmental status.

Gesell's schedules are considered less standardized and more subjective than the many other psychological tests (Anastasi, 1961). The restricted size and the homogeneous nature of the only described sample (the 107 infants in 1927) further limit its value. Moreover, some of the items are considered to have been rather arbitrarily placed (Stott and Ball, 1963). Gesell and his co-workers never reported a careful statistical analysis of the reliability or the validity of the schedules. Nevertheless, the wealth of thorough observations and the careful delineation of each of these behaviors have made the Gesell schedules the main source of material for many other infant tests (Stott and Ball, 1963).

The Viennese Test Series

Charlotte Buhler's Baby Tests, which were first released in German in 1928 and in English in 1930, resulted from intensive observations of children aged 2 months to 2 years. Like Gesell's Schedule, the Baby Tests were to provide standards by which normality of development could be assessed. Children at different age levels were observed for 24-hour periods. From these observations test items were developed to measure physical and mental control, behavior in social relationships, and manipulation of objects. The test included 10 items for every month in the first year and for each 3-month period in the second year.

In 1932 (translated in 1935) Buhler, Hetzer, and their colleagues presented the Viennese Series, a thorough revision of the earlier Baby Tests. These further investigations were guided by a desire both to study the child's personality and development in all its "fundamental dimensions" and to develop tests that would cover all of the "essential steps of development" from birth through 5 years. Based on earlier observation, six fundamental categories of development were identified: sensory reception, bodily movements, social behavior (including language), learning (and imitation), manipulation of materials, and mental productivity or thinking processes.

Each test in the Viennese Series had 10 items; tests were available monthly until 8 months, bimonthly through 18 months, and yearly from 2 through 5. Testing was done in an environment familiar to the child; the interest was in the child's natural, not optimal performance. Developmental age, age within each of the six categories, and the overall pattern of development were considered important in the diagnosis. It was hoped that these tests could be used to determine acceleration or retardation in the child's development in order to assess the normalcy of the child's personality, to predict further development, and to suggest the way for treatment, if necessary. Although some evidence of validity was given (Buhler and Hetzer, 1935), the generality of the tests was limited by the fact that the more than 500 children in the standardization group were drawn mainly from orphanages.

Shirley's Study of the First Two Years

In the late 1920s Mary Shirley was collecting data for the Minnesota Infant Study, one of the first longitudinal infant studies. Twenty-five infants from birth to 2 years were observed first in the hospital and then at home. Observations were made daily in the first week, once a week from 2 weeks to 1 year, and biweekly thereafter. Though Shirley's sample was too small to provide normative information on babies, her study was one of the first to describe comprehensive behavioral development in infancy. The study was initiated to trace the "roots of intellectual behavior . . . into the simplest acts on the infant" (Shirley, 1933, p. 3). Like Gesell, Shirley did not focus on intelligence *per se*. Shirley felt that in infancy, intellect had to be "used as a blanket term to cover almost everything the infant does" (1933, p. 3). In addition, since it would be difficult to determine how much each behavior type contributed to the development of intelligence, it was decided that all behaviors should be studied as carefully as possible.

Unlike Buhler, who was observing infants continuously for 24 hours at a stretch, Shirley gave her infants weekly timed exams lasting about 30 minutes each. It was felt that these exams allowed for more controlled observations. A wide variety of physical and behavioral tests were given. Tests for the youngest levels concentrated on physical development and on observation of the infant's reactions to sounds, tastes, and postural positions. Tests from 3 to 9 months concentrated on the infant's reaching and grasping behaviors. Tests for older infants considered children's behaviors toward pictures, mirrors, odors, various objects, and instructions. Some test items were original; others were borrowed from Kuhlmann (1922), Gesell (1926), Watson and Watson (1921), Stutsman (1931), and Wallin (1918).

The tests were scored by a point system in which different point values were assigned to each item. This system made the test somewhat cumbersome to score. Point scales were found to be highly erratic, suggesting that both level and rate of development were highly irregular, especially in the first year. These problems and the failure to try the tests out on a new and larger sample may have been partially responsible for the lack of widespread use of the tests. Shirley's work was probably most valuable for its early description of developmental sequences in a longitudinal sample.

California First Year Mental Scale

About the same time as Shirley was beginning her investigations in Minnesota, Bayley was beginning to develop scales of infant mental and motor development for use in the Berkeley Growth Study. In reviewing previous work, Bayley noted that "sufficient norms of infant behavior were already available; what was needed was exact determination of those behaviors which were 'significant as criteria of development' " (Bayley, 1933b, p. 10). Theoretical issues guided Bayley's research. She was interested in determining to what extent mental development was consistent over age—how patterns of behavior changed within the short but crowded period of infancy. Questions such as "What behavior is 'mental'?" "What specific behaviors in infancy precede later achievements?" "How dependent are later achievements on earlier ones?" and "What effect does environment have on development?" naturally led to the development of an infancy test that would, hopefully, predict future intelligence.

In 1933 Bayley published the California First Year Mental Scale

(1933*a*). It included 185 test items from birth through 3 years. However, norms and administration and scoring instructions were provided only for 115 items covering the first 18 months. The test contained original items as well as items from other tests. Items tapped motor maturation, eye–hand coordination, adaptive behavior, response to sound, visual maturation, language comprehension and production, and social responsiveness. Each item was age-placed to the nearest tenth of a month.

The test was standardized on a longitudinal sample from the Berkeley Growth Study. The children were mainly from upper-middle-class homes. From 52 to 61 infants were tested at each of the months through the first year. In the second year, 46–53 infants were tested monthly until 15 months, then every three months until 3 years.

Bayley's scales were the most well-researched scales of their time. Bayley provided extensive split-half reliability data (ranging from 0.51 to 0.95) and predictive validity information. According to Thomas (1970), the scales themselves never received general application outside the Berkeley Growth Study because of their inaccessibility and because the standardization group represented only upper-middle-class children. However, Bayley seemed less bent on "selling" her tests to the public for use as diagnostic tools than she was on the implications of her results for the understanding of mental development in general. She concluded that:

> . . . behavior growth of the early months of infant development has little predictive relation to the later development of intelligence. (p. 74)
>
> . . . We have measured at successive ages varying components of more or less independent functions; not until the age of 2 years do these composites exhibit a significant degree of overlapping with the aggregations of traits constituting "intelligence." (1933*b* p. 82)

The failure to secure high predictive validity, said Bayley, "can be explained by a series of shifts from one type of function to another as the child grows older" (1933*b* p. 74), by rapid, nonconsistent developmental changes, and possibly even from difficulties inherent in infant testing (e.g., temperamental problems and restricted behavioral repertoire). One might suspect that Bayley's investigation could have adversely affected the infant testing movement. Instead, it served to spur reconsideration of the nature of tests.

Iowa Tests for Young Children

A less well-known infant test series is the Iowa Tests for Young Children (Fillmore, 1936). Like other researchers in the 1920s, those in

Iowa were also working to establish a scale of mental development for children from birth to 3 years (Fillmore, 1936). The primary purpose of this scale was to assist in ongoing research at the Iowa Child Welfare Research Station.

To test early forms of the scale, home-reared children were brought to the laboratory about three times a year for mental and physical measurements; in some cases, medical examinations and nutritional advice were given. Many children were seen at each bimonthly age level; the exact numbers are unclear but seem to range between 60 and 200. Rigorous attempts were made to ensure consistent testing conditions across subjects. The final scale consisted of 49 items for use between the ages of 4.5 and 23.4 months. The items were similar to those of other previously published tests. Test reliability and predictive validity reports were rather low.

Unlike other test developers, Fillmore (1936) attempted to include only those test items that predicted later IQ. Unfortunately, this attempt did not result in much higher reliability or predictability, although it was a promising technique.

Issues in Infant Testing

After the flurry of infant test development in the 1930s, few new tests were introduced, the notable exceptions being the Griffiths abilities-of-babies scale (1954) and the Cattell infant scale (1940) (to be discussed in a later section of this chapter). Instead, a consolidation period began, as research on reliability, stability, and predictability flourished. This led to the gradual elimination of some, if not most, of the earlier tests from general usage. In fact, in Stott and Ball's survey of infant and preschool test usage in research and clinical settings in the 1960s, only the Cattell infant scale and the Gesell Developmental Schedules were used by a number of the respondents. The work of Shirley, Buhler, and Fillmore became largely referential, as test developers such as Cattell and Griffiths searched the early work for test items. Bayley's test was not popular in the 25 years following its inception but remained a research instrument until its revision in 1960.

The research also resulted in a number of hotly debated issues on the nature of intelligence as well as in a careful scrutiny of the existing tests themselves. These trends were due both to the need for a reliable and valid measure of intelligence in diagnostic settings and to the theoretical interest in the meaning of intelligence.

Primary Uses of the Infant Tests in the 1940s and 1950s

The widespread acceptance of infant testing paralleled the interest in preschool testing a decade earlier. The demand for these tests was primarily diagnostic. Adoption agencies found them especially useful. Throughout the 1940s and 1950s there was a dramatic increase in the number of adoptive homes in America. As Wittenborn (1957) reports, the number of adoptive petitions in Connecticut doubled in the decade from 1943 to 1952, numbering over a thousand by 1952. At the same time, the placement age was steadily lowering: in 1947–1948 only 9% of the cases in Connecticut were adopted before 6 months of age; by 1951–1952 a quarter of the cases were placed in the first half year of life. Thus the status of a child eligible for adoption had to be determined very early and the infant tests were the only diagnostic instruments available.

The tests were also used for other diagnostic purposes, as in cases of possible retardation, brain damage, and physical and sensory disabilities, and even for personality problems (Stott and Ball, 1963). Although infant test research was widely reported in the scientific journals, the research use was far overshadowed by the diagnostic use.

To obtain a clearer picture of who used the infant tests and how they were used, Stott and Ball (1963) conducted a survey of infant- and preschool-test users in the early 1960s. Questionnaires were sent to 750 individuals and centers. Both research and diagnostic settings were included in the sample, although unfortunately they were not treated separately in the survey results. Of the 330 surveys returned, 217 respondents were involved in some way with children under 6 years of age.

At least one of the early tests had been used by 93% of the respondents, and 81% of the respondents had used the tests for diagnostic purposes. A third also used the tests for preadoptive screening, for admission to special schools or programs, and for the testing of physically handicapped children. Not surprisingly, the tests were used for research purposes less frequently. Only 5% of the respondents had done general development or longitudinal studies; only 2% had been involved in validation studies. The most frequently cited research use was in studies of autism and anoxia.

Consolidation and Refinement of the 1930 Infant Tests

After the infant tests appeared, a variety of studies were initiated to assess the extent to which standardization, internal consistency, and test–retest reliability were adequate. In addition, the predictive validity from infancy to early childhood was carefully scrutinized.

Stability of Infant Intelligence Test Scores

With the proliferation of infant tests in the early 1930s, researchers became concerned with the extent to which measurements of mental abilities were stable. Two kinds of stability measures were considered: those dealing with the stability or consistency of measurement of a particular test within a testing session (internal consistency) and those dealing with the stability or consistency of scores within a particular infant test from one testing session to another (test–retest reliability).

Internal Consistency. To measure internal consistency, split-half coefficients are used. Werner and Bayley (1966) listed the split-half coefficients obtained for various early tests. With corrections for attenuation by the Spearman–Brown formula, correlation coefficients ranged from 0.51 to 0.95 for tests given within the first 18 months of life. Split-half coefficients averaged 0.81–0.84 for tests given within the first year. These results were generally considered acceptable.

Test–Retest Reliability. Test–retest reliability reports varied widely, depending on the particular test, the interval between tests, and the age at testing. For Two Buhler Baby Tests given a day apart, Herring (1937) reported that correlation coefficients ranged from 0.40 to 0.96 over the first 12 months of life. Conger (in Shirley, 1933) found little agreement between Linfert-Hierholzer test scores that were obtained two days apart on very young infants. For 1-, 2-, and 3-month-olds correlation coefficients were -0.24, $+0.44$, and $+0.69$, respectively. Shirley (1933) reported that week-to-week test scores correlated from -0.16 to $+0.69$ across the first 3–11 weeks of life.

Studies of the California First Year Mental Scale (Bayley, 1933b), the Kuhlmann–Binet (Driscoll, 1933), the Minnesota tests (Shirley, 1933), the Iowa tests (Fillmore, 1936), the Buhler Baby Tests (Herring, 1937), and the Gesell schedules (Richards and Nelson, 1939) all seemed to agree that correlations between scores from repeated testing sessions over the first 18 months were too low for any kind of individual prediction. The longer the interval between test sessions, the lower the reliability was. In Thorndike's (1940) review of reliability studies monthly test-retest reliability coefficients for tests given after the first four months of life were high enough to allow for reliable predictions, although predictions over longer time periods were not possible during the first two years of life.

Many explanations for the unreliability of content mental scores were advanced. First, since development was so very rapid, it might not proceed at a uniform rate from birth through 2 years, which would result in little stability. Second, those behaviors that might be used to measure "intelligence" at some stages of infancy might be very different from those used to measure "intelligence" at other stages of infancy. In fact, the quality of intelligence might be different at different periods within infancy. Third, the growing impact of environment and environmental fluctuations might account for the unreliability of the tests. And fourth, the experimenter's difficulties in motivating the child to perform and the child's small behavioral repertoire might further increase the unreliability of the tests and complicate the issue of what the tests were, in fact, measuring.

Predictive Validity of Early Infant Tests

It seems a common principle of tests and measurement that without retest reliability, there is little hope of predictive validity. One would have thought that the lack of retest reliability would be sufficient to erode confidence in the tests. Nevertheless, it was the predictive validity studies that ultimately determined each test's worth. In fact, concern with predictive validity was so important that no matter how well standardized or how reliable the infant test, if it did not predict to later measurements of intelligence, it was doomed to obscurity. Take, for example, the case of the Linfert–Hierholzer baby test. The Linfert–Hierholzer test was standardized on 300 infants (50 were tested repeatedly), while the Stanford–Binet test was only standardized on 10 three-year-olds and 51 four-year-olds, with 12 test items at each age (Stott and Ball, 1963, p. 133). Nevertheless, because the Linfert–Hierholzer test did not correlate with the 1916 Stanford–Binet test for 4-year-olds (Furfey and Muehlenbein, 1932), it never received widespread attention and was discarded.

The 1930s were a period of great disillusionment with infant tests, primarily because there were very few reports of high test validities. Even the studies that did give such reports were called into question. Cunningham (1934) found that 12-month scores on the Kuhlmann–Binet predicted to 2- and 8-year IQ scores, but her study was generally regarded as inconclusive because of the small sample size (Stott and Ball, 1963, p. 87). In two studies of the Buhler Baby Tests, one by Buhler (1930) and another cited by Buhler (Hetzer and Jenschke, 1930, as cited in Buhler, 1930), high predictive validities were also reported. However, in both studies small samples were used (24 and 25 infants), the ages of the subjects varied from 3 months to over 2 years, and test intervals varied from 3 to 14 months. In addition, predictive validities may have been amplified by the fact that classifications—normal, retarded, or advanced—were used instead of point scores.

Hallowell (1925–1927) reported that intellectual assessments of 142 children were reliable enough in 95% of the cases to be used for adoptive purposes; Gesell (1928) felt that his studies also showed consistency of mental growth. Bayley (1933b), however, criticized these studies on the grounds that age groups were not treated separately, the time intervals between tests were not considered, and the statistical treatments were unclear.

The majority of predictive validity studies in the 1930s yielded negative results. With a large sample, Driscoll (1933) observed that children's Kuhlmann–Binet scores from 12 to 24 months and from 24 to 36 months correlated only 0.58 and 0.57, respectively. Bayley (1933b) found that California First Year Mental Scales scores averaged over months 7, 8, and 9 of the first year correlated only 0.22 with scores at 2 years. Using ratings, Fillmore (1936) reported that children's scores on the Iowa Tests for Young Children at 5½ months correlated only 0.26 with scores at 18½ months.

In a sophisticated study by Nelson and Richards (1938), 6-month Gesell scores, 2-year Merrill–Palmer scores, and 3-year Stanford–Binet scores were related; the correlations were less than 0.50. Certain items, though correlating very little with the overall 6-month score, correlated highly with later intelligence scores. For example, awareness items, such as "regards pellet" and "splashes in tub," had low correlations with the overall 6-month Gesell score but acceptable correlations with the 2-year Merrill–Palmer score. In contrast, motor items, such as "secures cube" and "reacts to mirror," had high correlations with the 6-month Gesell test but lower correlations with later test scores. Observing that the predictive validity for several single items was higher than the predictive validity of the entire 6-month test, Nelson and Richards combined several highly predictive items in order to obtain the highest predictive validity possible. Multiple correlations using several highly predictive items from the 6-month test yielded a multiple R of 0.80 with 3-year Stanford–Binet scores.

Anderson (1939) also conducted a large-scale study of predictive validity about the same time as Nelson and Richards. Almost 100 infants were repeatedly tested in the first two years of life with a test composed of original items and items from the Gesell, the Buhler, and the Linfert–Hierholzer tests. The infants were also given a Stanford–Binet at 5 years. In general, Anderson found low or nonsignificant relationships between the 5-year-old IQ score and the earlier infant tests. Use of item analysis techniques helped increase the correlations to between 0.20 and 0.55. Very few items were shown to be useful in predicting later intelligence. The only two exceptions were alertness to the external environment in the early months and language items in the second year.

Thus infant intelligence testing emerged from the decade of the 1930s tarnished with disappointingly low reliabilities and, more important for that time, distressingly low predictive validities. A variety of explanations for the lack of reliability and validity were offered. Among them were the infant's limited behavioral repertoire, the failure to consider the infant's gestational age, difficulties in maintaining the attention and the motivation of the infant, the interference of temperamental characteristics such as activity level and alertness, and failure to make accurate clinical assessments of the infant's overall responsiveness to the testing session. More important, however, was the result that several theoretical assumptions had to be reevaluated. People began to question whether intelligence was, as had been hoped, a reliable, stable characteristic that developed continuously at a constant rate. In particular, the results of more sophisticated studies, such as those by Nelson and Richards (1938; Richards and Nelson, 1939) and Anderson (1939), lent support to arguments that intelligence varied not only quantitatively across the life span but qualitatively as well.

Intertest Item Consistency

It seems that the various test developers did look over each other's tests quite carefully. However, such cross-fertilization of ideas and borrowing of items did not result in the use of identical items. When similar items were used, they were placed at different ages. For instance, the fact that mirrors are of great interest to infants and elicit pleasurable responses was noted by those in the child study movement (Darwin, 1877; Preyer, 1888) and by those who were developing infant intelligence tests. An examination of the tests developed by Bayley, . . . Cattell, Buhler, Griffiths and Gesell reveals clearly that the mirror items themselves and the ages at which they occur are somewhat divergent across the five infant tests. The items and age ranges are presented in Table I.

The lack of consensus as to when various mirror responses occur is surprising and suggests that conclusive normative ages were not established by the test developers. The passing or failing of a similar item on different scales would often result in different intelligence scores. Regarding one's own image in the mirror "typically" occurs at either 5 or 8 months, while smiling at the image occurs at 5, 7, 8, or 10 months of age. Searching behind the mirror is placed at 10 months by Griffiths and at 18–20 months by Buhler.

Some of the divergence can be accounted for by the type of mirror used and the situation in which the behavior was elicited. However, there still remain large inconsistencies in the age at which certain behaviors were placed by the test developers in the 1930s and later. This is true even though all of the later tests were standardized on large numbers of infants.

Environmental Effects on Intelligence

Concurrent with the issue of predictability from early to later test scores was the issue of environmental effects on intelligence. From the beginning of the testing movement in America intelligence was seen as fixed or predetermined. For example, Goddard, who was the first to translate the Binet scale into English and the first to use it extensively, was a strong proponent of fixed intelligence. Of the infant test devel-

TABLE I
Mirror Test Items in Five Infant Tests

Test items	\multicolumn{17}{c}{Age in months at which item occurs}

Test items	4	5	6	7	8	9	10	11	12	13-14	15-17	18-20	21-23	24-26	27-29	30-32	36
Approaches image	Bayley																
Regards own image		Gesell			Buhler Griffiths												
Smiles at image		Gesell Bayley		Cattell	Buhler		Griffiths										
Vocalizes to image			Gesell Bayley														
Pats, feels image			Bayley	Cattell Gesell					Buhler								
Leans forward							Gesell										
Plays with image			Bayley				Griffiths										
Searches						Griffiths						Buhler					
Reaches toward mirror for object								Gesell	Buhler								
Reaches toward adult, not reflection										Buhler							
Refers to self by name														Gesell	Gesell		
Refers to self by pronoun																Gesell	
Refers to self by sex																	Gesell

opers Gesell was the best known for his adherence to a predetermined maturation; as late as 1954 Gesell was saying that "basic configurations, correlations, and successions of behavior patterns are determined by a process of maturation" (p. 371). So prevalent was this view that even when an early study found that nursery school attendance resulted in an increase in IQ (when compared to an appropriate control group), these differences were attributed to the inadequate standardization of the preschool scales (Goodenough, 1928b).

However, not everyone believed that intelligence could not be affected by environmental stimulation. In 1932 the first of a series of studies from the Iowa Child Welfare Station appeared (Wellman, 1932a, 1932b). This was the first of 11 papers that appeared in the next seven years and that generated a great deal of controversy. Children in a variety of settings (e.g., nursery schools, longitudinal studies, adoption settings, foster children of feebleminded women, and children in orphans' homes) were tested and retested in order to see if environmental circumstances would affect IQ scores. The various studies reported that participation in the Iowa Studies nursery schools resulted in IQ gains (Wellman, 1932a, 1932b), that children placed in adoptive homes in the first six months of life had higher IQ scores than those placed from 2 to 5 years of age (Skodak, 1939), that institutionalized children who were classified as feebleminded had IQ scores that declined (Crissey, 1937), and that children of feebleminded mothers, when placed in another home, had normal IQ scores (Skodak, 1939).

These findings were bitterly attacked. Goodenough (1939, 1940), one of the advocates of fixed intelligence, dismissed the Iowa findings for methodological and statistical reasons. The Iowa studies often had inadequate control groups. In addition, she felt that the data were based on two unacceptable assumptions: (1) that early test scores are predictive for intelligence in later childhood, and (2) that the reliability of the early tests is so high that measurement error and regression are inoperative.

Other attacks on the Iowa group were less rational. In what Stott and Ball (1963) termed the most violent article, Simpson (1939) said:

> But to claim miracle working at Iowa that cannot be duplicated in other parts of the country . . . , that is much worse than nonsense and ought to be exposed as such. (p. 366)

The controversy did result in a series of better-controlled studies on the impact of environment on IQ in the 1940s (e.g., Bradway, 1945;

Frandsen and Barlow, 1940; McHugh, 1943). However, the data were inconclusive, satisfying neither the so-called environmentalists nor nativists. The effects of environment on intellectual ability are still being debated today, especially in early-school enrichment programs. Although the argument takes a different form, the issues are the same.

The Second Wave of Tests

Child psychologists, although disillusioned by the failure of infant tests to show predictive validity, did not give up easily. Two approaches were taken toward the depressing validity studies of the 1930s. The less popular approach was to allow more room for clinical interpretation and subjective assessment instead of focusing narrowly on the child's performance skills. Hallowell (1941) argued that the qualitative aspects of performance—complexity and variety of responsiveness, attention span, and discrimination ability—had to be considered. McGraw (1942) developed a series of three laboratory tests in which a piece of plate glass was placed between the child and a lure so that the style quality of children's reactions rather than their particular behavior could be appraised. In both instances ratings were necessarily subjective; this subjectivity was considered highly valuable. However, these investigations did not report interobserver reliability measures.

The second and more popular approach was to improve and modify the older infant tests. This tack was taken by Cattell (1940), Shotwell and Gilliland (1943), and Griffiths (1954). Their attempts are briefly considered below.

Cattell's Infant Intelligence Scale

In an extensive study of the development of normal children from birth to several years of age at the Center for Research in Child Health and Development at Harvard University, Psyche Cattell was called upon to select psychological tests for the measurement of mental development in infants and young children. In the early years of the study existing infant tests were used (in particular the Gesell tests). Cattell (1940), however, was disappointed by these tests, listing seven drawbacks of the tests available at that time: (1) they lacked objective procedures for administration and scoring; (2) they included many personal-social items that were heavily influenced by home training; (3) they contained measures of large motor control that Cattell believed were not related to later mental development; (4) the scaling was often inadequate; (5) the tests covered limited age ranges; (6) test items were unequally distributed; and (7) the tests were often poorly standardized. Therefore Cattell developed her own scale for infants from 2 to 30 months. She drew heavily from the Gesell test items. Items were included only if they (1) showed a regular increase in percentage of passage from one age to another; (2) were easy to administer and were interesting to the child; (3) did not require cumbersome equipment; (4) measured performance not appreciably influenced by home training; and (5) were not dependent on the use of large muscles. At least five items were included at each age level—monthly in the first year, bimonthly in the second year, and quarterly in the third year. Precise objective directions were written for administering and scoring the test.

The tests were standardized on 274 middle-class children tested at 3, 6, 9, 12, 18, 24, and 30 months. Split-half reliabilities for tests from 6 through 30 months were high (from 0.71 to 0.90); the split-half reliability for the 3-month test was only 0.56. Though the Cattell test was designed to be a downward revision of Form L of the Stanford–Binet test, predictive validities for the younger infants were not terribly high. For 3, 6, 9, 12, 18, 24, and 30 months the correlations with 36-month-old Stanford–Binet scores were, respectively, 0.10, 0.34, 0.18, 0.56, 0.67, 0.71, and 0.83.

Other studies of the Cattell test have reported high test–retest correlations (Harms, 1951; Gallagher, 1953). However, predictive validity studies have been disappointing. Escalona and Moriarty (1961) reported zero correlations between either the Cattell or the Gesell tests at 7–8 months of age and school-age scores on the Wechsler Intelligence Scale for Children (WISC), and Cavanaugh (1957) found low correlations between the Cattell and the preschool Stanford–Binet tests.

Northwestern Intelligence Test

In the mid-1940s Shotwell and Gilliland (1943) developed a test to screen very young infants for adoption. The results were two tests (Gilliland, 1949, 1951): Test A measuring infants from 4 to 12 weeks and Test B measuring infants from 13 to 36 weeks. The tests were very similar to earlier tests in terms of administration and scoring. The 40 items on each test were heavily borrowed from the Gesell scales, although only those items that seemed to measure adaptability rather than physical coordination or reflexes were included.

Gilliland (1949, 1951) reported high split-half reliability coefficients for each test. However, the predictive validity of the tests was somewhat questionable. Gilliland (1949) reported small point differences between Kuhlmann–Binet or Cattell test scores and Test A; therefore he concluded that Test A was as valid as either of these other tests. However, the sample was small (n = 29) and composed entirely of mentally retarded children. There is only one other validity study (Braen, 1961). Infants ranging in age from 13 to 35 weeks were given both Test B and the Cattell test, and at 18 months they were given the Cattell. Early Cattell scores were correlated 0.39 with later Cattell scores; early Test B scores correlated 0.38 with later Cattell scores (Braen, 1961).

In reviewing the literature, Thomas (1970) concluded that the Northwestern scales "have not been adequately researched, nor do they appear to offer any advantages over existing scales" (p. 199). Though the goal of the tests—very early screening of infants for adoption—was an admirable one, it may have been unattainable, considering the difficulties involved in testing infants so young with traditional types of items and the great room for variation in the first year of life.

Griffiths Mental Development Scale

Ruth Griffiths's Mental Development Scale (1954), covering the ages from 2 weeks to 2 years, was designed as an improvement upon existing infant tests. Griffiths hoped that her assessment of what she regarded as innate general cognitive ability would help in early psychological diagnoses of infants.

The scale was divided into five subscales: locomotor, personal-social, hearing and speech, hand and eye, and performance. Each scale had 52 items; there were 3 items for each week in the first year and 2 items for each week in the second year. Though borrowing heavily from other tests, particularly the Gesell, Griffiths criticized earlier tests for their lack of speech items, especially in the first year. Believing that speech was a uniquely human intellectual task, Griffiths included twice as many speech items in her infant scale as anyone else. For the first year there were measures of imitation and monologue, of listening to sounds and conversation, of repetition of single sounds, and of babbling. Also

emphasized were the social nature of many of the items and the importance of social relationships to the infant's intellectual development.
Nevertheless, despite Griffiths's stress on the importance of the infant's relationship with others, her test included measures of the infant's
orientation toward, interaction with, and preference of other people
only during the first year; for infants in the second year all of the
personal-social items involved self-help skills that tapped the child's
relationship to objects, not people.

Griffiths standardized the tests on 571 London children using about
25 children for every month of testing. According to 1940 United States
census figures, Griffiths's English standardization sample seemed very
similar to the urban population of the United States. Test–retest reliabilities obtained from 60 children tested at variable ages, with test intervals
ranging from 7 to 70 weeks, were 0.87 (Griffiths, 1954). Griffiths did not
report predictive validity measures.

Other investigators have provided reliability and validity data. Hindley (1960) reported rather low test–retest correlations—ranging from
−0.13 to +0.56—for infants tested at 3, 6, 12, and 18 months. Hindley
(1960, 1965) and Roberts and Sedgley (1965) correlated the Griffiths scale
in infancy with Stanford–Binet scores at 5 years. Both studies reported
similar coefficients—from 0.30 to 0.46. Roberts and Sedgley reported
that infant scores taken at about 18 months of age were correlated less
than 0.40 with Binet scores at 7 years of age. Thus, while the Griffiths
test was viewed by many as an improvement over other infant tests
because of equal or better standardization efforts, higher test–retest
reliability, and higher predictive validity, the test was still inadequate for
individual predictions. Although the Griffiths test scores are highly
correlated (0.80s to 0.90s) with Cattell test scores (Caldwell and Drachman, 1964), the Griffiths has rarely been used in the United States,
probably because, according to Horrocks (1964), reported in Thomas
(1970), Griffiths will sell test materials only to those trained by her.

Trends and Issues in Infant Intelligence Testing: 1960s and 1970s

After the second wave of infant intelligence tests were developed, a
new round of evaluation and criticism began. Remember that the new
tests were more carefully designed than the tests of the 1930s: the testing

procedure was more standardized, the item selection was more rigorous, an adequate number of infants was used for normative purposes, the split-half reliability was adequate, and retest reliabilities, although often low, were at least reported. However, predictive validity lingered as an unresolved theoretical and practical issue. The new work on prediction was more sophisticated and more far-reaching than before, which allowed for a better understanding of the nature and prediction of early intelligence. The concern about prediction and related issues led to the development of a third wave of tests in the 1960s and 1970s. These tests were to serve a new purpose as the old notions of intelligence as a unitary factor became obsolete.

Predictive Validity and Related Issues

As the number of infant tests in use became fewer, as these tests were improved upon, and as research on their reliability and validity continued, it became increasingly clear that test scores from the first two years could not be used to predict preschool or school-age intelligence in normal samples. This was found in study after study (Bayley, 1949; Bowlby, 1952; Cavanaugh et al., 1957; Hindley, 1965; MacFarlane, 1953; McCall et al., 1972; Wittenborn et al., 1956).

Prediction in Impaired Populations

However, this was not true for all groups of infants. The results from studies of abnormally slow infants were particularly encouraging (Ames, 1967; Illingworth, 1961, 1972; Hallowell, 1941; Simon and Bass, 1956; Symmes, 1933). In general, the prediction of later IQ for infants who were classified as retarded or neurologically impaired was much better than prediction for a normal sample. Knobloch and Pasamanick (1960, 1966), whose work is the best of the early studies of neurological deficiency and later intelligence, may be mentioned. In these studies, the Gesell Developmental Schedule was used in infancy, the Stanford–Binet at later ages. Using large, heterogeneous samples including both normal and possibly impaired infants, Knobloch and Pasamanick reported substantial relationships between the first- and third-year ($r = 0.48$, 1960) and first- and 8–10-year ($r = 0.70$, 1966) IQ scores. In both studies, correlations were considerably higher in the abnormal than in the normal infant groups. In the 1960 study correlations for normals were 0.43, for abnormals 0.74. In the 1966 study correlations were 0.48 and 0.68, respectively. Such results caused many observers to agree with Drillien (1961) that it is "much easier to predict mental dullness in infancy than mental superiority."

However, a note of caution in interpreting many of the studies of low-scoring infants is necessary (see Thomas, 1970). Many may be criticized on methodological grounds. For example, in MacRae's study of adoptive children (1955), the early test scores may have influenced adoptive placement, thus exaggerating the correlations between early and later test scores.

Attempts to Increase Predictive Validity

A variety of methods for increasing the predictive validity of the tests was suggested and tested. One technique, introduced by Escalona, involved the use of clinical appraisals, category ratings, and testing under optimal conditions in conjunction with the infant tests (Escalona, 1950; Escalona and Moriarty, 1961; Gallagher, 1953; Simon & Bass, 1956). Persuasive as the argument for clinical assessment was, predictions were still less than 0.70. The failure to obtain high predictability was probably influenced by methodological problems, such as the deletion of large numbers of infant testing sessions, failure to describe the bases for clinical assessments objectively, and small sample sizes.

The use of multiple regression was a more promising technique for increasing predictive validity than was clinical assessment (Knobloch and Pasamanick, 1966; Werner *et al.*, 1968). Werner *et al.* (1968) were able to predict IQ at 10 years for normal children by using 20-month Cattell scores, pediatricians' ratings, social ratings, prenatal stress scores, and parents' socioeconomic class ($R = 0.58$). When the infant's Cattell score at 20 months had been under 80, the multiple correlation coefficient increased to 0.80. As can be seen, these investigators were relying less and less on individual IQ scores in infancy to predict later IQ.

Item Analysis and Predictive Validity

Item and factor analyses were also performed on various infant intelligence tests. Though item analyses revealed that some individual items, particularly verbal items, had higher predictive validity for later

IQ than overall test scores (Cameron *et al.*, 1967; Fillmore,1936; Hunt and Bayley, 1971; Nelson and Richards, 1938; Richards and Nelson, 1939), these correlations were still not high enough for reliable individual predictions. In an exploratory investigation Catalano and McCarthy (1954) found a high multiple correlation (0.52) between three phonological characteristics of infant speech at 13 months and Stanford–Binet scores at 45 months.

Factor analytic studies by Nelson and Richards (1938), Richards and Nelson (1939), and Stott and Ball (1963) were especially helpful in revealing reasons for differences in scores between various infant tests at the same age and at different ages and for differences in scores between the same tests at different ages. Considering the wide range in contents across tests, Stott and Ball remarked, "It is almost surprising that there is a degree of correlation between two simultaneously administered scales as seems to be present" (p. 221). According to Stott and Ball, infant scales were "more diversified" and covered a wider range of intellectual abilities than later tests. Whereas infant scales were judged to include measures of "divergent production"—creative abilities—later tests, such as the Stanford–Binet and the Merrill–Palmer tests had very few measures of creative abilities. The Stanford–Binet emphasized memory, the Merrill–Palmer manual skills.

The Third Wave of Tests

By the 1960s investigators were becoming reconciled to the fact that even improvements of existing tests would not lead to high predictive validity for normal children (Illingworth, 1961, 1972). Qualitative differences in intelligence across different age periods, the effects of varied environmental experiences, and the incidence of delayed maturation and unanticipated degenerative diseases were recognized as significant impediments to prediction. Thus Bayley's California First Year Mental Scale was revised and restandardized (Bayley, 1969), not so much, it seems, in the interests of increasing predictive validity, but to allow for a comparative assessment of current infant abilities. Alpern and Ball's (1972) Developmental Profile is another up-to-date comprehensive inventory of infant skills.

Unlike previously developed tests, the majority of new tests of the 1960s and 1970s have not been designed to test all aspects of mental development in infancy; they have been designed to fulfill particular purposes and measure specific types of behavior. Those interested in detecting mental subnormality set busily to work developing tests that would allow for the detection of mental deficiencies as close to birth as possible and that would be comprehensive, yet efficient. Some of the tests developed to this end are the Graham/Rosenblith Behavioral Examination of Neonates (Rosenblith, 1961), Prechtl's Neurological Examination (Prechtl and Beintema, 1964), the Composite Developmental Inventory for Infants and Young Children (Caldwell and Drachman, 1964), the Denver Developmental Screening Test (Frankenburg and Dodds, 1968), and the Neonatal Behavioral Assessment Scale (Brazelton, undated). The Frichtl–Peterson Tool for the Assessment of Motor Skills (Frichtl and Peterson, 1969) and the Koontz Child Development Program (Koontz, 1974) were developed specifically to evaluate and suggest treatments for retarded infants.

Those interested in more theoretical issues regarding mental development have set to work developing tests that would tap specific areas of development. Both cognitive and social skills have been translated into infant tests. The importance of sensorimotor skills to later development had been proposed by Piaget in the 1940s and 1950s but did not gain widespread acceptance in America until the 1960s. At least five tests have been developed to measure sensorimotor skills (Bell, 1970; Décarie, 1965; Escalona and Corman, 1969; Golden and Birns, 1968; Uzgiris and Hunt, 1966). Ricciuti's (1965) Object Grouping and Selective Ordering Tasks assess the development of categorizing skills in 1- to 3-year-old children, while the Fantz–Nevis Visual Preference Test (Fantz and Nevis, 1967) looks specifically at visual preferences from birth to 6 months of age. There are several tests that focus on early language development: the Communicative Evaluation Chart from Infancy to Five Years (Anderson et al., 1963); the Pre-linguistic Infant Vocalization Analysis (Ringwall, 1965); the Verbal Language Development Scale (Mecham, 1971); the Shield Speech and Language Developmental Scale (Shield Institute for Retarded Children, 1968); and the Bzoch–League Receptive–Expressive Language Scale for the Measurement of Language Skills in Infancy (Bzoch and League, 1971).

Renewed interest in social development has led to the search for measures of social competency. Two early tests of social skills are the Measurement of Social Competence (Doll, 1953) and the Ring and Peg Tests of Behavior Development (Banham, 1964). Several tests are currently being developed to assess the social competencies of children in day-care settings (Day Care and Child Development Council of America, Inc., 1973; Michalson and Lewis, 1975).

These very specific types of tests are movements away from a notion of general intelligence to emphasis on specific behaviors and skills as possible predictors of later development. Such tests hold great promise for a more precise analysis of the course of cognitive development in the early years of life.

REFERENCES

ALPERN, G. D., AND BALL, T. J., 1972, "Developmental Profile," Psychological Development Publication, Indianapolis.

AMES, L. B., 1967, Predictive value of infant behavior examinations, in "Exceptional Infant: The Normal Infant," Vol. 1, J. Hellmuth (ed.), Straub & Hellmuth, Seattle, Washington.

ANASTASI, A., 1961, "Psychological Testing," Macmillan, New York.

ANDERSON, D., 1939, The predictive value of infancy tests in relation to intelligence at five years, Child Development, 10(3):203.

ANDERSON, R. M., MILES, M., AND MATHENY, A. P., 1963, "Communicative Evaluation Chart from Infancy to Five Years," Educators Publishing Service, Inc., Cambridge, Massachusetts.

BANHAM, K. M., 1964, "Ring and Peg Tests of Behavior Development," Psychometric Affiliates, Munster, Indiana.

BAYLEY, N., 1933a, "The California First Year Mental Scale," University of California Press, Berkeley.

BAYLEY, N., 1933b, Mental growth during the first three years, Genetic Psychology Monographs, 14:1.

BAYLEY, N., 1949, Consistency and variability in the growth of intelligence from birth to 18 years, Journal of Genetic Psychology, 75:165.

BAYLEY, N., 1969, "Bayley Scales of Infant Development," The Psychological Corporation, New York.

BELL, S. M., 1970, The development of the concept of the object as related to infant–mother attachment, Child Development, 41:191.

BINET, A., AND HENRI, V., 1895, La mémoire des phrases, L'Année Psychologique, 1:24.

BINET, A., AND HENRI, V., 1896, La psychologie individuelle, L'Année Psychologique, 2:411.

BINET, A., AND SIMON, T., 1905a, Méthodes nouvelles pour le diagnostic du niveau intellectuel des anormaux, L'Année Psychologique, 11:191.

BINET, A., AND SIMON, T., 1905b, Application des méthodes nouvelles au diagnostic du niveau intellectuel chez les infants normaux et anormaux d'hospice et d'école primaire, L'Année Psychologique, 11:245.

BINET, A., AND SIMON, T., 1908, Le développement de l'intelligence chez les enfants, L'Année Psychologique, 14:1.

BINET, A., AND SIMON, T., 1914, "Mentally Defective Children" ("Les Enfants Anormaux," 1907) W. B. Drummond (trans.), Edward Arnold, London.

BOLTON, T. L., 1892, The growth of memory in school children, *American Journal of Psychology*, 4:362.

BOWLBY, J., 1952, "Maternal Care and Mental Health," Monograph Series, No. 2, World Health Organization, Geneva.

BRADWAY, K. P., 1945, An experimental study of the factors associated with Stanford–Binet IQ changes from the preschool to the junior high school, *Journal of Genetic Psychology*, 66:107.

BRAEN, B. B., 1961, An evaluation of the Northwestern Infant Intelligence Test: Test B, *Journal of Consulting Psychology*, 25:245.

BRAZELTON, T. B., undated, "Neonatal Behavioral Assessment Scale," Children's Hospital Medical Center, Boston.

BUHLER, C., 1930, "The First Year of Life," The John Day Co., New York.

BUHLER, C., AND HETZER, H., 1935, "Testing Children's Development from Birth to School Age," Farrar & Rinehart, Inc., New York.

BURT, C., 1921, "Mental and Scholastic Tests," King, London.

BZOCH, K. R., AND LEAGUE, R., 1971, "Bzoch–League Receptive–Expressive Language Scale for the Measurement of Language Skills in Infancy," Tree of Life Press, Gainesville, Florida.

CALDWELL, B. M., AND DRACHMAN, R. H., 1964, "Comparability of Three Methods of Assessing the Developmental Level of Young Infants," Pediatrics—SUNY, Upstate Medical Center, Syracuse, New York, p. 51.

CAMERON, J., LIVSON, N., AND BAYLEY, N., 1967, Infant vocalizations and their relationship to mature intelligence, *Science*, 157:331.

CATALANO, F. L., AND MCCARTHY, D., 1954, Infant speech as a possible predictor of later intelligence, *The Journal of Psychology*, 38:203.

CATTELL, J., 1890, Mental tests and measurements, *Mind*, 15:373.

CATTELL, J., AND FARRAND, L., 1896, Physical and mental measurements of the students of Columbia University, *Psychological Review*, 3:618.

CATTELL, P., 1940, 1960, 1966, "The Measurement of Intelligence of Infants and Young Children," The Psychological Corporation, New York.

CAVANAUGH, M. C., COHEN, I., DUNPHY, D., RINGWALL, E. A., AND GOLDBERG, I. D., 1957, Prediction from the Cattell Infant Intelligence Scale, *Journal of Consulting Psychology*, 21:33.

CHAILLE, S. E., 1887, Infants: Their chronological process, *New Orleans Medical and Surgical Journal*, 14:893.

CRISSEY, O. L., 1937, Mental development as related to institutional residence and educational achievement, *University of Iowa Studies on Child Welfare*, 13(1).

CUNNINGHAM, B. V., 1934, Infant IQ ratings evaluated after an interval of seven years, *Journal of Experimental Education*, 11(2):84.

DARWIN, C., 1859, "The Origin of Species," John Murray, London.

DARWIN, C., 1877, A biographical sketch of an infant, *Mind*, 2:285.

DARWIN, C., 1973 (originally published in 1872), "Expression of the Emotions in Man and Animals," D. Appleton, New York.

DAY CARE AND CHILD DEVELOPMENT COUNCIL OF AMERICA, INC., 1973, "Evaluating Children's Progress: A Rating Scale for Children in Day Care," Washington, D.C.

DECARIE, T. G., 1965, "Intelligence and Affectivity in Early Childhood," International Universities Press, New York.

DOLL, E. A., 1953, "Measurement of Social Competence," Educational Test Bureau (available from American Guidance Service, Circle Pines, Minnesota).

DRILLIEN, C. M., 1961, A longitudinal study of the growth and development of prematurely born children, Part VII: Mental development 2–5 years, *Archives of Diseases in Childhood*, 36:233.

DRISCOLL, G. P., 1933, The development status of the preschool child as a prognosis of future development, *Child Development Monographs*, No. 13.

ESCALONA, S., July 1950, The use of infant tests for predictive purposes, *Bulletin of the Menninger Clinic*.

ESCALONA, S. K., AND CORMAN, H., 1969, "Albert Einstein Scales of Sensori-motor Development," Albert Einstein College of Medicine of Yeshiva University, New York.

ESCALONA, S. K., AND MORIARTY, A., 1961, Prediction of school-age intelligence from infant tests, *Child Development*, 32:597.

ESQUIROL, J. D., 1838, "Des Maladies Mentales Considerées sous les Rapports Médical, Hygiénique et Médico-légal," J. B. Baillière, Paris.

FANTZ, R. L., AND NEVIS, S., 1967, Fantz–Nevis Visual Preference Test, Case Western Reserve, Cleveland.

FILLMORE, E. A., 1936, Iowa Tests for young children, *University of Iowa Studies on Child Welfare*, 11(4).

FRANDSEN, A., AND BARLOW, F. P., 1940, Influence of the nursery school on mental growth, *39th Yearbook of the National Society of Education*, Part II, 143.

FRANKENBURG, W. K., AND DODDS, J. B., 1968, "Denver Developmental Screening Test," University of Colorado Press, Denver.

FRICHTL, C., AND PETERSON, L. W., 1969, "Frichtl–Peterson Tool for the Assessment of Motor Skills," State Department of Mental Health, Champaign, Illinois.

FURFEY, P. H., AND MUEHLENBEIN, J., 1932, The validity of infant intelligence tests, *Journal of Genetic Psychology*, 40:219.

GALLAGHER, J. J., 1953, Clinical judgment and the Cattell intelligence scale, *Journal of Consulting Psychology*, 17:303.

GALTON, F., 1869, "Hereditary Genius," Macmillan, London.

GESELL, A., 1926, "The Mental Growth of the Preschool Child," Macmillan, New York.

GESELL, A., 1928, "Infancy and Human Growth," Macmillan, New York.

GESELL, A., 1954, The ontogenesis of infant behavior, in "Manual of Child Psychology," D. Carmichael (ed.), Wiley, New York.

GESELL, A., AND AMATRUDA, C. S., 1954, "Developmental Diagnosis," Paul B. Holber, Inc., New York.

GESELL, A., AND AMATRUDA, C. S., 1962, "Developmental Diagnosis: Normal and Abnormal Child Development, Clinical Methods and Practical Applications," Harper, New York.

GESELL, A., AND THOMPSON, H., 1934, "Infant Behavior: Its Genesis and Growth," McGraw-Hill Book Co., New York.

GILBERT, J. A., 1894, Research on the mental and physical development of school children, *Studies of Yale Psychological Laboratory*, 2:40.

GILLILAND, A. R., 1949, "The Northwestern Intelligence Tests: Examiner's Manual, Test A: Test for Infants 4–12 Weeks Old," Houghton Mifflin, Boston.

GILLILAND, A. R., 1951, "The Northwestern Intelligence Tests: Examiner's Manual, Test B: Test for Infants 13–36 Weeks Old," Houghton Mifflin, Boston.

GODDARD, H. H., 1908, The Binet and Simon tests of intellectual capacity, *The Training School*, 5:3.

GODDARD, H. H., 1910a, Four hundred feeble minded children classified by the Binet method, *Pedagogical Seminary*, 17:387.

Goddard, H. H., 1910*b*, A measuring scale for intelligence, *The Training School,* 6:146

Goddard, H. H., 1911, Two thousand normal children measured by the Binet measuring scale of intelligence, *Pedagogical Seminary, 18*:232.

Golden, M., and Birns, B., 1968, "Piaget Object Scale," Albert Einstein College of Medicine of Yeshiva University, New York.

Goodenough, F. L., 1928*a*, "The Kuhlmann–Binet Tests for Children of Preschool Age," University of Minnesota Press, Minneapolis.

Goodenough, F. L., 1928*b*, A preliminary report on the effects of nursery school training upon intelligence test scores of young children, *27th Yearbook of the National Society of Education,* 361.

Goodenough, F. L., 1939, Look to the evidence: A critique of recent experiments on raising the IQ, *Education Methods, 19*:73.

Goodenough, F. L., 1940, New evidence on environmental influence on intelligence, *39th Yearbook of the National Society of Education,* Part I, 307.

Goodenough, F. L., 1949, "Mental Testing," Rinehart, New York.

Griffiths, R., 1954, "The Abilities of Babies," University of London Press, Ltd., London.

Hallowell, D. K., 1925–1927, Mental tests for preschool children, *Psychological Clinic,* 16:235.

Hallowell, D. K., 1941, Validity of mental tests for young children, *Journal of Genetic Psychology, 58*:265.

Harms, I. E., 1951, A study of some variables affecting the reliability of intelligence test scores during late infancy, unpublished doctoral dissertation, State University of Iowa.

Herring, R. M., 1937, An experimental study of the reliability of the Buhler Baby Tests, *Journal of Experimental Education, 6*(2):147.

Hindley, C. B., 1960, The Griffiths Scale of Infant Development: Scores and predictions from 3 to 18 months, *Journal of Child Psychology and Psychiatry, 1*:99.

Hindley, C. B., 1965, Stability and change in abilities up to 5 years: Group trends, *Journal of Child Psychology and Psychiatry, 6*:85.

Horrocks, J. E., 1964, "Assessment of Behavior," C. E. Merrill, Columbus.

Hunt, J. McV., and Bayley, N., 1971, Explorations into patterns of mental development and prediction from the Bayley Scales of Infant Development, *Minnesota Symposium on Child Psychology, 5*:52.

Illingworth, R. S., 1961, The predictive value of developmental tests in the first year, with special reference to the diagnosis of mental subnormality, *Journal of Child Psychology and Psychiatry, 2*:210.

Illingworth, R. S., 1972 (originally published in 1960), "The Development of the Infant and Young Child, Normal and Abnormal," The Williams & Wilkins Co., Baltimore.

Itard, J. G., 1938, "The Wild Boy of Avergnon," G. Humphrey and M. Humphrey (trans.), Appleton-Century-Crofts, New York.

Jastrow, J., 1892, Some anthropological and psychological tests on college students—a preliminary survey, *American Journal of Psychology, 4*:420.

Kagan, J., 1971, "Change and Continuity in Infancy," Wiley, New York.

Knobloch, H., and Pasamanick, B., 1960, An evaluation of the consistency and predictive value of the forty week Gesell development schedule, *in* "Child Development and Child Psychiatry," G. Shagass and B. Pasamanick (eds.), Psychiatric Research Report of the American Psychiatric Association, No. 13, 10.

Knobloch, H., and Pasamanick, B., February 1966, Prediction from assessment of neuromotor and intellectual status in infancy, paper presented at American Psycho-pathological Association Meeting.

KOONTZ, C. W., 1974, "Koontz Child Developmental Program," Western Psychological Services, Los Angeles.

KRAEPELIN, E., 1895, Der psychologische Versuch in der Psychiatrie, *Psychologische Arbeiten, 1*:1.

KUHLMANN, F., 1911, Binet and Simon's system for measuring the intelligence of children, *Journal of Psycho-Asthenics, 15*:76.

KUHLMANN, F., 1922, "A Handbook of Mental Tests," Warwick & York, Inc., Baltimore.

LINFERT, H. E., AND HIERHOLZER, H. M., 1928, "A Scale for Measuring the Mental Development of Infants During the First Years of Life," Williams & Wilkins, Baltimore.

MACFARLANE, J. W., 1953, The uses and predictive limitations of intelligence tests in infants and young children, *Bulletin WHO, 9*:409.

MACRAE, J. M., 1955, Retests of children given mental tests as infants, *Journal of Genetic Psychology, 87*:111.

MCCALL, R. B., HOGARTY, P. S., AND HURLBURT, N., 1972, Transitions in infant sensorimotor development and the prediction of childhood IQ, *American Psychologist, 27*:728.

MCGRAW, M. B., 1942, Appraising test responses of infants and young children, *The Journal of Psychology, 14*:89.

MCHUGH, G., 1943, Changes in IQ at the public school kindergarten level, *Psychology Monographs, 55*(2).

MECHAM, M. J., 1971, "Verbal Language Development Scale," American Guidance Service, Inc., Circle Pines, Minn.

MICHALSON, L., AND LEWIS, M., 1975, Scales of socioemotional development, unpublished paper.

MOORE, T., 1967, Language and intelligence: A longitudinal study of the first eight years, Part I: Patterns of development in boys and girls, *Human Development, 10*:88.

MUNSTERBERG, H., 1891, Zur individual Psychologie, *Centralblatt für Nervenheilkunde und Psychiatric, 14*.

NELSON, V. L., AND RICHARDS, T. W., 1938, Studies in mental development, I: Performance on Gesell items at 6 months and its predictive value for performance on mental tests at 2 and 3 years, *Journal of Genetic Psychology, 52*:303.

PETERSON, J., 1925, "Early Conceptions and Tests of Intelligence," World Book Company, New York.

PRECHTL, H., AND BEINTEMA, D., 1964, "The Neurological Examination of the Full Term Newborn Infant," Heineman, London.

PREYER, W., 1888 (originally published in 1882), "The Mind of the Child," D. Appleton, New York.

RICCIUTI, H. N., 1965, Object grouping and selective ordering behavior in infants 12 to 24 months old, *Merrill–Palmer Quarterly, 11*:129.

RICHARDS, T. W., AND NELSON, V. L., 1938, Studies in mental development, II: Analyses of abilities tested at age of 6 months by the Gesell schedule, *Journal of Genetic Psychology, 52*:327.

RICHARDS, T. W., AND NELSON, V. L., 1939, Abilities of infants during the first 18 months, *Journal of Genetic Psychology, 55*:299.

RINGWALL, E. A., 1965, "Prelinguistic Infant Vocalization Analysis," State University of New York, Buffalo, New York.

ROBERTS, J. A. F., AND SEDGLEY, E., 1965, Intelligence testing of full-term and premature children by repeated assessments, in "Studies in Psychology," C. Banks and P. L. Broadhurst (eds.), University of London Press, London, p. 119.

ROSENBLITH, J. F., 1961, "Manual for Behavioral Examination of the Neonate as Modified by Rosenblith from Graham," Brown Duplicating Service, Providence, Rhode Island.

SEGUIN, E., 1907 (reprinted from original edition of 1886), "Idiocy: Its Treatment by the Physiological Method," Bureau of Publications, Teachers College Columbia University, New York.

SHARP, S. E., 1898–1899, Individual psychology: A study in psychological method, American Journal of Psychology, 10:329.

SHIELD INSTITUTE FOR RETARDED CHILDREN, 1968, Early identification and treatment of the infant retardate and his family, New York.

SHINN, M., 1900, "The Biography of a Baby," Houghton Mifflin, Boston.

SHIRLEY, M., 1933, "The First Two Years," University of Minnesota Press, Minneapolis.

SHOTWELL, A. M., AND GILLILAND, A. R., 1943, A preliminary scale for the measurement of the mentality of infants, Child Development, 14:167.

SIMON, A. J., AND BASS, L. G., 1956, Toward a validation of infant testing, American Journal of Orthopsychiatry, 26:340.

SIMON, T., 1900, Recherches anthropométriques sur 223 garçons anormaux agés de 8 à 23 ans, L'Année Psychologique, 6:191.

SIMPSON, B. R., 1939, The wandering IQ: Is it time to settle down? Journal of Psychology, 7:351.

SKODAK, M., 1939, Children in foster homes: A study of mental development, University of Iowa Studies on Child Welfare, 16(1).

STERN, W., 1924 (originally appeared in 1914), "Psychology of Early Childhood up to the Sixth Year of Age," Henry Hal, New York.

STOTT, L. H., AND BALL, R. S., 1963, "Evaluation of Infant and Preschool Mental Tests," Merrill–Palmer Institute, Detroit. Also, 1965, Monographs of the Society for Research in Child Development, 30(3), Serial No. 101.

STRAYER, G. D., 1911, "Age and Grade Census of Schools and Colleges," Government Printing Office, Report of the U.S. Bureau of Education, Bulletin #5, Washington, D.C.

STUTSMAN, R., 1931, "Mental Measurement of Preschool Children," The World Book Cc., New York.

SYMMES, E., 1933, An infant testing service as an integral part of a child guidance clinic, American Journal of Orthopsychiatry, 3:409.

TERMAN, L. M., 1916, "The Measurement of Intelligence," Houghton Mifflin, Boston.

TERMAN, L. M., KOHS, S. C., CHAMBERLAIN, M. B., ANDERSON, M., AND HENRY, B., 1918, The vocabulary test as a measure of intelligence, Journal of Educational Psychology, 9:452.

THOMAS, H., 1970, Psychological assessment instruments for use with human infants, Merrill–Palmer Quarterly, 16:179.

THORNDIKE, R. L., 1940, Constancy of the IQ, Psychological Bulletin, 37:167.

TRABUE, M. R., AND STOCKBRIDGE, F. P., 1922, "Measure Your Mind," Doubleday, New York.

UZGIRIS, I. C., AND HUNT, J. McV., 1966, An instrument for assessing infant psychological development, mimeographed paper, Psychological Development Laboratories, University of Illinois.

WALLIN, J. E. W., 1918, The peg form boards, Psychological Clinician, 12:40.

WATSON, J. B., AND WATSON, R. R., 1921, Studies in infant psychology, Scientific Monthly, 13:493.

WELLMAN, B. L., 1932a, Some new bases for interpretation of the IQ, *Journal of Genetic Psychology*, 41:116.

WELLMAN, B. L., 1932b, The effects of preschool attendance upon the IQ, *Journal of Experimental Education*, 1:48.

WERNER, E., AND BAYLEY, N., 1966, The reliability of Bayley's revised scale of mental and motor development during the first year of life, *Child Development*, 37:39.

WERNER, E. E., HONZIK, M. P., AND SMITH, R. S., 1968, Prediction of intelligence and achievement at 10 years from 20-month pediatric and psychological examinations, *Child Development*, 39:1063.

WISSLER, C. L., 1901, The correlation of mental and physical tests, *Psychology Review Monograph Supplement*, 3(6).

WITTENBORN, J. R., 1957, "The Placement of Adoptive Children," Charles C Thomas, Springfield, Illinois.

WITTENBORN, J. R., ASTRACHAN, M. A., DEGOUGER, M. W., GRANT, W. W., JANOFF, I. E., KUGEL, R. B., MYERS, B. J., RIESS, A., AND RUSSELL, E. C., 1956, A study of adoptive children, II. The predictive validity of the Yale developmental examination of infant behavior, *Psychological Monographs*, 70(2).

3   *Value and Limitations of Infant Tests: An Overview*

MARJORIE P. HONZIK

The development of intelligence during infancy is impressive and measurable. The anthropometrist measures growth in head size, which reflects the growth of the brain. The neuropathologist measures cerebral DNA to estimate cell number and possible damage from malnutrition or other causes (Winick, 1970). The psychologist measures behavioral change by means of careful observations of responses to specific tasks. In this chapter we shall review critically infant tests and their contribution to the understanding of mental growth in the first months of life.

The development of mental abilities in infancy is rapid and not easily measured. The adequacy of the tests, the skill of the examiner, and above all, the state of the infant affect mental measurement. Despite these limiting factors, pediatricians, psychologists, neurologists, and parents have found the results of testing to be crucial in the diagnosis of specific abilities and deficits; and research workers are turning with increasing frequency to tests to evaluate mental growth and its relevant determinants. We shall discuss sequentially the limitations imposed by the triad of infant, test, and examiner, and then consider the contribution of infant tests to diagnosis and research on infant intelligence.

THE INFANT

The growth of cognitive functions is intertwined with somatic growth, which makes the testing of the infant a challenge. The baby triples his body weight in the first year but the greatest changes occur in the brain, where there is some increase in cell number but marked

MARJORIE P. HONZIK · University of California at Berkeley.

increase in cell size, number of dendrites, and in the myelin sheath covering the nerve axons. The weight gain of the brain during early infancy is of greater proportion than the weight gain that takes place in any other somatic area (Dodgson, 1962). Accompanying structural growth are the marked changes in cognitive development that are revealed in the infant's changing perception of and reactions to his world.

The rapidly changing organism requires skillful management by the examiner, who must be continuously sensitive to and vigilant of the marked developmental changes as well as the continuously changing state of each individual child during the testing period.

The requirements of a good test are exacting. Not only does it have to yield reliable and valid scores, but it has to cover the repertoire of cognitive behaviors that are developing and changing from day to day; and clearly it must include materials that will elicit maximum responses at all developmental levels. The perfect assessment, then, takes place when the squalling, sucking, chewing, ever-moving baby is relatively quiescent, attentive, wide-eyed with interest, and above all, responsive to the tester and his toys. This idyllic situation is only achieved with effort on the part of all concerned.

Information processing begins at birth or earlier, but the baby has the greater problem during the paranatal period of accommodating to a life of independent breathing and assimilation of food. Somatic development and change create difficulties in testing at many stages of adjustment during the first years of life. In the immediately postnatal period the infant is often drowsy and unresponsive and the time periods available for testing are very short. Careful observations indicate that infants in the postnatal period are, on the average, alert only 10% of the time. The great ingestion of food relative to body size during the early postnatal months frequently leads to discomfort and colic, which intermittently interfere with the baby's responses. As this stage passes and he is more consistently comfortable, the baby's awareness of strange people and situations becomes apparent. "Awareness of a strange situation" or "fear of strangers" may be used as a test item (Bayley, 1969), but this apprehensive stage may make for less than optimal responses on certain test items. The teething child is often more interested in chewing the test equipment than in responding to it. The child who is learning to crawl and walk wants to practice these skills and is proportionately less interested in responding to form boards and problem situations. The skilled tester, using all the patience, perseverence, and charm that he or she can muster, usually can elicit the baby's best responses, but it is not always easy. This descriptive account suggests aspects of the baby's development that may result in errors of measurement in the test results, but it also suggests that we are considering the intellectual development of a living, vibrant, growing organism. The metamorphosis may not be as great as in the butterfly, but the sturdy, almost verbal 2-year-old has come a long way from his immature state at birth. Do the scores on infant tests document these changes? The purpose of this chapter is to answer this question.

INFANT TESTS

Infant tests reflect the concerns of their authors. Diagnosis was the primary objective of the Gesell (Gesell *et al.*, 1934, 1940, 1941), the Griffiths (1954), and the Brunet–Lézine (1951) tests. Cattell (1940) and Bayley (1933, 1969) were more interested in devising tests that could be used to study the development of mental abilities during the first years of life. However, all five tests have been used in major research projects and all have been and are being used in the diagnosis of individual children. More recently Uzgiris and Hunt (1966) in this country and Audrey Little in Australia have been assembling test items that more specifically test Piaget's stages. Another trend is the use of abbreviated screening tests. The most notable is the Denver Developmental Screening Test (DDST), which is being widely used by pediatricians in the United States and in a number of other countries.

Arnold Gesell of Yale was the pioneer in infant testing. His first degree was in psychology but his approach to infant testing is that of the pediatric neurologist, as indicated by the title of his handbook *Developmental Diagnosis* (with Amatruda, 1941). Griffiths (1954) expresses her indebtedness to Gesell, stating that the justification for a new test is the "urgency of the need for early diagnosis of mental condition in special cases." However, she shows greater concern about test standardization and the reliability of the scores than was true of Gesell.

All infant tests include many items first described by Gesell. The Brunet–Lézine test (1951) is a translation into French of the Gesell schedules, but the test items are arranged by age levels. The two tests constructed by American psychologists Bayley (1933, 1969) and Cattell

(1940) were developed as research instruments. These investigators were far more attentive than Gesell to the problems of test construction, sampling, and adequate standardization.

These five tests have been widely used. Their distinctive characteristics will be summarized before we discuss the contribution of infant tests to our understanding of intellectual development.

The Gesell Developmental Schedules

Gesell and Amatruda (1941) wrote that "developmental diagnosis is essentially an appraisal of the maturity of the nervous system with the aid of behavior norms." Many of the test items in his Developmental Schedules stem from this point of view. For example, he describes the stimulating value of the one-inch cube at successive ages: "grasps when placed in hand (4 weeks); ocular fixation when cube is placed on table (16 weeks); prehension on sight by palmer grasp (28 weeks); prehension by digital grasp (40 weeks)." These behaviors are classified as *adaptive behavior*. Other major fields of behavior, according to Gesell, are *motor*, *language*, and *personal-social*. The motor sequence includes both gross skills, such as sitting and walking, and fine motor skills, such as picking up a small sugar pellet or building with blocks. *Language* behavior is assessed in terms of comprehension as well as vocalizations and use of words. Gesell states that the *personal-social* behavior sequence, consisting of responses to people and self-help items, is "greatly affected by the kind of home in which the child is reared." In contrast, he writes of the *motor* scale that it "is of special interest because it has so many neurological implications," and of *language* behavior that it furnishes clues to the organization of the infant's central nervous system. These distinctions as to the determinants of the subscale scores have never been adequately tested. In fact, cross-cultural research on motor development suggests that child-rearing practices may in part determine gross motor skills. Experiential factors in the home affect not only *personal-social* behaviors but also *language* development and *adaptive* behavior, according to Bernstein (1961), Honzik (1967), and others.

The Gesell schedules yield developmental quotients or DQs obtained by the division of the maturity age by the chronological age of the child. Gesell writes that the "DQ represents the proportion of normal development that is present at a given age."

The Gesell schedules are based on extensive observations, but statistical evaluations of the normative findings are not presented, nor is there any attempt to assess the reliability or the validity of the DQs. Gesell's perceptive and almost eloquent descriptions of infant behavior have seldom been equaled:

> the baby can reach with his eyes before he can reach with his hand; at 28 weeks the baby sees a cube; he grasps it, senses surface and edge as he clutches it, brings it to his mouth, where he feels its qualities anew, withdraws it, looks at it on withdrawal, rotates it while he looks, looks while he rotates it, restores it to his mouth, withdraws it again for inspection, restores it again for mouthing, transfers it to the other hand, bangs it, contacts it with the free hand, transfers, mouths it again, drops it, resecures it, mouths it yet again, repeating the cycle with variations—all in the time it takes to read this sentence.

All subsequent authors of infant tests raided the Gesell schedules for test items, with appropriate acknowledgment of indebtedness. The test materials from the Gesell schedules found most frequently in other tests are the red ring and string, the red one-inch cubes, the sugar pellet, and the small dinner bell with handle. These materials are used in the early months to test visual and auditory responses, eye–hand coordinations, and problem solving.

A screening test that not only uses Gesell items but is modeled on it is the Denver Developmental Screening Test (DDST). This test deserves mention because of the care with which it was assembled and because of its wide use in the United States, Canada, and a number of European countries. Frankenburg and Dodds (1967) developed this screening test to "aid in the early detection of delayed development in young children." Frankenburg et al. (1971) reported on the basis of a few cases that the reliability and validity of this scale is fairly high. They concluded that this screening test used with infants in the first year of life misses approximately 13% of the cases who would obtain an abnormal rating on the Bayley test. Infants and young children earning an abnormal rating on the DDST average psychomotor development indexes (PDIs) of from 50 to 73 on the Bayley.

The Griffiths Scale of Mental Development

The Griffiths scale, published in 1954, resembles the Gesell schedules in some important dimensions. Ruth Griffiths is concerned with diagnosis; she is a perceptive observer of the behaviors of infants, and she wants to avoid any pretense of measuring "intelligence" in infancy. Her interest was in assembling a good and reliable test that detects deficits in the following areas of functioning: locomotion, personal-social, hearing and speech, eye and hand, and performance. These categories resemble those of Gesell, but Gesell's motor scale is divided into locomotion and performance; his language scale is called more precisely "Hearing and Speech"; and the adaptive scale is termed simply "Eye and Hand." An effort was made to standardize this scale on a representative sample of infants. The distribution of the paternal occupations of the 552 children tested was similar to that of employed males in the United States. A test–retest correlation of 0.87 was reported for 60 infants who were retested after an average interval of 30 weeks. Griffiths wrote that there is nothing necessarily fixed or permanent about an intelligence quotient as such. In addition, she wrote:

> . . . it has often puzzled the writer why psychologists should for so long have expected that the results of a single test, applied in some one particular hour of a child's life, under particular circumstances, should necessarily carry within it any particular implication of finality, or suggestion that if repeated the ratio of the child's performance to his age should remain unchanged. In no other field of diagnostic work is such a condition expected.

Brunet–Lézine Test

This test follows the Gesell schedules in dividing the test items into the four categories of motor, adaptive, language, and personal-social. However, it differs in that it is a point scale with six test items at each month level, followed by four questions that are asked of the mother or caretaker. The number of test items measuring each of the four behavior categories varies at the different age levels, but for the most part there are two *motor* and four *adaptive* items, and one *motor*, one *language*, and two *personal-social* questions. The test is scored according to the four categories and whether or not the score is based on an observation item or a question. The manual for this test is not available in the United States. The test is used extensively in Europe for diagnosis and was the test of choice in the Stockholm longitudinal study described by Klacken-berg-Larsson and Stensson (1968) and Brucefors (1972).

Cattell's Infant Intelligence Scale

This scale was assembled by Psyche Cattell to assess the mental development of a group of normal children in a longitudinal study conducted in the School of Public Health at Harvard. Cases were selected from prenatal clinics. This meant that well-to-do families were excluded from the standardization sample, as were those of the lowest economic levels. Cattell acknowledged "the vast amount of pioneer work of Gesell" and stated that his battery of tests was used as the foundation for her scale. However, Cattell excluded from her test, items of a personal-social nature, since they are influenced to a marked degree by "home training," and motor items involving the large muscles. Cattell provided objective procedures for administering and scoring the tests. Her test is an age scale with five items listed at each month level in the first year. The standardization was based on a total of 1346 examinations administered to 274 children, who were tested at ages 3, 6, 9, 12, 18, 24, 30, and 36 months.

The Cattell test has many good points. The items are of interest to the children. The instructions for administering and scoring are clear. Odd–even reliability was 0.56 for the 3-month test, but for the 6-month test it was 0.88, and at subsequent age levels it varied from 0.71 to 0.90.

There are two disadvantages to this test as compared with the Bayley series. Because the standardization testing was done at 3-month intervals the item placements at ages 2, 4, 5, 7, 8, 10, and 11 months are interpolated values. As a result, the transitions from age to age are less smooth than when standardization testing is done at monthly intervals. A second disadvantage is that the total number of test items covering the age period 2–12 months is 55, in contrast to over 100 items in both Bayley's California First Year Mental Scale and in the Brunet–Lézine. Griffiths's scale, which includes both locomotor and performance items, has 155 test items for the age period 1–12 months. Because the Cattell test is shorter than the other tests, it seldom tires the babies. It can usually be completed within a half hour.

The Bayley Scales of Infant Development

These scales, which include both mental and motor tests and a behavior record, are based on more than 40 years of research. Bayley published the California First Year Mental Scale in 1933. Her mental scale includes largely test items that are termed *adaptive* or *language* by Gesell, with a few *personal-social* and *motor* items. The test was assembled to test the children in the Berkeley Growth Study. This cohort was selected from two hospitals; one accepted clinic cases and the other only those who could pay for the delivery. All occupational classes were represented but a disproportionate number of the fathers were students or in the professions. From 47 to 61 babies were tested each month. The preliminary standardization was based on these tests. Split-half reliabilities were only 0.63 and 0.51 for the first two months but at subsequent ages ranged from 0.74 to 0.95.

The 1969 revision of the Bayley Mental and Motor Scales and Behavior Record includes new items and changes in the ordering of the test items. Standardization was done on a stratified United States sample of 1262 children, with from 83 to 94 tested at each age level. The split-half reliability coefficients for the 1969 scale are higher than those reported for the 1933 version of this test; from 0.81 to 0.93 (Werner and Bayley, 1966). Bayley (1969) wrote that the mental scale was designed to "assess sensory-perceptual acuities, discriminations, and the ability to respond to these; the early aquisition of 'object constancy,' memory, learning, and problem solving ability; vocalizations and the beginnings of verbal communication; and early evidence of the ability to form generalizations and classifications, which is the basis of abstract thinking."

This test was administered to approximately 50,000 eight-month-old babies born in 12 different hospitals; it was administered as a part of the collaborative study sponsored by the National Institute of Neurological Diseases and Stroke. These test results have been used in many investigations, which will be discussed later in this chapter.

Summary

These are the tests. Test–retest reliability where reported is adequate or good. What of the validity? All five tests have been widely used on research projects. It is only in the findings they have yielded that the value and thus the validity of the tests can be determined.

PREDICTION FROM INFANT TESTS

Gesell and Amatruda (1941) wrote "diagnosis implies prognosis." Griffiths did not expect her test score to be predictive. Cattell (1940) noted instances of marked variability in IQs of infants and young children on her test and concluded that "there is no age from birth to maturity at which it is safe to base an important decision on the results of intelligence tests alone." The purpose of her test, besides diagnosis, was "to add to existing knowledge as to the variability in the pattern of mental growth."

How well do these tests predict? As in most areas of human behavior, it depends! It depends on the integrity of the central nervous system, the genetic blueprint, in subtle and complex ways on experience, and, above all, on the interaction of all these factors. Investigators have begun to sort out the tangled skein and the picture is gradually becoming clearer.

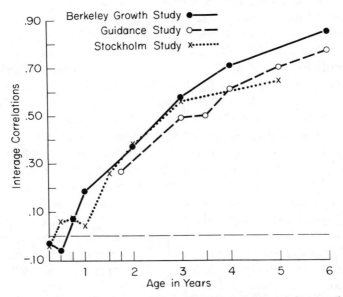

FIG. 1. Prediction of IQs on the Stanford–Binet, Form L or L-M, at eight years from earlier scores on the California Infant and Preschool Scales in the Berkeley Growth Study and the Berkeley Guidance Study and from earlier scores on the Brunet–Lézine in the Stockholm Study.

The Gesell, Griffiths, Brunet–Lézine, Cattell, and Bayley tests have all been used extensively in the prediction of later IQs from infant test scores. The method used to portray these results is by interage correlations. Agreement among investigators is high. In Figure 1 interage correlations between Bayley's infant test scores and Stanford–Binet Form L IQs at 8 years are shown for the Berkeley Growth Study sample (Bayley, 1949) and the Guidance Study sample (Honzik *et al.*, 1948) born in 1928–1929. These interage correlations are remarkably similar to those obtained for a Stockholm sample born between 1955 and 1961 and tested in infancy on the Brunet-Lézine, and tested at 8 years on Form L of the Stanford–Binet (Klackenberg-Larsson and Stensson, 1968; Brucefors, 1972). Neither of these longitudinal studies shows prediction of 8-year IQs from infant mental test scores, but both do show increasing prediction during the age period 1–3 years. This cross-validation of findings is impressive since the studies differ in three major respects: the infant tests used (Bayley versus Brunet–Lézine), cohort difference (Swedish versus United States samples), and a time period difference of 30 years.

These findings are further cross-validated by those of Cattell (1940), who reported that scores on her test at 3 months correlated 0.10 with 3-year IQs on the Stanford–Binet, and by those of Hindley (1960), who found a correlation of -0.13 between the 3- and 12-month test scores on the Griffiths for a London sample (see Table I). It should be noted here that whereas the babies in the Stockholm and London studies were tested at ages 3, 6, 12, 18, and 24 months, the babies in Bayley's Berkeley Growth Study were tested each month and the scores averaged for 3-month periods for purposes of determining the stability of test scores.

Table I shows that although the correlations over developmentally long time periods are negligible, adjacent ages yield moderately high *r*s. The findings of this table indicate what has become a truism in longitudinal studies of infants and children: the interage correlations are highly related to the age at testing and inversely related to the interval between tests. The negligible and even negative prediction from test scores obtained during the first months of life does not appear to be a chance phenomenon of one study but rather a developmental fact. What is the explanation? The moderate interage correlations between the 3- and 6-month scores of over 0.50 found in three different countries suggest that the changes in relative position are taking place gradually (Table I).

Brucefors *et al.* (1974), in an analysis of the test results for the Swedish sample, compared two groups of children who showed the

TABLE I

Interage Correlations of Infant Mental Test Scores Based on Five Different Tests

Investigator	Study site	Test	Approx. N	Interage correlations (in months)					
				3×6 r	3×12 r	3×36 r	6×9 r	6×12 r	6×36[a] r
Bayley (1949)	Berkeley	Bayley Calif. Infant Test	61	0.57	0.28	-0.09	0.72	0.52	0.10
Klackenberg-Larsson and Stensson (1968)	Stockholm	Brunet–Lézine	140	0.51	0.36	-0.08	0.70	0.59	-0.05
Hindley (1960, 1965)	London	Griffiths	29–80	0.53	-0.13	—	—	0.34	0.40
Cattell (1940)	Harvard	Cattell	35	—	—	0.10	—	—	0.34
Nelson and Richards (1939)	Fels	Gesell	48–80	—	—	—	—	0.72	0.46

[a] The 36-month test was the California Preschool Scale in the Bayley study and forms of the Stanford–Binet in the other four investigations.

greatest gains and losses over the age period 3 months to 8 years. The ascending group at 3 months had an average IQ of 84. The average IQ of this subsample at 8 years was 114 on the Terman–Merrill. The average IQ of the descending group was 111 at 3 months and 84 at 8 years. The rate of change in both of these extreme groups was gradual, with both groups earning the same score at about 18 months. Brucefors's preferred interpretation of the marked changes, which also account in part for the negative correlations between the 3-month and childhood mental test scores, is in terms of *activity level*. Less active infants may be less responsive to test stimuli in the early months and earn lower scores, but they may be acquiring information and developing skills that serve them well at a later age period.

Escalona (1968) wrote that "inactive babies show more sustained visual attention and do more tactile exploration of the immediate environment . . . up to at least 8 months than do active babies." In contrast, Escalona reported that "active babies, between the ages of 4 and 12 weeks, tend to develop responsiveness to relatively distant stimuli earlier, and acquire locomotion and the capacity for purposive manipulation of objects somewhat sooner." Escalona added that "the claim that activity level demonstrably affects the course of development does nothing to define the process or mechanisms that account for variations." She took as a working hypothesis that differences in activity level below the age of 8 months can be attributed to differences in the threshold for the release of movement. This hypothesis suggests a constitutional difference that predisposes the infant to react with activity or inactivity.

Support for the possibility that activity level may play a part in determining the age changes in mental test performance in infancy comes from Bayley and Schaefer (1964). They reported that the boys in the Berkeley Growth Study who had high IQs in later life were as infants calm, happy, and positive in their responses. They found that an abrupt shift in the nature of the correlations with the activity ratings at 18 months coincided with a drop in the boys' rs between mental and motor scores. They also found that activity in the child, his mental test scores, and hostility in the mother are correlated in the latter half of the first year but not thereafter. These authors concluded, "There is here a suggestion that hostile maternal behavior toward sons may goad them to activity and stimulate development until the boys begin to walk." They added, "If this is true, then we might postulate that the problems posed by active boys when they start running about and getting into things result in suppressive controls by mothers who are already hostile; at the same time, the accepting permissive mothers are encouraging activity in their relatively passive babies."

A similar trend was reported for the girls, but the impact of the mother's behavior on the girls' test score is much less clear. There is some evidence (Bing, 1963; Honzik, 1967) that the father's role is important in the development of the girls' cognitive skills, and the fathers were not rated in the Berkeley Growth Study. Taken together, these findings suggest that the road to high intellectual performance in later childhood is a complex one. Whether the baby is relatively active or inactive in the first year may itself make a difference, but these individual differences also have an impact on the caretakers, whose responses may further affect cognitive development. In sum, the fact of the low predictions of infants' mental test scores has led to hypotheses and perhaps a model of at least how some of the changes in mental test performance may occur.

Effect of Including Mothers' Reports on Test Scores and Interage Prediction

Correlations between test scores earned at 6 months and 3 years (Table I) indicate that predictions are higher for the Griffiths and Gesell tests than for Bayley's Infant Mental Scale and the Brunet–Lézine. This difference may be due to the fact that the mothers' reports of test behaviors are not included in the scores on the Bayley test but play an important part in the scores on the Gesell and the Griffiths. It is possible that the more intelligent and more educated mother or caretaker gives a clearer picture of the child's behavior than the less able mother, thus adding her capabilities to the individual differences in the babies' test scores. In some instances the mothers' reports would contribute to more accurate scores. For example, Honzik *et al.* (1965) found that infants who were "suspected" of having neurological impairment from their birth records vocalized with greater frequency during their mental tests at 8 months than was true of the normal control group. The conclusion was reached that the 8-month babies in the control group were more inhibited by the strangeness of the test situation, so vocalized less in the test situation and thus failed the vocalization items on the Bayley. On the

Griffiths and the Gesell scales the mothers' reports of vocalizing would have been credited. On future tests it would seem advisable to score a test with and without the caretakers' reports so that the advantages of both scores would be available. This is now possible on the Brunet–Lézine.

Vocalization Factor Score

Many researchers have concluded that early infant test scores are of little value because of the low negative interage correlations obtained when infant scores are compared with IQs obtained during childhood. Bayley's findings are among the most clear-cut in showing little or no prediction, and yet it was from a cluster analysis of the items of her test given each month to the children in the Berkeley Growth Study that a vocalization factor was obtained (Cameron et al., 1967). This factor score is moderately predictive to the age of 36 years, but for girls only (Bayley, 1968). The age of first passing each test item was the score used in the correlation matrix from which the vocalization factor was derived. Vocalization dimension definers include: vocalizes eagerness, vocalizes displeasure, says "da da" or equivalent, and says two words.

In the same year that Cameron et al. published the results of the vocalization factor score, Moore (1968) in England reported for the London sample that a "speech quotient" derived from the hearing and speech section of the Griffiths scale showed some constancy from 6 to 18 months in girls ($r = 0.51$, $p < 0.01$) but "virtually none in boys" ($r = 0.15$). This sex difference is of borderline statistical significance. Consistent with this finding is the failure of the boys' 6-month speech quotient to predict any later assessment, whereas that of the girls is significantly related to vocabulary at age 3 years. Moore concluded that "clearly, linguistic development runs a steadier course from an earlier age in female infants."

The sex difference in stability of vocalizations and a "speech quotient" was discovered independently from infant tests in London and Berkeley. Further confirmation of this finding was reported by Kagan (1971) in his study of continuity and change in infant behaviors. He found greater continuity and stability in the vocalizations of girls than of boys in a longitudinal study covering the first 3 years of life. He reported that the amount of vocalizing to facial stimuli was relatively stable in girls during the first year and that these vocalization scores predicted verbal behavior, but not overall IQ, at age $2\frac{1}{2}$ years. McCall *et al.* (1972) concluded from these three studies that vocalization in infancy may have a special salience for females that it does not connote for males with respect to predicting later mental test performance.

A Sex Difference in Prediction from Infant Tests

The greater stability of infant vocalizations in girls than in boys suggests that there might be a sex difference in prediction of infant test scores.

McCall *et al.* (1972) reported for the Fels longitudinal data that the 6-month Gesell DQs predicted $3\frac{1}{2}$-year Stanford–Binet IQs for girls ($r = 0.62$, $p < 0.01$), but not for boys ($r = -0.01$). This difference is statistically significant at the 0.02 level. For this same sample the 12-month DQs yielded a fairly high correlation with the 6-year Stanford–Binet IQs for girls ($r = 0.57$, $p < 0.001$), but not for boys ($r = 0.22$, $p < 0.05$). Hindley (1965) also reported a rather marked sex difference in the stability of girls' DQs on the Griffiths as compared with that of boys. Predictions of the 5-year Stanford–Binet IQs from the Griffiths DQs appear in Table II.

In contrast to these results, Klackenberg-Larsson and Stensson (1968) found no sex difference in DQ stability in the Stockholm sample,

TABLE II
*Predictions of 5-Year Stanford–Binet IQs
from Griffiths DQs*

	5-Year Stanford–Binet IQs	
Griffiths DQs	Boys ($N = 43$)	Girls ($N = 37$)
	r	r
6 months	0.24	0.41[b]
18 months	0.35[a]	0.48[b]

[a] $p < 0.05$ level.
[b] $p < 0.01$ level.

but they did find significant sex differences in mean DQ scores, favoring the girls at all age levels tested from 3 months to 5 years, and added that "the differences between the sexes are especially apparent in the language and personal-social scales."

Goffeney et al. (1971) reported the prediction of the Wechsler Intelligence Scale for Children (WISC) scores at age 7 years from the 8-month Bayley test scores for 626 children tested at the University of Oregon Medical School as a part of the Collaborative Project. The mothers in this sample were below average in socioeconomic status; 63% were black and 37% white. The correlations between the 8-month Bayley test scores and the IQs on the WISC were 0.27 ($p < 0.01$) for the females (0.30, $p < 0.01$ for the black and 0.28, $p < 0.01$ for the white females) and 0.12 ($p < 0.05$) for the males (0.01 ns for the black and 0.16, $p < 0.05$ for the

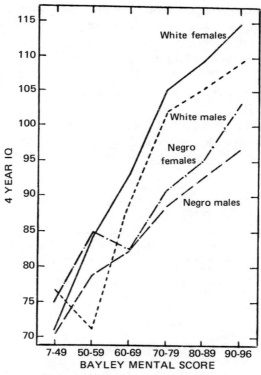

FIG. 2. Mean IQs on the Stanford–Binet, Form L-M, at 4 years according to scores on the Bayley Mental Scale at 8 months (Broman et al., 1975).

white males). Very similar correlations were obtained when the verbal IQs of the WISC were the predicted scores. The sex difference found in this study was minimally present for the total sample of 19,837 children in the Collaborative Project, which included cohorts born in 12 hospitals (Broman *et al.*, 1975). For this large sample, prediction of 4-year Stanford–Binet IQs from Bayley test scores is shown in Figure 2. This figure suggests a much higher relationship between the 8-month and 4-year test scores than is indicated by the correlation coefficients, which are 0.21 for white boys ($N = 4569$), 0.24 for black boys ($N = 5507$), 0.23 for white girls ($N = 4312$), and 0.24 for black girls ($N = 5507$). These coefficients are all highly significant at better than the 0.01 level because of the large number of cases. These samples included a few children with handicapping conditions that would increase the correlations beyond those found for a normal, neurologically intact sample. In other words, in this large study there is positive but extremely low prediction, which is of negligible practical significance. The sex difference suggests greater mental test stability in girls but is not significant.

Socioeconomic Status and Prediction

The effect of the interaction of socioeconomic status and infant test scores on prediction was described by Willerman *et al.* (1970) for a Collaborative Project subsample of 3037 babies born at the Boston Lying-In Hospital. This study shows that socioeconomic status has a significant effect on prediction for children earning low mental scores at 8 months. Children with low scores at 8 months living in homes of low socioeconomic status will do poorly on the 4-year Stanford–Binet, while children with low scores at 8 months living in homes of high socioeconomic status will earn above-average IQs at 4 years. Willerman *et al.* concluded that "poverty amplifies the IQ deficit in poorly developed infants," or stated another way, "infants retarded at 8 months were seven times more likely to obtain low IQs at age 4 years if they come from the lower socioeconomic status than if they come from a higher socioeconomic level." This is a provocative paper but there may be alternative interpretations. Some of the children earning low scores at 8 months may be "slow bloomers" who will eventually develop high verbal or other intellectual skills. The fact that these children live in homes of high socioeconomic status may not be the only determining factor. It may be that they are showing an increasing resemblance to parents who have similar skills. Support for this hypothesis comes from the study of adopted children by Skodak and Skeels (1949), who found that the IQs of adopted children who had never lived with their parents showed an increasing resemblance to the abilities of their own parents but little increase in resemblance to the educational level of the adopting parents during the age period 2–4 years.

Retardation and Minimal Brain Impairment as Factors in Prediction

Relatively high correlations between infant test scores and childhood IQs appear from time to time in the literature. The inclusion of children with very low scores usually accounts for these findings. MacRae (1955) reported a correlation of 0.56 ($p < 0.01$) between ratings based on either the Cattell or the Gesell tests, administered to 40 children under 12 months of age, and WISC IQs obtained at 5 years or older. This coefficient is considerably higher than that usually reported for normal children. We note that some of the children in this sample were living in a home for the mentally deficient. The purpose of the testing was for adoption. MacRae found that the ratings based on the infant test scores were very helpful. More than half the ratings of the babies did not change at all between the first and sixth year, and ratings of only two children changed by more than one rating category. The rating categories were definitely deficient, somewhat below average, average, somewhat above average, and definitely superior.

Knobloch and Pasamanick (1960) also reported significant correlations between infant test scores and later IQs. For 147 prematures considered normal, Gesell DQs at 40 weeks correlated with 3-year Stanford–Binet IQs 0.43; but for 48 children who were "neurologically or intellectually abnormal," the correlation rose to 0.74. These authors stated that correlations of the same order of magnitude were obtained for both white and black children in this Baltimore sample, suggesting the validity of the findings.

The results indicating greater stability in the test scores of low-scoring babies are of importance to neurologists, pediatricians, psychologists, and others who depend on infant tests in the diagnosis of mental impairment and subnormality.

DIAGNOSTIC VALUE OF INFANT TESTS

A majoi use of infant tests is in the diagnosis of mental defect. How accurate are these assessments? The fallibility of the tests themselves was suggested earlier in this chapter. On the other hand, the reliability of the tests is reasonably high and all tests are moderately predictive for low-scoring children. Before standardized tests were available, physicians, and especially pediatricians, had to depend entirely on their background of experience in making a diagnosis of mental defect. Their decisions would often have far-reaching effects on the lives of children, especially if institutionalization or adoption were being considered. To what extent does the information from an infant test help in the diagnosis? Illingworth (1960), a pediatrician, described in some detail the need for assistance in assessing the effects of such conditions as neonatal anoxia, head injury, virus encephalitis, or a subdural hematoma. He concluded from a review of the literature that "there is plenty of evidence that developmental tests, properly used, are of the utmost value." He went on to say, "No one, of course, should expect developmental tests when repeated to give a constant value." He stated that the objective test results should always be supplemented by a history and an evaluation of the quality of performance.

Studies specifically designed to assess the usefulness of infant tests in aiding pediatricians in their diagnosis of handicapping conditions was undertaken by Bierman et al. (1964) and Werner et al. (1968, 1971), using the data of the Kauai Pregnancy Study. In these extensive investigations of the pre- and postnatal development of all children ($N = 681$) born on the island of Kauai in 1954–1955, pediatricians rated the intelligence of the children at about 20 months of age as retarded, low normal, normal, or superior. A total of 93% were rated as normal; 5% as low normal; and 0.6% (1 girl and 3 boys) as retarded. These children were all tested on the Cattell at the same age, 20 months. The agreement between the pediatricians' appraisals and the Cattell IQs was not high ($r = 0.32$) but was statistically significant ($p < 0.01$). The 46% (16 out of 35 children) judged below normal by pediatricians at 20 months earned low IQs or were doing poorly in school at ages 5–9 years. The accuracy of these predictions of poor school performance was increased to 75% if the Cattell IQs were taken into account. Bierman et al. concluded that the test scores appear to be valuable to the pediatrician who does not want to err in the direction of giving a poor prognosis for a child who may later prove capable of adequate if not superior academic performance. Children who at 20 months had normal Cattell IQs, but were misjudged as below normal in intelligence by the pediatricians, were likely to have poor speech, show abnormal or slow motor development, and be of "poor physical status." Children judged *normal* by the pediatricians whose Cattell IQs at 20 months were below 80 were not doing well in school when 6–9 years of age: "from one half to two-thirds of these children were not capable of average academic work." In a follow-up at 10 years of all available children in the Kauai study, Werner *et al.* (1968, 1971) reported that the best single predictor of IQ and achievement at age 10 years was the Cattell IQ at age 20 months. For children with IQs below 80 at age 20 months, a combination of Cattell IQ and pediatricians' ratings of intelligence yielded a high positive correlation ($R = 0.80$) with the IQs on the Primary Mental Abilities tests at 10 years. That the results of this study yielded positive results using 20-month Cattell IQs is remarkable. There is probably no age at which testing is more difficult than at the end of the second year, when children want to be autonomous and are therefore negativistic and resistant to adult suggestions, requiring great skill on the part of the examiner.

Infant tests are used to detect the effect of handicapping conditions known to have occurred at an earlier time, such as rubella during the pregnancy or asphyxia during the neonatal period. Honzik *et al.* (1965) compared the 8-month Bayley mental test scores of a group of infants suspected of having neurological handicaps, on the basis of hospital records, with the scores of a matched normal control group from the same hospitals. In this study the birth records of more than 10,000 babies born in seven different hospitals were scrutinized for evidence of complications of pregnancy or delivery and distress during the neonatal period. Of this group approximately 2% were selected as possibly suspected of having brain impairment and were matched with a normal control group using the same records. The testers of the infants (128 males and 69 females) at 8 months were unaware of the neonatal appraisal as suspect or normal and rated most of the children "normal." The Bayley mental test scores, however, differentiated the suspect from the control group at between the 0.05 and the 0.01 levels of significance. There were also statistically significant differences in the performance on individual test items. This investigation is noteworthy in showing that infant mental tests at 8 months can be differentiating of deficits that are not obvious even to experienced testers.

Test scores do not always reflect the ill effects of asphyxia during delivery. Ucko (1965) reported no difference in the Griffiths DQs at 6 months of children who were anoxic during the neonatal period when they were compared with a matched normal sample from the London longitudinal study. A difference in the selection procedures in the two studies may account for the findings. Ucko was concerned only with the degree of anoxia or asphyxia. In the Honzik study the pediatrician making the decisions as to whether the infant was suspected of having neurological damage took into account evidences of neurological difficulty, describing the babies as follows: "Some[babies] were limp, others rigid, some sucked poorly . . . were frequently excessively irritable, and occasional opisthotonus was seen." Infants are tolerant of some degree of anoxia during the perinatal period, so that probably many of the infants in the Ucko study were not adversely affected by the asphyxia, while in the Honzik study only infants showing some evidence of ill effects were included.

GENETIC STUDIES USING INFANT TESTS

The only direct evidence of the effect of the genetic structure on intelligence comes from chromosomal studies. The advent of hypotonic treatment of cells led to accurate counts of the number of chromosomes in the cells of normal human beings and the possibility of correlating abnormal counts with tested abilities. One of the dramatic discoveries was that individuals with Down's syndrome, or mongolism, have an extra 21st chromosome. Individuals with this genetic makeup are noticeably slow in their mental and motor development, seldom earning IQs of more than 50. The Bayley scales have been used to compare the abilities of Down's syndrome infants reared at home versus those living in an institution (Bayley et al., 1971). The test scores reflected not only the low scores of these children but also the beneficial effects of a home environment. The mean Bayley IQ of the children reared at home was 50; in the hospital, 35. This difference is statistically significant ($p < 0.005$).

Resemblance in the mental abilities of family members is the most frequently used method of assessing the relevance of heredity. Erlenmeyer-Kimling et al. (1963) reported that for most relationship categories the median of the empirical correlations closely approaches the theoretical value predicted on the basis of the genetic relationship alone. The median empirical value of the parent–child correlations is 0.50; the median r for fraternal twins, 0.53; and for identical twins reared together, 0.87, and reared apart, 0.75. These coefficients are based on samples of parents and children of school age. Are the findings similar for infant test scores? The answer is interesting. Parent–child resemblance is negligible in the first months of life, and the characteristic statistic of 0.50 is not reached until the end of the preschool period (Bayley, 1954; Hindley, 1962; and Honzik, 1957, 1963). Skodak and Skeels (1949) reported a similar finding for children who were adopted in the first months of life. The correlations between the adopted children's IQs and their natural parents' IQs (or years of schooling) increased from a near-zero value at 2 years to statistically significant correlations ($p < 0.05$–0.01) at 4 years. The same increase in resemblance was not obtained between the children's IQs and their adoptive parents' years of schooling, although the children's above-average IQs reflected the good environments provided by their adoptive parents. These findings suggest that changes in IQ during the early preschool years are not entirely due to environmental factors. If we can assume that the increasing resemblance between the scores of the natural parents and their children's IQs is due to heredity, the genetic factor still accounts for very little of the total variance in the children's mental test performance.

Twin studies are the ones most frequently cited as showing the effect of genetic similarity on intelligence. Freedman and Keller (1963) tested a group of same-sexed twins every month during the first year on the Bayley scales. These investigators did not know the zygosity of the twins until after the testing period was over. They found that the intrapair difference on the combined mental and motor scales of the monozygotic twins was less in nearly all instances than that of the dizygotic twins ($p < 0.01$). Wilson (1972) and Wilson and Harpring (1972) reported within-pair correlations of monozygotic (MZ) and dizygotic (DZ) twins on the Bayley scales for a group of 261 pairs tested every three months during the first year (see Table III). These coefficients are similar to those found for older children and adults, except that the values for DZ twins are higher. The greater resemblance of fraternal twin babies than that of siblings is in all likelihood the result of the greater similarity in the experience of the twins than in the experiences of single-born children in the same family. There is also the possibility that the experiences of MZ twins are more similar than those of DZ twins. The greater similarity in the genetically similar MZ twins

Table III

Within-Pair Correlations of Twins
on Bayley Scales (261 Pairs)

Age in months	MZ[a] r	DZ[b] r
3	0.84[c]	0.67
6	0.82	0.74
9	0.81[c]	0.69
12	0.82[c]	0.61

[a] Monozygotic.
[b] Dizygotic.
[c] $p < 0.05$.

than in the less similar DZ twins suggests hereditary determination, but the crucial study requires that the twins be reared apart so that there is control of experiential factors.

A study by Nichols and Broman (1974), based on the 8-month Bayley tests given in the Collaborative Study, reported high intratwin correlations (0.84 for 122 pairs of MZ twins and 0.55 for 227 pairs of DZ twins) but a relatively low correlation of 0.22 for siblings. The low resemblance between the 4962 siblings tested at 8 months compared with the DZ intrapair r of 0.55 suggests that the experience of infants living in the same family can be very different and that the extent of the genetic similarity does not preclude great differences in test scores. There is always the possibility that the siblings were fathered by different men, but this is less likely to have occurred in the Collaborative Study, since the siblings were born and tested within a relatively limited time period. In fact, the authors referred to "full" siblings, suggesting that blood checks were done on the parents of these siblings. A significant finding in this study was that the high heritability estimate derived from the difference between the MZ and DZ correlations was due to the higher concordance of severe retardation in the MZ pairs. In the MZ sample, removal of all severely retarded children reduced the intrapair correlation of 0.84 to 0.55. Removal of severely retarded children had no effect on the DZ correlation of 0.55 or the sibling r of 0.22. These authors added that there was evidence that genetic factors are important in severe retardation on the Bayley scale, since the concordance ratio for retardation was significantly higher in the MZ than the DZ twins.

Environmental factors are also implicated in the very low test scores, since the incidence of retardation is significantly higher in the twin samples than among the single siblings.

EXPERIENCE AND INTELLIGENCE IN INFANCY

Interest in the effect of experience on the development of mental abilities has led to an upsurge of investigations of the possible effects of experience on the growth of intelligence in infancy.

The interaction of experience and heredity begins at conception, when the mother's nutrition and health begin to have their effect on the developing embryo. Infant tests are not needed to show the devastating effects of maternal rubella or Western encephalitis on the fetus but are being widely used to assess the effects of maternal and infant malnutrition on the development of the central nervous system (CNS) and intelligence.

Malnutrition

Both the Gesell and the Bayley infant tests have been used extensively in assessments of the effects of malnutrition on intellectual development. Cravioto and Robles (1965) tested the hypothesis that the effect of severe malnutrition on mental development varies as a function of the period of life at which malnutrition is experienced. Twenty infants hospitalized for severe protein–calorie malnutrition were tested on the Gesell scale during hospital treatment and during the rehabilitation period. On the first examination, just after the acute electrolyte disturbance had been corrected, all infants scored considerably below the age norms. During rehabilitation 14 of the children gained in DQs on the Gesell, but the 6 youngest did not, confirming the hypothesis that the younger the infant the greater the adverse effect of poor nutrition. Pollitt and Granoff (1967) cross-validated these findings in Peruvian children with marasmus using the Bayley scales. The scores of this group of previously marasmic infants were compared with those of their siblings who had no unusual medical history and whose measurements were within normal limits. It was found that while the siblings were developing according to age expectation, 17 of the 19 children recovered from marasmus had severe mental and motor retardation. From these studies and those of Mönckeberg (1968) and Chase and Martin (1969), Cravioto and Delicardie (1970) concluded that protein–calorie malnutrition occurring in the first year of life, if severe enough to retard physical growth markedly and to require hospitalization, may have adverse effects on mental development. These authors added that if the duration of the untreated episode is longer than four months, particularly during the first months of life, the effect on mental performance may be so intense as to produce severe mental retardation, which is incompletely corrected by nutritional rehabilitation. With all their limitations, both mental and motor scores of infant tests helped describe the findings objectively and indicate their significance.

Maternal Deprivation

The impetus for studies of the effect of experience on intellectual development has come in part from Bowlby's monograph (1952) describing the ill effects of maternal deprivation. This monograph was the stimulus for research on the ill effects of institutional care, which was reviewed by Ainsworth (1962), Casler (1961), and Yarrow (1961). Casler concluded in his review that in institutional care there is a lack or relative absence of tactile, vestibular, and other forms of stimulation, which accounts for some of the emotional, physical, and intellectual deficits. Casler (1965) later investigated the effects of extra tactile stimulation on infants living in an institution. He found that infants given specific tactile stimulation over a 10-week period performed significantly better on the Gesell Developmental Schedules than did a matched control group. This study, which used a rather small number of cases, should be replicated, but the findings are in line with those of comparative psychologists, such as Harlow (1958), as well as developmental psychologists (Bayley and Schaefer, 1964).

The next question is how long-lasting are the ill effects of institutional care and the good effects of supplemental stimulation. A partial answer is provided by Dennis and Najarian (1957), who tested all the children in a Lebanese crèche where health needs were met but the infants were minimally stimulated. They found that the infants' Cattell IQs were normal at age 2 months but averaged only 63 during the age period 3–12 months. Children tested at ages 4 and 5 years obtained IQs of approximately 90, although they had spent all their lives in the crèche. These results suggest that the period of limited stimulation during infancy had no lasting effect on mental growth. A similar finding was reported by Kagan and Klein (1973) in a cross-cultural study of Guatemalan infants. The rural Guatemalan infant spends most of his life in "the small dark interior of a windowless hut." He is usually kept close to his mother but is rarely spoken to or played with. Compared with American infants, he is extremely passive, fearful, unsmiling, and quiet. These Guatemalan infants were retarded with respect to "activation of hypotheses, alertness, onset of stranger anxiety, and object permanence." In marked contrast to the infants, the Guatemalan preadolescents were comparable to American middle-class norms on tests of perceptual analysis, inference, recall, and recognition memory. Kagan concluded that "infant retardation seems to be partially reversible, and cognitive development during the early years more resilient than had been supposed."

Apparently the effect of added stimulation may last no longer than that of relative deprivation. Rheingold and Bayley (1959) reported transitory gains in social responsiveness in institutionalized infants who were given "more attentive care" by one person from the sixth to the eighth month. These children performed no better on the Cattell test a year later than did a matched group who received no special attention.

Parent– Child Interaction and Infant Test Scores

Another approach to the problem of evaluating environmental influence is to relate infant test scores to socialization practices in the family. Baldwin et al. (1945) were among the first to relate parental behavior to the test scores of infants and young children. He reported that for 94 children in the Fels longitudinal study tested on the Gesell, DQ changes were related to "freedom to explore," "emotional warmth," and "acceleratory methods." These variables, described in different ways, have been found relevant to gains in IQ in a number of subsequent studies. Bayley and Schaefer (1964) reported for the small but intensively tested Berkeley Growth Study sample that boy babies whose mothers evaluated them positively, granted them some autonomy, and expressed affection for them were "happy, positive, calm infants." These boys tended to earn below-average scores on the Bayley tests in the first year but made rapid gains in the next few years, when they were likely to earn high IQs. The authors reported that, conversely, boys who scored high in the first year were active, unhappy, and negative with mothers who were hostile and punitive. These boys tended to have low IQs after 4 years. It is difficult to sort out cause and effect in these relationships. Were the boys' Bayley test scores higher in infancy *because* they were stimulated by the punitive mothers? To what extent did the positive, affectionate mother affect the cognitive development of her son? For girls in this study there was little correlation between the mother's behavior in the first two or three years and their later intelligence. These results were to some extent cross-validated in the much larger Guidance Study sample (Honzik, 1967). Ratings of the *closeness of the mother–son relationship* at 21 months correlated with the mental test scores of the boys at this age ($r = 0.29$, $p < 0.05$). This correlation increased to $0.48 < 0.01$ at 9 years and was still significant at age 40 years (Honzik, 1972). *Closeness of mother to daughter* correlated significantly with the daughter's IQ at 2 years but not thereafter.

In the London longitudinal study Moore (1968) reported a similar increasing correlation between the "emotional atmosphere of the home," "toys, books, and experience," and "example and encouragement" and the children's IQs at 3 and 8 years. The interesting phenomenon here is that although the family variables were rated when the children were aged $2\frac{1}{2}$ years, the correlations, and thus the predictions, of the 8-year IQs were all higher, and significantly so, than the 5-year IQs. Unfortunately Moore did not report the correlation between the family variables and the children's Griffiths DQs at ages 6 months and 12 months, so that age trends cannot be considered from infancy to middle childhood. A major conclusion to be drawn from the four longitudinal studies is that measurable experiences in the home in the first two years may show an increasing correlation with IQs during childhood. It is understandable that evidences of ability of the parents, such as their education or socioeconomic status, would show an increasing correlation with their children's test scores. It is more difficult to comprehend why variables like *mother–son closeness,* which is not related to parental ability, shows an increasing relation to the son's IQ. Actually, later measures of mother–son closeness do not show this correlation, which means that the warmth and concern that the mother has for her son in the early years has a greater effect on his later intellectual functioning than does concurrent favoring and protectiveness in adolescence (Honzik, 1966).

In a study of 41 black babies aged 5 to 6 months, Yarrow *et al.* (1972) differentiated the natural home environment into (1) inanimate stimulation and (2) social stimulation. These two types of environmental variables, obtained from time-sampling observations, were not highly correlated but did correlate significantly with Bayley's mental test scores. It is of interest in this study that the investigators considered the relation of other infant variables to *social* and *inanimate stimulation*. The infant variable *vocalization to bell* correlated significantly with social but not inanimate stimulation. *Goal-directed behaviors* correlated significantly ($p < 0.01$) with both social and inanimate stimulation. Yarrow *et al.* concluded that "it is likely that the infant's orientation to objects and to people very early becomes part of a feedback system with the environment. His smiling, vocalizing, and reaching out to people; his visually attending to and manipulating objects tend to be self-reinforcing and thus, to some extent self-perpetuating."

Two investigators have avoided the problem of inherited similarity of parents and children by studying the relation of the family milieu to infant test scores in adopted children. Beckwith (1971) correlated the Cattell IQs of 24 adopted infants with evaluations of their mothers' interactions with them in the home. Cattell IQs (at 8–10 months) were correlated with the infants' "social experience" ($p < 0.01$) and the extent to which he was "talked to," "touched," and "given an opportunity to explore the house." In this study no relationship was found between the infants' IQs and the adoptive parents' socioeconomic status, but the IQs did correlate with the natural mothers' socioeconomic class.

Another study of 40 adopted children at age 6 months was reported by Yarrow (1963). The maternal variables for the investigation were carefully chosen and covered three major maternal functions: (1) need gratification and tension reduction, (2) stimulation–learning conditions, and (3) affectional interchange. The maternal variables yielding the highest correlations with the 6-month Cattell IQs were *stimulus adaptation* ($r = 0.85$), *achievement stimulation* ($r = 0.72$), *social stimulation* ($r = 0.65$), and *physical contact* ($r = 0.57$). All these correlations were significant at the 0.01 level or better and were much higher than those reported for the natural mother and children. An important question here is how long-lasting the effects of the early infant experience are.

These adopted children were tested again on the WISC at 10 years (Yarrow *et al.*, 1973). Seven of the eight maternal variables assessed when these adopted children were aged 6 months correlated significantly with the WISC IQs at 10 years. However, when the correlations were computed for boys and girls separately, the findings were similar to those reported by Bayley and Schaefer (1964) and others: the relationships were negligible for the girls but highly significant for the boys. The range of rs for the girls was from 0.08 for *achievement stimulation* to 0.24 for *emotional involvement*. The range for the boys was from 0.43 ($p < 0.05$) for *achievement stimulation* to 0.68 ($p < 0.01$) for *physical contact*. These correlations, together with those of other investigators, clearly indicate the importance of early affective relationships and tactual stimulation to mental growth. Fortunately infant mental tests are available and have been used to evaluate the relation of the infant's experience to his test scores concurrently as well as in the prediction of later mental functioning.

SUMMARY

This chapter discusses the available infant tests and the difficulties involved in giving accurate and complete tests in the first year of life. It is noteworthy that the most clear-cut findings are those reported by investigators who are skilled in working with infants, are aware of the pitfalls inherent in assessing infants, and did much of the actual testing themselves. This is true of Bayley, Beckwith, Cattell, Gesell, Hindley, and others.

Reliability and Validity

The Bayley and Cattell infant tests are highly reliable and internally consistent as judged by the correlation of odd with even test items. Test–retest correlations are relatively high over short age periods but decline markedly as the time span between tests lengthens (Bayley, Brunet–Lézine, Cattell, Gesell, and Griffiths). The magnitude of the coefficients and the nature of the interage correlations have been cross-validated by studies in different countries by the use of different tests at different time periods, suggesting that a major determinant of these interrelationships is the rate of development of the human organism. Honzik (1938) noted that the magnitude of the rs varies with the age ratio of the first to the second test. Thus the r between the 3- and 6-month test scores is roughly 0.50, as is the correlation between the 3- and 6-year scores. This age ratio underestimates the magnitude of the rs as the children grow older but is suggestive of the changing rate of development of mental abilities with age.

Another index of the validity of the tests is the agreement between scores on different tests. Erickson *et al.* (1970) reported a correlation of 0.97 (*p* > 0.001) between the Bayley and the Cattell scores of children who ranged in ability from profoundly retarded to normal, suggesting a high degree of validity of the scores of the children in this ability range.

Prediction from Infant Tests

Predictions based on the test scores of infants depend not only on the growth processes but also on the effects of experience and on the nature of the tests used to measure the developing abilities. The following conclusions are reached from the studies discussed:

1. In neurologically intact infants, scores obtained on currently available tests during the first months of life are not predictive of later intelligence because of immaturity, rapidly changing behaviors, or the overriding significance of other behaviors such as the infant's relative *activity* during this age period (Bayley and Schaefer, 1964; Escalona, 1968).

2. Prediction of later intelligence test scores begins to occur in the second half of the first year in girls only (Hindley, 1960, 1965), and more especially in certain specific abilities, such as vocalizations (Cameron *et al.*, 1967; Kagan, 1971).

3. Prediction of later intelligence does not accelerate until after the second birthday (Bayley, 1949; Brucefors, 1972; Hindley, 1965; Honzik *et al.*, 1948).

4. Prediction is markedly more accurate for low-scoring infants, regardless of whether the low score is due to chromosomal aberrations (e.g., trisomy 21), infection (rubella during the pregnancy), injury, perinatal anoxia, or generalized subnormality of unknown etiology.

5. The effect of experience on test constancy is suggested by a study showing that the interage correlations are noticeably higher for children

living in the relatively constant environment of a day-care center (Ra-mey *et al.*, 1973).

Diagnosis

Evidence from many investigations attests to the value of infant mental tests in the diagnosis of even minimal neurological lags or deficits (Bierman *et al.*, 1964; Honzik *et al.*, 1965). Infant test scores are diagnostic of deprivation experiences as well as of the effects of enriched environments. However, the value of these scores is greater in the assessment of deficits than of superiority, since high scores on infant tests are less stable than average or low scores. Precocity in infancy may reflect early maturing or the effects of a great deal of stimulation rather than higher potential for later above-average cognitive functioning.

What can be done to improve diagnoses? The use of mothers' reports as additional information may add to the value of the examina-tion. It is often possible to determine the mother's estimate of the validity of the test by asking her if the baby responded to the test as she would expect him to or if she was surprised at what he could do.

The infant's reactions to the test and his cognitive style should be recorded and evaluated. These evaluations may prove more useful than the test scores. Freedman and Keller (1963) found that monozygotic twins were significantly more alike than dizygotic twins on Bayley's behavior profile, which is a part of the Bayley tests. Actually the behav-ior profile was more differentiating than the mental and motor scales in this study.

For more adequate diagnoses a greater effort should be made to measure specific abilities and new groups of abilities. Also the findings of investigations of cognitive functioning should be considered as possi-ble additions to the current tests. A premise of Fantz and Nevis's (1967) investigations was that "the early development of cognitive function is primarily through perception rather than action." They added that "later individual differences are more likely to be correlated with the early development of perception and attention than with action." Al-though it would not be feasible to duplicate Fantz's experiments in a testing situation, it would be possible to assess infants' attentiveness to schematic drawings as a part of the test. Lewis (1971) wrote that if one views *attention* and its distribution as an information-processing operation, attention can be viewed as a measure of cognitive functioning. Kagan (1971) reported social class differences in attentiveness in the first year, which further suggests its possible relevance to what is termed *intelligence* in the older child. *Attention* is easily assessed in the mental test situation, and if it proves diagnostic or predictive, it should be incorporated into the test score.

DISCUSSION

The value of infant tests is seriously questioned by Lewis (1973) and Lewis and McGurk (1972). This overview suggests why. Infant test scores are not stable over long periods of time, and their relationship to previous and concurrent experience is complex and only beginning to be understood. As Yarrow *et al.* (1973) wrote, "We are still in a rather primitive state with regard to concepts and methodology for handling the dynamic interplay among these sets of variables." Perhaps the key word here is *dynamic*. Growth is seldom simple and seldom occurs at a constant rate; instead it is rather highly interactive and occurs at a decelerating rate. A question that has not been raised but may prove highly relevant is whether experiences are more effective during periods of rapid or of relatively slower growth. Our hypothesis from what is known to date about intellectual development over the life span is that the effect of experiences, both those injurious and those beneficial to the organism's cognitive skills, is negatively related to growth and, thus, to age. In other words, the earlier the experience the greater the potential effect. This does not mean that the effects of experience are reflected immediately in the behavior of the infant. Some of the conditions, such as Western encephalitis or maternal care, are known to have more predictable effects on later cognitive development than on current cognitive skills. Another possibly confounding factor, suggested by the higher correlations between maternal care and infant scores in adopted than in own children, is that aspects of optimal maternal care may be negatively related to genetic potential. This was actually found in the Guidance Study, where the mother's education, which reflects her ability, was negatively related to the most relevant experiential variable, *closeness of mother and child* (Honzik, 1967).

The critiques of Lewis (1973) and Lewis and McGurk (1972) are valuable in asking some significant and cogent questions about attempts to measure "intelligence" in infancy. Infant tests obviously do not measure what is measured by the Stanford–Binet, the Wechsler, or primary abilities tests; they measure abilities and skills that, to a large extent, are the bases and precursors of later mental development. It is clear that the tests could be improved by the elimination of items that are more motor than mental and by the addition of new items suggested by recent research. Infant tests, with all their limitations, have served us well. Possibly their main value has been in diagnosis, but they have also contributed substantially to our understanding of the many factors contributing to the development of abilities in the first years of life.

CONCLUSION

The major question of this review is whether or not test scores accurately describe the growth of mental abilities and reflect the temporary and more permanent effects of experience. This we believe they do, and we believe that with amplification and careful use their value can be enhanced. Standards and reference points are needed and good tests can help serve this need. The purpose of infant testing is to determine the progress of an individual child or the mental development of all children. Prediction of later intellectual functioning is a worthy aim of infant tests but secondary to the more important objective of adding to our understanding and knowledge of the course of development of mental abilities in infancy and early childhood.

REFERENCES

AINSWORTH, M. D., 1962, The effects of maternal deprivation: A review of findings and controversy in the context of research strategy, *in* "Deprivation of Maternal Care: A Reassessment of Its Effects," World Health Organization, Geneva, Switzerland, p. 97.

BALDWIN, A. L., KALHORN, J., AND BREESE, F. H., 1945, Patterns of parent behavior, *Psychological Monograph, 58*(Whole No. 268).

BAYLEY, N., 1933, "The California First Year Mental Scale," University of California Press, Berkeley.

BAYLEY, N., 1949, Consistency and variability in the growth of intelligence from birth to eighteen years, *Journal of Genetic Psychology, 75*:165.

BAYLEY, N., 1954, Some increasing parent–child similarities during the growth of children, *Journal of Educational Psychology, 45*:1.

BAYLEY, N., 1968, Behavioral correlates of mental growth: Birth to 36 years, *American Psychologist, 23*:1.

BAYLEY, N., 1969, "Bayley Scales of Infant Development," Psychological Corp., New York.

BAYLEY, N., RHODES, L., GOOCH, B., AND MARCUS, M., 1971, Environmental factors in the development of institutionalized children, *in* "Exceptional Infant: Studies in Abnormalities," Vol. 2, J. Hellmuth (ed.), Brunner/Mazel, New York.

BAYLEY, N. AND SCHAEFER, E. S., 1964, Correlations of maternal and child behaviors with the development of mental abilities: Data from the Berkeley Growth Study, *Monographs for the Society for Research and Child Development, 29* (6, Whole No. 97).

BECKWITH, L., 1971, Relationship between attributes of mothers and their infants' IQ scores, *Child Development, 42:*1083.

BERNSTEIN, B., 1961, Social class and linguistic development: A theory of social learning, *in* "Economy, Education and Society," A. H. Halsey, J. Floud, and C. A. Anderson (eds.), Free Press, New York.

BIERMAN, J. M., CONNOR, A., VAAGE, M., AND HONZIK, M. P., 1964, Pediatricians' assessments of the intelligence of two-year-olds and their mental test scores, *Pediatrics, 34:*680.

BING, E., 1963, Effect of child-rearing practices on development of differential cognitive abilities, *Child Development, 34:*631.

BOWLBY, J., 1952, Maternal care and mental health, *Monograph Series,* No. 2, (2nd ed.), World Health Organization, Geneva, Switzerland.

BROMAN, S. H., NICHOLS, P. L., AND KENNEDY, W. A., 1975, "Preschool IQ: Prenatal and Early Developmental Correlates," Wiley, New York.

BRUCEFORS, A., 1972, Trends in development of abilities, paper given at Réunion de coordination des recherches sur la croissance et le développement de l'enfant normal, Institute of Child Health, London.

BRUCEFORS, A., JOHANNESSON, I., KARLBERG, P., KLACKENBERG-LARSSON, I., LICHENSTEIN, H., AND SVENBERG, I., 1974, Trends in development of abilities related to somatic growth, *Human Development, 17:*152.

BRUNET, O., AND LÉZINE, P. U. F., 1951, "Le développement psychologique de la première enfance," Éditions Scientifiques et Psychotechniques, Issy-les-Moulineaux.

CAMERON, J., LIVSON, N., AND BAYLEY, N., 1967, Infant vocalizations and their relationship to mature intelligence, *Science, 157:*331.

CASLER, L., 1961, Maternal deprivation: A critical review of the literature, Monographs of the Society for Research in Child Development, 26(2:Whole No. 80).

CASLER, L., 1965, The effects of extra tactile stimulation on a group of institutionalized infants, *Genetic Psychology Monographs, 71:*137.

CATTELL, P., 1940, "The Measurement of Intelligence in Infants and Young Children," Science Press, New York. Reprinted by Psychological Corp., 1960.

CHASE, H. P., AND MARTIN, H. P., 1969, Undernutrition and child development, paper read before the Conference on Neuropsychological Methods for the Assessment of Impaired Brain Functioning in the Malnourished Child, Palo Alto, California.

CRAVIOTO, J., AND DELICARDIE, E., 1970, Mental performance in school age children, *American Journal of Diseases of Children, 120:*404.

CRAVIOTO, J., AND ROBLES, B., 1965, Evolution of adaptive and motor behavior during rehabilitation from kwashiorkor, *American Journal of Orthopsychiatry, 35:*449.

DENNIS, W., AND NAJARIAN, P., 1957, Infant development under environmental handicap, *Psychological Monographs, 71*(7, Whole No. 436).

DODGSON, M. C. H., 1962, "The Growing Brain: An Essay in Developmental Neurology," Williams & Wilkins, Baltimore.

Erickson, M. T., Johnson, N. M., and Campbell, F. A., 1970, Relationships among scores on infant tests for children with developmental problems, *American Journal of Mental Deficiency*, 75:102.

Erlenmeyer-Kimling, L., and Jarvik, L. F., 1963, Genetics and intelligence: A review, *Science*, 142:1477.

Escalona, S., 1968, "The Roots of Individuality: Normal Patterns of Individuality," Aldine Publishing Company, Chicago.

Fantz, R. L., and Nevis, S., 1967, The predictive value of changes in visual preferences in early infancy, *in* "Exceptional Infant: The Normal Infant," Vol. 1, J. Hellmuth (ed.), Brunner/Mazel, New York.

Frankenburg, W. K., Camp, B. W., and Van Natta, P. A., 1971, Validity of the Denver Developmental Screening Test, *Child Development*, 42:475.

Frankenburg, W. K., and Dodds, J. B., 1967, The Denver Developmental Screening Test, *Journal of Pediatrics*, 71:181.

Freedman, D. G., and Keller, B., 1963, Inheritance of behavior in infants, *Science*, 140:196.

Gesell, A., and Amatruda, C., 1941, "Developmental Diagnosis," Paul B. Hoeber, New York.

Gesell, A., Halverson, H. M., Ilg, F. L., Thompson, H., Castner, B. M., Ames, L. B., and Amatruda, C. S., 1940, "The First Five Years of Life," Harper, New York.

Gesell, A., and Thompson, H., 1934, "Infant Behavior: Its Genesis and Growth," McGraw-Hill, New York.

Goffeney, B., Henderson, N. B., and Butler, B. V., 1971, Negro–White, male–female 8-month developmental scores compared with 7-year WISC and Bender Test Scores, *Child Development*, 42:595.

Griffiths, R., 1954, "The Abilities of Babies," McGraw-Hill, New York.

Harlow, H. F., 1958, The nature of love, *American Psychologist*, 13:673.

Hindley, C. B., 1960, The Griffiths Scale of Infant Development: Scores and predictions from 3 to 18 months, *Journal of Child Psychology and Psychiatry*, 1:99.

Hindley, C. B., 1962, Social class influences on the development of ability in the first five years, *Proceedings of the 14th International Congress of Applied Psychology, Child and Education*, 3:29.

Hindley, C. B., 1965, Stability and change in abilities up to five years: Group trends, *Journal of Child Psychology and Psychiatry*, 6:85.

Honzik, M. P., 1938, The constancy of mental test performance during the preschool period, *Journal of Genetic Psychology*, 52:285.

Honzik, M. P., 1957, Developmental studies of parent–child resemblance in intelligence, *Child Development*, 28:215.

Honzik, M. P., 1963, A sex difference in the age of onset of the parent–child resemblance in intelligence, *Journal of Educational Psychology*, 54:231.

Honzik, M. P., 1966, the environment and mental growth from 21 months to 30 years, *XVIII International Congress of Psychology Proceedings*, 11:28.

Honzik, M. P., 1967, Environmental correlates of mental growth: Prediction from the family setting at 21 months, *Child Development*, 38:337.

Honzik, M. P., 1972, Intellectual abilities at age 40 in relation to the early family environment, *in* "Determinants of Behavioral Development," F. J. Monks, W. W. Hartup, and J. de Wit (eds.), Academic Press, New York.

Honzik, M. P., Hutchings, J. J., and Burnip, S. R., 1965, Birth record assessments and test performance at eight months, *American Journal of Diseases of Children*, 109:416.

HONZIK, M. P., MACFARLANE, J. W., AND ALLEN, L., 1948, Stability of mental test performance between 2 and 18 years, *Journal of Experimental Education, 17*:309.

ILLINGWORTH, R. S., 1960, "The Development of the Infant and Young Child: Normal and Abnormal," E. & S. Livingstone, Ltd., Edinburgh and London.

IRETON, H., THWING, E., AND GRAVEM, H., 1970, Infant mental development and neurological status, family socioeconomic status, and intelligence at age four, *Child Development, 41*:937.

KAGAN, J., 1971, "Change and Continuity in Infancy," Wiley, New York.

KAGAN, J., AND KLEIN, R. E., 1973, Cross-cultural perspectives in early development, *American Psychologist, 28*:947.

KLACKENBERG-LARSSON, I., AND STENSSON, J., 1968, Data on the mental development during the first five years, *in* "The Development of Children in a Swedish Urban Community: A Prospective Longitudinal Study," *Acta Paediatrica Scandinavica,* Supplement 187, IV, Almqvist and Wiksell, Stockholm.

KNOBLOCH, H., AND PASAMANICK, B., 1960, An evaluation of the consistency and predictive value of the 40-week Gesell Developmental Schedule, paper presented at the Regional Research Meeting of the American Psychiatric Association, Iowa City.

LEWIS, M., 1971, Individual differences in the measurement of early cognitive growth, *in* "Exceptional Infant: Studies in Abnormalities," Vol. 2, J. Hellmuth (ed.), Brunner/Mazel, New York.

LEWIS, M., 1973, Intelligence tests: Their use and misuse, *Human Development, 16*:1.

LEWIS, M., AND McGURK, H., 1972, Evaluation of infant intelligence, *Science, 178*:1174.

MACRAE, J. M., 1955, Retests of children given mental tests as infants, *Journal of Genetic Psychology, 87*:111.

McCALL, R. B., HOGARTY, P. S., AND HURLBURT, N., 1972, Transitions in infant sensorimotor development and the prediction of childhood IQ, *American Psychologist, 27*:728.

MÖNCKEBERG, F., 1968, Effect of early marasmic malnutrition on subsequent physical and psychological development, *in* "Malnutrition, Learning and Behavior," N. E. Scrimshaw and J. E. Gordon (eds.), MIT Press, Cambridge, Massachusetts, p. 269.

MOORE, T., 1968, Language and intelligence: A longitudinal study of the first eight years, Part II: Environmental correlates of mental growth, *Human Development, 11*:1.

NELSON, V. L., AND RICHARDS, T. W., 1939, Studies in mental development, III: Performance of twelve-month-old children on the Gesell Schedule and its predictive value for mental status at two and three years, *Journal of Genetic Psychology, 54*:181.

NICHOLS, P. L., AND BROMAN, S. H., 1974, Familial resemblance in infant mental development, *Developmental Psychology, 10*:442.

POLLITT, E., AND GRANOFF, D., 1967, Mental and motor development of Peruvian children treated for severe malnutrition, *Review of Interamericana Psicologia, 1*:93.

RAMEY, C. T., CAMPBELL, F. A., AND NICHOLSON, J. E., 1973, The predictive power of the Bayley Scales of Infant Development and the Stanford–Binet Intelligence Test in a relatively constant environment, *Child Development, 44*:790.

RHEINGOLD, H. L., AND BAYLEY, N., 1959, The later effects of an experimental modification of mothering, *Child Development, 31*:363.

SKODAK, M., AND SKEELS, H. M., 1949, A final follow-up study of 100 adopted children, *Journal of Genetic Psychology, 75*:85.

UCKO, L. E., 1965, A comparative study of asphyxiated and non-asphyxiated boys from birth to five years, *Developmental Medicine and Child Neurology, 7*:643.

UZGIRIS, I. C., AND HUNT, J. McV., 1966, An instrument for assessing infant psychological development, mimeographed paper, Psychological Development Laboratories, University of Illinois.

WERNER, E. E., AND BAYLEY, N., 1966, The reliability of Bayley's revised scale of mental and motor development during the first year of life, *Child Development, 37*:39.

WERNER, E. E., BIERMAN, J. M., AND FRENCH, F. E., 1971, "The Children of Kauai: A Longitudinal Study from the Prenatal Period to Age 10," University of Hawaii Press, Honolulu.

WERNER, E. E., HONZIK, M. P., AND SMITH, R. S., 1968, Prediction of intelligence and achievement at 10 years from 20-month pediatric and psychologic examinations, *Child Development, 39*:1063.

WILLERMAN, L., BROMAN, S. H., AND FIEDLER, M., 1970, Infant development, preschool IQ, and social class, *Child Development, 41*:69.

WILSON, R., 1972, Twins: Early mental development, *Science, 175*:914.

WILSON, R. S., AND HARPRING, E. B., 1972, Mental and motor development in infant twins, *Developmental Psychology, 7*:277.

WINICK, M., 1970, Fetal malnutrition and growth processes, *Hospital Practice, 5*:33.

YARROW, L. J., 1961, Maternal deprivation: Toward an empirical and conceptual re-evaluation, *Psychological Bulletin, 58*:459.

YARROW, L. J., 1963, Research in dimensions of early maternal care, *Merrill–Palmer Quarterly, 9*:101.

YARROW, L. J., GOODWIN, M. S., MANHEIMER, H., AND MILOWE, I. D., 1973, Infancy experiences and cognitive and personality development at ten years, *in* "The Competent Infant: Research and Commentary," L. J. Stone, H. T. Smith, and L. B. Murphy (eds.), Basic Books, New York.

YARROW, L. J., RUBENSTEIN, J. L., PEDERSEN, F. A., AND JANKOWSKI, J. J., 1972, Dimensions of early stimulation and their differential effects on infant development, *Merrill–Palmer Quarterly, 18*:205.

4   *Toward an Epigenetic Conception of Mental Development in the First Three Years of Life*

ROBERT B. McCALL

Despite evidence to the contrary, "real intelligence" historically has been considered to be a relatively unitary trait, constant over age, and pervasive in its governance of nearly all mental behaviors (Hunt, 1961). Although it is currently fashionable to denigrate such a view, it is still prevalent to some extent. For example, the excitement in certain quarters about brain-wave tests of intelligence because scores reflect a unitary characteristic, are apparently constant over age, and are equally distributed among different cultural groups stands as testimony to the lingering vestiges of a unitary, developmentally constant "intelligence."

For decades such a concept has dominated the field of infant testing. Surely, it was reasoned, since a person is born with a certain amount of intelligence that remains with him throughout life, it should be possible to detect some aspects of intelligence even in a young baby. After all, intelligence simply grows in quantity with development (like height) but undergoes no qualitative changes, and one's relative standing remains the same over the years.

When infant tests could not predict from the first year of life to childhood IQ, the concept of a unitary, constant intelligence did not wither. Instead people blamed the infant tests for being unreliable (which they are not), or they claimed that the infant tests measured the wrong thing. Intelligence was really there in miniaturized adult form—if we only knew how to measure it.

ROBERT B. McCALL · The Fels Research Institute.

After several infant tests had been developed, none of which predicted later IQ from first-year scores, it began to appear that psychologists might never behaviorally ferret out the intelligence that hid within a human infant. This led to the ultimate retreat: the infant possesses intelligence, but he simply does not have the behavioral repertoire to display it. This argument wraps the unitary, constant notion of intelligence in a security blanket that can never be penetrated by the chilling winds of scientific inquiry.

There have always been dissenting voices. Gesell said he never intended his tests to measure "intelligence," and therefore he did not expect that they would predict later IQ. Stott and Ball (1965) and Bayley (1970) argued that mental performance underwent qualitative transformations and was not one thing that simply became more visible with development. And Piaget's (1952) comprehensive epigenetic view of development was in direct contradiction to the traditional conception of intelligence. As Piaget's influence gained in America, several investigators created assessments of infancy based upon Piagetian sensorimotor milestones (e.g., Uzgiris and Hunt and Corman and Escalona). While these Piaget-based assessments seem to have a certain face validity, there are far less actual psychometric data for these new forms of infant assessment than for the traditional methods. The upshot is a general dissatisfaction or disinterest in attempting to assess general mental development in human infants.

I believe we really have not taken Piagetian notions of development very seriously, and we have used infant tests to search for the wrong phenomena. It is ironic that the field of developmental psychology—presumably a study of *changes* over age—has spent much of its time looking for developmental continuities (Wohlwill, 1973). Finding little developmental stability, why haven't we inferred that changes are predominant and tried to describe such qualitative transitions in infant behavior?

In this paper I review selected portions of the data on stability and change in general infant test performance and then describe a slightly different strategy for viewing these data. I wish to persuade the reader that there are orderly and reasonable transitions that take the human infant successively through periods dominated by stimulus detection, exploration, imitation, vocal–verbal behavior, and symbolic language functioning. I will speculatively propose that despite these several qualitative transitions, there are one or two guiding themes that are not single abilities, skills, or g, but common functions served in turn by different sets of behaviors and skills.

Stability and Change in Infant Test Performance

Cross-Age Correlations

If infant tests reflect something of a unitary, developmentally constant "intelligence," then we should expect fairly strong age-to-age correlations among test scores within the infancy period and some prediction to childhood IQ.

Within Infancy

The issue of whether there are age-to-age correlations for infant tests was recently polarized by Lewis and McGurk (1972, 1973), Matheny (1973), and Wilson (1973). Lewis and McGurk argued for "no reliable relationship between successive measures of infant intelligence during the first 24 months of life" (1972, p. 1176), whereas Wilson presented moderate age-to-age correlations for a large sample of twins. Table I presents a few of the age-to-age correlations within the first three years of life for the precursor of the Bayley Infant Scale used in the Berkeley Growth Study as reported by Bayley (1949) and for the Gesell Developmental Schedule employed in the Fels Longitudinal Study. As might be expected, the correlations are higher the shorter the interval between assessments, and they tend to increase as the infant gets older. These values are more similar to those of Wilson's twins than those of Lewis and McGurk's singleton sample.

While the age-to-age correlations for infant test scores are not zero, neither are they impressively high. This is especially true when one considers the proportion of shared variance (obtained by the squaring of these test–retest rs) and when these correlations are compared with analogous figures for childhood IQ assessments. For example, a typical correlation for a one-year test–retest interval for IQ between 9 and 12 years of life exceeds 0.90, but such values are in the 0.50s for infant tests in the first two years.

These results are typical and lead to the conclusion that while there is some degree of correspondence in relative infant test performance

Table I

Age-to-Age Correlations for Infant Tests and Childhood IQ
from the Fels and Berkeley Longitudinal Studies

Fels, Gesell[a]

Mos.	6	12	18
12	0.59		
18	0.52	0.57	
24	0.40	0.57	0.71

Berkeley, California (Bayley)[b]

Mos.	(4, 5, 6)	(10, 11, 12)	(18, 21, 24)
(10, 11, 12)	0.52		
(18, 21, 24)	0.23	0.60	
(27, 30, 36)	0.10	0.45	0.80

Fels (above) and Berkeley (below), Stanford–Binet[c]

Years	9	10	11	12
9		0.90	0.82	0.81
10	0.88		0.90	0.88
11	0.90	0.92		0.90
12	0.82	0.90	0.93	

[a] Correlations between raw Gesell total scores for samples of 184–224 subjects
from the Fels study (McCall et al., 1972).
[b] Correlations between standardized scores averaged over available tests at the
three ages in months (from Bayley, 1949, p. 181).
[c] Stanford–Binet age-to-age correlations for the Fels study above the diagonal
(from Sontag et al., 1958, p. 28) and for the Berkeley Growth Study below the
diagonal (Bayley, 1949, p. 183).

across 6- and 12-month intervals, the degree of association is not strong,
especially when compared with analogous data from childhood IQ test–
retest performance of the same children. The changes in relative position from one age to the next are more impressive than the similarities.

Infancy to Childhood

Given the modest age-to-age correlations within the infancy period,
what is the level of prediction to childhood IQ scores for normal chil-

dren? A summary of such data is presented in Table II. These values represent correlations of test scores given to infants between 1 and 30 months of life with their childhood IQ scores obtained between 3 and 18 years. The correlation at any one test–retest interval represents the median over several different correlations reported by a variety of studies. These data follow the general trends observed for test–retest correlations within the infancy period (i.e., Table I), in which the correlations are highest over the shorter retest intervals and highest for older children. Generally speaking, there is essentially no correlation between performance during the first six months of life with IQ score after age 5; the correlations are predominantly in the 0.20s for assessments made between 7 and 18 months of life when one is predicting IQ at 5–18 years; and it is not until 19–30 months that the infant test predicts later IQ in the range of 0.40–0.55.

Perhaps other variables have diluted these predictions—such as the reliability of the tests and sex differences. First, the low correlations are not totally a function of the reliability of the infant test, which is approximately as reliable after the third month of life as the Stanford–Binet during childhood (McCall et al., 1972). Second, these predictive correlations have rarely been calculated separately for the sexes, and some studies report that predictability occurs at a younger age (e.g., 12 months versus 18–24 months) and attains higher levels for girls than for boys (McCall et al., 1972). Nevertheless, the basic trend observed in

TABLE II

Median Correlations between Infant Tests and Childhood IQ for Normal Children[a]

Childhood age (years)	Age in infancy (months)			
	1–6	7–12	13–18	19–30
8–18	0.01	0.20	0.21	0.49
	(12/4)[b]	(8/2)	(6/2)	(9/2)
5–7	0.01	0.06	0.30	0.41
	(7/5)	(5/4)	(5/4)	(16/4)
3–4	0.23	0.33	0.47	0.54
	(7/4)	(5/3)	(6/4)	(16/3)

[a] Reprinted from McCall et al. (1972) with permission from the *American Psychologist.*
[b] (Number of correlations involved in the median/number of different studies involved in the median)

Table II holds true for both sexes. Third, there have been some attempts to supplement the infant test with measures of the socioeconomic status of the parents to make multivariate predictions of childhood IQ. At the young ages the socioeconomic status of the parents predicts childhood IQ better than the infant test, and it is not until 12 months for girls and 18 months for boys that the infant test increases the predictability. Finally, some have tried to look at specific behaviors within the infant test battery for their potential to predict later IQ. There has been one, but only one, notable discovery: the propensity of infant girls to vocalize in the testing context during the first year of life has shown correlations as high as 0.74 with verbal IQ at 26 years (Cameron et al., 1967). This finding gains some support from other longitudinal studies (Kagan, 1969; McCall et al., 1972; Moore, 1967). However, apart from vocalization by female infants, the predictions of specific item clusters to childhood IQ are generally not higher than for the total infant test score (McCall et al., 1972).

Alternative Approaches

Whenever an expected relationship is not observed, it is possible that the "right" sample, age period, or combination of measures has not been tried. First, the above discussion concerns the relative lack of prediction from infancy to later IQ for essentially "normal" samples. Of course, what constitutes normality is a matter of definition, but an exceptionally low score on an infant test, even in the first few months of life and even if a pediatrician has not diagnosed the infant as high risk, has some contemporary and predictive significance regarding developmental progress (Honzik et al., 1965; McCall et al., 1972; Werner et al., 1968). But extremely high scores on an infant test in the first year are not predictive, and conversely, children who have IQs of 140 or higher at 4 years are essentially indistinct from the total population on the Bayley infant test at 8 months (Willerman and Fiedler, 1974). Thus, while the infant tests have diagnostic and predictive value when extremely low scores are involved, there is only modest cross-age consistency for "normal" samples, including those with very high scores (McCall et al., 1972).

Perhaps it is too much to ask that single infant scores should predict later IQ. For example, Gesell and others (Anastasi, 1968) have suggested that prediction to childhood IQ might be improved if the pattern of developmental change in infant test scores were considered. This approach has not been attempted in any serious way, though some preliminary analyses of the Berkeley Growth Study data have failed to reveal a relationship between pattern of infant test performance during the first two years of life and later IQ or change in IQ. Moreover, different patterns of IQ change between $2\frac{1}{2}$ and 17 years are not associated with infant test scores or changes in infant test performance during the first two years. Of course, infant test performance over the first two years of life and childhood IQ between $2\frac{1}{2}$ and 17 years may represent such gross developmental periods that important, but developmentally specific, relationships are obscured. These analyses are being continued.

Second, infant test scores might be supplemented with assessments of the child's personality or more specific parental behaviors. Child behaviors during the test session and in the home as well as specific parental–infant interaction variables have been shown to be modestly related to traditional and Piagetian test scores during the first two years of life (e.g., Bayley and Schaefer, 1964; Décarie, 1965; Matheny *et al.*, 1974; Wachs *et al.*, 1971). Whether prediction to childhood IQ would be enhanced significantly by the use of a combination of test scores (the total or specific item subsets) and such personality–social behaviors is still an open question.

Heredity–Environment and Infant Test Performance

The heredity–environment issue that has raged over childhood IQ performance has not been lost on infant testers. Before we take up this issue itself, it will be helpful to distinguish the general level of a child's performance from his developmental pattern or profile. *General level* denotes the average of a child's scores over some developmental period. In contrast, *developmental pattern* refers to the rises and falls in relative score over a given age span—whether the child increases, decreases, rises and then falls, etc. It is conceivable for general level and pattern to be independent of one another. That is, children could show rises in score value whether they averaged a developmental quotient (DQ) of 85 or 135. Further, two groups of children could have the same general level (e.g., DQ = 100) but some might show steep rises, others gradual declines, and still others U or inverted-U patterns. In actual fact, however, level and pattern are not independent, since infants having different age trends are also likely to have different general levels. The analysis of genetic correlates of differences in infant test performance has been done for the case in which general level and developmental profile are both permitted to determine the comparison groups as well as for the case in which only change in test score over age is involved. However, since general level and developmental profile are not independent in nature, this distinction is somewhat artificial.

Heritability

General Level Plus Developmental Pattern

Freedman and Keller (1963) reported that Bayley infant test performance between 2 and 12 months of age was more similar within monozygotic (MZ) than dizygotic (DZ) twins (20 pairs). Using the data from the Louisville Twin Study, Wilson (1972*a*, 1974; Wilson and Harpring, 1972) has also presented within-pair correlations for MZ and DZ twins. McCall (1972*a*; McCall *et al.*, 1973) compared siblings with unrelated children from the Fels sample, and Nichols and Broman (1974) presented correlations for monozygotic and dizygotic twins as well as for siblings from the Collaborative Perinatal Project. What can be concluded from these studies with respect to the heritability of the general level of infant test performance?

These data suggest extraordinarily consistent and high correlations within pairs of MZ twins—*r*s between 0.81 and 0.85, values that approach (and sometimes exceed) the reliability of the test based upon singleton infants. The correlations for DZ twins are less consistent but always lower than for MZs, *r*s ranging between 0.55 and 0.74 for samples containing different ages, races, and sexes. So far there appears to be some heritability for the general level of infant test performance since the within-pair correlations for MZ twins are higher than for DZ twins by approximately 0.07 to 0.30.

This conclusion is made suspect by a variety of methodological problems (McCall, 1972*a,b*; McCall *et al.*, 1973; Wachs, 1972; Wilson, 1972b) and the disturbing fact that the correlations for singleton siblings are fairly consistent across studies and very modest in size—0.15–0.37. If DZ twins and siblings both share 50% of their genes on the average, why is the correlation among DZ twins from two to five times larger than for siblings?

Nichols and Broman (1974) have provided a possible answer. In the

Collaborative Perinatal Project there was a tendency for serious retardation to be six to nine times more frequent among twins than among
single births. Obviously this figure depends on how one defines retardation, but Nichols and Broman used a very conservative definition in
which less than 1 in 10,000 children should be retarded if the distribution of scores were normal. Moreover, the incidence of severe retardation is almost twice as great among MZ as among DZ twins, and both
MZ twin members are twice as likely to be retarded as are both members
of DZ pairs. Therefore, there is heritability for severe retardation on the
Bayley at 8 months of age. But what happens to the MZ versus DZ
correlations when such retarded children are eliminated from the sample and only "normals" remain? When this was done, Nichols and
Broman reported that the correlations for MZ and DZ twins are virtually
identical—$r = 0.55$! Therefore *among normal twins* there is no evidence
for heritability of general level at 8 months of age.

But even after severe retardates are eliminated from the twin sample, the within-pair correlation for DZs is two to three times the correlation for siblings. McCall (1972a; McCall et al., 1973) and Nichols and
Broman (1974) have suggested that twins may have much more similar
prenatal environments than do siblings, as suggested by the fact that
concordance for retardation was 3.6 times more likely among DZ twins
than among siblings (Nichols and Broman, 1974). Since DZ twins and
singleton siblings are genetically comparable, some nongenetic factor
(e.g., prenatal environment) must be involved. Moreover, twins tend to
be tested at the same age on the same day, whereas a test at the same
chronological age may be administered to siblings in different calendar
years. Finally, no one really knows how much of the sibling correlation
is due to common environmental factors, since no one has tested unrelated infants reared in the same home as an environmental control for
the sibling relationship. In any case, the sibling correlations of 0.15–0 37
for infant test scores are substantially below the median sibling correlation of 0.55 (Jensen, 1969) for child and adult IQ.

The conclusion seems to be that there is heritability for serious
mental retardation detectable by infant tests, but when such severe
cases are eliminated there is no evidence for heritability of infant test
score among twins in the first year of life. Further, samples of twins are
not typical representatives of samples of singletons for nongenetic reasons—concordance for retardation is substantially more frequent among
DZ twins than among siblings, despite their genetic comparability.

Presumably, prenatal and perinatal environments are more similar and more risky for DZ twins than for siblings. Moreover testing procedures favor higher correlations for twins than for siblings. Finally, although siblings do correlate above zero, it is not yet possible to separate environmental from genetic contributors to this correlation, which is substantially lower than for childhood IQ. The evidence for a strong heritable component to infant test performance in the first year of life among normal infants is weak at best and more probably negligible (Scarr-Salapatek, 1974).

It is clear from the literature on the heritability of childhood IQ (Jensen, 1969), from the increasing correlations with development between the IQs of biological parents and their adopted children (Honzik, 1957), and from the emerging correlations with age between infant scores obtained from a parent (as an infant) and his child as an infant (Eichorn, 1969; McCall *et al.*, 1973) that there is a gradual increase in heritability for general mental test performance after the first year, which reaches adult levels between 4 and 6 years of age. These observations suggest that individual differences in mental test performance become progressively more closely associated with differences in the genetic composition of those individuals.

It is interesting to note that increasing heritability roughly coincides with the introduction of verbal items on the infant tests and the increased emphasis on verbal and abstract–symbolic reasoning on the IQ tests. Moreover, as heritability rises, so do the cross-age correlations between IQ retests. These observations are consistent with the proposition that the development of mental performance undergoes major qualitative shifts during the first few years of life, but that once verbal skills and abstract reasoning are available the general nature of behaviors called *intellectual* by our society is established and cross-age IQ correlations approach their highest levels.

Pattern over Age

When it comes to the heritability of the pattern of infant test performance over age, the issues are the same but the data on both sides of the argument are less decisive. Wilson (1972 *a,b*; 1974) and Wilson and Harpring (1972) have argued that MZ twins are more similar in their developmental profile for several developmental periods (e.g., 3–12 months, 12–24 months, 18–36 months, and 3–5 years) but not between 5 and 6 years. McCall (1972a,b; McCall et al., 1973) has criticized the results for the first two years of life and many of his comments also apply to Wilson's later publication (1974). In contrast to Wilson's twin data, McCall's analysis of the infant test scores from the Fels study indicated no greater pattern similarity for singleton siblings than for unrelated children during the first year, during the second year, and during the first two years, or for IQ test performance between 3 and 12 years, between 3 and 6 years, or between 6 and 12 years of age (McCall et al., 1973). Moreover, the issue is further complicated to the extent that the findings and implications of the Nichols and Broman (1974) data on the heritability of mental retardation among twins versus singleton siblings are also applicable to the pattern of test scores over age. Objectively one would conclude that the waters are too muddy and that there is no unambiguous evidence either way on the heritability of profile contour. In a less charitable moment, however, I am yet to be convinced of any genetic correlates of developmental profile of infant test or childhood IQ performance.

Environmental Influences

Regardless of the questions concerning the heritability data, it seems unequivocal that there is a major nongenetic component to individual differences in infant test performance that is larger than for childhood IQ. Nevertheless, it is quite another issue to specify what those environmental circumstances might be. Most attempts to relate traditional indices of between-family environmental differences to Gesell and Bayley test performance in the first year have been unsuccessful. For example, parental education and other presumed measures of socioeconomic status do not relate to mental test performance until 2–5 years of age (McCall et al., 1972). In contrast, socioeconomic status shows correlations between 0.25 and 0.50 for childhood IQ.

Of course, general SES may be too abstract and far removed from the actual functional parent–child interactions. These may nevertheless influence certain infant skills that in turn are masked when the total score is used. An indication that some of the environmental factors in infant and childhood test performance may be rather complicated and specific is implied in the sibling comparisons for developmental profile. If siblings are not more similar in their pattern of test scores over age, then changes within the infancy and childhood periods are apparently not related to those general intellectual characteristics of the home that are likely to be shared by siblings of that family. Such attributes as parental value for intellectual behaviors, reward for intellectual and academic performance, parental modeling of such behaviors, and the opportunity for educational and enriching experiences—factors that are frequently proposed as environmental determinants for IQ—are apparently not correlates of developmental change in infant and childhood mental test performance (though they may influence general level). One possible implication is that particular environmental events do not have the same influence on all children or even the same child at different ages (McCall et al., 1973).

One conclusion seems to be that there are major nongenetic factors affecting the general level and developmental pattern of infant test performance, and that these factors are probably not global in character or easily summarized under "general social status" or "intellectual climate of the home." In view of Nichols and Broman's (1974) data suggesting prenatal nongenetic influences on retardation rates among twins, perhaps one should search for early biological rather than social environmental influences on first-year infant test performance (see Chapter 8 by Hunt).

Interpretation

A summary of the above data represents a curious anomaly: both the heritability and the correlations between mental test performance and general indices of socioeconomic status increase with age. How can ostensible environmental and genetic contributions to mental test performance *both* increase? There are many possible explanations, but I favor one that emphasizes the proposition that the qualitative nature of mental performance—and thus its environmental and genetic determinants—changes over the infancy period. Thus nongenetic biological circumstances (e.g., prenatal environment, nutrition, state, and cooperativeness) may be related to infant test performance in the first few months because the test emphasizes basic perceptual alertness, neuromotor functions, and sensorimotor and social responsiveness—factors that may be relatively inconsistent within an infant from one testing to another. But such factors become less important with development, because the skills being tested emphasize vocabulary, verbal fluency,

reasoning, and memory—abilities that are influenced by social–educational experiences and that are more stable across time for an individual.
Thus the larger nongenetic variance in first-year infant test performance
may be a function of temporary biological and social factors that we have
largely failed to specify and measure, whereas the environmental factors
that influence later test performance are of a different genre, more
social–educational than earlier, more stable across time, and more commonly measured.

Actually the heritability values reported above, which inspired this
speculation, have very little implication for the nature of the development of mental performance. First, very low heritabilities (e.g., for first-
year test performance) do not necessarily imply that genes have no role
in infant mental development. Heritability values only reveal the extent
to which *differences between infants* are associated with differences in their
genotypes. Who would deny that the infant's neuromotor development
and general ontogeny of behavioral propensities and skills are not
heavily dependent upon genetic codes and programs? To interpret a low
or zero heritability as indicating that development of these characteristics is totally environmental is to postulate a new kind of creation.
Rather, *differences* between infants in their general level or developmental pattern of test performance are not predominantly reflections of
their differences in genetic composition. Indeed, as proposed above, it is
possible that early in infancy such development is so characteristic of the
species that differences between individuals simply constitute variations
in measurement error, contemporary emotional or attentional states,
cooperativeness, time since the last nap or feeding, and other uninter-
esting, transient, but nevertheless nongenetic variables.

But the converse of this argument is also true. Even though heritabilities for childhood IQ are high, this fact alone does not imply that
environment plays no role or that it makes a vastly subordinate contribution to the development of childhood mental skills. Again, heritabilities refer to the possible genetic correlates of differences between
individuals, not necessarily to the basic development of such characteristics in the species. Moreover high heritabilities themselves do not
provide an indication of how easily a phenotypic trait can be altered by
appropriate and timely intervention—hair color can be changed easily
but one's sex cannot. Phenylketonuria and TB once had high heritabilities, but these diseases are largely under medical control now. With
respect to IQ, a high heritability does not necessarily imply that it cannot

be changed, and Heber's Milwaukee project (Heber *et al.*, 1972) demonstrated that IQs can be raised as much as two standard deviations (e.g., 30 points) by early intervention and education.

In short, high or low heritabilities for general level or developmental profile do not tell us much about the dynamics of mental development in infants and children.

INFANT TESTS AS A PSYCHOMETRIC TOOL

Given the above discussion, what is the status of infant tests as a psychometric assessment technique?

A Question of Validity

First, the tests are clearly valuable in detecting abnormality and retardation. After reviewing the literature on the use of infant tests in detecting abnormality, McCall *et al.* (1972) concluded that "infant tests may have contemporary as well as predictive utility in identifying pathological and 'suspect' conditions in infancy, and a very low score on an infant test, even though a pediatrician does not classify the child as abnormal (and vice versa), may have diagnostic value" (p. 730).

However, with regard to essentially normal samples, test scores from the first year of life have essentially no practical utility in predicting later performance. In view of this fact, some have gone so far as to suggest that infant tests be abandoned as assessments of individual differences among essentially normal children (Lewis and McGurk, 1972, 1973). A frequent response to the empirical failure of infant tests to predict later IQ is that they were never intended to do so, and while they do not have predictive validity they have contemporary validity as an assessment of a child's current developmental status (e.g., Bayley, 1970). But somehow this claim is meaningless to many psychologists. Apparently, the faith in a constant, unitary intelligence is so strong that many feel that if the infant test has no predictive validity it has no validity whatsoever. What purpose is served to know a child's current developmental status if it tells nothing about that child's future performance?

Consider an analogous situation in pediatrics. A physician finds a newborn's birth weight an important piece of information, especially in conjunction with an estimate of the child's gestational age, despite the fact that among normal children birth weight does not predict stature in childhood. The "small-for-dates" newborn may have a variety of special problems that can be monitored or treated but that are unique to the newborn period. Birth weight is a valid sign of current status without much predictive utility. Analogously, infant tests are sensitive to behavioral and neurological abnormalities, and the infant test coupled with a skilled pediatrician can be quite valuable in diagnosing abnormality (McCall et al., 1972).

But does the infant test have contemporary validity for normal infants? Unfortunately there is precious little traditional psychometric validity data for normal samples, largely because there is no obvicus criterion against which the infant test can be evaluated. Pediatric judgment of developmental progress is a possibility, but the tests represent an attempt to make just such clinical impressions more objective and accurate. Indeed the tests have become the criterion of infant developmental status. The face validity of infant assessments is so great that there is relatively little "mental" behavior that characterizes an infant that is not represented on these tests. It is small wonder that each new infant test differs only slightly from its predecessors and correlates rather highly with them (McCall et al., 1972). This "criterion problem" may force us into accepting or rejecting infant tests largely on the basis of their face validity and contemporary utility.

White Elephant

Perhaps infant researchers have been chasing a white elephant. The assumption underlying the research reviewed above is that there is continuity in infant test performance during the first year or two of life, but the results are not profoundly supportive of that view, especially for the first year of life. Indeed a theme that recurs in the interpretation of these results suggests marked developmental transitions in the fundamental character of infant mental performance.

Ironically, developmental psychologists are not prone to investigate changes. The history of developmental psychology, especially within the context of longitudinal studies, represents the quest for continuity and stability and not the attempt to describe ontogenetic change. We have correlated scores and behaviors at one age with the same or different scores and behaviors at a very distant age. Having limited ourselves to this strategy, what else could we find? We either obtain significant correlations and pronounce the existence of stability, or we do not obtain such correlations and are left with the ambiguities of accepting the null hypothesis. Since the only acceptable scientific product of such a strategy is the "discovery" of continuity, our theoretical conceptions and statistical methods have denied us the privilege of observing development, a term that implies change and transformation with age (McCall, 1974; Wohlwill, 1973). In this sense, we have rarely studied infant mental development.

Assuming the infant tests are reliable samples of a significant portion of the infant's behavioral repertoire, it might be profitable to explore the test protocols for the purpose of describing such qualitative transitions in the development of mental behavior. If these transitions are marked, the determinants of one type of behavior at one age may be quite different from the determinants of another type of behavior at a developmentally distant age, and there may not be a sizable correlation between precocity at one age and precocity at quite another age. However, since it is reasonable to expect that a child who finishes a given stage early relative to other children should embark on the next stage (but not necessarily quite distant stages) relatively early, there may be correlational relationships among rather specific types of behaviors at adjacent developmental periods that might reveal the nature of these transitions. In short, perhaps we should shift our attention from an attempt to find stability and continuity to an attempt to describe and hypothesize about the nature of developmental change in infant mental behavior.

DEVELOPMENTAL TRANSITIONS IN MENTAL BEHAVIOR

Analysis of the Fels Data

McCall *et al.* (1972) recently attempted to pursue this course by examining responses to the items on the Gesell at 6, 12, 18, and 24 months for subjects in the Fels Longitudinal Study. The purpose was to look at more specific item clusters rather than total test scores and to determine paths of correlational association between item sets at one age and item sets at adjacent ages. Principal components analyses were performed on the item responses separately at each age, and then the component scores from these analyses were correlated across age.

The first principal components at each age correlated among themselves for both males and females. No other set of components showed such a strong correlational pattern across all the ages. Statistically these results are not surprising, but their advantage lies in the fact that the first principal components at each age contain fewer items than the total test, and one can be more specific about which behaviors are involved in these major developmental transitions.

At 6 months the items loading on the first principal component were interpreted to reflect visually guided exploration of perceptual contingencies. For example, the items "reaches for dangling ring," "lifts inverted cup," "bangs spoon on table," "splashes in tub," "conscious of fallen objects," and "pats table" all describe manipulation that produces some clear, contingent perceptual consequence. The fact that Piaget (1952) emphasized such behavior in his concept of circular response and that infants (e.g., in Rovee and Rovee, 1969; Siqueland, 1969; Watson, 1972) as well as animals (e.g., in McCall, 1965, 1966) will perform simple responses in order to produce a contingent perceptual event makes this interpretation appealing.

The exploration of perceptual contingencies at 6 months correlated with a mixture of sensorimotor and social imitation plus rudimentary vocal–verbal behavior at 12 months. While many items at 12 months have previously been interpreted to reflect fine motor skill, most of these items request the infant to imitate the examiner in performing a rather simple motor behavior, one that is well within the physical competence of the child. Consequently the items "rings bell in imitation," "imitates rattle of spoon in cup," "builds tower of two to three cubes," "puts cube in cup," "performance box," and "scribbles in imitation" all require the child to imitate the examiner's simple motor action. Also loaded on this component were several diverse behaviors that seemed to reflect the learning of social interactions and simple verbal skills (e.g., "waves bye-bye," "says three to five words," "says bye-bye or hello," and "plays peek or pat-a-cake"). This implies that social–verbal behavior and imitation of fine motor behaviors are related activities, and it seems reasonable that the child who develops the tendency to imitate does so in a social context, playing reciprocal sensorimotor and vocal–verbal imitation games with his parents. The similarity to Piaget's (1951) theorizing as well as to Hunt's (1961) interpretation of it is striking.

These behaviors at 6 and 12 months were correlated with verbal and motor imitation items (e.g., "scribbles in imitation," "repeats things said" and "throws ball in box") and especially verbal production ("names pictures," "repeats things said," "says five or more words," "requests things at table," "names watch," "uses two or more words together") and verbal comprehension ("points to several pictures," "points to parts of body") at 18 months.

By 24 months the main developmental trend was even more strongly verbal in character. While imitation was still present (e.g., "imitates simple drawn patterns," "puts cube in cup, plate, box"), the predominant theme featured the verbal skills of production and labeling ("names five pictures," "names watch," "asks for things at table by name," "names five familiar objects," "uses color names"), verbal comprehension ("points at several pictures," "listens to stories with pictures"), and fluent verbal production and grammatical maturity ("speaks in sentences," "tells name," "tells experiences," "uses pronouns," "asks for things at table by name," "knows prepositions").

These data provide a more specific description of the possible nature of transitions in mental behavior than might be obtained from a simple look at total scores. Although the analyses were not done with an *a priori* theory in mind, the results are remarkably consistent with Piaget's description of mental development in the first two years of life. That is, at 6 months the child is predominantly an explorer of perceptual consequences: he studies the perceptual–cognitive information or uncertainty in his environment. An important aspect of this exploration is the contingent consequences to his physical interaction with the environment. By 12 months his "environment" is more likely to include social beings with whom he engages in reciprocal imitation of sensorimotor and rudimentary verbal behaviors. As his ability increases to symbolize mentally, his language improves and he continues to imitate the verbal–vocal social behavior of adults as well as to demonstrate skills in vocabulary comprehension and production. By 24 months the dominant theme has evolved into grammatical fluency and production.

Very preliminary analyses are under way of the Berkeley Growth Study infant test data in collaboration with Dorothy Eichorn, Study Director, and Paul Mussen, Director of the Institute of Human Development, University of California at Berkeley. The early results of analyses similar to those reported above for the Fels data are quite concordant with these interpretations.

Speculations on a Theory of Epigenetic Developmental Transitions

Sensorimotor Behavior and Language

At a general level these observations are consistent with a Piagetian concept of epigenetic development in which qualitatively different behaviors build upon their predecessors, unfolding in a logical sequence. An important point is that there are relationships between diverse behavioral emphases (e.g., sensorimotor exploration, imitation, and language) within and across ages that suggest it would be profitable to consider early language, for example, as somehow emerging from, or at least related to, antecedent sensorimotor behaviors.

Formerly, many language scholars believed in innate language acquisition (e.g., McNeill, 1970). The infant was so dominated by inherited structures which predisposed him to language that almost no experience, save the presence of a language environment, was necessary for language to unfold according to a maturational schedule. Simplified, language began when the child uttered his first word. On the other side, researchers of sensorimotor and perceptual–cognitive behavior in early infancy rarely concerned themselves with language. They acknowledged that language was an important development, but no concerted attempt was made to view the phenomena of exploration, conjugate reinforcement, or sensorimotor imitation in early infancy as being related to the subsequent emergence of language. In contrast, Piaget described epigenetic transitions in which sensorimotor behavior became intimately meshed with the development of language, but American scientists studied only one behavioral aspect of Piaget's theory at a time and even then it was often not researched developmentally. In American research Piaget is popular in pieces, not for his developmental purview.

More recently there have been major shifts within the language community that are more friendly to the notion that early language might represent a logical outgrowth of sensorimotor behavior. No longer is early language thought to be simply the unfolding of an innate language, complete with its own grammar, that is manifested regardless of the adult language environment. Rather, it is now recognized that language develops because the child needs it to communicate something (Brown, 1973). Brown and others see early one- and two-word sentences not as exemplars of a pivot-open grammar but rather as servants to semantic goals. The child's early utterances are attempts to communicate or declare something meaningful, and the semantic categories that early language fulfills are remarkably similar to sensorimotor learning and behavior.

For example, prominent semantic functions of early language are *nomination, recurrence, nonexistence, location,* and *agent–action–object* declarations (Brown, 1973). The child's incessant naming of objects (e.g., "that ball") and requests for recurrence (e.g., "more ball") presupposes that the child recognizes objects and actions. Nomination is not unlike the Piagetian sensorimotor recognitory assimilation in which the child reels off a set of motor actions that have been habitually associated with a given object or event. The infant is likely to wander past a mechanical toy and give it a shove to produce a varied set of sights and sounds; in the same way, when he passes the stove he says "stove" and perhaps attributes a quality of heat to it by simply stating "hot." His requests for recurrence of objects or events are very similar to the circular reponses in which the child repeats an action to reproduce an interesting sight or sound. His propensity to declare the nonexistence of an object (e.g., "all-gone ball") presupposes the capacity of object permanence as well as an expectation that an object or an event should exist or occur in a given situation but that such an expectation has not been confirmed. Similarly he frequently utters pronouncements on the location of objects (e.g., "book table") that require a concept of object permanence and a memory in which he knows the object does not disappear but changes location (e.g., "where X?"). Such prerequisites are developed in early sensorimotor experience. Finally, when two- and three-word sentences arrive, they often fall into the agent–action–object category. Piaget believes that very early in infancy the child does not perceive agent, action, and object as independent from one another but comes to this perception through sensorimotor interaction with his environment. The child's experience with manipulating objects and observing the consequences of his manipulation represents a direct sensory analogue for agent–action–object verbal utterances (Brown, 1973).

The Fels data reveal correlations between early sensorimotor behavior and elementary language. These results may challenge the simplistic notion that language begins with the first word. While one must be careful not to infer that events that come developmentally early necessarily cause those that follow, a correlation at least suggests that maturational precocity at one stage relates to maturational precocity at a later stage. Further, there is the possibility that the correlation implies more than just stability in general development and maturation—perhaps such particular sensorimotor behaviors indeed represent necessary antecedent schema for language to build upon. At the very least such hypotheses cannot be so glibly dismissed as was once fashionable.

Developmental Themes

Although the behaviors at various points during the first three years of life differ in their qualitative details, they nevertheless seem to serve common purposes or themes. These purposes fall roughly into two classes. The first is the *reduction of perceptual–cognitive uncertainty*. The child takes in information about the world and frequently checks on the validity of that information. During the first year he explores the attributes of objects—their size, color, texture, weight, plasticity, and function. Later, he discovers there is something else to be learned about objects and events: they have names ("that ball"), locations ("book table"), and attributes ("big ball"), and are possessed by certain people ("Johnny ball"), etc.

A second pervasive function is a corollary of the first. The child has an influence on his environment—behaviors that we might call *affectance* (White, 1959). At first the child manipulates objects as if he were asking, "What can this object do?" Later, after he is more familiar with the nature of the object, the emphasis shifts from what the *object* can do to what *he* can do with the object (Hutt, 1970). When language is available, he may simply describe his affectance behaviors in the manner of a verbal circular response. For example, after throwing a ball down the stairs and out of sight, the child may describe the event (e.g., "ball go"), declare its disappearance or nonexistence (e.g., "all-gone ball"), or state a wish for its recurrence (e.g., "more ball"). Even one-word utterances often represent attempts to affect the environment, not just describe it, such as a request for milk expressed when the child says "milk" while pointing to the milk carton or holding an empty glass. And how effective is the defiant, "No!" in producing responses from a parent? Later, agent–action–object utterances are employed to affect environmental consequences (e.g., "I wanna cookie"). How analogous are the child's early manipulation of objects, circular responses, and gesturing to these simple verbal attempts to produce environmental (inanimate and social) consequences?

The proposal is that the reduction of perceptual–cognitive uncertainty—discovering the attributes and functions of objects and events in one's world—and the propensity of infants toward affecting their environment are themes or functions that underlie many of the diverse behaviors that evolve sequentially during the first three years.

Transitions

The data presented above suggest an orderly set of transitions guided by these themes. During the first few months the infant is simply a stimulus-detection device. He attends to objects as a function of their perceptual information, which may be embodied in their physical structure (e.g., contour density, brightness, and movement) or their discrepancy from familiar experiences. As the child's motor abilities develop, he uses them to serve exploration by moving himself near objects of interest and manipulating them to expose their various features. The process of acquiring perceptual information about an object is tantamount to attributing rudimentary meaning to it, since we call an object or an event "meaningful" partially as a function of the number of remembered associations called forth by its character and function. With the child's propensity to explore he discovers that objects roll, bounce, make noise, change shape, etc., when manipulated. Such contingent and/or conjugate reinforcement enhances the manipulatory behavior, and the child not only learns the static physical properties of an object but also what it can do. As the child becomes able to distinguish between himself as the agent and the action he performs and both of these from the object and its consequence, he explores different means to the same or different ends and what *he* can do with the object rather than what the object can do. Again the themes are perceptual–cognitive uncertainty and its corollary affectance.

It is at this point that sensorimotor imitation begins to play a more prominent role. At first, imitation tends to be adults imitating baby, who then repeats his own action. This is pseudoimitation because the child does not imitate a new behavior but merely repeats one that is already in his repertoire. Nevertheless such imitation games represent a social extrapolation of the exploration of perceptual–cognitive uncertainty and contingent consequences of the child's action. Perhaps the infant accidentally sighs and blows a bubble through his drool, the parent imitates him forthwith, the child repeats the action, and he is immediately rewarded by the parent who imitates him again. He is not only exploring the nature of this social object but also his social affectance.

Vocal behavior is a favorite activity for these pseudoimitation games. Moreover vocal behavior seems to serve the same functions as sensorimotor exploration: the reduction of perceptual–cognitive uncertainty through nomination (i.e., labeling or requests for labels, "dat?" or "what dat?"), attribution, location, etc., and social affectance (requests for recurrence or the 2-year-old's defiant, "No!"). Objects have size, shape, color, and now verbal labels. "I can make an object rock, fall, wiggle, and with language I can make other people vocalize, smile, talk to me, fetch me a cookie, and even get angry." If the functions that early language serves are well practiced in the sensorimotor period and transferred from the inanimate world to the social world by imitation, it is reasonable to expect that language comprehension precedes production at this stage (Blank, 1974).

The discussion above suggests that elementary vocalization and labeling, requests for recurrence, attribution, location, and agent–action–object utterances are simple verbal analogues to well-exercised sensorimotor behaviors. But why does more advanced language behavior develop? Blank (1974) has suggested that sensorimotor behavior, such as gestures and their verbal analogues, are inefficient next to more advanced verbal behavior and are nearly useless when it comes to expressing cognitions and affectance with respect to objects that are not present in the immediate environment. If a youngster wants to play with the big-wheeler that is on a shelf in the garage, it is about as efficient to point at it as it is to ask for it verbally. But how does a child at home obtain by gestures alone a big-wheeler that he saw yesterday on TV? Language is needed. And how does a young child respond nonverbally to a parent's demand, "How did this mess get here?" or "Why did you pour the ink in the bathtub?" No amount of gesturing can deal with "how" and "why" questions. Gesturing and sensorimotor actions simply become inefficient next to the potentiality of language for serving the goals of acquiring information and meaning about objects and affecting one's environment. Moreover, the social environment makes demands on the child that simply cannot be handled by gestural responses.

Parents model the appropriate verbal behaviors and reward the child for imitating them. In the simplest terms the themes of reducing uncertainty and affectance are the same; only the behavioral method has shifted from gestures to words.

Notice that beyond the level of elementary vocalization and verbal labeling and comprehension, more advanced language depends heavily on the symbolic function and memory. The most basic of these appears to be object permanence: the child must remember that an object exists after it has disappeared in order to declare its disappearance or nonexistence verbally and request its recurrence. Moreover there is no way for the child to handle the "not here" and "not now" situations that reward the development of advanced language concepts and communication skills without having representational thought and perceptual/verbal memory.

The sequence and nature of the behaviors that form the main set of developmental transitions in the Fels data are consistent with this developmental scenario.

ACKNOWLEDGMENT

Portions of the research reported in this paper were sponsored by Public Health Service grants NIE 6-00-3-0008 and HD-04160 to Robert B. McCall, by FR-15537, HD-00868, and FR-00222 to The Fels Research Institute, and by the Samuel S. Fels Fund of Philadelphia. The Fels data are the result of 45 years of effort by numerous staff individuals under the direction of Lester W. Sontag and now Frank Falkner and by the enduring faith of Samuel Fels and later the foundation that he endowed. I thank Carol Dodds, Dorothy Eichorn, Robert Kavanaugh, Rosemary Raterman, and Joanne Steinhilber for their several contributions to this paper.

REFERENCES

ANASTASI, A., 1968, "Psychological Testing," Macmillan, New York.
BAYLEY, N., 1949, Consistency and variability in the growth of intelligence from birth to eighteen years, *Journal of Genetic Psychology, 75*:165.
BAYLEY, N., 1970, Development of mental abilities, in "Carmichael's Manual of Child Psychology" (3rd ed.), Vol. 1, P. H. Mussen (ed.), Wiley, New York, p. 1163.
BAYLEY, N., AND SCHAEFER, E. S., 1964, Correlations of maternal and child behaviors with development of mental ability: Data from the Berkeley Growth Study, *Monographs of the Society for Research in Child Development, 29*(97).
BLANK, M., 1974, Cognitive functions of language in the preschool years, *Developmental Psychology, 10*:229.
BROWN, R., 1973, "A First Language," Harvard University Press, Cambridge, Massachusetts.

CAMERON, J., LIVSON, N., AND BAYLEY, N., 1967, Infant vocalizations and their relationship to mature intelligence, Science, 157:331.
DÉCARIE, T., 1965, "Intelligence and Affectivity in Early Childhood," International Universities Press, New York.
EICHORN, D. H., September 1969, Developmental parallels in the growth of parents and
their children, Presidential Address, Division 7, APA.
FREEDMAN, D. G., AND KELLER, B., 1963, Inheritance of behavior in infants, Science,
140:196.
HEBER, R., GARBER, H., HARRINGTON, S., HOFFMAN, C., AND FALENDER, C., December
1972, Rehabilitation of families at risk for mental retardation, progress report, Re-
habilitation Research and Training Center in Mental Retardation, University of
Wisconsin, Madison.
HONZIK, M. P., 1957, Developmental studies of parent–child resemblance in intelligence,
Child Development, 28:215.
HONZIK, M. P., HUTCHINGS, J. J., AND BURNIP, S. R., 1965, Birth record assessments and
test performance at eight months, American Journal of Diseases in Children, 109:416.
HUNT, J. McV., 1961, "Intelligence and Experience," Ronald Press, New York.
HUTT, C., 1970, Specific and diversive exploration, in "Advances in Child Development
and Behavior" Vol. 5, H. W. Reese and L. P. Lipsitt (eds.), Academic Press, New
York, p. 119.
JENSEN, A. R., 1969, How much can we boost IQ and scholastic achievement? Harvard
Educational Review, 39:1.
KAGAN, J., 1969, On the meaning of behavior: Illustrations from the infant, Child Develop-
ment, 40:1121.
LEWIS, M., AND McGURK, H., 1972, Evaluation of infant intelligence, Science, 178:1174.
LEWIS, M., AND McGURK, H., 1973, Testing infant intelligence, Science, 182:737.
MATHENY, A. P., Jr., 1973, Testing infant intelligence, Science, 182:734.
MATHENY, A. P., Jr., DOLAN, A. B., AND WILSON, R. S., 1974, Bayley's infant behavior
record: Relations between behaviors and mental test scores, Developmental Psychology,
10:696.
McCALL, R. B., 1965, Stimulus-change in light-contingent bar pressing, Journal of Compara-
tive and Physiological Psychology, 59:258.
McCALL, R. B., 1966, The initial-consequent-change surface in light-contingent bar press-
ing, Journal of Comparative and Physiological Psychology, 62:35.
McCALL, R. B., 1972a, Similarity in developmental profile among related pairs of human
infants, Science, 178:1004.
McCALL, R. B., 1972b, Similarity in IQ profile among related pairs: Infancy and childhood,
Proceedings of the American Psychological Association meeting, Honolulu, p. 79.
McCALL, R. B., 1974, Critique of a field, review of "The Study of Behavioral Develop-
ment," J. F. Wohlwill, Science, 184:673.
McCALL, R. B., HOGARTY, P. S., AND HURLBURT, N., 1972, Transitions in infant sensori-
motor development and the prediction of childhood IQ, American Psychologist, 27:728.
McCALL, R. B., APPELBAUM, M. I., AND HOGARTY, P. S., 1973, Developmental changes in
mental performance, Monographs of the Society for Research in Child Development, 38(3,
Serial No. 150).
McNEILL, D., 1970, The development of language, in "Carmichael's Manual of Child
Psychology," (3rd ed.) Vol. 1, P. H. Mussen (ed.), Wiley, New York, p. 1061.
MOORE, T., 1967, Language and intelligence: A longitudinal study of the first eight years,
Part I: Patterns of development in boys and girls, Human Development, 10:88.
NICHOLS, P. L., AND BROMAN, S. H., 1974, Familial resemblances in infant mental
development, Developmental Psychology, 10:442.

PIAGET, J., 1951, Play, dreams, and imitation in childhood, translation of La formacion du symbole chez l'enfant, by C. Gattegno and F. N. Hodgson, Norton, New York.

PIAGET, J., 1952, "The Origins of Intelligence in Children," International Universities Press, New York.

ROVEE, C. K., AND ROVEE, D. T., 1969, Conjugate reinforcement of infant exploratory behavior, Journal of Experimental Child Psychology, 8:33.

SCARR-SALAPATEK, S., February 1974, Genetic determinants of infant development: An overstated case, paper presented at the American Association for the Advancement of Science, San Francisco.

SIQUELAND, E. R., April 1969, The development of instrumental exploratory behavior during the first year of human life, paper presented at SRCD, Santa Monica.

SONTAG, L. W., BAKER, C. T., AND NELSON, V. L., 1958, Mental growth and personality development: A longitudinal study, Monographs of the Society for Research in Child Development, 23(68).

STOTT, L. H., AND BALL, R. S., 1965, Infant and preschool mental tests: Review and evaluation, Monographs of the Society for Research in Child Development, 30(101).

WACHS, T. D., 1972, Technical comment, Science, 178:1005.

WACHS, T. D., UZGIRIS, I. C., AND HUNT, J. McV., 1971, Cognitive development in infants of different age levels and from different environmental backgrounds: An explanatory investigation, Merrill–Palmer Quarterly, 17:283.

WATSON, J. S., 1972, Smiling, cooing, and "the game," Merrill–Palmer Quarterly, 18:323.

WERNER, E. E., HONZIK, M. P., AND SMITH, R. S., 1968, Prediction of intelligence and achievement at 10 years from 20 months pediatric and psychologic examinations, Child Development, 39:1063.

WHITE, R. W., 1959, Motivation reconsidered: The concept of competence, Psychological Review, 66:297.

WILLERMAN, L., AND FIEDLER, M. F., 1974, Infant performance and intellectual precocity, Developmental Psychology, 45:483.

WILSON, R. S., 1972a, Twins: Early mental development, Science, 175:914.

WILSON, R. S., 1972b, Technical comment, Science, 178:1006.

WILSON, R. S., 1973, Testing infant intelligence, Science, 182:734.

WILSON, R. S., 1974, Twins: Mental development in the preschool years, Developmental Psychology, 10:580.

WILSON, R. S., AND HARPRING, E. B., 1972, Mental and motor development in infant twins, Developmental Psychology, 7:277.

WOHLWILL, J. F., 1973, "The Study of Behavioral Development," Academic Press, New York.

5 Organization of Sensorimotor Intelligence

Ina C. Uzgiris

Introduction

Infancy is traditionally recognized as a distinct period in the course of human life; with regard to intellectual activity it is frequently considered to be not only distinct but different. Even those who do not view ontogenesis in terms of qualitative transformations seem to recognize a gap between functioning in infancy and in subsequent age periods. The apparent limitations on self-initiated activity, on physical mobility, and on communication with others during infancy have impressed numerous observers and have led to the conjecture that the infant's world may be quite unlike the world as known by the adult. Thus studies of infant intelligence have been concerned largely with charting those infant behaviors that seem to indicate progressive approximation to adult patterns of action, or those that seem to document acquisition of concrete information about the world. Since the importance of advance to adult and thereby uniquely human forms of intellectual activity is so clear, the relative neglect of forms of functioning characteristic of infancy itself need not be surprising.

In recent years the works of Piaget have served as one stimulus for greater interest in infant intellectual functioning. The model for the development of intelligence proposed by Piaget (1950, 1971a) recognizes the distinctiveness of intellectual activity during infancy but views this intellectual activity as an integral link in the evolution of human intelli-

Ina C. Uzgiris·Clark University.

gence. While noting that the infant's intelligence is "practical," directed
at obtaining results in the environment, Piaget insists that it is characterized by an organization that reveals its filiation with higher forms of
intellect. Since the infant does not possess language or a capacity for
representation, intellectual constructions during infancy have to be
based on perceptions and movements; hence the characterization of
infant intelligence as sensorimotor. Nevertheless Piaget (1970a) claims
that there is a "logic of actions" manifest in the coordinations between
schemes (i.e., the repeatable and generalizable aspect of actions) that
serves as the foundation for logicomathematical structures. In particular
a form of conservation revealed in the construction of the object concept
and a form of reversibility implicit in the coordination of displacements
and positions in space are taken by Piaget to indicate the sensorimotor
beginnings of these essential characteristics of operational thought.
Thus, among the four periods that Piaget recognizes in the development
of intelligence, the sensorimotor period represents the first structuration
of intelligence, which subsequently becomes integrated into the higher-
level structurations.

   The three books that deal with functioning in the sensorimotor
period stem from the middle years of Piaget's career (1952, 1954, 1962),
yet the general conclusions reached in these works have been reiterated
by Piaget in quite recent expositions of his theory (e.g., Piaget and
Inhelder, 1969). He has presented both an overall view of the changes in
intellectual activity during infancy and a more specific account of progress in the construction of such categories of reality as object, space,
causality, and time as well as of development in imitation and the
capacity for representation. In all cases development has been presented
in terms of a sequence of six stages. To the extent that the notion of stage
implies a distinct form of organization in intellectual activity, the issue of
congruence in the form of organization evidenced across different domains of functioning and within an interval of time arises with respect to
the sensorimotor period. The fact that progress in the various domains is
depicted in terms of the same number of stages suggests a coordination
among the transformations in each domain. On the other hand, the
claim that intercoordination between schemes constructed in different
domains is an achievement of sensorimotor development suggests that
congruence between functioning in various domains should be expected
only at the culmination of the sensorimotor period.

   The question is complicated by the fact that the term *stage* is used by

Piaget in several ways. Most generally it is applied to the major structurations in the development of intelligence, namely, the sensorimotor, the preoperational, the concrete–operational, and the formal–operational; these will be called *periods* in the present chapter. The implication of a qualitatively distinct organization is most clearly met by this usage of the term *stage* (cf. Pinard and Laurendeau, 1969). The problem of synchrony in the appearance of achievements in different domains of functioning that reflect structures characteristic of a given stage has been most extensively studied with respect to the period of concrete operations (e.g., Dodwell, 1963; Tuddenham, 1971), but the lack of congruence generally reported suggests that this question needs to be examined with respect to other periods as well. In addition the term *stage* has been used to refer to three levels in the development of cognitive structures within a given period; this yields the stage of entrance into a period, the stage of transition, and the stage of consolidation. From this viewpoint fluctuation in the application of newly forming structures is to be expected, and the issue of congruence of achievements across different domains of functioning is important only with respect to the stage of consolidation. The disparities usually covered by the term *horizontal décalage* would be expected to disappear once the structuration is fully elaborated. With respect to the sensorimotor period this would lead to an expectation of congruence in the level of functioning across domains only in the last one or two subdivisions of this period. Finally, Piaget has used the term *stage* to refer to the six subdivisions of the sensorimotor period.

The status to be given to the stages of the sensorimotor period is further complicated by the fact that Piaget has not attempted to characterize their organization in a formal way. He has provided numerous examples of behaviors that he considers indicative of a given stage in sensorimotor development, but he has confined his characterization of stages to the specific domain being considered. Consequently the sensorimotor stages tend to be discussed in the research literature not in terms of structures or levels of organization but in terms of exemplary behaviors. The recent statements by Piaget (1971b) claiming that intellectual activity in the sensorimotor period, as in subsequent periods, reflects overall structures—that is, organized wholes having the properties of self-regulation and transformation—would seem to fit the culmination of sensorimotor development better than each of the six stages. Consequently one question that will guide this examination of research on intellectual functioning in the sensorimotor period will pertain to congruence of achievement in different domains of functioning.

The claim for an invariant sequence of stages in Piaget's theory is predicated on the assumption of a hierarchical relationship between the stages. The sequence of the six sensorimotor stages describes the gradual differentiation of the assimilatory and accommodatory processes and their eventual coordination within a relatively stable structure. A critical outcome for the infant is the gradual objectification of reality and, as a complement, the evolution of the awareness of self as an agent in the world. Since many studies have been concerned with the sequential attainment of behaviors exemplifying the sensorimotor stages, this question will also guide my examination of the research literature.

A very brief characterization of the six stages in the development of sensorimotor intelligence proposed by Piaget is presented to facilitate discussion in subsequent sections of this chapter. More complete expositions of his views are readily accessible (e.g., in Hunt, 1961). The age ranges cited by Piaget for each of the stages have become widely accepted, although they were not meant to be normative except in the most general way.

Stage I, the use of reflexes, spans the period of birth to about 1 month of age. Although using the term *reflex*, Piaget seems to be interested in those activities of the infant that possess the characteristics of schemes, that is, possess generalizable and repeatable aspects. These reflexes or schemes are thought to be sustained through exercise, thus calling the processes of assimilation and accommodation into play. The infant is seen as active in making contact with the environment, yet at the same time dependent on such contacts for coming to know the world in which he exists. Stage II, the stage of secondary circular reactions, spans the period of 2–4 months of life and is marked by the appearance of new adaptations termed *habits*. The use of schemes, which entails the processes of assimilation and accommodation, is said to lead eventually to somewhat stable modifications in the schemes. These modified schemes, which also come to be repeatedly used, indicate the beginnings of differentiation in the infant's activities. Although the behavioral examples resemble instances of conditioning, Piaget insists that the behavioral changes reflect an integration of new elements into existing schemes and not an association between an arbitrary sign and some behavioral response. Stage III, the stage of secondary circular reactions, spans the period between around 4 and 8 months of life. It is characterized by Piaget as a transition period between activity based on simple habits and intelligent activity. The assimilation of accidentally produced outcomes engenders repetition of schemes so as to reproduce those outcomes, which entails an accommodation to the circumstances at hand. This is said to lead to new coordinations between schemes as well as to a gradual dissociation between goals and means, since the same means come to be used in more and more varied contexts.

The achievement of coordination between means and ends marks the beginning of intelligent activity for Piaget. While the transformation involved in becoming able to intend goals prior to embarking on the means for their attainment was stressed more in Piaget's earlier writings, nevertheless the reorganization taking place between stages III and IV is clearly a major landmark in sensorimotor development. Stage IV, the coordination of secondary schemes and their application to new situations, spans the period between 8 and 12 months. The variety of schemes constructed at the previous stage come to be coordinated with each other in goal-directed sequences. The important novelty stressed by Piaget is that the coordinations of schemes involved in the goal-directed sequences are freely constructed in each situation, albeit from well-practiced schemes, indicating the differentiation of means from goals. Stage V, the tertiary circular reaction stage, spans the first half of the second year, between about 12 and 18 months of age. This stage is marked for Piaget by an increase in the importance of the accommodatory process, so that schemes are repeated less in order to preserve them unchanged and more so as to incorporate new elements of reality into them. This observed variation in infant's activities is described by Piaget both as an interest in novelty and as experimentation or groping leading to invention. In goal-directed activities the infant appears capable of trial-and-error learning, since the scheme serving as means is flexible enough to be varied systematically and thus to be adjusted to the goal. Although Piaget insists on interpreting trial-and-error learning as a process directed by both the goal of the action and the scheme serving as the initial means, not as a blind process, he nevertheless assigns considerable importance to such activity within intelligent action.

While the differentiation between means and ends achieved in stage IV is an important mark of intelligent activity, Piaget suggests that from the vantage point of stage VI, the three preceding stages might be grouped together, in that they all reflect adaptation through adjustment to a concrete situation by overt activity, by taking into account the constraints of the situation gradually and only subsequent to acting in it. Stage VI, the invention of new means through mental combinations, is distinguished for Piaget by the fact that new coordinations appear as if through insight, sudden understanding, or some similar process. Rather than viewing it as the sudden appearance of true intelligence, Piaget prefers to consider it a direct outgrowth of development in the previous stages. Beginning around 16–18 months of age, the infant is said to become capable of internalized groping, of covert activity, so that the overt action finally engaged in appears already adjusted to the requirements of the situation. Obviously one of the most interesting questions concerning sensorimotor development pertains to this process of internalization, to the mechanisms that make possible such abbreviation and condensation, so that previously overt acts come to serve as signifiers of reality and can be acted upon covertly. Acquisition of language is thought to facilitate this internal activity greatly, but not to be responsible for its initial appearance. In this way, also, Piaget insists that stage VI sensorimotor intelligence is but a completion of the accomplishments of previous stages.

Most of the current research on sensorimotor intelligence has been directed toward systematization and replication of Piaget's observations, which form the foundation for his characterization of the six stages in sensorimotor development. In addition to the problems of sequence and of congruence of functioning across various domains, some of the studies permit examination of differences in sensorimotor development among groups of infants differing in cultural, socioeconomic, or other environmental circumstances. In the section that follows, results from studies using systematic assessment procedures will be discussed with respect to these problems. Then a conception of four levels of organization in sensorimotor intelligence, founded on Piaget's ideas but focusing more on the structuration of the infant's actions, is presented together with some observations from a longitudinal study of functioning in the first two years.

Assessment of Sensorimotor Intelligence

Scales for Assessment

Albert Einstein Scales of Sensorimotor Development (SSD)

Following the systematic observation of a large sample of infants in New York City, three scales spanning the period of sensorimotor intelligence have been constructed by Escalona and Corman (unpublished), with the help of a number of co-workers. These scales were designed to establish the stage in sensorimotor functioning. The Prehension Scale, the Object Permanence Scale, and the Space Scale have been distributed in mimeographed form (no date) and have been used in several studies. The introduction to the manual for these scales mentions that work on a Causality Scale is in progress.

The Prehension Scale spans the first three stages in sensorimotor development, although the items are scored in terms of evidence for stage II or stage III functioning. It contains 16 items, which have been administered to 51 infants between 5 and 35 weeks of age and to 14 infants studied longitudinally. Corman and Escalona (1969) have reported that Green's Index of Consistency (I) is 0.66 for this scale and commented that none of the infants studied longitudinally manifested behaviors at a higher level before passing items at a lower level on this scale.

The Object Permanence Scale includes 18 items and spans stages III through VI. It has been administered to 113 infants between 5 and 26 months of age and to 15 infants followed longitudinally. Scored in terms of stages, this scale is reported to be perfectly ordinal (I = 1.00). A more interesting finding obtained by Corman and Escalona (1969) pertains to the degree of completion of one stage prior to entrance into the following one. They found progression from one stage to another to be much more gradual than might be expected from a view of stages as sudden transformations. For example, infants entering stage IV were found to pass, on the average, 82% of the items at the previous stage, but the range was from 40% to 100%. Similarly infants entering stage VI were found to pass, on the average, 74% of the items at stage V, but the range was from 20% to 100%. From these data it appears that there is considerable variability in infant functioning across specific situations, if all the items used as indices of a particular stage are in fact equally appropriate for its assessment.

The Space Scale also spans stages III to VI and includes 21 items. It has been administered to 83 infants between 5 and 26 months of age and to 16 infants studied longitudinally. An invariant order in the attainment of stages was found (I = .98), but completion of items at one stage prior to entry into the next was again variable. On the average, infants achieved 76% of items at stage IV prior to entry into stage V, but the range was from 25% to 100%; similarly, infants achieved 56% of items at stage V prior to entry into stage VI, with a range of 20–100% (Corman and Escalona, 1969). These findings clearly suggest the need for additional studies concerning the correlates and implications of variability in stage-level functioning even within a single domain. If such variations are meaningful, then scoring infant development by stages glosses over important differences; however, until the meaning of these variations is understood, scoring in terms of number of items passed, which has been adopted by some investigators, does not seem to be justified. In the latter case the assumption is made that the greater the number of actions performed at one stage level, the greater the advancement within that stage and (implicitly) the sooner the entrance into the subsequent stage. Such quantitative relationships do not follow clearly from Piaget's theory of sensorimotor development and need specific investigation.

These SSD do not seem to have been administered to a single sample of infants and comparisons of stage-level congruence across domains have not been reported. In studies by other investigators the Object Permanence Scale has been the most frequently used.

Casati–Lézine Scale

This scale was constructed in France and was described by Casati and Lézine (1968) in a monograph that provides instructions for its administration. Information concerning the performance of 305 infants tested between 6 months and 2 years of age with this scale and 2 infants tested longitudinally is presented by Lézine et al. (1969). The scale is composed of four tests, each containing a variable number of items.

The first test concerns object search. It spans stages III through VI and contains seven items. The items appear to be selected for the purpose of diagnosing each stage and therefore are usually assigned two per stage, one to indicate entry into a stage and the second to indicate its completion. Their findings are presented in terms of the percentage of infants passing each item at each month of age. With very few exceptions a greater percentage of infants was found to pass each item at each successive month of age (the exceptions indicating a reduction by one or two infants). Similarly the item indicating entry into a stage was passed by a greater percentage of infants than the item indicating completion of that same stage at every month of age, with very few exceptions. Although formal scaling analyses were not performed, it is reported that there were only two individual instances of success on a higher-level item following failure on a lower item.

The second test concerns the use of intermediaries, such as a string, supports (a cloth and a pivoting board), and a rake or stick, in order to obtain an object placed out of reach. The four string items span stages IV and V, while the support and stick items span stages IV through VI, containing seven and six items, respectively. Again, with few exceptions a greater percentage of infants was found to pass each item at each successive month of age; the exceptions seem small enough to be due to sample variations. For all of the items used, a greater percentage of infants passed the item marking the entry into each stage than the item marking completion of that stage. Examination of individual protocols revealed four instances in which an infant succeeded on a higher-level item following failure on a lower item.

The six items in the test for exploration of objects span stages IV through V. The objects used in the test are a mirror and a box. The group results indicate a regular increase in the percentage of infants passing each item with age and a larger percentage of infants passing the lower of the two items marking each stage. In individual records, only one instance of inversion in the sequence was reported.

The fourth test, concerned with combination of objects, is applicable at stages V and VI. The eight items concern the combination of a tube and a rake or a tube and a chain. For this test the increase in percentage of infants passing each item at each successive month of age is less regular, although the higher-level items are passed by fewer infants than the lower-level items at most ages. The division of items as indexing stage V versus stage VI seems to be the least clear for this test.

Each infant in the sample was administered the various tests, so that examination of congruence in stage level across tests was possible. Findings pertinent to this issue have been presented by Lézine *et al.* (1969), but the discussion of these findings is deferred to a subsequent section of this chapter. These tests have been used by other investigators and their findings provide information concerning the performance of different groups of infants on them.

Infant Psychological Development Scales (IPDS)

Uzgiris and Hunt have constructed a set of seven scales that are also derived from Piaget's original observations, but they are not scored in terms of sensorimotor stage level. These scales have been available in mimeographed form (Uzgiris and Hunt, 1964, 1966, 1972), and results on the 84 Illinois infants observed in situations contained in these scales have been published (Uzgiris and Hunt, 1975). The infants ranged from 1 to 24 months of age and were examined with each of the scales.

The first scale pertains to Visual Pursuit and Permanence of Objects and has 14 steps. It attempts to tap the same domain of functioning as the Object Permanence and Object Search Scales described previously. Given the central importance attributed by Piaget to the construction of the notion of object in the sensorimotor period, it is not surprising that all scales include an assessment of this domain. The second scale pertains to the Development of Means for Obtaining Desired Events and has 13 steps. This scale contains situations similar to those grouped by Casati and Lézine as the Use of Intermediaries and, at the higher levels, is directed to the same domain as their Combination of Objects Test. The two scales pertaining to Imitation (Vocal and Gestural) have 9 steps each. Although recently there have appeared a few studies concerned with imitation in infancy (e.g., Giblin, 1971; Maratos, 1973), no other imitation scales have been constructed.

The scale pertaining to Development of Operational Causality has 7 steps. It is concerned with progress in objectification of causality, which is considered by Piaget to be involved in the construction of reality. Similarly the scale pertaining to the Construction of Object Relations in Space deals with objectification of space. It has 11 steps and is concerned with the same domain as the Space Scale from the SSD. The scale

TABLE I

Summary of Results for the Infant Psychological Development Scales

Scale	Observer reliability (% agreement)	Infant performance stability (% agreement)	Scalability (Green's I)	Correlation with age (r)
Visual pursuit and permanence of objects	96.7	83.8	0.97	0.94
Development of means	96.2	75.5	0.81	0.94
Imitation—vocal	91.8	72.6	0.89	0.88
Imitation—gestural	95.7	70.0	0.95	0.91
Development of operational causality	93.7	71.2	0.99	0.86
Construction of object relations in space	96.9	84.6	0.91	0.91
Schemes for relating to objects	93.0	79.0	0.80	0.89

pertaining to the Development of Schemes for Relating to Objects has 10 steps and is directed at a more general assessment of the differentiation and coordination of schemes. It seems to be related to the Exploration of Objects Test included by Casati and Lézine.

These scales have been administered twice within a three-day period to each infant in the sample in order to obtain an indication of stability of infant performance. The steps in each scale were analyzed for ordinality, and correlations of performance with chronological age were also determined. These results for the IPDS are summarized in Table I.

Other Scales

Two scales grounded in Piaget's theory have been constructed by Décarie (1965, 1972). The scale concerned with the development of the object concept has eight items scored in terms of stage level. It was the first systematic scale to be derived from Piaget's observations. In Décarie's sample of 90 infants between 3 and 20 months of age, no infant was found to pass an item indexing a higher stage after failing on an item indexing a lower stage. The correlation between stage level and chronological age was found to be 0.86. A scale pertaining to the development of causality has been recently reported (Décarie, 1972). This scale is also scored in terms of stage level and contains 15 items. Décarie appears to have constructed these scales to meet the needs of her research and not to serve general assessment purposes. An interesting feature of both of these scales is that the infant's level of progress may be assessed with respect to persons and with respect to inanimate objects. Bell (1970) has also constructed an object concept scale in the context of a study of infant attachment to the mother; this scale closely resembles many of the other scales. However, although the various scales are similar, their proliferation makes generalization across studies a difficult task.

A Cognitive Development Scale based on Piaget's work has been reported by Mehrabian and Williams (1971). It contains 28 items concerned with observing responses, denotation and representation, object stability, causality, and imitation. These items are organized into a single scale and are scored mostly in terms of pass–fail, although a few items have a larger range of scores, but without consideration for stage level. The scale has been administered to a sample of 196 infants from the Los Angeles area, ranging between 4 and 20 months in age. As a result of multidimensional homogeneity analysis the authors concluded that the entire scale measures a unitary ability. Many of the items were found to show a low correlation with age, but a test–retest correlation of 0.72 was reported for 43 infants retested after an interval of four months. This scale is directed to assessing those cognitive achievements that are considered particularly relevant for development in representational ability.

In addition a number of investigators have studied individual situations originally described by Piaget, which are also contained as items in one or another of these scales; however, since these studies were not focused on assessing the level of sensorimotor development (even though stage designations have sometimes been used), they are excluded from this review. Without doubt, studies pertaining to object concept development form the most numerous group among such more limited investigations.

Problem of Stage Sequence and Congruence

Invariant Sequence

The expectation of an invariant progression through the sequence of stages in the sensorimotor period has been generally substantiated by evidence for scalability found for the various scales and by the observation of an orderly advance in terms of stages with increase in chronological age. However, the results from a few studies complicate this rather clear-cut finding.

As might be expected, two of these cautionary studies relied on longitudinal observations. Using the Casati-Lézine scale, Kopp et al. (1974) tested a sample of 24 infants at monthly intervals between the ages of 7 and 18 months. Although an increase in the percentage of infants achieving each stage level was generally obtained, the progression was considerably less regular than that reported by Lézine et al. (1969) for their cross-sectional sample. In order to examine the variability in performance, Kopp et al. (1974) calculated a percentage of decline for each infant, representing the percentage of tests on which the infant scored lower than in the previous testing. For all infants combined, the percentages of decline were not very high, but they did occur, reaching 20% at 15 months of age and ranging between 14% and 16% for tests occurring between 13 and 18 months of age. The authors stated that declines from one stage to the previous one were less frequent but were also observed.

In a different report on apparently the same sample of infants Kopp *et al.* (1973) presented the results of scalability analysis for three of the Casati–Lézine tests. With respect to the Object Search Scale the reproducibility index I was found to be acceptably high at each of five ages (9, 12, 15, 18, and 20 months), although at 12 months of age it reached only 0.75. Similarly, for the Use of Intermediaries (Strings) I = 1.00 except at 15 months of age, when it reached only 0.65. However, for the Use of Intermediaries (Support), I implied an acceptable level of scalability only at 9 and again at 20 months of age. These results indicate that although there is a definite order in sensorimotor attainments, individual infants do backslide in concrete test situations, more at some ages than at others and more in some domains of functioning than in others.

Somewhat similar results were obtained for the IPDS in a longitudinal study of a sample of 12 infants (Uzgiris, 1973a). A pattern of transitional performance was quite common: an infant would succeed in a situation at a higher level than previously, would drop back in the next session, and would again succeed at the higher level in the following session and continue to succeed subsequently. In comparison with the cross-sectional sample, exceptions from the postulated order of attainment were infrequent. With the exception of the Object Permanence and the Causality Scales, the order for a single pair of two adjacent steps appeared to be inverted for the sample as a whole on each of the scales. These inverted pairs of steps were not concentrated at any one age period. In addition individual infants were observed to attain the higher of two adjacent steps first on almost every scale, although these irregularities appeared to be due to idiosyncratic factors in that generally no more than one or two infants showed any particular inversion. Such individual inversions were more frequent on some scales than on others, occurring most frequently in the Development of Means Scale. Since these scales are not scored according to stage level, each irregularity should not be interpreted as indicating variability in stage progression. In this context it must be remembered that Corman and Escalona (1969) found little consistency among infants in achievement of items indexing a particular stage prior to entry into the next stage. To the extent that adjacent steps on the IPDS may be considered to index the same sensorimotor stage, variability in order of achievement should not be surprising.

A study conducted by Miller *et al.* (1970) investigated the effect of order of presentation of items on infant performance, using the Object Permanence Scale from the IPDS. Three age groups of infants were presented appropriate items from the scale either in the order of difficulty (the usual administration procedure) or in a random order. The youngest infants (6 and 8 months) were administered situations 1–8, the middle group (10 and 12 months) situations 4–12, and the oldest group (14, 16, and 18 months) situations 8–16. With the constricted range of test situations, the scalability analysis did not yield an acceptable I coefficient for any of the age groups in either of the two administration conditions. Examination of their graphs suggests that the largest deviations from the postulated sequence occurred on two tasks, which might be because of a different construal of those tasks by these investigators. On the other hand, when assumptions about performance on nonadministered items were made so that each infant was scored on the complete scale, I still exceeded the 0.50 value suggested by Green as minimal for scalability under both conditions of administration.

It must be emphasized once more that an invariant order of achievement is claimed only for the sensorimotor stages and not for samples of tasks that might be selected to index one of these stages. In fact, examples of backsliding in the behavior of individual infants on specific tasks may be found among Piaget's observations as well. Variation in performance from one day to another and from one task to another is to be expected; what seems to be needed is better explication of criteria for determining the consolidation of a stage, subsequent to which backsliding within the same domain ought not to occur except in very unusual circumstances. However, as long as particular performances on a single task are treated as equivalent to stage achievement, findings of regressions and inversions for individual infants are bound to be reported.

Stage Congruence across Domains

The classification of sensorimotor functioning into domains has been somewhat arbitrary. Theoretically each domain should pertain to activities based on a unitary cognitive structure. The domains individually discussed by Piaget were chosen on theoretical grounds; however, their structuration and types of interdependence were suggested rather than explicitly analyzed by him. Those who have grounded their work in Piaget's observations have either accepted Piaget's classification of domains or have arrived at more circumscribed groupings of competencies on some intuitive basis. Consequently the theoretical meaningfulness of comparisons across domains so variously formed may be questioned, since the findings of lack of congruence would have different implications, depending on whether the two domains might be said to rely on a single structure. A more formal characterization of structures and levels of organization for sensorimotor intelligence would certainly facilitate the evaluation both of tasks presented to infants and of findings regarding congruence in performance on such tasks. With these limitations in mind the available research on stage congruence may be examined.

One of the first attempts to examine congruence in sensorimotor development across domains was carried out by Woodward (1959), not on infants but on severely mentally retarded children. A total of 147 children, ranging up to 16 years in age, were administered a variety of tasks described by Piaget, which were scored in terms of stage level. Overall, Woodward reported that success on two tasks classified as indicative of the same stage was significantly related for this sample. In addition, when the children were assigned to a stage of sensorimotor development on the basis of their performance on various problem-solving tasks (items similar to coordination between schemes and to the use of means or intermediaries in other scales) and also to a stage in object concept development, considerable consistency in stage level was obtained (87% of the children were classified at the same stage in both). Less consistency was obtained when stage in problem-solving was compared to stage based on type of circular reactions shown (43% were classified in the same stage in both). Given the considerable variability in level of development in different domains that has been observed in children attaining concrete operations, Woodward's findings are impressive. One may be tempted to attribute these results to the nature of her population, which might be viewed as no longer advancing, having been somehow arrested in intellectual development.

A similarly impressive degree of stage consistency across domains has been reported by Lézine et al. (1969). Comparing stage congruence across their tests taken in pairs, they found an overall percentage of concordance to be 71%, ranging from 58% to 87% for individual pairings of tests. For example, the stage on Object Search was equivalent to that obtained in the Use of Intermediaries (Strings) for 74% of the infants, equivalent to that obtained in Object Exploration for 72% of the infants, and equivalent to that obtained in the Use of Intermediaries (Rake-Stick) for 59% of the infants. Among the discrepancies found, over 80% amounted to a discrepancy by a single stage. It may be of interest to note also that the infants tended to be advanced most frequently on the Object Search Test. However, Lézine *et al.* carried out such analyses for various age groups separately as well; it turned out that stage congruence was more prevalent at some ages than at others. Overall there was highest congruence at 9 and 10 months of age and lowest congruence at 14 and 15 months of age, with the percentage of concordance generally lower in the second year of life. This observation complements the finding by Kopp *et al.* (1974) of greatest instability in performance on longitudinal testing around 15 months of age. Since the same tests were used in both studies, the findings may also be a function of the tasks used, although it is intriguing to consider this instability as evidence for a period of transition and reorganization prior to the consolidation achieved at stage VI.

Findings from a study using the Casati–Lézine tests on a group of Ivory Coast infants have been recently reported by Bovet *et al.* (1974). They reported that stage concordance was obtained in 65% of the test comparisons, ranging from 30% to 85% for specific pairs of tests. Their sample of 73 infants covered a similar age span, ranging from 6 to 24 months in age.

In a study of the relationship of language development to sensori-motor level, Zachry (1972) employed the IPDS but transformed the scoring to a stage-level system. For his sample of 24 infants, ranging in age between 13 and 23 months of age, he found considerable variation in stage level across the six domains tapped by these scales. All infants scored in at least two stages, and 9 infants scored in all three stages assessed. An interesting finding reported by Zachry pertains to the scale combinations on which infants scored at stage VI. All 22 infants who reached stage VI were at stage VI on object permanence; thus the four infants who scored at stage VI on only one scale did so on object permanence. All infants who scored at stage VI on one additional scale added object relations in space. Thereafter, however, the combinations of scales were more varied. Nevertheless a Guttman scalar analysis suggested an orderly sequence in stage VI development as follows: object permanence, object relations in space, imitation, causality, and then development of means. These results suggest that there may be orderly consolidation at the stage VI level.

The congruence of infant achievements across domains has been examined in several studies without reference to stage level. An extensive correlational analysis of infant scores on the IPDS (Uzgiris, 1973a) indicated few substantial correlations for pairs of scales at any single month of age between 2 and 24 months. The only notable clusters of correlations were obtained between scores on the Object Permanence and the Object Relations in Space Scales for the period of 5–8 months of age, and between scores on the Object Relations in Space and the Development of Means Scales for the period of 4–6 months and, also, 14–19 months. Even taking into account the small size of the sample, these results are at variance with expectation. One problem with this type of correlational analysis is that chronological age is used to group infants. If it is assumed that infants progress at different rates and that congruence across domains may be expected only at times of stage consolidation, then carrying out such analyses by age would tend to obscure any meaningful pattern in the results. In fact, the examination of infants grouped in terms of their object permanence scores suggested more interesting patterns of development for the same data.

In a study by King and Seegmiller (1973) infants living in Harlem were administered the IPDS at 14, 18, and 22 months of age. The performance of these infants was compared across domains at these three age levels. The results are again subject to the limitations of analysis by chronological age. Although all correlations were rather low, the greatest number of significant correlations was obtained at 14 months of age. The Object Permanence Scale scores were significantly related to those on the Object Relations in Space, the Development of Means, the Causality, and the Gestural Imitation Scales. In addition scores on the Object Relations in Space Scale were significantly correlated with scores on Development of Schemes, Causality, Development of Means, and Gestural Imitation. Similarly scores on the Causality scale were significantly correlated with scores on the Object Relations in Space and the Development of Schemes Scales. The one scale that did not correlate with any of them pertains to Vocal Imitation. On the other hand, at 18 and 22 months of age there were practically no significant intercorrelations among the scales. The almost single exception was the correlation between scores on the Development of Schemes Scale with Vocal Imitation at 18 months and again at 22 months.

The suggestion that grouping infants by chronological age may mask developmental relationships is supported by the correlational results obtained by Kopp *et al.* (1974) for the Casati–Lézine tests. Although considerable stage-level congruence has been reported for these tests, Kopp *et al.* obtained only eight significant correlations for all the age levels analyzed and no more than two at any one age level. In addition most of the significant correlations involved items from the Use of Intermediaries Tests. On the other hand, Gottfried (1974) reported a significant correlation between scores on the Object Permanence Scale from the SSD and scores on the Development of Schemes Scale from the IPDS for a sample of 207 New York City infants tested at around 11 months of age. However, although significant, the magnitude of this correlation was similar to those obtained in other studies, simply illustrating the dependence of correlational studies on sample size.

Thus it may be concluded that the strategy of correlational analysis for narrow age groups is not likely to be successful in demonstrating interdependencies between achievements in different domains. It may be that progress during the sensorimotor period is not very well coordinated across different domains of functioning. Such a conclusion would gain support from studies demonstrating considerable modifiability of rate of progress in specific domains (e.g., Gaiter, 1972; Paraskevopoulos and Hunt, 1971; Hunt *et al.* 1975). However, before we accept this conclusion, it would seem important to consider what interdependencies should be theoretically expected and then to obtain evidence regarding them in the most direct and suitable way.

Clearly the problem of domain definition cannot be avoided. A study by Silverstein *et al.* (1976) may be taken as an example of attempting to deal with this problem. Using the data obtained by Uzgiris and Hunt (1972) and by King and Seegmiller (1973), they performed a hierarchical cluster analysis and a factor analysis on these data. Three very similar factors were obtained for both samples. The first factor was defined by scores on the Causality, the Object Relations in Space, and the Development of Schemes Scales; the second by the Object Permanence, the Development of Means, and the Gestural Imitation Scales; and the Vocal Imitation Scale alone defined the third factor. Such an analysis suggests that at least the IPDS are neither uniformly interrelated nor completely independent. In this context it may be noted that a scalogram analysis of the Bayley Mental Scale items (Kohen-Raz, 1967) also resulted in several ordinal sequences rather than in a unitary scale.

Progression with Age

Age Sequence

The clearest result that has been obtained with all the different measures of progress in sensorimotor functioning is the regular relationship of such progress to chronological age. All who constructed the various sets of scales to assess sensorimotor development have reported high and significant correlations of scores with age (Corman and Escalona, 1969; Casati and Lézine, 1968; Décarie, 1965; Uzgiris and Hunt, 1972). Subsequent studies have also generally obtained regular increments in scores with age, at least for samples of infants taken as a group (e.g., Lewis and McGurk, 1972; King and Seegmiller, 1973; Uzgiris, 1973a; Paraskevopoulos and Hunt, 1971). Some exceptions have been found only in protocols of individual infants tested repeatedly. Nevertheless, since these results have been obtained in studies using different tests, different populations of infants, and even scoring procedures such that items presented as alternative indicators of a stage were added up to give a quantitative score, the results should be considered robust. They satisfy the minimal validity requirement for these scales.

Rate of Progression with Age

Another question frequently addressed in the literature pertains to the correlation of individual scores over age. The expectation of high correlations presupposes either uniform rates of progress or stable rates for individuals. This question is foreign to a Piagetian view of developmental progress. Nevertheless it seems to arise from the attempt to transpose the scales that have been devised to assess the level of sensorimotor development into psychometric devices, which are grounded in a different set of assumptions (see, for example, Furth, 1973; Uzgiris, 1973b; Uzgiris and Hunt, 1972). A number of studies have examined correlations between scores at one age level and scores at some subsequent age level with the expectation that those infants who attained the highest scores at the earlier age should be the ones to attain the highest scores at the later age. If, however, developmental progress is viewed as discontinuous, there seems little reason to expect such correlations, especially if achievement is scored in terms of stage level; that is, the initially more advanced infant might be extending the range of functioning at some given stage level during the intertest interval, while the initially less advanced infant is reaching that stage level, so that at the second testing, both may be at the same stage, reducing any interage correlation. Similarly, unless it is proposed that coordination of each stage is equally rapid, there seems little reason to expect similarities in rates of progress through them. In fact the evidence appears to indicate a lack of consistency in rate of progress over age.

King and Seegmiller (1973), in the study already referred to, correlated the scores obtained by infants at 14 months with their scores at 18 and 22 months on the IPDS. By and large they found nonsignificant correlations between scores on the various scales over the intervals used. Aside from the questions that may be raised about seeking such correlations on conceptual grounds, it should be pointed out that the age range chosen in this study was not optimal, since coordination of sensorimotor intelligence is thought to be accomplished somewhere between 16 and 24 months. Since the scales are designed to assess the presence of various coordinations in sensorimotor functioning and not the ease or the breadth of their application, the scales would not be likely to detect many individual differences between 18 and 24 months. For the interval between 14 and 22 months, involving a longer time span, the correlation for a total score obtained from all the scales was moderate ($r = 0.56$) and significant.

Negligible interage correlations were also obtained by Lewis and McGurk (1972) for scores on the Object Permanence Scale from the SSD. For infants tested at 3, 6, 9, 12, 18, and 24 months of age, they obtained significant correlations only between scores at 3 months and scores at 12 and 18 months. The authors concluded that "there is no indication that successful performance at the simpler level is predictive of an infant's ability to succeed on the more complex items when he is older" (p. 1176). Yet the more strictly correct conclusion from these data is that the rank of an infant's performance at one level when compared to that of others in the sample does not predict the infant's rank among others at a higher level at a later age. Given the view of development in which these scales are grounded, should such prediction be expected? On the other hand, speaking strictly again, to the extent that the scales are ordinal, successful performance at the simpler level is predictive, since successful performance at a higher level will not be shown without the lower-level achievement.

In a third study on this same issue (Uzgiris, 1973a) consistency in rate of development was examined by correlation of the age of achievement for the various steps in the Object Permanence and the Development of Means Scales from the IPDS. With few exceptions most of the intercorrelations were low; however, the correlations were higher between those steps that might be taken to mark the entry into a new stage. For example, on the Object Permanence Scale the age for finding a simply hidden object (usually taken to indicate stage IV) correlated significantly with the age for finding an object hidden by means of an invisible displacement (early stage VI), which in turn correlated with the age for finding an object through a series of invisible displacements (consolidated stage VI). In general, however, the possibility that there might be regularities in progression through developmental cycles has not been adequately studied, since the available studies have not differentiated between items indexing entrance into a stage and items marking extension of functioning within the same stage when interage correlations are calculated.

Influence of Environmental Conditions

Although rapidity of progress through the stages of sensorimotor intelligence is not a question of central concern for a stage theory of development, the correlation of specific environmental conditions with the achievement of given levels of functioning is of interest, since such correlations provide leads concerning the prerequisites for particular achievements.

In her study of object concept development Décarie (1965) included in her sample infants from three different backgrounds: infants living in their natural homes, infants living in foster homes, and institutionalized infants. However, since the effect of the infant's circumstances on development was not a major concern in this study, only minimal characterization of the conditions in the foster homes or the institution was provided. Whatever the actual differences between these environments, they did not account for much of the variance in object concept ranks (over 3%), even though their contribution was statistically significant.

Golden and Birns (1968) were more directly interested in the influence of environmental conditions and compared home-reared infants from three socioeconomic groups on the Object Permanence Scale from the SSD. No significant differences in achievement were obtained for any of the age groups tested (12, 18, and 24 months). Since the range of scores was similar for each of the socioeconomic groups, it does not seem that a ceiling effect is responsible for these findings.

Similarly Cobos *et al.* (1972) reported that 292 infants tested with the same Object Permanence Scale in Bogotá showed no significant differences in performance when contrasted by social class. Also these infants did not score significantly lower than the New York sample. On the other hand, malnourished infants had significantly lower scores after the age of 10 months when compared to well-nourished youngsters from the same population. Unfortunately specific scores at different ages have not been reported for this study. An investigation of a sample of Guatemalan infants (Lester *et al.*, 1974) did report the number of infants at each stage of object concept development. Although no other study that has used the Object Permanence Scale from the SSD has reported results in such a way as to permit a direct comparison, the finding that 75% of the infants tested at 18 months of age had entered stage VI appears comparable to the result obtained by most other studies.

A related study by Wachs *et al.* (1971) used the IPDS to examine groups of infants of 7, 11, 15, 18, and 22 months of age from two socioeconomic levels. On the Object Permanence Scale a significant difference in favor of infants in the higher socioeconomic group was obtained only at 11 months of age. Thus this finding does not contradict the report of Golden and Birns (1968). However, on the Development of Means Scale a significant difference was obtained in favor of infants at the higher socioeconomic level for every age group except the 15-month-old group. The Vocal Imitation Scale was administered only to the three oldest groups, and significant differences on it were obtained for every age group tested. However, on the Development of Schemes Scale there were no significant differences due to socioeconomic level for any of the age groups. However, the more interesting aspect of this study pertains to correlations obtained between a variety of specific characteristics of the home environments and achievement on the IPDS for the sample of infants as a whole. Various home environment characteristics correlated with infant achievement at different age levels, but there were some consistencies. The study concluded that intensity of stimulation, variety of changes in the environment, and exposure to spoken language were the most significant dimensions of the environment with regard to infant achievement at this period.

Recently Wachs (1973) reported on the results from a longitudinal study of 39 infants living in varying home environments. Detailed observations were made in the infants' homes at regular intervals during the second year of life, and the infants were administered the IPDS at 15, 18, 21, and 24 months of age. Correlations between achievement level on the IPDS and the home environment ratings during the preceding three months revealed a number of significant relationships. Various characteristics of the environment were most consistently related to achievements assessed by the Object Permanence, the Foresight (a branch of Development of Means), the Development of Schemes, and the Vocal Imitation Scales. Wachs specified four categories of environmental characteristics that appear to be particularly relevant to early intellectual functioning: (1) the predictability and regularity of the environment for the child; (2) the adequacy of the stimulation offered the child; (3) the intensity of stimulation (related negatively), when accompanied by lack of possibilities for withdrawal from it; and (4) verbal stimulation. The importance of these findings lies not in the demonstration of the influence of environmental conditions but in the demonstration that different characteristics of the infant's environment are related to specific achievements at different intervals in the infant's life. Unless one assumes that all the important characteristics of environments are positively interrelated, findings such as these support the notion that rates of progress shown by individual infants should vary from one interval to the next.

The studies described so far suggest that most environments provide sufficient support for object concept development during the first two years of life. In contrast, Paraskevopoulos and Hunt (1971) reported considerable lag in the achievement of various levels in object construction for three groups of Greek infants: those being reared at home, those in a model orphanage, and those in a municipal orphanage. As might be expected, the infants in the municipal orphanage were the oldest when they reached specific levels in object construction on a modified form of the IPDS. Since the major variable differentiating the orphanages was the infant–caregiver ratio, it is intriguing to speculate that object concept development might depend more on interpersonal interaction than has been suspected. The studies that have obtained no differences in object construction between comparison groups have sampled infants living with their families; Paraskevopoulos and Hunt used institutionalized infants. It should be noted also that several studies have reported some relationship between the quality of infant–mother attachment or the infant's response to separation and object concept development (Bell,

1970; Décarie, 1972; Serafica and Uzgiris, 1971). In this connection it may be mentioned that Paraskevopoulos and Hunt obtained similar differences between the three rearing conditions on the Vocal Imitation Scale, which would be expected to be sensitive to interpersonal stimulation, but not on the Gestural Imitation Scale.

A more general view of environmental influence may be obtained by a comparison of the stage in sensorimotor functioning reached by infants of particular ages in different cultural environments. The Casati–Lézine tests have been administered to infants of comparable age in France (Lézine *et al.*, 1969), the Ivory Coast (Bovet *et al.*, 1974), and the United States (Kopp *et al.*, 1974); the last study was longitudinal, while the first two were of cross-sectional design. Moreover the comparison of these studies is complicated by the fact that the Ivory Coast results were presented for groups within a three-month age span rather than at specific ages. Nevertheless a comparison of the three studies reveals some interesting trends. On most tests an earlier entry into stage VI was reported for the United States infants; this result may be due to longitudinal testing or to less stringent scoring criteria as well as to more rapid advancement. In addition two overall trends stand out in this comparison: (1) the relative advance of the Ivory Coast infants compared to the French infants at the 6–8 month period, which is in line with the precocious sensorimotor coordination of the African infant noted in studies using other assessment techniques, and (2) the dependence of the ordering of the groups on the specific test employed. For example, the Combination of Objects test, which seemed quite difficult for French and United States infants even at 18 months of age, was much easier for the Ivory Coast infants; however, these same infants were not as proficient in the Use of Intermediaries as the French or United States infants, while all performed comparably on the Object Search test. Again, if the tests can be assumed to index the different stages adequately, these results suggest that there is considerable independence in the organization of different domains of functioning throughout the sensorimotor period. In addition studies like those being conducted by Wachs should help to explicate the environmental supports most needed for the coordination of particular achievements.

Correlations with Other Measures

Many considerations complicate a direct comparison of measures of sensorimotor development with other measures of infant intellectual functioning. Even when the comparisons are done contemporaneous_y, the conceptual grounds for expecting a parallel ranking of individuals on different measures are not clear. If we assume that both measures provide valid assessments, a biological inclination toward either rapid or slow achievement of competencies has to be postulated in order to predict a high correspondence between various types of measures. To the extent that different infant competencies are differentially dependent on the presence of environmental supports, specific previous learnings, and specific opportunities, and to the extent that such supports and opportunities vary, high correspondence between achievements need not occur. In addition, if the measures of sensorimotor development, in fact, index the level of organization of actions, while the psychometric devices assess degrees of competence along dimensions that have been found to detect individual differences, they should produce largely unrelated rankings of infants. It has been pointed out in earlier sections that a conception of sensorimotor development in terms of transformations in overall structures does not demand complete congruence of functioning within different domains, particularly during the earlier stages. Even more, it does not seem necessary to expect congruence between assessments using different criteria to determine advancement. The complications are further increased when the comparisons between assessments are made over time, since either the importance of intervening experiences must be discounted or they must be assumed to be comparable for every infant in the group.

Given these considerations, the general pattern of low correlations between different assessment measures is unremarkable. Lewis and McGurk (1972) correlated scores on the Object Permanence Scale (SSD) and Bayley's Mental Development Index for six age levels between 3 and 24 months of age. At 6 months the correlation between these two measures was significant ($r = 0.60$), but these measures were essentially unrelated at all subsequent testings. Similarly Golden and Birns (1968) obtained a significant correlation between performance on the Cattell and on the Object Permanence Scale at 12 months of age ($r = 0.24$), but the correlations between these same measures were not significant for infants at 18 and 24 months of age. King and Seegmiller (1973) correlated individual IPDS scores with scores on Bayley's Mental Scale and on Bayley's Psychomotor Scale separately. At 14 months of age Bayley's Mental Scale correlated significantly with most of the IPDS scores, except for Object Permanence and the two imitation scales (rs between 0.32 and 0.42). The significant correlations with Bayley's Psychomotor

Scale were fewer and somewhat lower. On the other hand, the different measures were practically unrelated to each other at 18 months. At 24 months scores on the Development of Means, the Development of Schemes, and the Vocal Imitation Scales correlated with Bayley's Mental Scale scores. It may be interesting to note that the Development of Schemes Scale, which does not seem to cluster together with object concept development (taken to be at the core of sensorimotor development), is the one scale that was found to correlate at all three age levels with a psychometric measure of intellectual functioning. The other two correlations at 24 months were probably due to some overlap with respect to early language and problem-solving tasks.

Although Gottfried (1974) dealt only with infants around 11 months of age, he obtained significant correlations between Bayley's Scales and both Object Permanence (SSD) and Development of Schemes (IPDS) scores. The Mental Scale scores correlated more highly ($r = 0.47$ for Object Permanence and $r = 0.69$ for Schemes) than the Motor Scale scores ($r = 0.34$ and $r = 0.53$, respectively). For a single assessment at 12 months of age Honig and Brill (1970) reported a significant correlation ($rho = 0.43$) between the total score on six Piagetian scales and the Cattell IQ for a group of 40 infants, although the Object Permanence Scale scores did not yield a significant correlation with the Cattell. Overall these studies suggest, first, that any significant correlations are more likely to be obtained in the first year of life than in the second, possibly because all tests during the first year rely on the infant's fairly limited repertoire of actions for test items, even if the performances are given different interpretations. Second, object concept development, of central importance theoretically for sensorimotor development, hardly relates to performances measured by psychometric tests. Third, Bayley's Mental Scale correlates more highly than the Psychomotor Scale with the level in sensorimotor functioning during infancy.

There are hardly any reports on the relationship between measures of sensorimotor functioning and psychometric tests over some interval of time. Wachs (1975) has obtained correlations between IPDS performance at various ages in the second year and Stanford–Binet scores at 31 months of age for a sample of 20 infants. His results indicate that at each successive age level a greater number of the scales are significantly related to the Stanford–Binet scores at 31 months. However, until additional studies are carried out to test the predictability of intellectual functioning in early childhood, no definite implications can be drawn for the relationship between the rate of coordination of sensorimotor functioning and intellectual functioning in later periods.

LEVELS OF ORGANIZATION IN SENSORIMOTOR INTELLIGENCE

Introduction

It has been pointed out already that a more formal characterization of levels in the development of sensorimotor intelligence than has been explicitly presented by Piaget would be desirable for the study of sensorimotor functioning in infancy. Evaluation of the adequacy of various tasks as indices of some one level of functioning would be facilitated as well as the comparison of functioning in different domains, which are usually assessed by diverse tasks. Without such characterization the growing correlational data may divert research from sensorimotor intelligence to questions concerning task conditions or subject variables.

To start a characterization of the levels in sensorimotor functioning it may be useful to reiterate a distinction made by Piaget (1970b) between experience that leads to knowledge of physical reality and "logicomathematical" experience, or experience that is derived from the subject's own actions upon objects and that abstracts the relations imposed on the objects. It seems that an analogous distinction might be made in the consideration of the infant's interactions with the world. In discussions of infant actions the word *scheme* is used to refer to the pattern inherent in actions, but it is applied without distinction to actions that provide both types of experience for the infant. Thus *scheme* is used to refer to activities such as sucking, shaking, or throwing, by means of which the infant may be expected to discover the actual properties of various objects, and also to the regulative aspects of activities such as joining, ordering, or conserving, from which the infant may be expected to discover the relations present in coordinations of actions irrespective of the objects employed. When Piaget mentions the "logic of actions" evident in sensorimotor functioning (Piaget and Inhelder, 1969), it seems reasonable to assume that he is referring to this latter aspect of infant actions. My suggestion is that the interweaving of understandings regarding the properties of objects and understandings derived from the coordination of actions may be critically involved in the transition to higher levels of development in infancy.

In the section that follows a beginning characterization of four levels in sensorimotor intelligence is given together with some observational data that illustrate the form of activities expected to be seen at each level. Whether there is a prior form of functioning characteristic of the neonatal period is left open in this formulation. The data come from a longitudinal study of 12 infants who have been observed at regular intervals from the age of 1 month up to 2 years, using the IPDS (a description of procedure has been given in Uzgiris, 1973a). A correlational analysis of the performance of these infants across domains at various chronological ages was not very productive. However, a more selective analysis of contingencies between specific achievements from different domains suggested some meaningful interrelationships and led to the delineation of four distinct levels of functioning.

Levels of Organization

Level of Simple Undifferentiated Actions

At this level, roughly analogous to Piaget's stages II and III, infant actions have the character of single unit behaviors, lacking in evidence of internal differentiation. Knowledge of object properties appears to be limited, and the infant's repertoire of schemes is applied to objects indiscriminately. Shifts from one scheme to another occur in rhythmic alternation without coordination between successive schemes. Among the infants observed in the longitudinal study, the predominant actions on objects during this period consisted of mouthing, looking, and some variety of shaking or banging; however, these activities were not combined with each other in a regulated way. In addition they were applied to one object at a time; that is, the infant did not construct relations between objects in such a way that there would be the opportunity to abstract understanding of relations from his own actions.

The transition to the next higher level may be linked to three parallel developments. First, the application of different schemes to the same object in close succession or simultaneously, as the infant begins to monitor his own behavior visually, may be expected to substantiate objects as reality elements at the intersection of diverse schemes, each object providing particular resistances to assimilation by the different schemes. This development may be observed in the appearance of the "examining" scheme (Uzgiris, 1969). All 12 infants observed longitudinally engaged in examining objects prior to showing behaviors that would place them at the next level in sensorimotor development. Second, interaction with responsive objects—whether inanimate objects designed to provide regular but varied inputs, such as musical toys, or persons, who regularly respond to the infant's vocal and facial overtures—may be expected to promote a primordial differentiation of self as agent. Again all the infants in the longitudinal sample were observed to make attempts to reproduce interesting spectacles and to evolve "procedures," i.e., actions that may be transplanted from one concrete situation to another when the infant is confronted with interesting events during this period. It may be worthy of note that in analyzing traditional infant tests, McCall *et al.* (1972) isolated a main component at 6 months of age that was heavily defined by items concerned with the exploration of test materials or with the production of perceptual consequences through actions. Third, the execution of different schemes in close succession even on different objects may be expected to lead to the first coordination of actions through the simple relation of "joining." Once such joining of schemes appears, the construction of two-unit actions and means–ends relations becomes feasible.

Level of Differentiated Actions

The entrance into this level may be equated with the transition to stage IV in Piaget's theory. This level may be characterized by the appearance of subcomponents in actions achieved through coordination of the simple schemes. During transition, the infant's repertoire of schemes at first simply expands and then is more discriminately applied to objects in accord with their diverse characteristics. To concretize, the repertoire of schemes composed of mouthing, grasping, looking, and hitting expands to include a variety of manipulations such as shaking, striking, dropping, stretching, tearing, crumpling, and so forth. Similarly, upon expansion of the repertoire of schemes, the initial combination of schemes through joining gives way to more diverse interrelations between schemes. Means–ends differentiation in behavior fosters the selective joining of schemes and the implicit coordination in terms of "ordering" or "inclusion"; the combination of reciprocal schemes allows the discernment of the "inverse" relation. Such developments may be observed in sequences of actions to remove obstacles, to employ intermediaries in the attainment of goals, to explore properties of objects, and also to explore spatial and causal relationships between objects. Coordinated sequences of actions appear first with respect to single objects (e.g., letting fall and picking up, crumpling and straightening) and then with multiple objects (e.g., putting an object into another and taking it out, building up a structure and knocking it down). The generally repetitive character of many infant behaviors may be seen as examples of the application of the "joining" scheme to most actions in the infant's repertoire.

A number of observations on my longitudinal sample of infants illustrate the developments at this level of functioning. With respect to object concept development, while the correlations in the age of achievement between one step in the sequence and other steps were not high overall, indicating little individual consistency in the rate of progress, the correlations between the age of beginning search for an object completely covered by a screen and the extension of the search to a number of separate screens were fairly high. For my sample the beginning of search for a partially covered object (which does not require a differentiated action) correlated slightly ($r = 0.31$) with the beginning of search for a completely covered object; however, the beginning of search for a completely covered object correlated substantially ($r = 0.76$) with search for an object under one of two or one of three screens, and moderately ($r = 0.53$) with search for an object following a series of visible displacements.

A number of associated achievements appeared in other domains during the interval spanned by the extension of object search from one to a number of locations (for my sample, an interval of four months, on the average). In terms of schemes shown in relation to objects, 10 of the 12 infants were not actively dropping objects and observing their fall at the beginning of this interval, but 11 of the 12 were engaging in this activity at the time they searched for objects following a series of visible displacements. It seems to me that the dropping activity involves a two-component action, since the object is released by the infant to move through space and is then visually relocated. Similarly, while none of the 12 infants showed differentiated schemes at the beginning of this interval, 11 of the 12 engaged in such activities at the end. It seems to me that most differentiated schemes involve two-component actions, often tied by an inverse relation, as, for example, crumpling and straightening. The infant's caretaker may play an important role in facilitating the construction of more complex actions. Many of the games played with infants have the character that the social partner performs one link in a sequence of actions, completing the organization. For example, in the early dropping of objects and exploration of their movements through space, infants depend on someone else for the retrieval of those objects. Later infants construct sequences of dumping and retrieval on their own, taking over the function previously filled by the social partner. It may be important to study the extent to which sensitivity to the structurations being worked on by infants, and willingness to fill in appropriate gaps during interactions with them forms a part of "good mothering," reflected in the correlation between rate of infant development and maternal "interest," or "responsiveness to baby," typically found in studies concerned with environmental influences on early development.

In the domain of imitation 10 of the 12 infants did not imitate sound patterns familiar to them at the beginning of this interval, but only 2 did not do so by the end. Also none of the 12 infants imitated complex actions composed of familiar schemes at the beginning, but only 5 did not do so by the end. The development in imitation at this level seems to involve the taking of the modeled action as a goal with an attempt to construct appropriate action to reproduce it; hence it may be treated as requiring the capacity for differentiated actions. Some instances of an infant's reproducing only an aspect of the modeled act are quite instructive. In another domain, while 11 of the infants did not make use of relationships between objects, such as that of support, at the beginning of this interval, all did so by the end. It seems that a number of achievements in different domains requiring a differentiation of action from goal in order to commence at least a two-component action appear in parallel and thus indicate the beginning of the structuration of actions. It may be of interest to note that in studying the taking into possession of multiple objects, Bruner (1970) observed the appearance of the strategy of setting one object in reserve while picking up another in infants of roughly the same age as the age of infants at this level of development in my sample.

What does not occur at this second level is an immediate modification of actions as a result of their outcome. The schemes appear to function still as elementary units; the coordinations observed take place between available schemes. If a constructed sequence of actions is unsuccessful, the infant's ability to modify the sequence seems limited to a fresh construction of another sequence from schemes already in his repertoire, without an immediate modification of any single scheme in the sequence. Thus, while outcomes do regulate actions, the regulation is global, leading to a reconstruction of the whole action sequence rather than to the modification of a component of the sequence. In novel problem situations the attainment of a solution through gradual approximation or through the observation of demonstrated solutions does not seem to take place.

Level of Regulation by Differentiated Feedback

This level in sensorimotor development may be characterized by the beginning of regulation of actions by their outcomes and thus by a gradual modification of actions so as to attain various goals. Even global responsivity to feedback from outcomes may be expected to promote objectification of reality and an increasing selectivity in actions. Toward the beginning of the second year several changes in infants' behavior toward objects is evident: there is a reduction in the number of schemes applied to particular objects, and there is a conventionalization of the schemes applied. Probably because of awareness of the social outcomes of actions (i.e., differential adult responses to hitting and hugging of dolls or mouthing and rolling of toy cars) as well as progress in imitation of novel actions, the activities of infants begin to reflect culturally approved modes of interacting with objects, particularly those objects that are miniaturizations of objects important in adult life. The responsivity to outcomes in the social domain may be expected to contribute to self–other differentiation, especially with respect to self and other as centers capable of instigating action. This differentiation may be observed in "showing–sharing" schemes, through which the infant manifests both an expectation of responsiveness from the social partner and a recognition that such responsiveness has to be instigated by the other person. Increase in the variety of relations through which schemes come to be coordinated contributes to construction of sequences of actions composed of multiple component-schemes. This, in turn, seems to distance the schemes further from particular contexts of application and to increase the flexibility of coordinations into which they enter. In short, individual schemes may be said to become more context-free as well as to include more mobile action components.

One of the important coordinations established at this level involves the relation of compensation, which might be considered to be an outgrowth of the inverse relation between two schemes established at the previous level. The relation of compensation seems to be involved in the regulation of action by outcome in a differentiated way. Even in novel problem-solving situations, given a differentiated effect of feedback, available schemes can be adjusted immediately through compensatory coordinations with other schemes in response to perceived outcomes. Thus action sequences no longer seem to be constructed and reconstructed as totalities but tend to be modified in their components to suit the demands of the situation. The trial-and-error behavior, or "groping," to use Piaget's term, exhibited by infants in problem-solving situations may be taken as evidence of such compensatory regulation. The attainment of behavioral regulation by differentiated feedback would be expected to promote imitation of novel events and perfection of skilled actions.

The most prominent feature of various achievements at this level is the alteration of actions through gradual approximation, the taking into account of correspondence between outcome and goal. Since new forms of actions are thus constructed, it may be that it is in this sense that Piaget has talked of the appearance of an interest in novelty at the fifth sensorimotor stage. The appearance of regulation by outcome is most clearly evident in the infant's activities in relation to objects, in imitation, and in means behavior. For example, at the time when infants begin to search for an object in several locations or under a number of screens, practically none show activities with objects that indicate a social influence on their actions. However, very soon afterwards the social influence on their actions becomes evident, so that instead of examining, banging, dropping, and stretching, they begin to push toy cars around, to hug dolls or cuddly animal toys, to build with blocks, and to put necklaces around their necks, the actions specific to each object. Furthermore, at about this time varied relationships between objects—for example, one serving as an extension of another—begin to be exploited to obtain desired goals. The use of these relationships is often achieved through a gradual modification of initially ineffective actions.

In regard to imitation the infant's behavior indicates not only an attempt to reconstruct the model by means of known schemes but also the ability to recognize failure to reproduce the model accurately. It was noticed that infants imitated unfamiliar gestures visible to them more readily when they were performed in relation to an object than when they were presented as gestures. For instance, sliding a piece of paper back and forth was imitated more readily than the sliding action alone. This suggests that an act with a definite result may facilitate reproduction by providing an outcome for the infant to work toward. The successive modifications that the infants showed in gradually approximating the model presented by the examiner are also illuminating. This level corresponds roughly to the appearance in the domain of object construction of search for objects hidden by means of an invisible displacement in one or a number of locations (i.e., where the infant has to infer the location of the object when it is not found where it was seen to disappear)—for my sample between 14 and 15½ months, on the average. Thus, at the appearance of search for an object hidden by an invisible displacement under one of three screens, 10 of the 12 infants regularly showed socially influenced activities with objects. Similarly, at the same point the majority of infants (7 of the 12) began to imitate novel sounds presented by the examiner directly, after a period of responding to them by varied vocal responses.

All infants attempted to imitate novel visible gestures by means of gradual approximation at the time they began to search for an object hidden by an invisible displacement, although only 5 of the 12 imitated novel gestures directly. In addition most infants at this point seemed to recognize centers of causality in objects and therefore learned from demonstrations how to activate objects or produce spectacles, frequently through gradual approximation. Thus, while a diversity of new achievements may be observed to occur in parallel at this level, including a great deal of specialization in actions, the appearance of regulating relationships between outcomes and actions (with compensation and correction of successive actions) seems to be the main advance in structural organization.

Level of Anticipatory Regulations

This level is assumed to characterize the culmination of sensorimotor intelligence and to bridge the practical intelligence of infancy and the representational intelligence of early childhood. The beginnings of language may be seen as both an outgrowth of and a further instrument for the coordinated intellectual functioning of this period. The appearance of make-believe play may be viewed as evidence for decontextualization of schemes in that their application to objects is no longer governed exclusively by the evident properties of the object. Anticipatory coordi-

nation of schemes would seem to account for both inference and evocation of absent aspects of reality. The extensive network of coordinations
between schemes constructed at the previous level of functioning may
be thought to allow for the regulation of sequences of actions, in many
instances, prior to overt execution of those sequences and prior to
feedback from actual outcomes. Thus sequences of actions appear to be
coordinated not through after-the-fact compensations but by means of
anticipatory compensations, resulting in preadapted overt behavior.
This change may be seen as analogous to the change that takes place
during skill acquisition in a task such as target tracking from compensatory to anticipatory regulation, so that the perfected skill seems to be
governed by foresight.

The notion of object attained at this level of functioning may be
thought to stand for the invariance inherent in a group of spatial
displacements and a coordinated network of schemes applicable to
objects. Accordingly, the infant may be expected not only to conserve
the object through a series of inferred displacements but also to be
sensitive to the identity–nonidentity of objects. The ability to coordinate
actions by means of anticipatory regulations may be expected to promote self–other distinction and to lead to increased appreciation of
others as spontaneous and less predictable (in contrast to inanimate
objects) centers of action manifest in the self-consciousness and wariness sometimes observed in children at this level of development.

If the achievement of the highest level in object construction—i.e.,
the beginning of search for objects following a series of invisible displacements with the ability to reconstruct the path of an object in
reverse—is taken as an index for this level of development (21–23
months of age on the average in my sample), a number of parallel
achievements in other domains may be noted. By the time the infants in
my sample began to search for objects following a series of invisible
displacements, all were engaging in activities showing a social influence, all were imitating novel sounds directly, and all were imitating
novel visible gestures directly. They were beginning to imitate novel
invisible gestures, i.e., facial gestures, which one cannot see oneself
perform and thus from which one cannot obtain direct visual feedback.
However, by the time these infants began to reconstruct the path of the
object in reverse, 9 of the 12 were imitating even invisible gestures
directly. Similarly, at the same time 9 of the 12 infants were imitating
new words regularly, which they were just starting to do at the begin-

ning of this level. In regard to activities with objects the naming of objects in recognition appeared, which should be distinguished from the use of a verbal label, since it involves the examining of an object and the use of the name to express the possibilities suggested by the object, often in the context of interacting with another person. In my sample 10 of the 12 infants were naming objects in recognition by the time they constructed a reverse path in their search for objects. In addition their activities with objects frequently revealed evocation of objects or events that were not within their perceptual field at the moment (i.e., the beginning of symbolic play). Furthermore, if they found direct access to a desired object blocked, the majority of infants by this time constructed detours through space and thus were able to reach their goal.

Evidence for the construction of solutions to problem situations without overt groping was also obtained at this level: all infants began to show foresightful behavior in one problem situation (necklace and container) and 8 of the 12 did so in another (the solid ring). It seems that the coordination achieved between the construction of multicomponent actions and the regulation of action sequences by their outcomes at this level allows for a nonovert adaptation of actions or, in other words, thought.

The four levels of organization in sensorimotor intelligence that have been outlined seem to be supported by the occurrence of a number of achievements in rough parallel, all of which may be interpreted as exemplifying a particular level. The parallels are, however, rough and the question of synchrony in achievements across domains in sensorimotor functioning is still open.

SUMMARY AND CONCLUSIONS

The available literature on infant functioning during the sensorimotor period demonstrates that an orderly sequence is manifested in the achievement of a number of competencies. The regularity of these sequences and their high correlation with chronological age are among the most consistently reported findings. However, with respect to a number of other questions the evidence is far from definitive.

The difficulties stem to a large extent from an imprecise conception of stages in sensorimotor intelligence. If a stage progression is posited, then questions about transition from one stage to the next must be separated from questions pertaining to modifications in functioning at a particular stage. However, since determination of stage level is often based on performance in a particular task, the separation of stage transition from change in performance on a task becomes difficult. Moreover investigators vary in their choice of tasks for indexing stage level and most do not try to present their rationale for choosing a particular task. The greatest uniformity obtains in tasks used to assess stages in the construction of the object.

There seems to be consensus that development in sensorimotor functioning is multifaceted and must be assessed in more than one domain. However, the delineation of domains, the choice of domains to be used in assessment, and the choice of tasks within those domains are rarely clearly explicated. The domains represented in the different scales that have been constructed to assess progress in sensorimotor functioning vary from scale to scale. Even when the same domain appears to be represented within two assessment scales, the tasks included to tap functioning within that domain differ. Thus it is well nigh impossible to deal with the question of congruence in the level of cognitive functioning across domains. The one apparent consistency concerns the reported relative advance in object concept development as compared to other domains of functioning (Lézine *et al.*, 1969; Uzgiris, 1973*a*; Zachry, 1972). Since a multifaceted conception of sensorimotor intelligence contrasts with the unitary view of intellectual progress adopted by most psychometric tests for infants, the problem of domain definition seems to deserve further effort.

A more explicit characterization of four levels in the organization of sensorimotor intelligence has been proposed in this chapter with the intent of facilitating a formal analysis of the various tasks used to assess sensorimotor functioning. Unless the diversity of task performances is shown to possess a formal similarity (which might be termed their structure), the tie of these assessment procedures to Piaget's theory of intellectual development becomes dubious. Without such a tie the status of these performances becomes no different from that of the various items contained in the standardized infant intelligence tests. It is apparent to me that my evidence for the four levels in organization of sensorimotor intelligence is minimal; yet it seems important to begin to seek evidence in these terms.

The issue of ways to conceptualize individual differences in functioning within Piaget's theory is not unique to the sensorimotor period;

it is critical only because much of our interest in infant functioning is related to interest in individual variation. The most frequent method of examining individual differences is by means of rates of progress. However, if sensorimotor intelligence is the foundation for subsequent intellectual development, it will be coordinated and then reorganized by most children at an early age. Are the differences of a few months in achieving some level of functioning of real interest? On the other hand, if it is implicitly expected that the rate of progress shown at one level will be continued at the next, this expectation cannot be sustained. There are few theoretical reasons for expecting stability in rate of progress, and all the empirical evidence points to the contrary. A different way of thinking about individual differences might be to consider the domains or even specific contents in which an individual excels as well as the solidity of such excellence, i.e., its breadth over diverse tasks. Similarly individuals might differ in their readiness to reorganize their constructions upon exposure to special situations providing supports for higher-level functioning, i.e., there may be differences in openness to developmental change. It is important to search for ways to think about individual differences that would be meaningful in the context of Piaget's theory, for the problems of the normative approach have been sufficiently revealed with other types of assessment procedures. In relation to this point it may be of interest to note that the achievement of stages in object construction has been shown to vary little with socioeconomic level or with cultural group, yet it is considered to be a core achievement of sensorimotor intelligence. In addition the correlations between level in object construction and scores on standard infant intelligence tests are negligible, suggesting that variation on levels of object construction is not akin to that demonstrated on standardized tests. On the other hand, higher correlations are obtained between infant intelligence test scores and level of sensorimotor functioning in domains that may be more strongly intertwined with specific contents. The relationship may be due to the overlap in content, yet this strengthens the suggestion that one meaningful approach to individual differences may be in terms of contents within which the highest levels of organization are revealed.

It is evident to me that the gains that might accrue from adopting Piaget's approach to the conception of intellectual development in infancy are still far from exhausted as far as assessment of infant intelligence is concerned.

REFERENCES

BELL, S. M., 1970, The development of the concept of object as related to infant attach-ment, *Child Development*, 41:291.

BOVET, M. C., DASEN, P. R., AND INHELDER, B., 1974, Étapes de l'Intelligence Sensori-motrice chez l'Enfant Baoulé, *Archives de Psychologie*, 41:363.

BRUNER, J., 1970, The growth and structure of skill, *in* "Mechanisms of Motor Skill Development" K. Connolly, (ed.), Academic Press, New York, p. 63.

CASATI, I., AND LÉZINE, I., 1968, "Les Étapes de l'Intelligence Sensori-motrice," Les Éditions du Centre de Psychologie Appliquée, Paris.

COBOS, L. F., LATHAM, M. C., AND STARE, F. J., 1972, Will improved nutrition help to prevent mental retardation? *Preventive Medicine*, 1:185.

CORMAN, H., AND ESCALONA, S., 1969, Stages of sensorimotor development: A replication study, *Merrill–Palmer Quarterly*, 15:351.

DÉCARIE, T. G., 1965, "Intelligence and Affectivity in Early Childhood," International Universities Press, New York.

DÉCARIE, T. G., 1972, "La Réaction du Jeune Enfant à la Personne Étrangère," Les Presses de l'Université de Montréal, Montreal.

DODWELL, P. C., 1963, Children's understanding of spatial concepts, *Canadian Journal of Psychology*, 17:141.

ESCALONA, S., AND CORMAN, H., Albert Einstein Scales of Sensorimotor Development, unpublished manuscript.

FURTH, H. G., 1973, Piaget, IQ and the nature–nurture controversy, *Human Development*, 16:61.

GAITER, J. L., 1972, The development and acquisition of object permanence in infants, unpublished master's thesis, Brown University.

GIBLIN, P. T., 1971, Development of imitation in Piaget's sensorimotor period of infant development (stages III–VI), *Proceedings* of the 79th Annual Convention of the American Psychological Association, 6:137.

GOLDEN, M., AND BIRNS, B., 1968, Social class and cognitive development in infancy, *Merrill–Palmer Quarterly*, 14:139.

GOTTFRIED, A. W., 1974, Interrelationships between and nomological networks of psychometric and Piagetian measures of sensorimotor intelligence, unpublished doctoral dissertation, New School for Social Research.

HONIG, A. S., AND BRILL, S., 1970, A comparative analysis of the Piagetian development of twelve month old disadvantaged infants, presented at the American Psychological Association Convention, Miami, Florida.

HUNT, J. McV., 1961, "Intelligence and Experience," Ronald, New York.

HUNT, J. McV., PARASKEVOPOULOS, J., SCHICKEDANZ, D., AND UZGIRIS, I. C., 1975, Variations in the mean ages of achieving object permanence under diverse conditions of rearing, *in* "Infant Assessment and Intervention," B. Friedlander, G. Kirk, and G. Sterritt (eds.), Brunner/Mazel, New York.

KING, W. L., AND SEEGMILLER, B., 1973, Performance of 14- to 22-month old black, firstborn male infants on two tests of cognitive development, *Developmental Psychology*, 8:317.

KOHEN-RAZ, R., 1967, Scalogram analysis of some developmental sequences of infant behavior as measured by the Bayley infant scale of mental development, *Genetic Psychology Monographs*, 76:3.

KOPP, C. B., SIGMAN, M., AND PARMELEE, A. H., 1973, Ordinality and sensory-motor series, *Child Development*, 44:821.

KOPP, C. B., SIGMAN, M., AND PARMELEE, A. H., 1974, Longitudinal study of sensorimotor development, *Developmental Psychology*, 10:687.

LESTER, B. M., KOTELCHUCK, M., SPELKE, E., SELLERS, M. J., AND KLEIN, R. E., 1974, Separation protest in Guatemalan infants, *Developmental Psychology*, 10:79.

LEWIS, M., AND McGURK, H., 1972, Infant intelligence, *Science*, 178:1174.

LÉZINE, I., STAMBAK, M., AND CASATI, I., 1969, "Les Étapes de l'Intelligence Sensori-motrice," Les Éditions du Centre de Psychologie Appliquée, Paris.

MARATOS, O., 1973, The origin and development of imitation in the first six months of life, presented at the British Psychological Society Annual Meeting, Liverpool.

McCALL, R., HOGARTY, P., AND HURLBURT, N., 1972, Transitions in infant sensori-motor development and the prediction of childhood IQ, *American Psychologist*, 27:728.

MEHRABIAN, A., AND WILLIAMS, M., 1971, Piagetian measures of cognitive development up to age two, *Journal of Psycholinguistic Research*, 1:113.

MILLER, D. J., COHEN, L. B., AND HILL, K. T., 1970, A methodological investigation of Piaget's theory of object concept development in the sensory-motor period, *Journal of Experimental Child Psychology*, 9:59.

PARASKEVOPOULOS, J., AND HUNT, J. McV., 1971, Object construction and imitation under differing conditions of rearing, *Journal of Genetic Psychology*, 119:301.

PIAGET, J., 1950, "Psychology of Intelligence," Routledge and Kegan Paul, London.

PIAGET, J., 1952, "The Origins of Intelligence in Children," Norton, New York.

PIAGET, J., 1954, "The Construction of Reality in the Child," Basic Books, New York.

PIAGET, J., 1962, "Play Dreams and Imitation in Childhood," Norton, New York.

PIAGET, J., 1970a, "Genetic Epistemology," Columbia University Press, New York.

PIAGET, J., 1970b, Piaget's theory, *in* "Carmichael's Manual of Child Psychology," P. H. Mussen (ed.), Wiley, New York, p. 703.

PIAGET, J., 1971a, "Biology and Knowledge," University of Chicago Press, Chicago.

PIAGET, J., 1971b, The theory of stages in cognitive development, *in* "Measurement and Piaget," D. R. Green, H. P. Ford, and G. B. Flamer (eds.), McGraw-Hill, New York, p. 1.

PIAGET, J., AND INHELDER, B., 1969, "The Psychology of the Child," Basic Books, New York.

PINARD, A., AND LAURENDEAU, M., 1969, "Stage" in Piaget's cognitive-developmental theory: Exegesis of a concept, *in* "Studies in Cognitive Development," D. Elkind and J. H. Flavell (eds.), Oxford University Press, New York, p. 121.

SERAFICA, F. C., AND UZGIRIS, I. C., 1971, Infant–mother relationship and object concept, *Proceedings* of the 79th Annual Convention of the American Psychological Association, 6:141.

SILVERSTEIN, A. B., McLAIN, R. E., BROWNLEE, L., AND HUBBELL, M., 1976, Structure of ordinal scales of psychological development in infancy, *Educational and Psychological Measurement*.

TUDDENHAM, R. D., 1971, Theoretical regularities and individual idiosyncrasies, *in* "Measurement and Piaget," D. R. Green, M. P. Ford, and G. B. Flamer (eds.), McGraw-Hill, New York, p. 64.

UZGIRIS, I. C., 1969, Some antecedents of the object concept, paper presented at a symposium on the object concept at the meetings of EPA, Philadelphia.

UZGIRIS, I. C., 1973a, Patterns of cognitive development in infancy, *Merrill–Palmer Quarterly*, 19:181.

UZGIRIS, I. C., 1973b, Infant development from a Piagetian approach: Introduction to a symposium, presented at the American Psychological Association Convention, Montreal.

UZGIRIS, I. C. AND HUNT, J. McV. 1964, A scale of infant psychological development, unpublished manuscript.

UZGIRIS, I. C., AND HUNT, J. McV., 1972, Toward ordinal scales of infant psychological development, unpublished manuscript.

UZGIRIS, I. C. AND HUNT, J. McV., 1975, "Assessment in Infancy," University of Illinois Press, Urbana.

WACHS, T. D., 1973, Utilization of a Piagetian approach in the investigation of early experience effects, presented at the American Psychological Association Convention, Montreal.

WACHS, T. D., 1975, Relation of infant performance on Piaget's scales between 12 and 24 months and their Stanford–Binet performance at 31 months, *Child Development*.

WACHS, T. D., UZGIRIS, I. C., AND HUNT, J. McV., 1971, Cognitive development in infants of different age levels and from different environmental backgrounds, *Merrill–Palmer Quarterly, 17*:283.

WOODWARD, M., 1959, The behavior of idiots interpreted by Piaget's theory of sensorimotor development, *British Journal of Educational Psychology, 29*:60.

ZACHRY, W., 1972, The relation of language development to sensorimotor level in second-year infants, unpublished doctoral dissertation, Memphis State University.

6   An Evolutionary Perspective on Infant Intelligence: Species Patterns and Individual Variations

Sandra Scarr-Salapatek

Since selection can and did occur in terms of developments at all ontogenetic points, the entire life span is a product of evolutionary adaptation, and a psychologist interested in causes of behavior must simultaneously consider phylogeny and ontogeny, difficult as it may seem. [Freedman, 1967, p. 489]

Any attempt to construct an evolutionary view of infant intelligence should raise a certain skepticism in the reader's mind. What, after all, is the nature of intelligence in infancy? And how shall the validity of an evolutionary account be judged? Not, certainly, by its predictive power for the future evolution of infant behavior! On the first question I shall defer largely to Piaget (1952), whose descriptions and explanations of infant intelligence I find consistent with an evolutionary view. On the second question, a few words about evolutionary theory may be helpful.

The central tenet of evolutionary theory is natural selection, an exceedingly simple idea. Organisms differ from one another. They produce more young than the available resources can sustain. Those best adapted survive to pass on their genetic characteristics to their offspring, while others perish with fewer or no offspring. Subsequent generations therefore are more like their better-adapted ancestors. The result is evolutionary change (Ghiselin, 1969, p. 46). Elaborations of the

SANDRA SCARR-SALAPATEK · University of Minnesota.

idea of natural selection, as it applies to periods in the life span, learned characteristics, and speciation, appear throughout this chapter.

An evolutionary account of any human behavior is by definition a historical reconstruction. We cannot observe our behavioral past. There are limits, however, to the fancifulness of a useful evolutionary construction: the known facts must fit and contrary facts must be few and isolated. Most important, the hypothetical account must be open to falsification; it cannot contain statements that could explain every possible outcome—and thus be unfalsifiable. These criteria are especially important for *ad hoc* theories, since predictions about human evolution cannot be tested within the life span of any investigator. Some testable hypotheses can be generated, however, about phenomena not directly used to construct the account. The implications of the theoretical construction will, hopefully, extend beyond the immediate boundaries of its most central facts. In these ways evolutionary views can be scientifically tested.

Within an evolutionary framework I want to make a radical argument about the natural history of human, infant intelligence. The argument revolves around the primary nature of early intelligence—a nonverbal, practical kind of adaptation. Sensorimotor behaviors must, I think, have emerged very early in primate evolution, certainly before man split off from the great apes. There is simply too high a degree of parallelism in the early intelligence of apes and man to suggest independent, convergent evolution. The phylogeny of infant intelligence seems to be very ancient history.

The ontogeny of infant intelligence has a distinctive pattern and timing. The species pattern, I would argue, is not an unfolding of some genetic program but a dynamic interplay of genetic preadaptations and developmental adaptations to features of the caretaking environment. Individual variation is limited by canalization, on the one hand, and by common human environments, on the other. From the common behavioral elements to be seen among individuals, one can abstract a species pattern to describe and contrast with the patterns of other species. One must be ever mindful, however, that what exists are individuals, each different from the other; a species-typical pattern is an abstraction from reality. The development of infant intelligence has both a species-typical pattern and individual variation. How and why the species theme and individual differences exist is the subject of this chapter.

Four hypotheses about the nature and evolution of human infant intelligence are basic to my argument:

1. That infant intelligence evolved earlier in our primate past than ontogenetically later forms of intelligent behavior and remains virtually unchanged from the time that hominids emerged.
2. That selection pressures that resulted in the present pattern of sensorimotor intelligence acted both on the infant himself and on the caretaking behaviors of his parents.
3. That infant intelligence is phenotypically less variable than later intelligent behavior because it has been subjected to longer and stronger natural selection.
4. That the phenotypic development of infant intelligence is governed both by genetic preadaptation (canalization) and by developmental adaptation to human physical and caretaking environments.

An Evolutionary View of Infant Intelligence

The Nature of the Sensorimotor Period

The primary tasks of infant primates are to survive the first two years and to learn to operate effectively in the physical and social environment. The attachment system is of critical importance to survival and to learning species-appropriate social interactions. Sensorimotor skills are critical to survival and to adaptation in the physical and social worlds. As several authors have noted (e.g., Bell, 1970; Bowlby, 1969, 1973), the development of social attachments is intertwined with increasing cognitive skills, such as object or person permanence. I divide the cognitive and affective domains here more for convenience of discussion than for any good conceptual reasons. Infant primates' survival depends upon the protection of their caretakers while they become competent to explore and learn. The increasing distance permitted between infant and mother is correlated with increasing sensorimotor skills. Both serve survival and adaptation.

Infant primates are remarkably curious and open to learning how to be practical experimenters. The presymbolic skills of human infancy that Piaget has so richly described also characterize our nearest primate relatives. The great apes and even Old World monkeys master sensorimotor skills that are very like those of human infants.* Later in the life

* I do not claim that other mammals are not capable of some aspects of sensorimotor intelligence, such as object permanence. The manipulative, tool-using skills, however, are largely limited to species with good prehension.

span human and nonhuman primates show different forms of adaptation. Different selective pressures, particularly those that led to man's cultural revolution, have produced quite dissimilar forms of childhood and adult intelligence.

Man's gradual accumulation of culture has great relevance to his evolution past infancy. Culture provided new environments to which childhood and adult adaptations could occur. As McClearn (1972) said:

> First steps toward culture provided a new environment in which some individuals were more fit, in the Darwinian sense, than others; their offspring were better adapted to culture and capable of further innovations; and so on. The argument can be made that, far from removing mankind from the process of evolution, culture has provided the most salient natural selection pressure to which man has been subject in his recent evolutionary past. (p. 57)

The pressures of culture on intelligence are self-evident. The greater the ability of some individuals to learn and to innovate, the more likely they were to survive to reproduce, and the more likely it was in the long run that their progeny would have even greater fitness in the new environment. But I would argue that the symbolic cultural revolution had practically no effect on the evolution of infant intelligence.

The distinctly different nature of infant intelligence was recognized by Florence Goodenough, who noted:

> The unsettled question as to whether or not true intelligence may be said to have emerged before symbolic processes exemplified in speech may have become established. Attempting to measure infantile intelligence may be like trying to measure a boy's beard at the age of three. (quoted by Elkind, 1967)

Sensorimotor intelligence is qualitatively different from later symbolic operations, whose evolution may have quite a different history. I do not propose a common primate history for formal operations, or even for concrete operations, although some symbolic and conceptual skills are shared by apes and man (e.g., Premack, 1971). I do propose that the natural history of sensorimotor intelligence is independent of skills that evolved later and that there is no logically necessary connection between them.

Indeed, the empirical connection between sensorimotor skills and later intellectual development is very tenuous (Stott and Ball, 1965). Children with severe motor impairments, whose sensorimotor practice has been extremely limited, have been shown to develop normal symbolic function (Kopp and Shaperman, 1973). The purported dependence of symbolic activity on sensorimotor action has not been demonstrated. One reason for the lack of correlation may be different sources of individual variation. If sensorimotor and symbolic skills have different genetic bases, they could well be uncorrelated. Sensorimotor skills are best seen as a criterion achievement; that is, individual differences are found in the *rate* but not the final *level* of sensorimotor development. Symbolic intelligence has individual differences in both rate and level of achievement, and the rate of development is correlated with the final level (witness the substantial correlations between IQ at ages 5 and 15). Infant intelligence is characterized by universal attainment by all nondefective species members. Its evolution is more ancient history than symbolic reasoning, and individual differences do not have the predictive significance of variations in later intelligence.

Infant Learning

The fact that human infants learn is of paramount importance to understanding the evolution of infancy and infant development. All normal babies interact with their social and physical worlds, structure and interpret their experiences, and modify their subsequent interactions. As Piaget has described, human infants set about learning in a graded sequence of intellectual stages that reflect their growing awareness of the effects of their actions and of the properties of the physical and social worlds around them.

A critical feature of human learning is its flexibility. In infancy we see the major transitions from reflex organization to a flexible, experimental approach to the world. By 1–1½ years babies have become impressive, practical experimenters. The rapid development of practical intelligence leaves the rest of the preadolescent period for mental adaptations. While formal operational thought may not develop in all normal species members, sensorimotor intelligence does.

In a brilliant and provocative paper Bruner (1972) outlined the nature and uses of immaturity for human development. He identified the "tutor-proneness" of the young, their readiness to learn through observation and instruction. Infants are ever ready to respond to novelties provided by the adult world. Further, they use play, according to Bruner, as an opportunity to work out their knowledge in safety— without the consequences that would befall adults who were in the initial stages of learning sensorimotor skills and how to be a responsible social animal. The distinctive pattern of immaturity lends itself to more flexible adaptation for the species. The usefulness of opportunities for learning depends upon the behavioral flexibility of the infant to acquire by learning what has not been "built into" the genome.

Two facts of human evolutionary history are particularly salient for infancy: the necessity of infant–mother dyads and the consistent availability of a larger human group into which the dyad is integrated. No surviving infant was without a social context throughout human history.* The evolution of infant development has occurred, therefore, in the context of normal infant environments. This context has, I think, profound implications for the lack of developmental fixity (Lehrman, 1970) in infant behavior. Foremost, it has been unnecessary for selection to build into the genotype those behaviors that all infants would develop experientially in their human groups. All normal infants would have close contact with mothers and other conspecifics and with tools and material culture, thus giving them opportunities to learn object manipulation, social bonds, and a human language. What has evolved genotypically is a bias toward acquiring these forms of behavior, a bias that Dobzhansky (1967) calls human educability.

The Evolution of Infancy

Infancy is a mammalian theme. A period of suckling the dependent young evolved as an efficient way to increase the survival chances of fewer and fewer offspring. Extended care of the dependent young is a burden and a risk for their parents, however, but it is of greatest evolutionary importance to the mammalian pattern of reproduction and parental behavior. The more an organism is protected from the vicissitudes of the environment, the greater the role of intraspecific competition. What one offspring requires of its parents are energy and resources not available to another offspring of those same parents. It became advantageous to have fewer and better-equipped offspring rather than many offspring and to have long life spans. Both competition for females and demands for long parental care put a premium on long life

---

* The few reported cases of feral children, even if they are believed, have contributed little to the human gene pool and the subsequent evolution of infant behaviors.

span, and this again decreased the number of offspring still further (Mayr, 1970, pp. 338–340).

Primate infancy is an elaboration (exaggeration?) of the mammalian pattern: a single infant born not more than once a year and requiring years of parental care. What advantages can such a pattern confer? Highly developed parental care allows a fundamental change in the genetics of behavioral development. Primate infants have a more "open program" for learning than other mammals. Such an open program requires a far larger brain in the adults who provide the care and in the infants who must learn what information is needed. Primate intelligence is a coadapted product of evolutionary changes in the duration and the intensity of infant dependence and parental care. No one product could have evolved independently of the others.

I would argue, however, that the pattern of development for human infants in the sensorimotor period was basically established in common with other closely related primates. The later evolutionary history of apes and man led to species differences in the degree of immaturity at birth, the degree of flexibility in learning, and the length of the socialization period. In considering infancy alone, however, I am struck by incredible similarities in the sensorimotor period, similarities that should be considered apart from the later, more obvious differences. Prolonged infancy evolved as a primate variation on the mammalian theme. Human infancy is a further evolution of the primate pattern. Contemporary apes have evolved patterns of infant development that still share much with the human species. These similarities originated in our common primate past.

Every period of the human life span is a product of selection (Mayr, 1970, p. 84). Multiple pressures, which we can only speculate about *post hoc*, must have played interacting roles in the evolution of prolonged infancy. LaBarre (1954) argued for an increasing specialization of human infants in *brains*. One-seventh of the newborn's weight is brain. With limitations to the female pelvic girth infants were born less and less mature to assure the safe passage of the big-brained fetus into the world. Changes in adult behaviors must have accompanied the increasingly long dependence of a less mature infant:

> Curiously enough, as human females became better mammals (through sexual availability and permanent breasts) and as human males increased in constancy of sexual drive, the human infant seems simultaneously to be specializing in mammalian infancy. In helplessness and dependency, human

babies and children are about as infantile as mammalian infants come.
(LaBarre, 1973, p. 29)

LaBarre's account of the coordinated changes in adult male, adult
female, and infant adaptations includes the structure of the family,
which, he says, depends upon the sexual availability of the female to
keep the father home, on the father's strong sexual drive, and on the
infant's attachment relation with his mother (LaBarre, 1954). LaBarre's
account of the evolution of human immaturity is highly speculative.
Mayr (1970, p. 407) argued that brain size could have increased still
further if (1) the female pelvic size increased; (2) pregnancy were short-
ened; or (3) more brain growth were postnatal. Any of these adaptations
would permit further evolution of brain size (although no increase in
brain size has occurred in the last 30,000 years of man's evolution,
presumably because there is no longer a selective premium on it).
Omenn and Motulsky (1972) noted that human newborns are delivered
at a less advanced stage of development than newborn apes and monkeys, a fact that they attribute to two adaptational differences. First, the
female pelvis narrowed with the adaptation to bipedal locomotion, and
the restriction in the bony birth canal required earlier birth of fetuses.
Second, the slow maturation of human infants is ideally adapted to the
molding of species-specific behaviors by social input.

It is impossible at present to decide which set of factors in evolutionary history accounted for the correlated shifts in infant intelligence,
immaturity, and parental behaviors. They are coadapted. The total
phenotype is, after all, a compromise of all selection pressures, some of
which are opposed to each other (Mayr, 1970, p. 112). The evolution of
neoteny and infant intelligence most likely represents a compromise
solution among pressures on adults to provide increased infant care (a
liability), pressures for increasing brain size and flexible learning ability
(a benefit, we presume), reproductive economy, and other factors we
can only guess.

Restrictions on Phenotypic Variability

In the case of infant intelligence, the flexibility in learning that is
typical of humans must have some bounds. Species adaptation depends
upon a rather limited range of behavioral phenotypes. Some character-

istically human patterns need to emerge in every individual. There are two principal mechanisms for limiting the possible number of phenotypes that develop: *canalization* by genetic preadaptation and *developmental adaptation*.

Canalization is a genetic predisposition for the development of a certain form of adaptation, guided along internally regulated lines. Environmental features are necessary for complete development or for the full expression of the adaptation, but the direction of the development is difficult to deflect. Environmental inputs that are necessary for canalized development to occur must be universally available to the species, else this form of adaptation would not work.

Embryologists, particularly Waddington (1957, 1962, 1971), have long recognized the "self-righting" tendencies of many aspects of growth. The difficulty of deflecting an organism from its growth path (which Waddington calls a *creod*) is expressed in the idea of canalization. Canalization restricts phenotypic diversity to a limited species range while maintaining desirable genetic diversity. If all genetic diversity were phenotypically expressed, there would be such enormous behavioral differences among people that it is difficult to see how any population could reproduce and survive (Vale and Vale, 1969). There are obviously functional equivalences in many genotypes (they produce similar phenotypes) for the most basic human characteristics.

Canalization is a very conservative force in evolutionary history. A well-knit system of canalization tends to restrict evolutionary potential quite severely. It accounts for the maintenance of particular phenotypes throughout a family of related species for no obvious reason, since a different phenotype seems to serve another taxon equally well in the same environment (Mayr, 1970, p. 174). In the case of infant intelligence the similarities among primate species suggest a relative immunity to recent evolutionary pressures.

A major reason for the perseverence of particular phenotypes is that new characters or traits are produced not by isolated mutations but by a reorganization of the genotype. It requires a genetic revolution to break up a well-buffered developmental pattern. Second, most genetic variability can be hidden by canalized development and therefore be immune to selective pressures:

> A tight system of developmental homeostasis helps to shield the organism against environmental fluctuations. However much genetic variation

there is in a gene pool the less of it penetrates into the phenotype, the smaller
the point of attack it offers to selection. (Mayr, 1970, p. 39)

The total genome is a "physiological team." No genes are soloists;
they must play harmoniously with others to achieve selective advantage
because selection works on the whole person and on whole coadapted
gene complexes in the population. As Dobzhansky (1955) has said,
evolution favors genes that are "good mixers," ones that make the most
positive contributions to fitness against the greatest number of genetic
backgrounds.

Selection is always for coadapted gene complexes that fit a developmental pattern. The sheer number of gene differences between individuals or species is not a good measure of overall difference. To express
individual or population differences as differences in the number of
nucleotide pairs of the DNA is like trying to express the difference
between the Bible and Dante's *Divine Comedy* in terms of the frequency
of letters used in the two works (Mayr, 1970, p. 322). The developmental
pattern of infant intelligence is, I would argue, a strongly buffered
epigenotype that is shared by our closest primate relatives. To break it
up would require multiple rewritings of the primate manuscript.

Compared with canalization, *developmental adaptation* is a more flexible arrangement to ensure survival in varied possible environments. The
genetic program does not specify a particular *response* to any environment, but it specifies a generalized *responsiveness* to the distinctive
features of environments within a permissible range of variation. In
practice it is very difficult to distinguish between *developmental adaptation*
and *genetic preadaptation* (through selection) because they serve the same
goal, i.e., to limit the possible behavioral phenotypes that develop.

The contrast between canalization and developmental adaptation is
not a distinction between genetic and environmental determinants of
development. Every human characteristic is genetically based (because
the entire organism is), but a useful distinction can be made between
genetic differences and nongenetic differences. *Nongenetic* means simply
that the differences between two phenotypes are not caused by genetic
differences. The capacity of a single genotype to produce two or more
phenotypes is itself genetically controlled, of course (Mayr, 1970). The
notion of a genetic blueprint for ontogeny means that each genotype has
its own canalized course of development, from which it is difficult to
deflect. In the case of strong genetic canalization, individual phenotypic

differences are presumably genetic because one genotype cannot produce a variety of phenotypes. In the case of weak canalization, one genotype can and does produce multiple phenotypes among which the differences are not genetic.

Two puzzling examples of human adaptation illustrate the difference between genetic adaptation as a result of natural selection and developmental adaptation as a result of genetic flexibility (strong versus weak canalization). Milk "intolerance" normally develops in most humans after the preschool years. The ability to digest large quantities of milk in adulthood is the result of prolonged lactase activity in some populations that have practiced dairying for the past several thousand years. Is the continued secretion of lactase in adulthood a developmental adaptation to continued milk drinking past weaning? Or is it a result of natural selection for lactase activity in those peoples for whom some selective advantage was derived from milk in their adult diets?

The second example is adaptation to life at high altitudes. One feature of high altitudes is reduced oxygen concentrations in the air. Peoples in Ethiopia and in the Andes at elevations above 10,000 feet typically have large lung capacities and deep "barrel chests." Peoples who live at lower altitudes have smaller chests and lung capacities. Is this primarily a developmental adaptation or a result of natural selection for adaptation to a high-altitude niche?

In both cases, either a developmental or a selective adaptation would accomplish the same goal of better utilization of the available resources—in one case nutrition, in the other case oxygen. For reasons beyond the comprehension of this author, the case of milk"intolerance" seems to be primarily the result of natural selection acting on the gene frequencies for lactase activity past childhood (Gottesman and Heston, 1972). The second case—adaptation at high altitudes—is primarily a developmental phenomenon. We know these explanations to be the primary ones because in the case of lactase activity, continued milk drinking into later childhood does not maintain lactase activity in intolerant people at levels adequate for comfortable absorption of a significant portion of one's nutrition through milk, and discontinued milk drinking does not terminate lactase activity in people who are genetically tolerant of milk. In the lactose-tolerant group loading the stomach with milk at any time results in renewed lactase activity. In the lactose-intolerant case lactase activity declines despite continued stimulation through milk consumption.

The high-altitude example could well have represented genetic selection for life under unusual oxygen tension (Baker, 1969). After 15,000 years in the high Andes, however, Peruvian Indians who descend to the lowlands have children with little evidence of barrel-chestedness, and Indians who migrate from lowland to highland areas have children who exhibit the phenomenon. Harrison (1967) reported that Amharic Ethiopians who migrate from 5000- to 10,000-foot altitudes develop some chest enlargement even in adulthood.

What kinds of human behavioral characteristics are likely to show developmental adaptation more than genetic preadaptation? Omenn and Motulsky (1972) proposed that older (in an evolutionary sense) forms of adaptation are more likely to have limited genetic variability and a higher degree of canalization. Specifically, the brain stem, the midbrain, and the limbic structures that evolved earlier are less polymorphic than cortical areas of the brain. Behavioral characteristics associated with higher cortical centers are newer evolutionary phenomena and likely to develop more variable phenotypes. Behaviors associated with older areas of the brain, those we share with other primates, are genotypically and phenotypically less variable. Their development is more highly canalized. This hypothesis has clear implications for infant intelligence, as contrasted with later forms of intelligence.

EVIDENCE ON CANALIZATION AT SPECIES, POPULATION, AND INDIVIDUAL LEVELS OF ANALYSIS

To evaluate the research evidence on the canalization of infant intelligence, we must coordinate the data gathered with several methodological approaches. Ethological and comparative studies of primates speak to the canalization of infant intelligence at a species level. Behavior genetic studies of variation analyze sources of individual differences within populations, and cross-cultural studies deal with population differences in development. Four operational definitions (or primitive models) are proposed to integrate comparative and ethological descriptions of species patterns with analytical studies of variation, including population and individual levels of analyses. Predictions can be made from any of the four:

1. Functional equivalencies in both genotypes and environments are interpreted as strong canalization at a species level. If neither geno-

typic nor environmental differences contribute much to phenotypic diversity, there will be a restricted range of individual differences, moderate heritability, and a distinctive species pattern.

2. Functional differences in genotypes but equivalencies in environments are interpreted as strong canalization at an individual, not a species, level. If genetic differences are the primary contributors to phenotypic differences, then heritability will be high within a population and between populations, if the distribution of genotypes is different.

3. Functional equivalencies of genotypes but not environments are interpreted as weak canalization at individual and population levels, with low heritabilities and a weak species pattern.

4. Functional equivalencies of neither genotypes nor environments will yield extreme individual phenotypic variation and moderate heritabilities within and between populations, if genotypes are differently distributed.

The implications of an evolutionary account for varied data on infant intelligence can now be tested. If infant intelligence indeed evolved early in primate history, if its development is to some extent canalized, and if both genotypes and environments are largely functionally equivalent, then contemporary primates should share a similar pattern of infant intelligence, individual diversity within the human species should be restricted, and the heritability of sensorimotor intelligence should be moderate, not high.

Infant Intelligence as Species-Specific Behavior

The notion of species-specific behavior is an abstraction from the reality of individual variation. Some behavioral geneticists deny the concept of "species-typical" any heuristic value (Bruell, 1970); others would support its usefulness as a statement about the highly leptokurtic shape of the distribution of individual differences within a species, measured on a species-comparative scale. Genetically conditioned homogeneity within a species is seen as a species-specific character; genetically conditioned heterogeneity is seen as individual variation within a species (Gottesman and Heston, 1972).

There is confusion inherent in the contrast between genetically conditioned homogeneity and heterogeneity in behavioral characteristics because (1) the notion of species-specific behavior is always an abstraction; (2) complex behaviors are always polygenic and to some degree phenotypically heterogeneous; and (3) the degree of phenotypic homogeneity is always relative to the scale on which the phenotype is measured. For example, take linear height. In the human population adult heights vary between, say, 3 feet and 7 feet, with the median height being about 5 feet 6 inches. From a within-species vantage point the distribution is somewhat leptokurtic, with perhaps 95% of the world population distributed between 5 feet and 6 feet 2 inches. If we scale human heights on a species-comparative scale from 0.01 inches to 240 inches (from protozoans to giraffes), the human distribution appears strongly leptokurtic. A "species-typical" height of about $5\frac{1}{2}$ feet represents a useful value in relation to other species. Actually, of course, the human variation is quite large if one's perspective is intraspecific. And so it is with nearly all human behaviors.

Robin Fox (1970) has argued for the usefulness of the species-specific concept. Language capacity is one obvious example, but kinship, courtship and marriage arrangements, political behaviors, and male groups that exclude females appear to be other species-specific human traits. There are limits, he argues, to what the human species can do and to what we can understand in another's behavior. There must be "wired-in" ranges for the information-processing capacity that responds only to certain kinds of inputs. Our ability to process information and to respond to the inputs of another's behavior are strongly tied to our phylogeny and to timing in the life cycle.

We are faced with an apparent paradox: that species-specific behaviors do not exist but are an abstraction from the reality of individual variation, yet the concept of species-typical does have heuristic value on a species-comparative scale. We can better approach the problem of variation and the species-typical concept, I believe, by looking at what limitations there are on variability within species, and by what mechanisms variation is limited.

Biases in Learning

Though it hardly needs saying, human infants tend to learn some things rather than others. One example is language acquisition, for which underlying sensitivities to speech sounds, both comprehension and production, combine with the stimulation of a language environment to produce a speaking human child. Another example is hand–eye coordination. At around 3 months normal infants gaze extendedly at their hands as though they were detached objects. One might think that visually guided reaching followed from such accidental experiences. In fact, blind infants "gaze" at their hands in prolonged fashion at about the same age as seeing infants (Freedman, 1974). The canalization of arm–hand motor development seems to bring all infants' hands within their visual range at that point in development. Experience with hand regard doubtless plays a role in subsequent coordinations, but the opportunity for hand–eye coordination to develop has not been left to experiential chance.

Seligman (1970) has shown that mammals come to a learning situation with a good deal of built-in bias to learn particular things. It is simply not the case that any stimulus can be equally well associated with any response or reinforcement. I would argue that human infants have built-in biases to acquire certain kinds of intelligent behaviors that are consonant with primate evolutionary history, that these biases are programmed by the epigenotype, and that human environments guarantee the development of these behaviors through the provision of material objects that are assimilated to them.

We seldom emphasize the role of common human environments in development, being attuned as we are to look at distinctive features. The environments for highly canalized behaviors like walking are seldom even studied. Lipsitt (1971, p. 499) gave a charming description of an infant who is "ready" to walk being propped up on his legs and flopped back and forth between adults. The acquisition of walking undoubtedly has experiential components that can be studied (Zelazo, 1974). On the other hand, all human environments seem to provide the necessary and sufficient conditions for walking to begin between 10 and 15 months. Only physically infirm infants (handicapped, malnourished) and those deprived of firm support (Dennis, 1960) fail to walk during infancy.

A similar point can be made about language acquisition. All normal, hearing infants have a human language environment, regardless of which language is spoken, that provides the necessary and sufficient conditions for acquisition. Infant intellectual development has some of the same properties in that it follows a species pattern of sensorimotor skills that assimilate whatever material objects the culture offers. The overall species patterns for motor, language, and cognitive development seem to be well ordered by the chromosomes and the common human environment. While experimental interventions may accelerate the acquisition of these behaviors, all normal infants acquire them in due time, and it is not clear that acceleration has any lasting impact on subsequent development.

Deprivation Effects

If infant intelligence is highly canalized at a species level, one would predict that environmentally caused retardations of sensorimotor development would be overcome once the environmental causes were eliminated. Canalization implies such an outcome. Recently Kagan and Klein (1973) published a cross-sectional study of infant and childhood development in Guatemala. Their assessment of infant development in an Indian village suggested to them that the children were behaviorally quite retarded at the end of the first year. Older children in the same setting, however, approached the performance levels of United States children on a variety of learning and perceptual tasks. From the observation of "retarded" infants and intellectually "normal" older children, they concluded that human development is inherently resilient, that is, highly canalized at the species level:

> This corpus of data implies that absolute retardation in the time of emergence of universal cognitive competences during infancy is not predictive of comparable deficits for memory, perceptual analysis, and inference during preadolescence. Although the rural Guatemalan infants were retarded with respect to activation of hypotheses, alertness, and onset of stranger anxiety and object permanence, the preadolescents' performance . . . were comparable to American middle class norms. Infant retardation seems to be partially reversible and cognitive development during the early years more resilient than had been supposed. (p. 957)

What Kagan and Klein (1973) suggested about canalization is that the caretaking practices of rural Guatemalans significantly retard the rate of infant development but that this deflection is only temporary because later child-rearing practices compensate for the early deprivation. In Waddington's terms the Guatemalan infants' mental development is asserted to have been temporarily deflected from its canalized course by environmental deprivations but to have exhibited the same kind of "catch-up" phenomenon claimed for physical growth among children who have been ill or malnourished for brief periods of time. Unfortunately, serious ceiling effects on the later tests make it difficult to judge whether or not the older Guatemalan children have intellectual skills typical of United States white children. Thus arguments for the canalization of infant intelligence at a species level are not well supported by this study.

The Guatemalan data do suggest that environmental deprivation can retard sensorimotor development. Studies of institutionalized infants (White, 1971; Dennis, 1960) also support the conclusion that social and physical deprivation retard infant intelligence. One can question, however, whether or not sensorimotor skills fail to emerge eventually in even moderately deprived infants. While there is no question that the rate of acquisition is affected, is there any evidence that infants who have any contact with physical and social objects fail to develop criterion-level sensorimotor skills by 2–3 years of age?

Clearly one could design a featureless, contactless environment that would turn any infant into a human vegetable. Extreme deprivation will prevent the emergence of the species-typical pattern. But the more interesting questions are how much input is necessary for adequate sensorimotor development and how many naturally occurring environments fail to provide the necessary conditions for criterion level development.

The proposal that sensorimotor intelligence is to some degree a canalized form of development does not require that the behaviors emerge in an environmental vacuum. *Canalization does not imply that species-typical development will occur under conditions that are atypical of those under which their evolution occurred.* It does imply that within the range of natural human environments most genotypes will develop similarly in most environments.

The Guatemalan data suggest that in at least one naturally occurring human environment the rate of sensorimotor development is slower than in some other conditions. An alternate explanation is also available, however: that the differences observed are due to genetic differences between groups in the rate of sensorimotor development. Whether the differences between Guatemalan and United States infants are genetic and/or environmental, the data provide some evidence against an extreme canalization position. There must be some developmental adaptation to enriched or impoverished environments and/or some group differences in genotypic responsiveness to sensorimotor environments that affect the rate of infant intellectual development. There is no evidence, however, that nondefective genotypes and naturally occurring environments are not equivalent in producing, eventually, the species-typical pattern.

Other Primates

The ethological, comparative evidence suggests that we share with at least the great apes a primate form of infant intelligence. The homologous, intelligent behaviors of infant apes and humans strongly suggest common origins in our primate past. During the first 18 months of human life there are few intellectual accomplishments that are not paralleled in nonhuman primates, particularly the apes. Both develop object concept, imitation, spatial concepts, cause–effect relations, and means–ends reasoning. In brief, both young apes and young humans become skillful, practical experimenters.

Our knowledge of chimp intellectual development comes primarily from home-reared animals, whose progress on form-board problems and the like exceeds that of their human infant companions in the first year of life (Hayes and Nissen, 1971). Even at the age of 3, Viki, the Hayeses' chimp, closely resembled a human child of 3 on those items of the Gesell, Merrill–Palmer, and Kuhlmann tests that do not require language:

> Viki's formal education began at 21 weeks with string-pulling problems. At 1 year she learned her first size, form, and color discriminations. By $2\frac{1}{2}$ years of age she could match with an accuracy of 90% even when a 10-second delay was imposed. (Hayes and Nissen, 1971, p. 61)

Viki was reared in a human child's environment, and her nonlinguistic attainments are impressive. Certainly her sensorimotor intelligence was as adequate as that of a human infant. In the wild Van Lawick-Goodall's (1971) observations confirm the excellent sensorimotor intelligence of chimps at later ages, but few data are available on their intellectual development in the first year of life.

Hamburg (1969) noted the many similarities between man and chimpanzees in the number and form of chromosomes, in blood proteins, in immune responses, in brain structure, and in behavior. The more we see of their behavior, he said, the more impressed we are by their resemblance to man: "This is not to imply that we inherit fixed action patterns. The chimpanzee's adaptation depends heavily on learning, and ours does even more so!" (p. 143).

Hamburg further suggested that there are probably important biases in what chimps and humans learn: "Our question is: Has natural selection operated on early interests and preferences so that the attention of the developing organism is drawn more to some kinds of experiences than others?" (p. 144). Both chimp and human infants attend to physical problem-solving tasks and to relational problems in their environments.

The nature of learning processes in chimp and human infants is virtually the same. Both profit particularly from observational learning, a skill that is a forte of primate adaptation. From observing the behavior of conspecifics, primates imitate and then practice the observed sequences of behavior over and over again:

> The chief mode of learning for the non-human primate is a sequence that goes from observation to imitation, then to practice. They have full access to virtually the whole repertoire of adult behavior with respect to aggression, sex, feeding, and all other activities. The young observe intently, and then imitate, cautiously at first, all the sequences they see. Then they may be seen practicing these sequences minutes or hours after they have occurred. This observational learning in a social context becomes extremely important for the young primates. It takes the place of active instruction on the part of adults, which never seems to occur. (Hamburg, 1969, p. 146)

The active instruction of human infants by adults probably exceeds that provided by other primate parents. In most parts of the world, however, infants are not instructed on the development or use of sensorimotor schemes. Although both home-reared chimps and human infants may profit from active instruction, it is not clear that the normal development of sensorimotor intelligence requires more than *opportunities* for exploration and learning.

The Gardner's chimp, Washoe, exhibited observational learning of even the most "unnatural" behaviors, like signs, although most of the signs were deliberately taught to her. She learned the sign for "sweet" from the Gardners' use of it in connection with her baby-food desserts. Later reinforcement of her use of the sign increased the reliability of her use of "sweet," but she acquired it from observation (Gardner and Gardner, 1971). She freely combined signs in novel utterances, reflecting her primate ability to make flexible combinations.

What differences, then, exist between the chimp and the human infant in sensorimotor intelligence? I would argue that the differences are in degree, not in kind. As Bruner (1972) has said, the difference between apes, monkeys, and man is in the *flexible use* and *combinatorial quality* of schemes, not in the schemes themselves. This is especially true in infancy, in which the greater cortical development of the human species has only barely begun to show its eventual effects. Human infants may exceed chimps in the combinatorial quality of their schemes, but the evidence is not so striking that observers of chimpanzee infants have noticed any great differences from human infants.

There is no question that after the age of 3, chimps and human children are intellectually different. Despite extensive tutoring in sign language and conceptual skills, Washoe's and Viki's problem-solving skills at 4 years were hardly a match for those of an ordinary 4-year-old child. In infancy, however, their skills were entirely comparable to those of a normal human infant.

The commonalities between apes and man in sensorimotor intelligence suggest that within each species most genotypes and environments are functionally equivalent in producing the recognizable species (perhaps, panprimate) form of development. The commonalities also suggest that this ancient phylogenetic adaptation has been highly resistant to evolutionary change—a characteristic of canalized behaviors.

Early forms of development are always more similar to other species' early forms than later, more differentiated forms. The most extreme statement of this point of view is that ontogeny recapitulates phylogeny. Although we have all been taught to reject this rigid view, there is a perfectly good observation that has been thrown out in the process. Embryologists can tell the difference between a human embryo and a fish embryo even though both have gill slits, but the embryonic forms share more in common than adult forms of the two taxons. It is not too great a leap, I hope, to note that early behavioral forms among primates share more in common than later behavioral forms. This is not to say that chimps and human infants have identical forms of behavior, only that they share more in common in the first 18 months than they do in later life.

An elaboration of this view, suggested by John Flavell, would propose that early human behavior has qualities that are pan-mammalian (e.g., sucking); later in the sensorimotor period, we can no longer refer to pan-mammalian but only to pan-primate forms of behavior. By adolescence, human intelligence is uniquely human, and other primate intelligence is unique to those species. The progressive divergence of intellectual development is analogous to the progressive differentiation of embryos. At no point are species forms indistinguishable, but early forms share more in common than later ones.

The restricted range of individual variation is another characteristic of canalization at a species level. Such individual differences as exist arise in the *rate* of sensorimotor development, not in the level eventually attained. Differences in the rate of sensorimotor development are small, relative to later intellectual differences. The overall pattern of sensorimotor intelligence is quite homogeneous for the species since criterion performance is accomplished in 15 to 20 months for the vast majority cf human infants. When one compares this restricted range of phenotypic variation with the range of intellectual skills of children between 11 and 12 years, for example, it is readily apparent that sensorimotor skills are a remarkably uniform behavioral phenomenon.

The hypothesis that infant intelligence is a more highly canalized form of development than later intelligence does not mean that environmental influences are inconsequential, either for development or for individual differences. Even strongly canalized behaviors respond to experience. Learning strongly affects the subsequent sexual behavior of castrated male cats, whose normal sexual development requires only opportunities to perform. Male cats castrated after copulatory experience are vastly superior in sexual performance to inexperienced castrates. Nest building in rabbits improves steadily over the first three litters, even though the differences among strains of rabbits in nest-building skills are largely due to genetic differences (Petit, 1972). Rather, I would argue that infant intelligence shows some signs of canalization in the timing and the general outline of its program but clearly develops in response to the sensorimotor environment. Later intellectual development, particularly around adolescence, seems to have a far less definite form and timing for all members of the species.

All nondefective infants reared in natural human environments achieve all of the sensorimotor skills that Piaget has described. (Do you know anyone who didn't make it to preoperational thought?) This is not a trivial observation, or at least no more trivial than the observations that all nondefective human beings learn a language, are attached to at least one caretaker, achieve sexual maturity, and die in old age, if not before. One cannot say that all nondefective human beings develop formal operational logic, learn a second language, are attracted to the opposite sex, or have musical talent. There is a fundamental difference between these two sets of observations: in the first case, everyone does it; in the second case, only some do.

Uniformity of achievement may be due to limited genetic variability, to canalized development that hides genetic variability, to uniform environments, or to some combination of the three causes. The evidence suggests to me that there is less genetic variability in infant than in later intelligence, that much of the genetic variability that exists is hidden in a well-buffered, epigenetic system, and that many environments are indeed functionally equivalent for the development of sensorimotor skills. I would argue that the genetic preadaptation in sensorimotor intelligence is a strong bias toward learning the typical schemes of infancy and toward combining them in innovative, flexible ways. What human environments do is to provide the materials and the opportunities to learn. For the development of sensorimotor skills, nearly any natural, human environment will suffice to produce criterion-level performance.

Canalization at the Individual Level

Wilson (1972a, 1972b) has argued, on the basis of his data on twins' development, that infant mental development is highly canalized at the individual level, difficult to deflect from its genotypic course, and unaffected by differences in an average range of home environments. If Wilson is correct, the heritability of infant intelligence scores should be very high, phenotype variation fairly large, and the data should fit canalization model 2 (p. 177 of this chapter):

> Therefore, the hypothesis is proposed that these socioeconomic and maternal care variables serve to modulate the primary determinant of developmental capability, namely, the genetic blueprint supplied by the parents. On this view, the differences between twin pairs and the similarities within twin pairs in the course of infant mental development are primarily a function of the shared genetic blueprint.
>
> Further, while there is a continuing interaction between the genetically determined gradient of development and the life circumstances under which each pair of twins is born and raised, it requires unusual conditions to impose a major deflection upon the gradient of infant development. (Wilson, 1972b, p. 917)

The primacy of "genetic blueprints" for development is a view shared by Sperry (1971). With respect to the importance of infancy and early childhood, Sperry said:

> The commonly drawn inference in this connection is that the experiences to which an infant is subjected during these years are primary. I would like again to suggest that there might be another interpretation here, namely, that it is the developmental and maturational processes primarily that make these years so determinative.
>
> During the first few years, the maturational program is unraveling at great speed. A lot of this determination seems to be inbuilt in nature; this is becoming increasingly clear from infant studies. I think we ought to keep our

> minds open to the possibility that the impression these first years are so
> critical is based to a considerable extent on the rapid unraveling of the
> individual's innate character. (p. 527)

Two lines of evidence have been used to support a strong canalization position on individual differences in infant mental development: family correlations and studies of individual consistency over time.

Family Studies

Table I shows the results of four family studies of twins and siblings, using infant mental tests.

Wilson's conclusion about the "genetic blueprint" for development is based on the very high monozygotic (MZ) correlations obtained on the same day by co-twins (Wilson and Harpring, 1972). The co-twin correlations at the same point in time were much higher, in fact, than the month-to-month correlations for the same infant.

Nichols and Broman's (1974) data from the Collaborative Study support Wilson's findings of high MZ correlations. Monozygotic twins could hardly have been more similar. The two studies differ, however, in their results for dizygotic (DZ) pairs. The genetic correlation between DZ co-twins is estimated to be between 0.50 and 0.55, the larger figure based on parental assortative mating. But note that Wilson's DZ pairs were considerably more similar than expected. Wachs (1972) replied that "This degree of correlation indicates the operation of nongenetic factors in the dizygotic twins' mental test performance." Indeed, Nichols and Broman's dizygotic twins displayed the level of similarity predicted by a genetic model. Both same- and opposite-sexed twins have correlations of 0.50 ± 0.09, which are well within the 95% confidence interval around 0.5 in this study.

Now look at the siblings. Although they share the same percentage of genes in common, on the average, as dizygotic twins, the Fels study and the Collaborative Study found them to be far less similar in mental development during infancy. With sample sizes between 656 and 939 pairs, Nichols and Broman reported average correlations of about 0.20 for siblings; McCall reported 0.24. There is no question that sibs are less similar than DZ twins and that the explanation must be based on the greater environmental similarity of twins, both pre- and postnatally.

The comparison of sibling and DZ twin results is puzzling. The maximum heritability that can be obtained for any characteristic is twice

TABLE I

Infant Mental Scale Correlations for Related Pairs in the First Year of Life

Author	Date	Test	Age (months)	Twins						Siblings				Estimates of genetic variance	
				MZ	(N)	SSDZ	(N)	OSDZ	(N)	SS	(N)	OS	(N)	Twins 2($riMZ-riDZ$)	Sibs 2(ri)
Wilson	(1972b)	Bayley	3	0.84		0.67								0.34	
			6	0.82		0.74								0.16	
			9	0.81	(~82)	0.69	(~101)[a]							0.24	
			12	0.82		0.61								0.42	
Nichols and Broman	(1974)	Bayley													
		Whites	8	0.83	(48)	0.51	(41)	0.56	(62)	0.17	(887)	0.22	(939)	0.64	0.39
		Blacks	8	0.85	(74)	0.43	(47)	0.57	(78)	0.22	(656)	0.16	(745)	0.84	0.38
		Total	8	0.84	(122)	0.46	(88)	0.58	(140)	0.21	(1543)	0.20	(1684)	0.76	0.41
McCall	(1972a)	Gesell	6 & 12							−0.24	(142)	—			0.48
Freedman and Keller	(1963)	Bayley	2–12	Variance within MZ pairs significantly lower than variance within DZ pairs (N = 20)											

[a] There were a few opposite-sex pairs included.

the sibling correlation (Falconer, 1960). This calculation assumes that *all* of the variance between sibs is genetic and that no environmental variance is present. For behavioral traits this is an absurd assumption, and the heritability should most often be less than twice the sib correlation. A comparison of the McCall and the Nichols and Broman sibling data with the latter's twin results quickly shows a substantial difference in calculated heritability. Twice the sibling correlation varies around 0.40; heritabilities based on the twin results are much higher, around 0.75.

Since twins are nearly always tested on the same day, while sibs may be tested at slightly different ages, Nichols and Broman (1974) examined their data for age differences between sibs at testing, which were inconsequential. Then they tested for uniform correlations across the range of scores to assess the influence of extremely low scores. Extreme scores, which are much more frequent for twins in general, also showed greater concordance than higher scores among MZ twins. After eliminating the twin pairs in which one or both scored less than 50, Nichols and Broman found that the MZ correlation was reduced to 0.63, while the DZ correlation increased slightly to 0.57. Low scores had inflated the heritability estimate by a factor of 6! Although the best estimate of heritability for a population should include some low scores, the distribution of scores in a twin sample should represent the population distribution. Nichols and Broman concluded:

> These results suggest that the influence of genetics (differences) on scores on the Bayley Mental exam is greatest at the low end of the distribution, and underline the need for caution when interpreting twin correlations. (p. 5)

The hypothesis that a "genetic blueprint" programs individual infant mental development does not stand up as well as the high MZ correlations would lead us to believe.

Canalization of Patterns of Infant Mental Development

There is an additional hypothesis that deserves mention: that patterns of change in infant mental development are programmed by the individual genotype. Waddington (1971) proposed that the degree of canalization can vary depending upon the alleles present at relevant loci, which would suggest that some genotypes are better buffered than others. Wilson (1972a) found that the profiles of scores obtained from the MZ twins over the first two years were significantly more similar than those obtained from DZ pairs, that is, that MZ co-twins show more similar responses to their common environments. McCall (1970) found no similarity in sibling profiles of intellectual development. Apart from the methodological arguments, which I will not detail here (see McCall, 1970, 1972b; McCall et al., 1973; Wilson, 1972b; Wilson and Harpring, 1972), there is a substantive question again about the interpretation of twin data. Co-twins must share very common rearing environments as well as genotypes. In infancy the effects of shared prenatal environments may be more important than they are at later ages. Sibling data provide a crucial check on the generalization of twin results.

Continuity in Development

Continuity in developmental levels and profiles has been used as evidence for canalization. In longitudinal studies of singletons less continuity of intellectual level has been found in infancy than in later years (Bayley, 1965). Although one recent study with a small sample failed to find any continuity (Lewis and McGurk, 1972), there are most often correlations of 0.2–0.6 in mental levels across the first two years. Wilson (1972a; Wilson and Harpring, 1972) has attributed the lower correlations among ages under 2 to the genetic blueprint, which has genotypically different spurts and lags in its course. Others have argued for discontinuities in the skills being tested at various ages (Stott and Ball, 1965; McCall et al., 1973).

Continuity from infant to later development can be observed for some infants who score poorly on infant mental scales. They more often remain retarded than others who are not impaired in early life. But the prediction from the first year to later childhood is greatly enhanced by consideration of the caretaking environment, which, if poor, increases the risks for poor development of "retarded" infants (Willerman et al., 1970; Scarr-Salapatek and Williams, 1973; Sameroff and Chandler, 1975). Infants who perform poorly in the first year but who have middle-class families are rarely retarded by school age. Infants at risk for retardation whose families are lower class show greater continuity in poor development (Willerman et al., 1970; Scarr-Salapatek and Williams, 1973).

The reasons for later retardation may vary between middle-class and lower-class groups, but the continuous caretaking environment is at least one apparent difference. Sameroff and Chandler (1975) presented a transactional model that ascribes consistency both to organismic variables and to caretaking environments that support and maintain responses in the system. For example, infants with "difficult" temperaments are more likely to evoke assaultative behavior from their caretakers, whose battering increases the probability of more maladaptive behavior by the infants, and so forth. It is not clear that continuity in infant mental development can be attributed primarily to individual genetic blueprints.

Canalization at the Population Level: Group Differences

If infant development is highly canalized at a species level, one might expect to find universal patterns and rates of infant behavioral development, regardless of differences in child-rearing practices. No one has recently argued that the *sequences* of infant behavioral acquisitions are different across cultures. Piaget's descriptions of the important sensorimotor stages seem to apply to all normal infants. Differences in *rates* of development, however, have been noted for infants and older children of various cultural groups.

There are at least three problems with the cross-cultural paradigm in studies of canalization. First, genetic differences in rates of development may exist between populations. Relatively isolated gene pools may have evolved somewhat different patterns of infant development. Second, cross-cultural studies are fraught with methodological problems (Pick, in press; Warren, 1972) that may apply less to infant studies than to studies of older children but that cannot be ruled out entirely. Third, the cultural practices that may, in fact, affect rates of infant development may not be identified by investigators, who may be at a loss to know what comparisons to make. These three problems—possible genetic differences, methodological problems, and identification of relevant environmental contingencies—make the interpretation of cross-cultural research on infant development difficult. Nevertheless, what has been observed?

Compared to United States white infants, those reared in other groups have been observed to be accelerated or retarded in sensorimotor development. African infants have often been found to be precocious (Warren, 1972; Freedman, in press), particularly in the early appearance of major motor milestones, such as sitting, standing alone, and walking.

Although some investigators have related the precocity of African infants to child-rearing practices (Geber, 1958), U. S. black infants have also been found to be precocious in the same ways (Bayley, 1965; Nichols and Broman, 1975; Knobloch and Pasamanick, 1953). The similar pattern of precocity of urban United States black infants and rural African infants would seem to reduce the efficacy of a cultural argument to explain the phenomenon.

Navaho infants have been reported to be somewhat retarded in motor development, an observation that has been attributed to the cradle board but that may reflect gene pool differences. The latter explanation is particularly interesting in light of Freedman's (in press) report of the flaccid muscle tone and paucity of lower limb reflexes in Navaho newborns.

Several other reports of behavioral differences among newborns from different populations are suggestive of gene pool differences (Brazelton et al., 1969; Freedman, in press), although prenatal differences are not easily ruled out. In a particularly well-designed study Freedman and Freedman (1969) did show differences between small samples of Chinese-American and Caucasian-American newborns whose mothers were members of the same Kaiser-Permanente hospital group. Presumably many possible differences in prenatal life could be ruled out as competitive hypotheses.

There are few comparable studies of infant mental or language development cross-culturally. We do not know when object permanence or first words appear in various groups; a first step toward studies of canalization at a population level should certainly include the simple description of the existing group variation.

The evidence from cross-cultural studies suggests that there are variations among groups in the rates of infant development. The origins of these differences are possibly cultural in part and probably genetic in part. Further studies at a descriptive level would clarify the degree of variation among groups in developmental patterns. Studies of infants from two gene pools—some of whom were reared by members of their own culture, compared to others adopted into families of a different group—would clarify the roles of genetic and environmental differences among groups. If canalization is strong for infant development in both groups, then rearing conditions should not affect the differences among infants from different gene pools nor the similarities among infants from the same gene pool. Opportunities for such studies exist, as in the cases of black and Asian infants adopted into United States Caucasian families. Is their rate of infant development similar to Caucasian infants in the same families or to infants from the same gene pool reared by members of their own group?

Whither Studies of Canalization?

Hypotheses about the strong canalization of infant development at species, population, or individual levels have not been thoroughly investigated as yet. Studies of canalization at an individual level can benefit from several research strategies. Adoptive studies also provide a useful technique to examine the influence of shared genotypes and shared environments. Comparisons of infants with their biological relatives can be made for groups reared by their own parents and others reared by adoptive families. Further family studies of siblings and half siblings, reared together and apart, would enhance our knowledge of genotypic differences in development. An ingenious natural experiment can be found in the families of adult monozygotic twins. In the family constellations are MZ twins, siblings, parents and their children, half sibs, and separated "parent"–child pairs (composed of the MZ twin with the co-twin's children). A beautiful part of the design is the intactness and normality of the families who are related in all of those varied ways.

High heritabilities of infant development within a population would suggest that the environments sampled are functionally equivalent and that genotypic differences are important sources of variation. This would be evidence for the canalization of that development within the context of average infant environments. Current evidence from twin and sibling studies of mental development leaves this model in doubt, however, even for the one population studied. There is even less evidence available for the canalization of mental development at a population level.

At a species level an argument can be made for considerable restriction in phenotypic variation and for a recognizable species pattern, a pattern shared with our closest primate relatives. Whatever the sources of variation, there is a typical form of sensorimotor intelligence that develops over the first 18 months of human life. This pattern, I would argue, depends upon the functional equivalence of most genotypes and environments within the species. Canalization of infant sensorimotor intelligence is not a genetic blueprint for the emergence of particular responses. It is , rather, a preadapted responsiveness to certain learning opportunities. The full development of the sensorimotor skills depends upon the infants' encountering the appropriate learning opportunities, but most human environments are rich in the physical and social stimuli that infant intelligence requires. Differences in rates of sensorimotor development are not yet assignable to genetic or environmental causes, but they are relatively unimportant variations on a strong primate theme.

ACKNOWLEDGMENTS

I want to express my gratitude to Professors William Charlesworth and John Flavell for their careful, critical reviews of the manuscript. Their challenging ideas have been sometimes incorporated in the chapter, but they are not responsible for any errors of presentation. The research and review were supported by the Grant Foundation and the National Institute of Child Health and Human Development (HD-06502 and HD-08016).

REFERENCES

BAKER, P., 1969, Human adaptation to high altitude, *Science, 163*:1149.
BAKER, P., AND WEINER, J., 1966, "The Biology of Human Adaptability," Oxford, New York.
BAYLEY, N., 1965, Comparisons of mental and motor test scores for ages 1–15 months by sex, birth order, race, geographical location, and education of parents, *Child Development, 36*:379.
BELL, S. M., 1970, The development of the concept of the object and its relationship to infant–mother attachment, *Child Development, 41*:291.
BOWLBY, J., 1969, "Attachment and Loss" (Vol. 1: *Attachment*), Basic Books, New York.
BOWLBY, J., 1973, "Attachment and Loss" (Vol. 2: *Separation*), Basic Books, New York.
BRAZELTON, T. B., ROBEY, J. S., AND COLLIER, G. A., 1969, Infant development in the Zincanteco Indians of southern Mexico, *Pediatrics, 44*:274.
BRUELL, J., 1970, Behavioral population genetics and wild *Mus musculus* ,in "Contributions to Behavior Genetic Analysis: The Mouse as a Prototype," G. Lindzey and D. D. Thiessen (eds.), Appleton, New York, p. 261.
BRUNER, J. S., 1972, The nature and uses of immaturity, *American Psychologist, 27*:687.
DENNIS, W., 1960, Causes of retardation among institutional children: Iran, *Journal of Genetic Psychology, 96*:47.
DOBZHANSKY, T., 1955, A review of some fundamental concepts and problems of population genetics, *Cold Spring Harbor Symposium on Quantitative Biology, 20*:1.
DOBZHANSKY, T., 1967, On types, genotypes, and the genetic diversity in populations, *in* "Genetic Diversity and Human Behavior," J. Spuhler (ed.), Aldine, Chicago, p. 1.
ELKIND, D., 1967, Cognitive development, *in* "Infancy and Early Childhood," Y. Brackbill (ed.), Free Press, New York, p. 361.
FALCONER, D. S., 1960, "Introduction to Quantitative Genetics," Ronald Press, New York.
Fox, R., 1970, The cultural animal, *Encounter, 42*:31.

Freedman, D. G., 1967, A biological approach to personality development, in "Infancy and Early Childhood," Y. Brackbill (ed.), Free Press, New York, p. 469.

Freedman, D. G., 1974, "An Ethological Perspective on Human Infancy," Erlbaum, New York.

Freedman, D. G., and Freedman, N. C., 1969, Behavioral differences between Chinese-American and European-American newborns, Nature, 24:1227.

Freedman, D. G., and Keller, B., 1963, Inheritance of behavior in infants, Science, 140:196–198.

Gardner, B. T., and Gardner, R. A., 1971, Two-way communication with an infant chimpanzee, in "Behavior of Non-Human Primates," A. M. Schrier and F. Stollnitz (eds.), Academic Press, New York, p. 117.

Geber, M., 1958, The psychomotor development of African children in the first year, and the influence of maternal behavior, Journal of Social Psychology, 47:185.

Ghiselin, M., 1969, "The Triumph of the Darwinian Method," University of California Press, Berkeley.

Gottesman, I. I., and Heston, L. I., 1972, Human behavior adaptations: Speculations on their genesis, in "Genetics, Environment, and Behavior," L. Ehrman, G. S. Omenn, and E. Caspari (eds.), Academic Press, New York, p. 105.

Hamburg, D. A., 1969, Sexual differentiation and the evolution of aggressive behavior in primates, in "Environmental Influences on Genetic Expression," N. Kretchmer and D. N. Walcher (eds.), United States Government Printing Office, Washington, D.C., p. 141.

Harrison, G. A., 1967, Human evolution and ecology, in "Proceedings of the Third International Congress of Human Genetics," Johns Hopkins University, Baltimore.

Hayes, K. J., and Nissen, C. H., 1971, Higher mental functions of a home-raised chimpanzee, in "Behavior of Non-Human Primates," A. M. Schrier and F. Stollnitz (eds.), Academic Press, New York, p. 59.

Kagan, J., and Klein, R. E., 1973, Cross-cultural perspectives on early development, American Psychologist, 28:947.

Knobloch, H., and Pasamanick, B., 1953, Further observations on the behavioral development of Negro children, The Journal of Genetic Psychology, 83:137.

Kopp, C. B., and Shaperman, J., 1973, Cognitive development in the absence of object manipulation during infancy, Developmental Psychology, 9:430.

LaBarre, W., 1954, "The Human Animal," University of Chicago Press, Chicago.

LaBarre, W., 1973, The development of mind in man in primitive cultures, in "Brain and Intelligence," F. Richardson (ed.), p. 21.

Lehrman, D., 1970, Semantic and conceptual issues in the nature–nurture problem, in "Development and Evolution of Behavior," L. R. Aronson, E. Tobach, and E. Shaw (eds.), Freeman, San Francisco, p. 12.

Lewis, M., and McGurk, H., 1972, Evaluation of infant intelligence, Science, 178:1174.

Lipsitt, L. P., 1971, Discussion of paper by Harris, in "The Biopsychology of Development," E. Tobach, L. R. Aronson, and E. Shaw (eds.), Academic Press, New York, p. 498.

Mayr, E., 1970, "Populations, Species, and Evolution," Harvard University Press, Cambridge.

McCall, R. B., 1970, IQ pattern over age: Comparisons among siblings and parent–child pairs, Science, 170:644.

McCall, R. B., 1972a, Paper presented at the meeting of the American Psychological Association, Honolulu.

McCall, R. B., 1972b, Similarity in developmental profile among related pairs, Science, 178:1004.

McCall, R. B., Appelbaum, M. I., and Hogarty, P. S., 1973, Developmental changes in mental performance, *Monographs of the Society for Research in Child Development*, 38(3, Whole No. 150).

McClearn, G. E., 1972, Genetic determination of behavior (animal), *in* "Genetics, Environment, and Behavior," L. Ehrman, G. S. Omenn, and E. Caspari (eds.), Academic Press, New York, p. 55.

Nichols, P. L., and Broman, S. H., 1974, Familial resemblance in infant mental development, *Development Psychology*, 10:442.

Nichols, P. L., and Broman, S. H., 1975, "Preschool IQ: Prenatal and Early Developmental Correlates," Wiley, New York.

Omenn, G. S., and Motulsky, A. G., 1972, Biochemical genetics and the evolution of human behavior, *in* "Genetics, Environment, and Behavior," L. Ehrman, G. S. Omenn, and E. Caspari (eds.), Academic Press, New York, p. 129.

Petit, C., 1972, Qualitative aspects of genetics and environment in the determination of behavior, *in* "Genetics, Environment, and Behavior," L. Ehrman, G. S. Omenn, and E. Caspari (eds.), Academic Press, New York, p. 27.

Piaget, J., 1952, "The Origins of Intelligence in Children," International Universities Press, New York.

Pick, A. D., 1975, The Games Experimenters Play: A Review of Methods and Concepts of Cross-Cultural Studies of Cognition and Development, *in* "Handbook of Perception," E. C. Carterette and M. P. Friedman (eds.), Academic Press, New York.

Polansky, N. A., Borgman, R. D., DeSaix, C., and Smith, B. J., 1969, Mental organization and maternal adequacy in rural Appalachia, *American Journal of Orthopsychiatry*, 39:246.

Premack, D., 1971, On the assessment of language competence in the chimpanzee, *in* "Behavior of Nonhuman Primates," A. M. Schrier and F. Stollnitz (eds.), Academic Press, New York.

Sameroff, A. J., and Chandler, M. J., 1975, Reproductive risk and the continuum of caretaking casualty, *in* "Review of Child Development Research" (Vol. 4), F. D. Horowitz, M. Hetherington, S. Scarr-Salapatek, and G. Siegel (eds.), University of Chicago Press, Chicago.

Scarr-Salapatek, S., and Williams, M. L., 1973, The effects of early stimulation on low-birth-weight infants, *Child Development*, 44:94.

Seligman, M. E. P., 1970, On the generality of laws of learning, *Psychological Review*, 77:406.

Sperry, R. W., 1971, How a developing brain gets itself properly wired for adaptive function, *in* "The Biopsychology of Development," E. Tobach, L. R. Aronson, and E. Shaw (eds.), Academic Press, New York, p. 27.

Stott, L. H., and Ball, R. S., 1965, Infant and preschool mental tests: Review and evaluation, *Monographs of the Society for Research in Child Development*, 30(Whole No. 101).

Vale, J. R., and Vale, C. A., 1969, Individual differences and general laws in psychology, *American Psychologist*, 24:1093.

Van Lawick-Goodall, J., 1971, "In the Shadow of Man," Dell, New York.

Wachs, T., 1972, Technical comment, *Science*, 178:1005.

Waddington, C. H., 1957, "The Strategy of the Genes," Allen & Son, London.

Waddington, C. H., 1962, "New Patterns in Genetics and Development," Columbia University Press, New York.

Waddington, C. H., 1971, Concepts of development, *in* "The Biopsychology of Development," E. Tobach, L. R. Aronson, and E. Shaw (eds.), Academic Press, New York.

WARREN, N., 1972, African infant precocity, *Psychological Bulletin, 78*:353.
WHITE, B. L., 1971, "Human Infants: Experience and Psychological Development," Prentice-Hall, Englewood Cliffs, New Jersey.
WILLERMAN, L., BROMAN, S. H., AND FIEDLER, M., 1970, Infant development, preschool IQ, and social class, *Child Development, 41*:69.
WILSON, R. S., 1972a, Twins: Early mental development, *Science, 175*:914.
WILSON, R. S., 1972b, Similarity in developmental profile among related pairs of human infants, *Science, 178*:1005.
WILSON, R. S., AND HARPRING, E. B., 1972, Mental and motor development in infant twins, *Developmental Psychology, 7*:277.
ZELAZO, P. R., 1974, Newborn walking: From reflexive to instrumental behavior, paper presented at the annual meetings of the AAAS, Symposium on Psychobiology: The Significance of Infancy, San Francisco.

7 Early Learning and Intelligence

JOHN S. WATSON

There are three important ways that learning in infancy might be related to what could be termed an infant's intelligence. For one, early learning experiences might be determined by the level of intelligence of the infant. If that were so, then the amount and/or form of early learning could be expected to reveal something about the level of the infant's intelligence that existed at the time of the learning. Another way a relationship could exist between early learning and intelligence is if intelligence were an effect as opposed to a cause of learning. Were that the case, then one could expect to observe some appreciable relationship between the amount and/or form of early learning and the infant's subsequent level of intelligence. Finally, and quite separate from being either a cause or an effect of intelligence, early learning might yet stand in a useful predictive relationship to later expressions of intelligence. In this chapter each of these three potential relations between infant learning and intelligence is considered with respect to past and future relevant research. Before we turn to that discussion, however, it is necessary to say a few words about what is meant by *learning* and *intelligence* as these terms are used in this chapter.

DEFINITION OF TERMS

Learning is used here to refer to the process in which an individual's behavior or disposition to behave is changed by experience—with the exception of changes caused by the direct biological effects of fatigue, physical injury, or drugs. This definition is meant to include such

JOHN S. WATSON · University of California at Berkeley.

traditional learning phenomena as operant and classical conditioning, sensitization and habituation, and imitation and observational learning, as well as such things as the adaptations of sensory motor schema described by Piaget (1952). This broad definition is consistent with the nonexclusive stance taken by most recent reviews of infant learning (e.g., Brackbill and Koltsova, 1967; Lipsitt, 1969; Fitzgerald and Porges, 1971; Sameroff, 1971; Schaffer, 1973).

Intelligence is used here to refer to the dispositional property or properties of an individual that function in the determination of efficiency and quality of cognitive behavior and cognitive adaptation to the individual's experience. The reference to cognitive behavior and adaptation is purposely loose enough to remain compatible with most variants of professional definition (e.g., Bayley, 1970; Anastasi, 1958; Stevenson, 1970; Mussen *et al.*, 1974) and hopefully consistent with common usage as well. About the only classes of behavior meant to be excluded are those of a purely emotional, motivational, or accidental form. The reference to "dispositional property" is a relatively technical philosophical point that deserves brief elaboration. The reference is to the conceptual tradition of Carnap (1938) and Ryle (1949) as integrated with an assumption of materialism (e.g., Armstrong, 1968; Weissman, 1965). Briefly stated, this involves two assumptions about intelligence. One is that the property may be said to exist even when it is not being substantiated by criterial behavior, e.g., an individual may be said to be very intelligent even at times when his behavior is ordinary or when he is not behaving at all. The second assumption is that individual differences in intelligence refer to a real (i.e., material structural) variable as opposed to an intervening (i.e., mathematical relational) variable introduced to simplify behavioral laws (MacCorquodale and Meehl, 1948). From this perspective, intelligence is viewed as one of a variety of ability or capacity constructs that have frequent usage in both professional (e.g., Baldwin, 1958) and common-sense explanations of behavior (e.g., the "naïve" theory of action as constructed by Heider, 1958).

The acceptance of intelligence as an ability construct introduces the opportunity to make a distinction that is almost inevitably raised in either lay or professional considerations of ability. The distinction concerns the extent of ability that exists at the present time ("actual ability" according to Baldwin, 1958) as contrasted to the maximal extent of ability to exist at some future time in the life of the individual ("potential ability" according to Baldwin). Clearly this distinction has been a central concern of the intelligence testing field from the time Binet accepted the task of sorting Parisian children into those who would versus those who would not come to have the ability to succeed in formal schooling. We shall return to this distinction between actual and potential intelligence at a later point in the discussions of the three forms of relationship between early learning and intelligence.

Before turning to those discussions, however, one final point should be made concerning the use of the terms *learning* and *intelligence*. These terms will often be used as if they referred to single entities, i.e., as if learning were a unitary process or intelligence a unitary trait. This will be done for the sake of simplicity in discussions that do not require maintaining a differentiated conception of the terms. However, it should be noted that the weight of existing evidence indicates that intelligence is more likely a set of traits than a single trait (Anastasi, 1958; McCall *et al.*, 1972) and learning appears to proceed in a variety of rather independent processes (Stevenson, 1970). The choice to simplify reality with mostly undifferentiated references to learning and intelligence should not cause any misrepresentation of the relations to be discussed, and indeed it should be quite possible to substitute particular learning processes or intellectual traits for the general references in almost any of the discussions. In fact, it is worth keeping in mind that any of the relationships may be stronger for certain processes and traits than for others.

INTELLIGENCE AS A DETERMINANT OF EARLY LEARNING

Let us begin consideration of the three potential relationships by focusing on the possibility that an infant's learning is in some degree determined by his intelligence. To a certain extent this possibility appears to flow directly from the general definitions of the two terms. If one accepts that intelligence is in part embodied by the disposition (or dispositions) to adaptive change in cognitive behavior with respect to experience and that learning is the process of behavioral or dispositional change resulting from experience, then it follows logically that whenever learning involves adaptive change in cognitive behavior, that learning should be influenced by—and to that extent reveal—the individual's intelligence. In short, higher intelligence should express itself in faster or better learning. At least this should be so when the learning involves adaptive changes in cognitive behavior.

Studies that have compared traditional measurements of intelligence with learning scores of various kinds have observed only modest levels of correlation between the two variables. In a recent review of this area Stevenson (1970) concluded that while the extent of the relation does not appear to be as low as early studies implied (e.g., Garrett, 1928; Garrison, 1928; Husband, 1941; Simrall, 1947), the correlations observed in more recent studies (e.g., Duncanson, 1964; Stake, 1961; Stevenson *et al.*, 1968; Stevenson and Odom, 1965) have only been in the moderate range of $r = 0.20$–0.40. Moreover the higher correlations appear to be limited to learning situations involving "verbal material, tests of the ability to acquire associations, and material similar to that found in intelligence tests" (Stevenson, 1970). One is left to wonder, therefore, whether the modest correlations that have been found are reflections of truly general functional relationships between intelligence and learning or whether they reflect relationships that depend on relatively specialized response capacities (e.g., verbal skills) that are relevant to the shared content of these particular intelligence and learning tasks. So then, while the general definitions of intelligence and learning lead to the expectancy that higher intelligence will display itself in superior learning capacity, the available data do not forcefully substantiate this logical expectation.

It is clearly too early to conclude that early learning capacity and intelligence are independent, however. As has been observed by previous reviewers of children's learning (e.g., Brackbill and Koltsova, 1967; Stevenson, 1970), studies that have examined this question are surprisingly few in number. If the scarcity of such studies of children seems remarkable, then the void of such studies of infants (i.e., under 2 years) should seem even more so. A variety of infant intelligence tests has been available for decades (Bayley, 1970), and techniques for studying learning and conditioning in infants have proliferated in the last 15 years (Brackbill and Koltsova, 1967; Lipsitt, 1963, 1969). So why does there appear to be no single study in which the MA or IQ scores of infants have been related to some aspect of their performance in a standard learning situation (e.g., operant or classical conditioning)? Perhaps it is that researchers on infant behavior are less diversified in their experimental versus differential psychological training and/or interests than those researchers working with older subjects. On the other hand, perhaps infant researchers have been discouraged from initiating such a study since they are aware that the weight of existing evidence implies that (1) learning has at most a moderate relation to intelligence in older age levels and (2) that intelligence test performance in infancy has little relation to intelligence test performance at the older age levels (Bayley, 1970).

Regardless of what has led to the existing lack of data concerning the relation of intelligence and learning in infancy, there would seem little doubt that it is yet an empirical relation worth investigating. The failure to find a substantial relationship at older age levels should not be too discouraging. The relation could well change with age. The complexity and even the forms of learning are extended with age and experience for the normal child (Gagné, 1965). Along with this transition in capacity there would seem little doubt that as the child matures, his dominant or focal learning experiences are occurring primarily in his more complex and advanced forms of learning. If one accepts intelligence as a determining factor of the efficiency and quality of cognitive adaptation to experience, then it should not be surprising to find that the form of learning that is associated with intelligence in infancy is different from the form associated with intelligence in older children or adults. Continuing this line of reasoning, one might sensibly search for potential relationships between simple instrumental learning and intelligence in early infancy even though there is a fair amount of evidence to imply that the efficiency of such nonverbal learning is minimally, if not slightly negatively (Brackbill and Koltsova, 1967), associated with intelligence in older children.

McCall et al. (1972) has made a related point concerning the potential transition of item structure in intelligence tests across the course of infant development. Basically his point is that we might do far better in our attempt to understand and predict the developmental course of infant intelligence if we were to focus on the behaviors that are at the center of the infant's intellectual organization at the time of testing. In other words, intelligence may be expressed in different behavioral functions at different times. A reasonable source of such variable expression would be the systematic variation resulting if intelligence were expressed most clearly in those behavior patterns that were most subject to the influence of the infant's present stage of cognitive adaptation. Thus, as the thrust of development shifts from one area of cognitive behavior to another, there would be an associated shift in the assessment value of the behavior from the different areas.

On the basis of a separate component analysis of intelligence test performance at each of four ages in a longitudinal sample of infants, it would seem that a transition in the behavioral expression of intelligence does occur in infancy (McCall *et al.*, 1972). The principal component structure of test performance appeared to change from one age to the next across the four assessments that were obtained at 6, 12, 18, and 24 months of age. Moreover the highest-order components at each age displayed the largest interage correlations. These latter correlations were considerably higher than the interage correlations of whole test scores. Thus it would seem that to obtain the best picture of the continuity of intellectual development requires weighting behavior differently at different ages. In addition, on the basis of McCall's interpretation of the behavioral content of the major components at each age, it would seem that the wave of intellectual advance passes from a behavioral area akin to instrumental learning at 6 months, to motor imitation at 12 months, to verbal imitation at 18 months, and on to more elaborate verbal association learning at 24 months. Interestingly enough this rough picture of the developmental transformation in the behavioral expression of intelligence would seem basically compatible with either the hierarchy of learning processes proposed by Gagné (1965) or the stages of sensorimotor intelligence proposed by Piaget (1952). But more interesting than the broad theoretical compatibility of McCall's data is the fact that they imply that early expression of intelligence may be most appropriately assessed by an examination of the kind of simple nonverbal learning that appears to have so little relation to intelligence at later ages.

With the implication that instrumental learning may embody a central expression of intelligence at around 6 months of age, one may wonder whether this remains so at even earlier ages or whether another form of learning—classical conditioning, for example—might provide the central expression of intelligence in younger infants. This would seem a reasonable possibility, particularly if one tends to view classical conditioning as a simpler form of learning than instrumental or operant conditioning. On the other hand, Sameroff (1971) has made a strong case for viewing classical conditioning as a developmentally more advanced form of learning than operant conditioning on the bases of both empirical data and Piagetian theory. If Sameroff is right, then perhaps one should expect instrumental learning to provide an earlier expression of intelligence than classical conditioning. That may depend, of course, on whether intelligence is best displayed by a learning capacity at the time it is emerging or at the time it is reaching consolidation. For instance, Lewis (1969, 1971) has found that habituation rate appears to reach a developmental peak at about 12–13 months. While this learning capacity surely emerges much earlier—at least by 6 months and possibly by birth—Lewis found a significant association between relative speeds of habituation at 12–13 months and intelligence test performance at $3\frac{1}{2}$ years of age. If this correlation is accepted as indicating an expression of existing or actual intelligence in the 12-month-old (Lewis does propose viewing the habituation measure as an index of "cognitive efficiency"), then habituation would appear to be an example of a learning capacity that expresses intelligence at the stage at which the capacity is reaching developmental consolidation.

In the void of empirical data about the direct relations between learning capacities and intelligence in infancy, the variety of reasonable theoretical expectations for the developmental order of learning forms that best express intelligence is a very large variety. The purpose of the present discussion has not been to argue for any particular sequence in which intelligence might be seen to determine, and thus to be expressed in, various forms of early learning. The purpose has been to argue that while few, if any, researchers have been moved to invest energy in studying the relations between an infant's intelligence and his developing learning capacities, this area of study would seem to be a potentially fruitful one for both the practical objective of finding early measures of intelligence and the theoretical objective of charting the early relations between intelligence and the capacity to learn.

Cognitive Processes within Learning

It was said earlier that the expectation of observing a relationship between early learning and intelligence followed from the possibility that early learning would be determined by intelligence, and it was said that that possibility appears to flow directly from the general definitions of the two terms. However, this logical expectancy flows from only one portion of the general definition of intelligence, the portion referring to the dispositional property (or properties) for cognitive adaptation to the individual's experience. The remaining portion of the general definition simply refers to the existing status (in terms of efficiency and quality) of cognitive behavior as opposed to the readiness to adapt or change that behavior as a function of experience. Both portions of the definition were included because they both have historical precedence. However, it is worth noting that Binet did not define intelligence in terms of the capacity for cognitive adaptation, and some researchers have been led to conclude firmly, if not convincingly, that intelligence can not be defined as the ability to learn the kinds of behaviors intelligence tests test (e.g., Simrall, 1947). For the sake of discussion let us assume that a valid conventional definition of intelligence does not include the portion referring to the capacity to adapt cognitive behavior to experience. Could one propose that early learning might yet reveal an infant's existing level of intelligence? The answer would seem to be clearly yes, and it would seem worth considering how this might be so whether or not one seriously contemplates excluding the adaptation portion of the definition of intelligence.

Characteristically studies of conditioning or learning represent the learning process with some single score indicating change in rate or relative probability of the focal behavior. If learning is a unitary process, then it makes good sense to look for the best single score to represent this process. However, if learning is itself the product of some set of component processes, then it is possible that rate or probability of behavior might change while one or more component processes remained unaltered by experience. This point relates to the question whether intelligence is revealed by early learning in that it is possible to conceive of learning being dependent on a component cognitive process that is in some way assessable in the learning situation but that is not necessarily altered by it. Some work by this writer on the component processes of instrumental learning in early infancy can serve to illustrate the form of cognitive-process assessment being considered here. The major point to be made is that while a relatively stable cognitive process may be centrally involved in an act of learning, it is possible that other factors may operate to mask its role and thus to limit the extent to which summary scores of the total learning function can provide a reliable estimate of an underlying cognitive process. As shall be seen, however, less contaminated measures of the component processes may be readily available.

Watson (1966, 1967) has described early instrumental learning as involving "contingency analysis," "contingency memory," and "response recovery." It is proposed that when an infant perceives the occurrence of an interesting event, he will seek to establish the relationship that may exist between that event and some aspect of his behavior.

It is assumed that the event's occurrence will arouse the infant to search his memory records of stimuli and responses under the guidance of a primitive "learning instruction" of the form "find and repeat the response that preceded the occurrence of the interesting stimulus." The effect of making these assumptions is that three separate processes arise as internal to instrumental learning. First, there is the process of memory involving the assumption that an active short-term memory trace of recent stimuli and behavior will fade in time, i.e., the process termed *contingency memory*. Second, there is the process of seeking out the response trace as marked by its temporal relation to the stimulus trace, i.e., the process termed *contingency analysis*. And third, there is a role played in learning by the temporal distribution of the effective behavior, i.e., the *response recovery* process. If the infant had no memory, then no learning could occur. If analysis time were longer than trace storage time, then no learning could occur. And if response recovery did not occur before trace storage had faded, then even if the correct response had been selected from memory, the selection could not be confirmed if it were forgotten by the time the response occurred again.

It is not important that the reader accept this specific three-component model of early instrumental learning. For the sake of the model's illustrative function, it is only important that the reader note that of the three processes proposed in this model only two resemble cognitive acts. The third, speed of response recovery, is a process that one might imagine to be reliably measurable, but neither common sense nor professional experience would lead one to view this motoric variable as representative of what might come under the category of a cognitive process. By contrast, both contingency analysis and contingency memory have the appearance of processes traditionally associated with the cognitive variables assessed by intelligence tests, i.e., analytic thinking and short-term memory. We might suspect that greater intellectual capacity would be composed of quicker and more accurate contingency analysis as well as a more retentive contingency memory. Yet, even if this were so, variation in response recovery time could effectively mask the expression of these cognitive variables in summary learning scores (e.g., rate and asymptote). What is needed in a case like this is some means of measuring the component processes in a manner independent of the criterial measurement of the overall learning.

In the work with the contingency awareness model of early infant learning, a recent methodological development looks promising as regards its potential for assessing individual learning records and providing direct measurement of speed of contingency analysis and temporal length of contingency memory. Watson (1974) analyzed the interresponse times of 8-week-old infants who were exposed to a mobile that turned contingent upon head movement for some infants and feet movement for others. The distributions of interresponse times of rewarded responses were found to deviate from chance expectancy when analyzed in terms of the critical time demarcations of one and seven seconds. The specific time demarcations were originally derived from analysis of grouped data on instrumental eye movements (fixations) of 8- and 12-week-old infants (Watson, 1967). The more recent data are notable because they were obtained with a method that was applied to individual response records and because the statistical assessment was focused on the shape of the distribution of interresponse times, which makes the assessment quite independent of traditional indices of learning as provided by general response rate. Although the work to date has not examined the question of the existence of reliable individual differences in contingency analysis and memory times for infants of a specific age, the new method of interresponse time analysis would seem to open the way for approaching the question of individual differences in the two cognitive variables while bypassing the masking effects of the response recovery variable as the latter affects response rate.

It is too early to tell whether the interresponse time distribution analysis will make a definitive contribution to the examination of the potential link between early instrumental learning and the infant's existing level of intelligence. Nevertheless the example illustrates a form of component analysis of learning that ought to be applied to infant learning before any final conclusions are drawn to the effect that early learning is not determined by an infant's intelligence.

Early Learning as a Determinant of Intelligence

Whether or not an infant's intelligence affects his learning, one may yet ask whether his learning affects his subsequent intelligence. That is, is it the case that learning experiences in infancy play a role in determining an individual's intelligence at some point following the learning? Surely an affirmative answer to this question was implicit within J. B. Watson's claim that he could produce an adult befitting any walk of life if only given the opportunity to manipulate the individual's learning experiences from birth (Watson, 1924). That claim caused a storm of professional debate and a flurry of popular interest that have never really subsided during the course of the subsequent half century. The concern for and credibility of teaching people to be more intelligent have risen sharply, however, since the publication of Hunt's *Intelligence and Experience* (1961). Enrichment programs have proliferated at both the level of small experimental studies (Hess and Bear, 1968; Starr, 1971) and at the level of national demonstration projects (e.g., Head Start, Follow Through, "Sesame Street"). Yet it must be noted that this growth of investment in the proposed learning-determines-intelligence function is a growth that has been nurtured more by faith than by fact. Little more is known today than was known in J. B. Watson's day about how experience might be arranged to increase the intelligence of the average healthy child.

Of course one might remark that it should not be surprising that we have accumulated so little knowledge about affecting the intelligence of the average healthy child, since the average healthy child has rarely been the object of study in experiments or the object of concern in demonstration projects. Rather, effort has been concentrated on the less-than-average—or at least the expected-to-be-less-than-average (e.g., the disadvantaged and the institutionalized). While the social and moral virtue of this specialized effort is unquestionable, it has very likely introduced a special handicap to the effectiveness of the inquiry. It seems obvious that the choice of techniques and material incorporated into most enrichment studies has been guided by the environmental model provided by the surroundings of children judged to be develop- ing in a normal and healthy way, i.e., the middle-class home.

There is an understandable appeal to this modeling procedure when we consider the pragmatic goal of raising the less-than-average up to par. Yet it must be recognized that the procedure leads to replications rather than experiments on environmental effects. The problem with such replications is that whether or not they work, the results will probably make little difference to our understanding of the learning– intelligence relation. For instance, if it could be demonstrated that introducing disadvantaged children to a middle-class environment leads to a normal (i.e., middle-class) distribution of intelligence, we would know little more than we knew to start with concerning the basis of the environmental effect. We would have learned that there is apparently no difference between the disadvantaged and the middle-class child as regards the effect of the middle-class environment on intelligence. We also would have learned that the two environments have different effects on the development of intelligence in disadvantaged children. Yet we already knew that the middle-class environment supported the growth of normal intelligence in the middle-class child. So the only real gain in information about the effect of learning on intelligence would be that something in the way the two environments differ makes a significant difference to the growth of intelligence in the disadvantaged child.

We may engage in *ex post facto* speculation about the dimensions of observed contrast between the two environments that we would guess are the determinative variables for intelligence, but until we can demonstrate that manipulation of these variables can either raise intelligence beyond the middle-class average or depress it below the disadvantaged average (the latter being a study we could not morally engage in), then our grasp of the environmental effect on intelligence would be far from firm. We would be little better than the simple farmer who notices that his corn grows better in field A than in field B. He is wise enough to put all his corn in field A, but he is unable to improve productivity of that field and he has no clear idea why it is better for corn than is field B. It seems fair to say that for all our effort to affect the growth of intelligence over the past 50 years, we have not done much better than the simple farmer has with his corn. When a developmental psychologist is confronted by a young mother who earnestly wants to aid, if possible, the development of her child's mind, even the most ardent of environmentalists can do little more than repeat middle-class child-rearing ideology and thus direct her to our field A.

If our lack of progress in obtaining clear and conclusive evidence about the learning-determines-intelligence function is a surprise to anyone, then it might be an even greater surprise to learn how rarely the subjects of enrichment studies have been infants, i.e., less than 2 years old. Our efforts with school-age and preschool-age children have been bountiful, particularly in the past decade. Infants, however—because of their inaccessibility, their need for individual treatment, or their enigmatic form of humanity—have received only a fraction of the attention given to older children. From either a historical or a theoretical vantage point this lack of attention to infants is rather surprising. Both J. B. Watson and Hunt accentuated the importance of development during infancy. Both carried out empirical studies of infant behavior. However, neither they nor the many researchers influenced by them were moved to invest much energy in the specific task of discovering what (if any) learning experiences in infancy will affect the growth of intelligence.

Considering the pervasive, almost pernicious, interest in intelligence rating in our society and the similar commitment to control in American behavioral psychology, one might well expect to find many experiments on the infant learning-determines-intelligence function. After all, what would it take to carry out a basic study of this type? Randomly assign infants to two groups. Give the infants in one group a special learning experience. Then give a posttest of intelligence, immediate and/or delayed, to both groups. If the experimental group tested statistically significantly higher than the control group, that would be rousing evidence for the effectiveness of the learning experience. Replication of the effect and refinement of controls would be pursued, of course. Yet the basic study would not be insubstantial on its own. So where are these studies? Given the interest in the topic and the simplicity of the basic design of the study, we might expect to uncover a profusion of them in the literature. For some reason, however, they are few and far between. And for the most part those that do exist have either introduced a relatively short (two weeks or less) learning experience (e.g., Schaffer and Emerson, 1968), or like the majority of studies with older children, they have involved the presentation of middle-class experiences to disadvantaged or institutionalized infants (e.g., Rheingold, 1956; Dennis and Sayegh, 1965).

Although there have as yet been no reports of successful attempts to enrich intellectual development in middle-class infants, there have been two impressive experiments with non-middle-class infants that cannot be classified as merely replication studies for the inquiry into the learning-determines-intelligence relation. Both White's work with institutionalized infants (White, 1968, 1969, 1971) and Heber's work with disadvantaged infants (Heber et al., 1971, 1972) reported experimental effects that placed their average experimental subjects beyond the level of cognitive capacity expected at that age in healthy middle-class infants. In a series of experiments, White provided special handling and altered the immediate (crib) environment of infants in an effort to accelerate the development of visual and prehensile skills. The results of this work make it clear that the introduction of various modifications within the first six months of life can appreciably alter the growth of sensorimotor capacity, and it seems that the development of visually directed reaching can be accelerated so that it becomes established at 5 months rather than at 7 months. White argued that visually directed reaching is very possibly the major developmental accomplishment of an infant's first half year, and therefore to advance its arrival by two months is probably a very meaningful advance in cognitive–perceptual life for the infant.

By contrast to the rather specific behavioral acceleration in White's work, Heber reported more general enrichment effects. Disadvantaged infants were given massive amounts of individual attention and educational instruction by a special teacher who was with the infant seven hours per day for five days a week from 3 months of age onward. The Gesell Developmental Schedule was given at 6 months of age and every four months thereafter up to 22 months. On the 18- and 22-month tests, the experimental subjects were performing substantially above age norms, while control subjects performed at the norm for their age. The enrichment program continued for these infants in various ways over the next three years. Periodic tests of intelligence were obtained during this period and the initial enrichment effect was maintained, if not slightly improved upon. At 5 years of age, the experimental group obtained an average IQ score of 118, while the control group's average score was 92.

The White and Heber experiments are both important contributions to the investigation of the learning-determines-intelligence relation, but they are important for different reasons. White's study provides a good example of how the *form* of learning experiences can be structured to effect at least certain aspects of early cognitive–perceptual skill. Although it is not clear how extensively intelligence might be affected by a limited number of relatively specific learning experiences, White's results of specific environmental manipulations provide the welcome beginnings of an articulation in our meager knowledge about the learning-determines-intelligence relation. By contrast, Heber's experiment is perhaps best viewed as an example of how the *intensity* of early learning experiences can be advantageously manipulated. Although it is not clear what aspects of the experiential manipulation were effective, the general effect was so massive (i.e., the resulting IQ scores' being higher than expectable for middle-class children) that the study must stand as inspiration for much further theoretical and empirical work.

What is needed, of course, is a series of studies as precise as White's in their experiential manipulation, as powerful as Heber's in their experimental effects, and then as generalizable to the middle-class as to the disadvantaged or institutionalized infant. Fowler (1972) made what is perhaps the clearest effort to date to fill this need. However, because of an unfortunate sampling distribution in his small samples of advantaged and disadvantaged infants, it is impossible to tell whether his intensive program of cognitive enrichment administered to experimental groups led to significantly greater gains in intelligence scores over the gains observed in control groups.

Moreover, if we ever wish to examine the causal connection between early learning and later intelligence, we have to separate the criteria for the cause from the criteria for the effect. As it is, the definitions of intelligence and learning allow for the possibility that the dispositional property whose change serves as the criterion of learning is a cognitive capacity whose change is simultaneously serving as the criterion of a change in intelligence. Surely we can imagine that the same environmental exposure will result in different amounts of learning for different individuals. If learning is a cause of change in intelligence, then the amount of learning should be related to the amount of change in intelligence. But if the same disposition is taken to serve as evidence of both the learning and the change in intelligence, then a test of the relation between the two is impossible because there is no freedom for the relation to be less than perfect. What is required, of course, is a separation of criteria either by content or by time. Without that we have, at best, evidence that change in intelligence is related to the opportunity for learning. Most existing studies, including White's, Heber's, and Fowler's, suffer this limitation. The problem is that a situation offering an opportunity for learning may offer other things as well, e.g., emotional arousal. There are already many nonexperimental (i.e., correlational) studies that imply that early learning is a positive influence on the development of intelligence (e.g., see the reviews by Hunt, 1961, and White, 1971). If experimental studies of the early learning-intelligence relation are to take full advantage of their potential to sort out cause and effect, then they will have to incorporate separate measures of learning and intelligence. When and if that is accomplished, we would not only know how to arrange enriching environments for infants, we would very likely have generated the basis for a far more differentiated picture of the learning-determines-intelligence function.

Early Learning as a Means for Predicting Intelligence

It is conceivable that infant learning is neither a cause nor an effect of intelligence but that it yet may provide a useful predictive relationship to future individual differences in intelligence. Learning might simply "expose" individual differences in intelligence that were not visible in its absence. This distinction between learning-exposes-intelligence and the previously discussed learning-determines-intelligence or intelligence-determines-learning is not immediately obvious. In an effort to draw this distinction most simply and clearly, it is helpful to consider a hypothetical analogy from the domain of motor development. There is no intention of implying any meaningful relationship between the development of motor and intellective capacities. The point to be made is strictly limited to the conceptual level as regards the development of *any* capacity (i.e., dispositional property). The analogy will be followed quickly by a consideration of some real and potentially relevant data.

Let us assume that we are interested in the development of the capacity for throwing a ball, specifically the capacity to throw it fast. Further assume that we and our friends in professional baseball are aware of the following hypothetical facts: (1) neither periodic nor prolonged training in childhood has any appreciable effect on the average speed with which adults are capable of throwing a baseball; (2) when tested in a situation in which they are enticed to throw a baseball, adults throw it with an average speed of 50 mph (sd= 10 mph); (3) when tested in a situation in which they are enticed to throw a golf ball, 18-month-old infants throw it with an average speed of 15 mph ($sd = 5$ mph); and (4) the correlation between throwing capacity at 18 months and adulthood is $r = 0.10$. We can imagine that this very modest association of capacity at the two ages might have some theoretical interest to physical anthropologists, but it would surely be of little interest to our practical-minded friends in professional baseball.

Now assume that we decide to introduce a short-term training program prior to testing. The training consists of practice trials interspersed with exposure to a model who illustrates efficient foot and leg movements and oppositional arm action. When the subject reaches asymptotic performance, the test situation is presented. It is conceivable that the following facts might emerge: (1) it is still true that neither periodic nor prolonged training in childhood has any effect on the average speed with which adults are capable of throwing a baseball; but immediately following a training program, (2) 18-month-olds throw the golf ball with an average speed of 20 mph (sd = 5 mph) and (3) adults throw the baseball with an average speed of 55 mph (sd = 10 mph); (4) the correlation between the capacity to throw the ball before versus immediately following the training program is r = 0.20 for 18-month-olds and r = 0.90 for adults; and most notably (5) the correlation between throwing capacity following training at 18 months and throwing capacity in adulthood, with or without training, is r = 0.70. These new facts would be of additional theoretical interest for researchers focused on the development of physical capacities. And it is easy to imagine that those people who are interested in improving the quality of professional baseball would be very excited about the new-found predictive relationship between throwing capacity at 18 months and adult capacity. Even though childhood training would not be expected to affect later throwing capacity, the predictive power of 18-month-old capacity would yet be a fact having significant practical value. It could be used to select those children to whom special attention might be given to encourage an interest in the sport and for whom it might be most fruitful to provide special training in other capacities that are required by the sport, e.g., fielding and batting.

One might explain the predictive power of the posttraining capacity at 18 months by proposing that the test score following training reflects the capacity of the individual to learn to throw a ball. The ability to throw a ball at any age could be assumed to depend on past learning, and so the posttraining score at 18 months predicts the adult capacity to throw (with or without training) because it distinguishes between individuals who are versus those who are not likely to learn to throw well over the course of experience between 18 months and adulthood. However, in the present hypothetical example there is strong evidence that adult capacity to throw is not appreciably affected by learning, in as much as neither periodic nor prolonged training in childhood affects adult capacity.

There is an alternative explanation of the predictive power of the posttraining capacity at 18 months that is more consistent with all the facts at hand. One might propose that the capacity to throw a ball at any age is dependent on both experience in throwing and physical characteristics (e.g., skeletal, neurological, and muscular) that are largely governed by an individual's genetic and maturational status. With a modest and yet critical amount of experience the differences between individual levels of capacity are almost totally accountable in terms of differences in genetic and maturational status. Yet with less than the critical level of experience, differences in capacity might be predominantly accountable in terms of the amounts of experience individuals did have.

One may further assume that if the probability of certain experiences is relatively constant in an individual's environment, then his likelihood of having been exposed to some minimal level of these experiences will increase as time passes (i.e., as he ages). Now if early physical status were correlated with adult physical status, then the assumptions made so far would lead to an expectancy that (1) capacity in ball throwing would be more closely associated with physical status in adulthood than it is in early childhood because of the adult's greater likelihood of having been exposed to the critical level of experience, and (2) the provision of training prior to the assessing of capacity in childhood should increase the predictive relation between childhood capacity and adult capacity, since it would increase the extent to which physical status would be a major factor in the accounting of individual differences in childhood capacity. This explanation would be consistent with the facts that average capacity changes by a large amount with age and yet is little affected by periodic or prolonged training in childhood. The large age differences are attributed to maturation. It should also be noted that there would be nothing mysterious about the fact that training 18-month-olds has a large effect on the predictive correlation while it has only a small effect on the average level of capacity at that age. The situation would be one in which the training affects the distribution around the mean by affecting the performance of some individuals more than the performance of others, though not affecting any individuals very much. In terms of this hypothetical example, then, the distribution of capacity following training at 18 months is more closely aligned with the distribution of adult capacity than is capacity prior to training at 18 months.

One way of labeling this distinction between capacity prior to and following short-term training is to call the former *manifest capacity* and the latter *latent capacity*. Each is a dispositional property statement about the existing status of an individual, and thus each is a form of what Baldwin (1958) termed "actual capacity." Furthermore each is to be distinguished from future states of capacity such as Baldwin's "potential

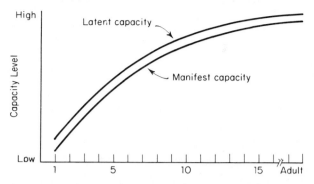

FIG. 1. Hypothetical growth curves of manifest and latent capacity illustrating case of parallel growth.

capacity," which refers to the maximal capacity that the individual has the possibility of attaining in the future. Figure 1 presents a hypothetical graph illustrating a simple and parallel age change in the mean values of manifest and latent capacity. Figure 2 presents a more complicated and nonparallel age change in the two forms of existing capacity. One can imagine that the differences in the relations illustrated in Figure 1 and Figure 2 might exemplify the contrast in growth functions of separate types of behavioral capacity (e.g., ball throwing versus memory for digits), or the difference between Figure 1 and Figure 2 might exemplify the contrast in growth functions arising for a single type of behavioral

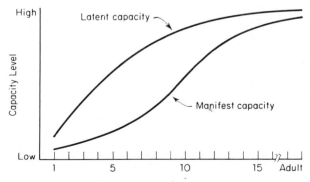

FIG. 2. Hypothetical growth curves of manifest and latent capacity illustrating case of nonparallel growth.

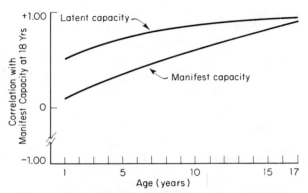

FIG. 3. Hypothetical graph of correlations of both manifest and latent capacity at successive ages with manifest capacity at 18 years.

capacity as this develops in two quite different environments (e.g., middle versus lower socioeconomic class). Figure 3 illustrates the contrast that could conceivably exist between the predictive validities of the correlations between manifest capacity in adulthood (defined as 18 years or older) and the two measures of capacity at earlier ages.

Returning to the example of ball throwing, it should be clear that the learning experience involved in the assessment of latent capacity would not be viewed as either a cause or an effect of the future level of manifest capacity, nor would it be viewed as a cause or an effect of the association between the present state of latent capacity and the future state of manifest capacity. The role of the short-term training seems best described as one of exposing the association between present and future capacity. Surely the difference in performance observed prior to, versus following, training is attributable to learning during the training procedure, but one would not contend that the difference in predictive validity of manifest versus latent capacity is itself an effect of learning—at least not in the sense as we normally use the term *learning*. We would say a subject learned his new level of behavior (e.g., he learned to throw a ball at 26 mph), but we would not say that he learned the new level of predictive validity (e.g., he learned to display a closer association between his present and his future capacity to throw a ball relative to the capacities of other children). Indeed we have no way to conceive of how such a thing could be learned!

How does this hypothetical example help us understand real-world relationships between learning and intelligence? If it helps, it does so by illustrating a potential relationship between infant learning and future intelligence, which is neither of the form intelligence-determines-learning nor of the form learning-determines-intelligence. In an analogy with the motor capacity example, early learning may simply provide a means of exposing underlying (i.e., latent) differences in intellectual capacity that happen to have a greater developmental stability than those differences in intellectual capacity that are visible without the provision of a special learning experience. It is interesting to note that while the developers of intelligence tests have long been concerned with the possibility of contaminating effects that might be introduced by experience in the taking of an intelligence test (Anastasi, 1958), the fact that individuals will improve with experience has not been closely examined for its potential use in improving the predictive validity of early test scores.

This writer could find no evidence that learning has ever been put to use as an "exposing agent" in the attempt to predict adult intelligence from measures of infant intelligence. However, the previously mentioned study by Simrall (1947) provides some relevant data, although it is neither a study of infants nor a study of predictive relations between early and adult intelligence measures. Recall that Simrall provided high school children training on intelligence test behavior and found that their gains in performance were unrelated to their pretraining scores. She concluded from this fact that the performance gain (i.e., the learning) was unrelated to intelligence (i.e., the original performance scores). But we may conclude something quite different. We may conclude that the predictive value of the new performance (original performance plus gain) can be very different from the original performance. Had the gains been perfectly correlated with the original scores, then addition of the gains to the original scores would not appreciably change the predictive value of the sum score from that of the original. If intelligence test performance gains are as independent of original scores in infancy as they are in older children (and we have no reason to believe that they would not be), then the stage is clearly set for looking at the potential interplay of latent intelligence in infancy and intelligence test performance in later years. Whether one's concerns are with the practical problems of prediction or with the theoretical implications of dispositional continuity, one thing seems clear at the start. Any attempt to assess latent intelligence in infancy should be encouraged by the fact that it has little chance of uncovering lower associations between intellectual capacity in infancy and adulthood than have to date been obtained with existing tests of manifest infant intelligence (e.g., Bayley, 1970).

Summary and Conclusions

In this chapter we have considered the potential relation between early learning and intelligence in terms of three specific forms that the relation might take: intelligence-determines-learning, learning-determines-intelligence, and learning-exposes-intelligence. We have considered these three forms separately, but of course it is quite possible that two or more forms may coexist and even interact with one another. For example, intelligence may determine learning, which in turn determines subsequent intelligence. However, before much energy is spent on working through the potential interweavings of these forms, it should be clear that we should first invest sufficient energy in establishing the existence of a substantial fabric for any of these forms. Earlier, more general reviews have noted with some astonishment just how little we know about the relation of learning and intelligence (Stevenson, 1970; White, 1971). When one limits one's sight to infancy, the extent of our knowledge is shrunk nearly to nil. Thus to a large extent this chapter has been an exercise in differentiating an empirical vacuum. If there is any merit to such an exercise, it is perhaps that in dividing a problem we may reduce our reluctance to attack it.

References

Anastasi, A., 1958, "Differential Psychology" (3rd ed.), Macmillan, New York.

Armstrong, D. A., 1968, "A Materialist Theory of the Mind," Humanities Press, New York.

Baldwin, A. L., 1958, The role of an "ability" construct in a theory of behavior, in "Talent and Society," D. C. McClelland, A. L. Baldwin, U. Bronfenbrenner, and F. L. Strodtbeck (eds.), D. Van Nostrand, Princeton, New Jersey.

Bayley, N., 1970, Development of mental abilities, in "Carmichael's Manual of Child Psychology" (3rd ed.), Vol. 1, P. H. Mussen (ed.), Wiley, New York.

Brackbill, Y., and Koltsova, M. M., 1967, Conditioning and learning, in "Infancy and Early Childhood," Y. Brackbill (ed.), Free Press, New York.

CARNAP, R., 1938, Logical foundations of the unity of science, *in* "International Encyclopedia of Unified Science," Vol. 1, Part 1, University of Chicago Press, Chicago.

DENNIS, W., AND SAYEGH, Y., 1965, The effect of supplementary experiences upon the behavioral development of infants in institutions, *Child Development*, 36:81.

DUNCANSON, J. P., 1964, "Intelligence and the Ability to Learn," Educational Testing Service, Princeton, New Jersey.

FITZGERALD, H. E., AND PORGES, S. W., 1971, A decade of infant conditioning and learning research, *Merrill–Palmer Quarterly*, 17:79.

FOWLER, W., 1972, A developmental learning approach to infant care in a group setting, *Merrill–Palmer Quarterly*, 18:145.

GAGNÉ, R. M., 1965, "The Conditions of Learning," Holt, Rinehart, and Winston, New York.

GARRETT, H. E., 1928, The relation of tests of memory and learning to each other and to general intelligence in a highly selected adult group, *Journal of Educational Psychology*, 19:601.

GARRISON, K. C., 1928, The correlation between intelligence test scores and success in certain rational organization problems, *Journal of Applied Psychology*, 12:621.

HEBER, R. D., GARBER, H., HARRINGTON, S., AND HOFFMAN, C., 1971 and 1972, Rehabilitation of families at risk for mental retardation, unpublished progress reports, Research and Training Center, University of Wisconsin, Madison, as cited in Mussen, Conger, and Kagan, 1974, p. 352.

HEIDER, F., 1958, "The Psychology of Interpersonal Relations," Wiley, New York.

HESS, R. D., AND BEAR, R. M. (eds.), 1968, "Early Education," Aldine, Chicago.

HUNT, J. McV., 1961, "Intelligence and Experience," Ronald, New York.

HUSBAND, R. W., 1941, Intercorrelations among learning abilities, III: The effects of age and spread of intelligence upon relationships, *Journal of Genetic Psychology*, 58:431.

LEWIS, M., 1969, A developmental study of information processing within the first three years of life: Response decrement to a redundant signal, *Monographs of the Society for Research in Child Development*, 34(9).

LEWIS, M., 1971, Individual differences in the measurement of early cognitive growth, *in* "Exceptional Infant," Vol. 2, J. Hellmuth (ed.), Brunner/Mazel, New York.

LIPSITT, L. P., 1963, Learning in the first year of life, *in* "Advances in Child Development and Behavior," Vol. 1, L. P. Lipsitt and C. C. Spiker (eds.), Academic Press, New York.

LIPSITT, L. P., 1969, Learning capacities of the human infant, *in* "Brain and Early Behavior," R. J. Robinson (ed.), Academic Press, New York.

MacCORQUODALE, K., AND MEEHL, P. E., 1948, Hypothetical constructs and intervening variables, *Psychological Review*, 55:95.

McCALL, R. B., HOGARTY, P. S., AND HURLBURT, N., 1972, Transitions in infant sensori-motor development and the prediction of childhood I.Q., *American Psychologist*, 27:728.

MUSSEN, P. H., CONGER, J. J., AND KAGAN, J., 1974, "Child Development and Personality" (4th ed.), Harper & Row, New York.

PIAGET, J., 1952, "The Origins of Intelligence in Children," International Universities Press, New York.

RHEINGOLD, H. L., 1956, The modification of social responsiveness in institutionalized babies, *Monographs of the Society for Research in Child Development*, 21(2).

RYLE, G., 1949, "The Concept of Mind," Barnes and Noble, New York.

SAMEROFF, A. J., 1971, Can conditioned responses be established in the new-born infant? *Developmental Psychology*, 5:1.

SCHAFFER, H. R., 1973, The multivariate approach to early learning, in "Constraints on Learning: Limitations and Predispositions," R. H. Hinde and J. Stevenson-Hinde (eds.), Academic Press, London.

SCHAFFER, H. R., AND EMERSON, P. E., 1968, The effects of experimentally administered stimulation on developmental quotients of infants, British Journal of Social and Clinical Psychology, 7:61.

SIMRALL, D., 1947, Intelligence and the ability to learn, Journal of Psychology, 23:27.

STAKE, R. E., 1961, Learning parameters, aptitudes, and achievements, Psychometric Monographs, (9).

STARR, R., 1971, Cognitive development in infancy: Assessment, acceleration, actualization, Merrill–Palmer Quarterly, 17:153.

STEVENSON, H. W., 1970, Learning in children, in "Carmichael's Manual of Child Psychology" (3rd ed.), Vol. 1, P. H. Mussen (ed.), Wiley, New York.

STEVENSON, H. W., HALE, G. A., KLEIN, R. E., AND MILLER, L. K., 1968, Interrelations and correlates in children's learning and problem solving, Monographs of the Society for Research in Child Development, 33(7).

STEVENSON, H. W., AND ODOM, R. D., 1965, Interrelationships in children's learning, Child Development, 36:7.

WATSON, J. B., 1924, "Behaviorism" (rev. ed., 1930), Norton, New York.

WATSON, J. S., 1966, The development and generalization of "contingency awareness" in early infancy: Some hypotheses, Merrill–Palmer Quarterly, 12:123.

WATSON, J. S., 1967, Memory and "contingency analysis" in infant learning, Merrill–Palmer Quarterly, 13:55.

WATSON, J. S., 1974, Early infant learning: Some roles and measures of memory, thinking, and trying, paper presented at Annual Meeting of the British Psychological Society, Bangor, North Wales.

WEISSMAN, D., 1965, "Dispositional Properties," Southern Illinois University Press, Carbondale.

WHITE, B. L., 1968, Informal education during the first months of life, in "Early Education," R. D. Hess and R. M. Bear (eds.), Aldine, Chicago.

WHITE, B. L., 1969, Child development research: an edifice without a foundation, Merrill–Palmer Quarterly, 15:50.

WHITE, B. L., 1971, "Human Infants: Experience and Psychological Development," Prentice-Hall, Englewood Cliffs, New Jersey.

8 Environmental Risk in Fetal and Neonatal Life and Measured Infant Intelligence*

JANE V. HUNT

The fetus and neonate may be exposed to a variety of exogenous influences that are potentially damaging to the brain during the time that brain growth and differentiation are most rapid. The major categories of insult are the introduction of neurotoxins into the body, the withholding of essential nutrients, and the disruption of the mechanisms of oxygen and carbon dioxide exchange. These are environmental to the extent that they are caused or controlled by environmental manipulation. At the level of cell metabolism these environmental influences may not be mutually exclusive and may be interdependent. Brain systems undergoing active organization are most vulnerable to damage from adverse conditions such as malnutrition (McKhann et al., 1973) and anoxia (Sumi et al., 1973), suggesting not only that the effects of an insult may be more intense when it is encountered in early life but also that the specific time of encounter may influence the precise nature of these effects.

The developmental consequences of early insult and the complex interaction of morphological, histochemical, and behavioral effects may be studied systematically for subhuman species to explore the corre-

* Data for this discussion were generously provided by Dr. William H. Tooley, Professor of Pediatrics and Director of the Neonatal Follow-up Clinic at the University of California at San Francisco. (Study supported by the National Heart and Lung Institute, Grant # HLO 14201.)

JANE V. HUNT·University of California at Berkeley.

spondence between brain and behavior (Rosenzweig, 1971; Quimby *et al.*, 1974). Such direct relations are difficult to document for the human infant except in extreme situations leading to early death. It has been suggested that behavioral studies can stand alone and are currently perhaps more productive in delineating the range of effects on human development (Escalona, 1974).

The developing infant demonstrates behaviors that we associate with human intelligence (although many of them may also be noted in other primates), such as visual following, smiling and vocalizing to a social approach, and reaching for objects. The behaviors indicate an awareness of ongoing events and demonstrate the integration of behavior to produce a directed, purposeful response. The specific behaviors we can observe in any infant depend upon the level of awareness reached and also upon the development of other abilities, such as motor control, not usually considered directly related to intelligence. Standard assessments of infant mental development, such as those of Bayley (1969), Gesell (Gesell and Amatruda, 1947), and Cattell (1940), provide empirical evidence for a sequence of observable behaviors in infancy, with both the order and the timing of these behaviors being predictable within limits. These tests are designed to define normal limits and to measure individual differences. Appropriate use as a standardized measure of mental development assumes that the infant observed is not physically handicapped, e.g., blind or palsied.

The rapid pace and predictable sequence of mental development during the first two years permits a sensitive monitoring of both depressed function and delayed organization of behavior. The theoretical importance of these early behavioral deviancies lies in their relevance to the growth and expression of intelligence in later life. Developmental delays in infancy are frequently associated with later deficiencies in intellectual functioning (Werner *et al.*, 1968; Drillien, 1964; Hunt *et al.*, 1974; Holden, 1972). The finding of a similar correspondence between early developmental lags and later learning deficits in monkeys asphyxiated at birth (Sechzer *et al.*, 1971) suggests the possibility of controlled studies of the developmental sequelae of specific insult. Nevertheless unique aspects of human experience and intelligence require direct study to determine the full consequences of adverse events.

The demonstration of an association between human infant development and later intellectual attainment is complicated by the mediating effects of later environment on the growth and differentiation of the brain beyond infancy (Drillien, 1961; Knobloch and Pasamanick, 1963; Willerman *et al.*, 1970). Except in cases of devastating damage to brain structures in infancy, these mediating effects are expected to be potent and, often, controlling. However, these same mechanisms of biological and environmental interaction are operating in infancy, the period of most rapid behavioral change. The observation of transient or delayed behavioral effects in infancy in response to perinatal events suggests such interaction. Studies in infant development may, then, provide a model for the study of long-term consequences of early events and may suggest the patterns of biological and environmental influence on intelligence. Also, studies of infant outcome, whether or not they are predictive, and precisely because they do not reflect the total long-term effects of environmental differences, may be the most appropriate way of determining some direct relations between biological insult and behavior.

OVERVIEW OF RESEARCH METHODS AND STRATEGIES

Studies of naturally occurring risk factors and subsequent infant development rarely demonstrate cause and effect because of the difficulty of manipulating or controlling all relevant variables. Risk factors may be difficult to quantify or to pinpoint in time, and they may be confounded or interrelated. Environmental variables in infancy that alter the course of normal development may also be operative for infants previously exposed to risk. Traits observed in normal neonates interact with the environment to influence developmental tendencies, and similar effects may be found in suspect or damaged neonates. Research that examines the relations between infant status and prior adverse events is enhanced by a model that incorporates these considerations of the intensity, duration, and timing of the insult, concurrent risk factors, neonatal status, and environmental variables in infancy.

If one is to study the consequences of risk factors for infant development the sample must be drawn from a population for whom the relevant fetal and neonatal data have been documented, and the infants must be identified soon after birth for developmental testing. The testing requirement virtually eliminates retrospective studies as a model because routine mental testing of infants is not common, as it is for school-aged children. To define the sample, one of three general methods is used, although there are a number of variations within each model. These are (1) the large, prospective study of a normal population to identify the small, but predictable, abnormal group within it; (2) the study of a discrete population defined by a specific etiological factor thought to be relevant for subsequent development; and (3) the sample defined by the neonatal risk status of the infant. All of these methods are also used to examine outcome in childhood, and indeed this has been the primary concern of many studies. The interested reader is referred to recent reviews in Jordan (1971) and Broman et al., (1975) and to reviews by McKeown and Record (1971) and Sameroff and Chandler (1975).

The Large Prospective Study

Longitudinal studies of normal populations have been instituted both in this country and abroad in an effort to relate a number of perinatal variables to intellectual outcome. These studies do not usually focus attention on outcome in infancy, even though infant status may have been assessed, because of a greater interest in outcome at childhood.

One example of the prospective study is the Collaborative Project for the study of cerebral palsy, mental retardation, and other neurological and sensory disorders of children. This project enrolled 44,000 pregnant women between 1959 and 1965 and followed one or more pregnancies and the development of the children born to these women through the combined efforts of thirteen selected medical institutions in the United States (Mendelson, 1967; Broman et al., 1975). Status in infancy was assessed at 8 months of age with an early research version of the Bayley Scales of Infant Development. Infant status was considered for the first 20,000 pregnancies in a report by Berendes (1964), who noted a relation between abnormal outcome at 8 months and obstetrical factors of placenta previa, abruptio placentae, and cord complications, and also a relation between abnormal outcome and gestational age, maternal age, and maternal education. The close association between gestational age and mental test score at 8 months is due, in large part, to the fact that test scores were not adjusted for prematurity. A comparison of Bayley mental scale performance and the one-year neurological examination for infants with gestational ages at or below 35 weeks indicates a considerably larger percentage of abnormal scores on the developmental scale. Because the obstetrical complications of placenta previa and abruptio are associated with prematurity, these factors are confounded. Cord complication, more common in the full-term infant, was examined in relation to birth weight. For the infants of low birth weight (2001–2400 g) the importance of tight cord loops was demonstrated for the one-year neurological examination but lost much of its significance for the 8-month developmental score because of the high incidence of abnormal scores for this weight group in the nonaffected population. Cord complications appeared to be only slightly related, if at all, to abnormal outcome for the group with birth weight at or above 2501 g. The author pointed out, "it is incumbent on us to sort out the effects of a complication from the effects of the prematurity that stems from the complication" (Berendes, 1964, p. 314).

In a subsequent analysis of data from the Collaborative Study (Churchill and Berendes, 1969) the offspring of 116 diabetic mothers were found to differ significantly from controls in Bayley mental and motor scale scores at 8 months and in Binet IQs at 4 years of age. A further comparison within the diabetic group also yielded significant score differences on these measures when mothers who did or did not evidence acetonuria in the last trimester of pregnancy were compared. The incidence of prematurity was greater for the diabetic group than for the matched controls and for the acetone-positive diabetics when compared with the acetone-negative group. To control for prematurity, comparisons were restricted to those pairs in which the acetone-positive diabetic member had a gestational age equal to or greater than the nondiabetic control ($N = 20$). The differences in Bayley test performance (mental and motor) were greatly reduced and no longer significant; however, the IQ differences at age 4 years remained significant for this small group, suggesting the possibility of a delayed effect on mental abilities.

A large prospective study of a normal population is the Kauai Pregnancy Study (Yerushalmy et al., 1956; French et al., 1958), which located and followed the 3000 pregnancies and subsequent offspring of virtually all the pregnant women living on the Hawaiian island of Kauai in 1954–1955. The children were followed longitudinally into school age (Werner et al., 1971). The Cattell Infant Intelligence Scale was administered at 20 months of age. A clinical rating of adverse factors in the fetal, antenatal, and neonatal periods was made by pediatricians who first scored the severity of some 60 selected complications or events that could occur and then gave an overall perinatal stress rating (none, mild, moderate, or severe) to each infant. In general, the value of the overall score corresponded to the value assigned to the most severe condition present. Statistically significant differences in mean Cattell IQs were found among the four perinatal stress groups. When the proportion of children with IQs under 85 was examined, it was found to be more than doubled for the group with severe complications when compared to the group with none. The stability of prediction from 20 months to IQ at age 10 years was examined for this group (Werner *et al.*, 1968) and found to be high for those who tested below IQ 80 at 20 months. In contrast to all other severe handicaps, only one infant of the nine judged to be severely mentally handicapped (IQ below 70), but with no physical problem, was recognized prior to the special testing of the study at age 20 months.

Because the Kauai study encompassed an entire population of a community, the demographic data are pertinent. For this sample, 56% were free of prenatal and perinatal complications, 31% had mild complications, 10% were rated moderate, and 3% were in the severe category. For those who survived to age 2 years, no sex differences were noted in the incidence of perinatal complications by degree of severity, nor was there an influence by ethnic group, age of mother, socioeconomic status, or mother's intelligence. Easy access to medical care was considered to be the significant factor in eliminating socioeconomic factors from perinatal complications. Low birth weight (below 2500 g) was more frequently encountered—and less likely to present developmental problems than anticipated—in this racially mixed population. More than half of these small infants required no special neonatal care. Postmaturity (gestational age of 42 weeks or more), as judged by the menstrual dates of the mothers, was not found to increase the likelihood of IQ below 80 at 20 months or any other unfavorable outcome.

Prospective studies are necessarily limited in their potential to relate specific perinatal events to outcome in infancy because of the low incidence of any specific event in a largely normal sample of births. The perinatal stress rating used in the Kauai study suggests a method of grouping the kinds and intensities of perinatal insult and emphasizes the importance of considering the interaction of a number of perinatal problems. The enormous data pool of the Collaborative Project allows for continuing evaluations of specific groups, as demonstrated by the study of infants with diabetic mothers. These prospective studies also provide useful demographic data on the expected incidence and relative influence of a class of insults on a larger segment of society. They can answer questions concerning the relative importance of a range of biological and environmental variables to the incidence of handicap in a population.

Studies of Specific Risk Factors

The environmental variables suspected of causing damage in prenatal and perinatal life can be defined in such a way as to provide either a greater or a lesser correspondence to their specific effects on brain physiology. The indirect factors that can be related to behavioral effects may be difficult to interpret but may point the way for more specific investigations. Examples include the effects of closely spaced pregnancies; twinning; geographical, seasonal, and secular variations; and maternal social class, age and parity. Although these general factors will not be discussed in detail, their importance is recognized. The interested reader is referred to a more comprehensive review of studies of prenatal environment by Ferreria (1969).

Difficulties in interpretation are illustrated in a review of research related to the development of twins by McKeown and Record (1971). They point out that estimates and interpretations of the correspondence in twin intelligence differ widely, as do the observed differences between twins and single births. Although the lower IQs found for twins in comparison with singleton siblings are widely interpreted as being accounted for by risk factors associated with twin pregnancies and deliveries (cf., Holley and Churchill, 1969), Record et al., (1970) presented evidence that this may not be the case. They examined data for 148 twins who were raised as singletons because of the fetal or neonatal death of the co-twin and found that their IQ was comparable to that of singleton siblings. They concluded that the lower IQ usually associated with twinning is determined largely by postnatal environmental effects. Similarly the interpretation of results indicating lower IQ in children of mothers with shorter intervals between pregnancies may be interpreted as confounded with social class, as reflecting nutritional inadequacies in the mother, or as reflecting the same social effect as noted for twins. Holley et al., (1969) compared the intelligence of children of closely spaced pregnancies with a control group in a longitudinal sample that was controlled for the socioeconomic characteristics of the families. They found lower means for the experimental group in Bayley mental scale scores at 8 months and in IQ at age 4 years. They concluded that although the environmental effect of a close-aged sibling might be controlling development by 8 months, the findings of lower birth weight not attributable to gestational age in the closely spaced group and a higher incidence of neurological abnormalities at 1 year of age suggest the importance of biological influences.

An intermediate group of variables can be specified, but the exact timing and severity of the insult to the fetus and neonate are often difficult to determine. Included in this category are maternal malnutrition and drug addiction. The more direct factors often have the advantage of greater specificity in relation to physiological mechanisms and permit more precision in describing the parameters of timing and intensity. They can be replicated and can be extended, through studies of lower animals, to their neuroanatomical correlates in mammalian and primate development. Examples are drugs of labor and delivery and neonatal hypoxia and hyperoxia.

Even when the timing and intensity of exposure to a specific insult are determined with some confidence, it is difficult to establish causality. A particular insult can be demonstrated to have a significant relation to outcome, but there are almost always exceptions to the effect that suggest multiple factors interacting in its expression. A dramatic example, although unrelated to intelligence, is the effect of thalidomide taken during the first trimester of pregnancy. The teratogenic effects of this drug are well publicized. Less well known is the finding, according to Apgar (1964), that 80% of the mothers who took thalidomide during early pregnancy had normal babies. It is presumed that either genetic or environmental factors, or both, operated to produce the difference in outcome. When investigating the more general environmental effects on infant development, one is aware of the need for eventual reduction or explanation of these effects, ultimately in biological terms (cf., Montague, 1971). In the more specific studies there is an equal need to question the possibility of attendant, correlated variables and to look for interaction effects.

Drugs of Labor and Delivery

The effects on the fetus and neonate of maternal and fetal exposure to drugs during pregnancy is reviewed by Bowes *et al.* (1970) and Kelsey

(1973). Bowes *et al.* concluded, "The proven untoward influences are relatively few, in view of the great number of drugs taken by or given to pregnant women" (p. 23). Although obvious fetal and neonatal problems may not be evident, there remains the possibility of more subtle effects on neonatal behavior and on developmental rates in infancy. Some methodological problems in evaluating the effects of drugs used during labor and delivery on newborn infant behavior were considered by Kraemer *et al.* (1972). They report the results of a survey of obstetrical drug management and of two neonatal studies for a population ($N = 156$) all delivered at the same hospital. The authors reported interaction effects among parity, length of labor, and drug use during labor and delivery and concluded that all may simultaneously affect some parameters of neonatal behavior. The authors pointed out that parity and length of labor may influence decisions made regarding drug use and also that some drugs may prolong labor. They concluded that because drug decisions are not random and not without effect on other variables, data should be analyzed to allow for the associated factors.

An illustrative study of drug effects on infant intelligence is that of Conway and Brackbill (1970). They compared the behavior of small groups of clinically normal, full-term infants delivered to mothers who had received no anesthesia during delivery, local anesthesia, or general (inhalation) anesthesia. Selection of subjects was distributed among the patients of obstetricians known to prefer one of these three treatment procedures. Neonatal evaluation measures included the administration of the Graham scale (Graham, 1956) and a measure of habituation to an auditory orienting response; the research version of the Bayley scales was administered at 4 weeks of age. A rating of the potency of total medication used during labor and delivery was made by two independent obstetricians, who considered the use of analgesics and tranquilizers as well as anesthetics of delivery. For the 17 infants tested on the Bayley scales at 4 weeks the correlation between the potency of medication and mental scale scores was not significant but was suggestive, and potency was significantly correlated with the motor test scores and with the neonatal habituation measure. When analgesic dosage was controlled, some differences were seen that appeared to favor the group exposed to less anesthetic, although the groups being compared were very small. There were no significant correlations among the ratings of medication level and length of labor, birth weight, maternal age, or parents' education and income. The Bayley scales and the habituation measure were readministered at age 20 weeks to 15 infants. The Bayley scores no longer showed the directional trends they did at 4 weeks, although there were some apparent effects remaining in habituation rate. The authors conceded the need for a larger study.

A subsequent study included 44 infants (Brackbill *et al.*, 1974). All shared common normal features of pregnancy, delivery, and neonatal health. For 25 of the infants the type and dose of delivery anesthetic was constant and the independent variable was a commonly used analgesic (meperidine). The other 19 infants were those whose mothers had received a variety of kinds and levels of anesthetics and analgesics. As in the earlier study the independent variable was the score of potency of medication. For both groups behavioral results were not related to maternal age, parity, forceps usage, type of feeding, birth weight, gestational age, or time to first inspiration. The habituation response obtained during the first few days of life was significantly correlated with the use of meperidine, including parameters of dose level and time of administration during labor, and also with the premedication potency score. Similar neonatal effects of anesthesia were demonstrated by Moreau and Birch (1974), but the duration of these short-term effects was not reported.

Neonatal Hypoxia and Hyperoxia

The adjustment of the newborn infant to an extrauterine environment poses a variety of threats to the maintenance of physiological homeostasis. Sudden demands are superimposed on an organism that has been making continuous adjustments during fetal life and that may have been just previously stressed by experiences related to the birth process. The factors of functional maturity and perinatal stress influence newborn adaptation and also represent potential independent sources of insult. One threat that has been recognized in medical literature for more than a century is oxygen deprivation, particularly as it is encountered in perinatal and neonatal life.

Measures of oxygen deprivation preceding birth are often inferential, based on indications of fetal distress and the condition of the infant immediately following birth. The assessment of blood oxygen levels from the umbilical cord and the fetal scalp have assisted in determining the extent of perinatal hypoxia. Neonatal blood oxygen levels are determined by implanted catheters, a procedure that may be accomplished immediately after birth, or by other blood-sampling techniques. For the neonate, then, the duration and extent of oxygen deprivation need not be inferential except for the inference that the measured blood values reflect related values in brain tissues. This assumption may be confounded by other physiological events that can affect oxygen transport to the brain and also by the presence of oxygen antagonists in the circulating blood that can interfere with oxygen take-up by brain cells. Neonatal hyperoxia is typically an iatrogenic condition related to resuscitation efforts and therefore may be confounded with anoxia. Anoxia is closely associated with other abnormal physiological states, including carbon dioxide retention (hypercarbia) and abnormal acid–base balance (acidosis). These states can also be measured in the blood.

Despite the precise measures of blood oxygen available in the neonatal period, a less than perfect correspondence can be expected between these measures and the demonstration of effects on infant mental development. Fetal and perinatal events, maturational status, and the interaction of other variables of neonatal physiology are relevant to outcome. For the anoxic infant the likelihood of some of these antecedent or concurrent complications is high.

Neonatal oxygen sufficiency and subsequent development were examined directly by Apgar *et al.* (1955). Blood oxygen levels were measured for 404 randomly selected newborn infants during the first three hours of life. Later 65 of the infants were tested on the Gesell schedule and 243 were given complete Stanford–Binet tests in childhood. No significant correlation was found between scores for either test and oxygen content or oxygen saturation of neonatal blood. The 22 infants with the lowest blood oxygen levels (below 3 vol percent during the first 10 minutes of life) had a range of scores on both tests and a Stanford–Binet mean IQ of 104.7. The IQs were normally distributed for this population, with a 3.6% incidence of mental retardation. The retarded children did not differ from the others in neonatal blood oxygen measures. The importance of these measures of blood oxygen levels in the first hours of life to subsequent development in infancy and childhood was judged to be insignificant for this normal population.

The duration of oxygen deprivation is important to outcome, as demonstrated by Windle (1969), who examined the brain pathology and behavioral development of monkeys totally asphyxiated during or immediately following delivery. Although 6 minutes of total oxygen deprivation was not damaging, asphyxiation for 8 minutes or more invariably resulted in structural brain damage and at least transient neurological signs. Exposure to 17 minutes of asphyxia produced monkeys who failed to breathe spontaneously and required resuscitation at birth. Longer periods of asphyxia were associated with more severe depression in the neonate and with greater brain pathology. Some monkeys were permitted to live for varying periods of time and brain pathology was compared with behavioral effects at different ages up to 3 years. By 1 month of age the infant monkeys had lost some of the neurological abnormalities that had been noted in the neonatal period but were delayed and abnormal in motor development, exhibited low activity level and dull facial expression, and lacked normal curiosity for their age. At 1–3 years the monkeys lacked manual dexterity and were docile and unemotional. Psychological tests at 9–10 years of age showed inferior memory and learning compared with nonasphyxiated controls. Brain pathology was noted, with evidence for continuing neuronal degeneration in the originally affected brain regions.

In relating the effects of oxygen deprivation to outcome it may be important to distinguish between acute anoxia and hypoxia. Relatively prolonged hypoxia may occur in fetal life if the oxygen supply to the fetal brain is limited for any reason and in neonatal life if the infant has problems of blood gas exchange. Two examples in the newborn are patent ductus arteriosis ("blue baby") and respiratory distress syndrome (hyaline membrane disease). Acute anoxic episodes may occur before birth if the oxygen supply is completely suppressed or after birth if the infant fails to breathe initially or has apneic episodes after respiration has been established. Myers (1969) compared the effects on the brain in monkeys subjected either to prolonged fetal hypoxia at term or to acute neonatal anoxia. The two insults resulted in distinct patterns of pathology in the brain. Brain changes in hypoxia varied according to degree of insult (determined by fetal blood monitoring) as well as duration of insult. The lesions produced by hypoxia mimicked those found in human cerebral palsy, and the most severely compromised hypoxic monkeys demonstrated acute cerebral necrosis. In contrast, the pathology following acute anoxia was limited to brain stem structures. The author stressed the importance of other blood gas measures in hypoxia, including carbon dioxide levels and acid–base balance.

In studies of human infant oxygen deprivation, duration and intensity of insult are often inferred. *Perinatal anoxia* appears in the literature as a generic term, frequently used to include all indications of oxygen insufficiency in prenatal, antepartum, and neonatal life. Although the importance of oxygen deprivation is not restricted to the newborn, there are problems in defining terms when direct measures are not available. Reviews of research relating perinatal anoxia to mental development emphasize the considerable discrepancies in results (Bailey, 1968; Gottfried, 1973; Sameroff and Chandler, 1975), although the consensus would seem to favor the use of multiple criteria of perinatal events and neonatal status as predictors of later developmental abnormalities. Gottfried (1973) cited five studies in which anoxia was defined by clinical signs or apnea and that assessed infant mental development. In three of these (all controlled for prematurity) a difference was found that favored the nonanoxic groups, but the two studies that were also longitudinal found no comparable differences in childhood IQ. He cited a total of 10 prospective studies in which childhood IQ was measured; significant results were found in childhood only in 2 of these (Graham et al., 1962; Schacter and Apgar, 1959). The significant effect on IQ found by Graham et al. (1962) at 3 years of age was no longer noted when these children were 7 years old (Corah et al., 1965).

Brown et al. (1974) noted that the clinical criteria most widely used to designate asphyxia are not, by themselves, usually predictive of developmental problems. (Their criteria included some specific antepartum disorders known to influence fetal physiology, indications of fetal distress, low Apgar scores, need for assisted ventilation at birth, severe neonatal respiratory distress syndrome, and abnormal acid–base and blood gas status.) They investigated the predictive consequences of adding seven neonatal behavioral criteria (feeding difficulty necessitating tube feeding, apneic or cyanotic attacks, apathy, convulsions, hypothermia, "cerebral cry," and persistent vomiting). From a group of 760 asphyxiated newborn infants 94 were selected as having one or more of these additional criteria (mean number slightly more than three), and 93 infants were subsequently followed to a mean age of 21 months. By this age 20 had died, and 24 others had a functionally significant handicap. The total number of neonatal behavioral abnormalities was associated with outcome, and 90% of the infants with five or more symptoms died or had serious handicaps. In 32 cases birth injury was thought to be responsible for the asphyxia, while the remainder were considered cases of "pure" asphyxia. The outcome at 21 months favored the group with birth injury. In this group relatively fewer infants died or had severe handicaps, and more appeared to be completely normal by neurological examination (55% as compared with 26% for the group with primary asphyxia). Abnormal muscle tone was "present and prominent" in many of the 94 infants during the newborn period, and patterns of muscle tone were related to outcome. Normal flexor tone, appropriate to gestational age, was never associated with subsequent death or moderate to severe handicap, although 26% of these infants had some minor, residual neurological sequelae at 21 months.

The evidence from man and monkey suggests that a definition of anoxia can include parameters of intensity and duration of insult. Sophisticated methods of fetal monitoring are available for use with the human infant (cf., Caldeyro-Barcia et al., 1968). When clinical signs are used to define anoxia, they can be described and specified in some detail to allow interpretation of conflicting results. The degree and duration of insult may perhaps be inferred from the neonatal condition of the infant (Windle, 1969; Brown et al., 1974), particularly if a distinction is made between primary oxygen insufficiency and symptoms of anoxia related to other primary insults (Brown et al., 1974).

The physiological status of the neonate can be measured to study the effects of respiratory disorders and treatment procedures, including measures of the correlates of suffocation such as hypercarbia and acidosis. Hyperoxia, a condition that can occur when the neonate is exposed to high levels of exogenous oxygen during treatment, can be measured. In the newborn, hyperoxia is associated with retinal damage (cf., Silverman, 1969), and the adverse effects on the nervous system of high oxygen concentrations have long been known (cf., Bert, 1943).

Predictor Variables

It is possible to define a cluster of discrete perinatal insults for investigation of developmental outcome. When this alternative is used, the hypothesis shifts from the expectation of specific effects related to duration and intensity of a single variable to the prediction of some developmental effects from a defined group of variables. Such a construct may permit an examination of interactive effects.

The study by Honzik et al. (1965) is illustrative. Birth records of 197 cases, previously selected as potentially neurologically damaged or normal, were reevaluated by independent pediatricians. The cases were grouped in four categories: not suspect, possibly suspect, suspect, or definitely suspect of neurological handicaps. Following the categorization, the birth records were again reviewed and the kinds and degrees of insult leading to the classifications were determined and reported by the authors. The infants were tested at 8 months of age on the Bayley scales of mental and motor development. For both sexes the test scores significantly discriminated among groups, and the definitely suspect group was most clearly differentiated. Specific items of the mental scale were examined, and some item differences were found that characterized the most suspect infants (relatively poor coordination, short attention span, distracted, hypo- or hyperactivity, less success on tasks requiring eye–hand coordination and problem solving). An interesting item difference, pertaining to both sexes, was a tendency for the suspect infants to vocalize more in the test situation. The authors suggested that this difference may have been due to less awareness of the novel situation (and less wariness) in the suspect group. They pointed out that the correspondence between mental score and definitely suspect status is less than perfect, i.e., some of the suspect infants tested well within normal limits.

A large prospective study of 1005 infants (the St. Louis Baby Study) was inaugurated more than a decade ago at the University of Missouri at St. Louis, and results pertaining to outcome in infancy have been reported (Jordan, 1971; Jordan and Spaner, 1970, 1972). An operational definition of early developmental adversity was constructed and further refined into four discrete categories: specific disorders of pregnancy and gestation, of delivery, of neonatal life, and of combinations of any of these three. Membership in the multiple category excluded membership in any of the first three categories. Included in these four categories were 507 infants, and 498 controls were selected systematically from the same population pool. The predictive power of the four categories was determined by multiple linear regression analysis for a number of outcome variables in infancy that included developmental measures at 12 and 24 months. Developmental level was assessed at 12 months by Jordan's *ad hoc* development scale (Jordan, 1969), constructed for report by unsophisticated mothers. It sampled domains of locomotion, personal development, speech and hearing, and fine coordination. The Stanford–Binet test was given to a subsample of 102 children at 24 months. Jordan (1971) reported significant relations between development at 12 months and both the first category (disorders of pregnancy and gestation) and the third (neonatal factors). At 24 months significant relations were found between Binet mental age and both the neonatal and the multiple factors. The biological predictors of development were robust at 12 months but declined sharply at 24 months. Social class, not significantly related to the developmental score at 12 months, was significantly· associated with mental age at 24 months.

These illustrative studies of predictor variables suggest that the grouping of discrete insult variables, clearly defined, is a powerful research strategy. Measures of developmental delay in infancy are, in themselves, not specific, and the predictive value of nonspecific insult clusters suggests that multiple causes may be operating to produce this effect. The indication of differences in specific item performance related to intensity of insult and the demonstration of age-related predictors suggest the potential of this line of inquiry.

Studies Defined by Neonatal Risk Status

Another method of sample selection is from membership in a population known to be at risk for developmental problems. This technique increases the likelihood of developmental problems in the sample beyond that of a normal population and lends itself to a consideration of individual differences in outcome for children with some common potential for insult. These differences may be explored by further definition of biological factors or by a consideration of the effects of subsequent environmental events on development. Some examples of highrisk groups are preterm infants, undergrown infants (i.e., small for gestational age), infants of diabetic mothers, infants with erythroblastosis fetalis (Rh blood factor incompatibility), and infants who develop neonatal respiratory distress syndrome. These examples suggest that there is no common denominator in group definition other than the knowledge that these conditions are accompanied by a high incidence of neonatal mortality and pose a threat to normal development. They are not mutually exclusive nor necessarily discrete, for there are more explicit distinctions within some conditions, such as the causes of prematurity or fetal undergrowth, that may be important determinants of outcome. The relative success of neonatal environmental intervention may, in part, depend upon these distinctions (Drillien, 1972). The individual differences within high-risk groups provide an important source of hypotheses for the effects of perinatal risk factors on development.

Some groups of high-risk infants are followed by longitudinal evaluations of physical and mental status that study the effects of neonatal intensive care (cf., Drillien, 1964; Amiel-Tison, 1969; Lubchenco et al., 1974; Stahlman et al., 1973; Outerbridge et al., 1974). The purposes of these studies are twofold: to investigate the outcome of patients subjected to specific, innovative techniques of intervention during neonatal life and to determine the general effects of intensive care on survival rates and the developmental status of the survivors. The recognition of subtle handicaps not easily determined in infancy, such as mild mental retardation and learning disorders, has prompted follow-up investigations of survivors into childhood. During the past decade, novel techniques of intensive neonatal care have been introduced, and the concept of such care for the newborn has become less exceptional. A secular trend has been noted for increased survival rates in treated neonates and for decreased incidence of severe handicaps in infancy for certain high-risk populations (Stahlman, 1969; Hunt et al., 1974). The effect of some recent innovations in treatment on childhood status remains to be determined.

Measures of Neonatal Status

The assessment of newborn behavior provides a measure of differences within and among high-risk categories. Such a referent can be used as an outcome measure of fetal or perinatal insult and as a predictor of subsequent development. Neonatal behavioral observations have been formalized into clinical and research instruments by Apgar (1953), Graham (1956), Rosenblith (1961), and Brazelton (1973).

The Apgar scale, based on five neonatal criteria, gives an index of the infant's condition immediately after birth, with a score of 10 representing normal status and a lower score indicating some signs of abnormal or depressed function. The observations are made at 1 and 5 minutes of age. Although there were some indications of a relation between Apgar scores and IQ at 4 years of age for some subgroups in the data of the Collaborative Project (Drage et al., 1969), the scores had no real predictive value for the major subgroups of the study (Broman et al., 1975).

The Graham–Rosenblith and Brazelton scales measure the status of infants during the newborn period and assess a range of normal and abnormal behaviors. Neither scale generates a total score, but each yields clusters of behaviors that can be used to discriminate infants. For example, performance on the Brazelton scale has been described for infants of low birth weight at 1 and 4 weeks (Scarr and Williams, 1971) and for infants born to drug-addicted mothers (Soule *et al.*, 1973). Rosenblith (1973, 1975) reported significant relations between measures from the Graham–Rosenblith scale and performance on the Bayley scales at 8 months of age for a sample of children in the Collaborative Project. This report included previously published data relating discrepancies in tension between upper and lower limbs (Rosenblith and Anderson, 1968) and hypersensitivity to light (Anderson and Rosenblith, 1964) to outcome in infancy.

The demonstration of individual differences in the normal newborn and the very young infant has changed our perception of the infant as a passive receiver of the environment to that of an interactive and selective user of the environment. Early differences in temperament and activity level are assessed by the neonatal scales. These traits may persist and influence the infant's response to environmental events (Escalona, 1968) and the reciprocal social responses given to him by others (Thomas *et al.*, 1968). These early determinants of infant–environment interaction may be important for high-risk infants (Allen *et al.*, 1971; Scarr-Salapatek and Williams, 1973).

The Preterm Infant

Infants born prematurely are, as a class, disadvantaged in making the necessary adaptations to extrauterine life and at risk for sustaining significant brain damage and developmental problems (cf. Caputo and Mandell, 1970). The degree of risk, although strongly related to the degree of prematurity as measured by either gestational age or birth weight, is influenced by other factors. These include the causes of prematurity, the quality of neonatal care, and features of the postnatal environment.

Drillien (1972) studied the relation between etiological factors and developmental outcome at 1–3 years for 283 children with birth weights of 2000 grams or less. Developmental quotients were divided into five levels and outcome was compared for varied etiologies. She concluded that there are three main causes of premature delivery and intrauterine growth retardation. These are (1) developmental abnormalities of the fetus, reflecting adverse factors in early gestation (these infants are at highest risk of moderate or severe handicaps); (2) adverse factors in late pregnancy, such as hypoxia and malnutrition (with increased likelihood of mild degrees of mental retardation and minor neurological abnormalities); and (3) "those who are prematurely delivered 'by accident,' are potentially normal at birth, and whose later status depends largely upon postnatal care."

Braine et al. (1966) studied the development of 346 preterm infants who weighed 2100 grams or less at birth and 50 full-term control infants. The infants were all black single births and largely economically disadvantaged. The Cattell infant test was given to 83 infants at $7\frac{1}{2}$ months of age and to 248 infants at $13\frac{1}{2}$ months, ages adjusted for prematurity. A number of neonatal and maternal complications were analyzed in relation to developmental status, and patterns of impairment were investigated. The test scores at both ages (adjusted for prematurity) were positively related to birth weight. In the females significant impairment was found only in the lowest-weight group; a more general trend was found in the males. In this sample, already economically disadvantaged, socioenvironmental differences contributed to the impairment found, but only in the less intact groups, and the authors did not attribute this effect to specific pre- or postnatal factors. They noted that "quite extreme levels of underprivilege" were necessary for the environmental effect to be manifest. The male preterm infants did significantly less well than females of the same birth weight on the mental test at $13\frac{1}{2}$ months; no sex differences were found in the full-term control infants. Because the incidence and severity of complications were about the same for both sexes, the developmental difference was attributed to greater vulnerability in the males.

The outcome of preterm infants weighing less than 1500 grams at birth has been investigated by medical centers providing intensive neonatal care. The prognosis for such very small infants has been reported in the past as generally poor (Drillien, 1964; Lubchenco et al., 1963). However, more recent studies have indicated a more favorable outcome (Rawlings et al., 1971; Calame and Prod'hom, 1972; Alden et al., 1972; Dweck et al., 1973; Fitzhardinge and Ramsay, 1973).

We have recently begun to analyze the perinatal and developmental data for a group of preterm infants weighing 1500 grams or less at birth. The group is being followed longitudinally at the University of California at San Francisco as part of a larger study of children who required intensive neonatal care. The study includes infants born since 1965. A preliminary analysis of the entire sample suggests that it has remained

TABLE I

Mental Test Performance of Preterm
Infants with Birth Weight ≤ 1500 Grams
(IQs Adjusted for Prematurity)

Age	N	IQ	SD
6 months	42	96.95	21.11
12 months	49	97.35	15.43
24 months	46	89.93	14.78

consistent for major socioeconomic variables. Intensive neonatal care has undergone many changes, and a previous report (Hunt *et al.*, 1974) compared outcome in infancy for the preterm group born in 1965 through 1968 with that born in 1969 through 1972. Both the survival rate and the percentage of infants with normal development had increased significantly between the two time periods.

Infant assessments have included the Cattell Infant Intelligence Scale or the Bayley mental scale at 6, 12, and 24 months. To date, 76 children in the preterm group have reached the age of 12 months, and one or more infant tests have been given to 67 of them; the remainder have been tested at older ages only. Table I indicates the numbers tested at each age and the results by age group. Because maturational differences related to gestational age are expected (cf. Parmalee and Schulte,

TABLE II

Pearson Product Moment Correlations—IQ at 6, 12, and 24 Months; Gestational Age;
Standard Deviation of Birth Weight to Gestational Age; Apgar Score at 5 Minutes of
Age; Socioeconomic Status of Family and Midparent Education

	IQ_{12}	IQ_{24}	GA	sdBW/GA	$Apgar_5$	SES	MPE
IQ_6	0.358^a	0.477^b	-0.066	0.263^a	0.395^b	-0.188	-0.010
IQ_{12}		0.684^c	-0.165	0.281^a	0.036	0.084	0.253
IQ_{24}			0.100	0.092	-0.066	-0.019	0.235
GA				-0.722^c	0.346^b	0.044	0.014
sdBW/GA					-0.289^a	-0.129	0.026
$Apgar_5$						0.047	0.277^a
SES							0.656^c

[a] $p < 0.05$
[b] $p < 0.01$
[c] $p < 0.001$

1970), all IQs are adjusted for prematurity at 6, 12, and 24 months. This is done by the conversion of the weeks of prematurity to months and the subtraction of this value from the infant's chronological age. The adjusted age is then used to compute the score. Gestational age is determined by menstrual history. Correlations among the infant IQs and other variables that were found to be normally distributed are presented in Table II. These include gestational age (GA) and the standard deviation of birth weight for gestational age (sdBW/GA), as determined from Usher's data (Usher, 1969). The latter measure gives an indication of how small or large each newborn infant is in comparison with other infants of comparable prematurity. Infants who are very small for gestational age (three standard deviations or more below average) are considered "small for dates" or "runts." Table II also includes the Apgar score at 5 minutes of age and family variables of socioeconomic status (SES) and midparent education (MPE).

IQs at all three infant ages are positively correlated; the strongest relation is between 12 and 24 months. IQ at 6 months is related to IQ at older ages and to the Apgar score at 5 minutes of age, suggesting the possibility of transient effects of neonatal status on early development. The significant correlation between Apgar score and GA is not unexpected in this population of small preterm infants, for whom survival itself is related to relative maturity at birth. However, the correlation between Apgar score and IQ at 6 months is even more noteworthy because it exceeds the expected correlation between Apgar score and GA. The high correlation between the two family variables (SES and MPE) is expected, and neither, again as expected, is significantly related to IQ in infancy. The Apgar score correlates in a low but significant manner with MPE, suggesting that the causes of prematurity might be pursued in this group. The index of sdBW/GA is negatively correlated with the Apgar score but positively correlated with IQ at 6 and 12 months.

Risk factors associated with developmental delays in preterm infants are not usually normally distributed. Instead they are dichotomous (sex, presence or absence of neonatal respiratory distress syndrome) or unidirectional (incidence of decreasing birth weight below 1500 grams). For this preliminary analysis risk variables and developmental outcome are compared by the division of the sample into groups by normal and low IQ. In a previous report (Hunt et al., 1974) it was demonstrated that no child from the preterm group who had a low IQ in childhood (IQ

Table III

IQ Distribution at 12 Months (N = 49) or 24 Months
(N = 12) for Preterm Infants with Birth Weight ≤ 1500
Grams (IQ Adjusted for Prematurity)

IQ	Males	Females	Total	Tested 24 mo.
Normal Group (IQ > 90)				
> 115	4	3	7	(1)
100–115	10	12	22	(3)
91–99	5	7	12	(3)
Total > 90	19	22	41	(7)
Low Group (IQ ≤ 90)				
84–90	6	3	9	(3)
68–83	4	3	7	(0)
52–67	4	0	4	(2)
Total ≤ 90	14	6	20	(5)

below 84 on the Binet, i.e., one standard deviation) had an IQ above 90 at 12 months of age. However, some who had scores of 90 or below in infancy were normal in childhood. Many of the children in the present study are still well under 4 years of age. For purposes of comparison the 12-month IQ scores are divided at IQ 90 for "normal" and "low" groups, so that no retarded children should thereby be included in the normal group but that some potentially normal children will be included in the low group. Table III shows the distribution of IQ scores at 12 months for the normal and the low groups. In those instances in which a 12-month IQ is not available, the score at 24 months is used (12 cases out of 61). Because the average IQ at 24 months is lower than at 12 months (see Table I), errors in assignment may be biased toward overinclusion in the low group.

In Table IV the groups with normal and low IQs at 12 months are compared for sex differences, birth-weight variations, presence or absence of neonatal respiratory distress syndrome (RDS), and secular trends. The group with low IQ includes a disproportionate number of males. As expected, the group with the highest birth weight (1251–1500 grams) has the best outcome in infancy, with proportionately greater

Table IV

Distribution of Cases in Normal and Low IQ Groups at 12 Months by Sex, Birth Weight, Presence of Respiratory Distress Syndrome, and Period of Birth

	Normal (IQ > 90)	Low (IQ ≤ 90)
Male	19	14
Female	22	6
Birth weight: 1251–1500 g	25	7
1001–1250	11	7
≤ 1000	5	6
RDS	14	9
No RDS	27	11
Born 1965–1968	14	15
1969–1973	27	5

numbers in the normal group. Those infants who did not develop RDS have a relatively better outcome than those who did. More children born since 1969 have had normal infant development than have those born in the earlier period.

As noted above, the Apgar scores at 5 minutes of age approximate a normal distribution. This very unusual finding attests to the high-risk status of these preterm infants. In a normal population an Apgar score at 5 minutes of age of 9 or 10 points (normal score) is most frequent and lower scores are encountered with decreasing frequency. Table V shows the distribution of Apgar scores at 1 and 5 minutes of age for the preterm group. A large proportion of these small infants is in a very depressed condition at birth, as evidenced by Apgar scores of 1 or 2 points for 22 infants. By 5 minutes of age only one child is in such a state, and the

Table V

Distribution of Apgar Scores at 1 and 5 Minutes of Age for Small Preterm Infants

Score:	9–10	7–8	5–6	3–4	1–2	No data
1 min	1	11	25	16	22	(1)
5 min	11	35	19	7	1	(3)

TABLE VI

Incidence of Most Extreme Value Ever Recorded for Arterial Blood Gas Measures of pH, PCO_2 and PO_2 for Preterm Infants of Low and Normal IQ

	Normal (IQ > 90)	Low (IQ ≤ 90)
Lowest pH recorded:		
≥ 7.2 (normal)	19	8
7.10–7.19	11	3
7.00–7.09	8	4
< 7.00	1	1
Total	(39)	(16)
Highest PCO_2 recorded:		
< 50 (normal)	10	4
51–69	12	4
70–89	13	5
90–100+	4	3
Total	(39)	(16)
Lowest PO_2 recorded:		
≥ 50 (normal)	16	3
40–49	6	1
30–39	5	8
20–29	9	1
< 20	1	1
Total	(37)	(14)
Highest PO_2 recorded:		
≤ 100 (normal)	3	0
101–199	14	4
200–299	11	4
300–399	7	5
> 399	2	1
Total	(37)	(14)

modal value is a score of 7 or 8 points. This comparison suggests the vigorous resuscitation efforts of immediate intensive neonatal care.

One of the major concerns in resuscitation and continuing intensive neonatal care is to restore and maintain physiological homeostasis. This outcome is pursued by active environmental manipulations, such as increasing levels of exogenous oxygen and infusing with sodium bicarbonate (cf., James, 1969). Arterial blood oxygen (PO_2) and carbon dioxide (PCO_2) tensions and determinations of acid–base balance (pH) are used (with other measures) to monitor the success of these manipulations. Table VI displays the range of abormal values encountered in the normal- and low-IQ groups, determined by the calculation of the lowest or the highest abnormal value ever recorded for each infant. Three of these—low pH, high PCO_2, and low PO_2—occur in asphyxia; the fourth variable, high PO_2, represents hyperoxemia, a higher than normal level of arterial oxygen that occasionally can occur during treatment. (Very high arterial oxygen levels are less frequent for those infants born during the later years of intensive neonatal care, reflecting more precise monitoring and changing treatment practices.)

The lowest pH recordings ($\leqslant 7.09$) are about equally distributed between normal- and low-IQ infants, and so are the highest PCO_2 values (70–100+). Low PO_2 values (20–29) are not unusual for the normal infants, and high PO_2 (101–299) is more common than normal values. For none of the four variables is there a range in which low IQ is clearly associated with any extreme value and hence no direct indication that reaching an abnormal value is, *per se,* indicative of damage.

Data from the blood measures have been analyzed to determine the number of minutes that each preterm infant experienced some abnormal states. This is done by a determination of the cumulative minutes above or below a specific level (i.e., PO_2 below 50, 40, and 30 mm Hg; PCO_2 above 50, 60, 70, and 80 mm Hg). The relation between the duration in minutes and the IQ group is illustrated for some abnormal states in Table VII.

Most of the infants in both the normal- and the low-IQ groups had no minutes of pH below 7.1 as neonates, and none in the normal group sustained such a value for more than 30 minutes. (Four infants in the low-IQ group actually had durations above 60 minutes and one above 90 minutes.)

High PCO_2 values (above 80) were also unusual for either IQ group, but 8 of the 39 infants of the normal group had from 1 to 60 minutes at this level, and one had more than 60 minutes. For the low-IQ group 6 of 18 had durations of more than 60 minutes. (Although not shown in Table VII, 5 of these 6 had this high PCO_2 value for more than 240 minutes.) Values for PCO_2 and pH are not independent, but there seems to be evidence in Table VII that duration of pH below 7.1 is usually considerably shorter than is duration of PCO_2 above 80 for both IQ groups and that durations related to low IQ are also different.

TABLE VII

*Minutes at Certain Abnormal Physiological States for
Infants of Normal and Low IQ*

	Minutes	Normal (IQ > 90)	Low (IQ ⩽ 90)
*p*H < 7.1	0	29	13
	1–30	10	2
	> 30	0	4
PCO$_2$ > 80	0	30	11
	1–60	8	1
	> 60	1	6
PO$_2$ < 40	0	21	5
	1–60	8	5
	61–180	7	0
	> 180	2	4
PO$_2$ > 100	0	4	0
	1–500	22	6
	501–1000	7	4
	1001–2000	2	1
	2001–3000	3	1
	> 3000	0	2

Low arterial oxygen in the small preterm neonate (PO$_2$ below 40) is less unusual than are the abnormal measures of *p*H and PCO$_2$. Many of the normal IQ infants had up to 180 minutes, and 2 had even longer durations. A relatively larger proportion of the infants with low IQ (4 of 14) had this low blood oxygen value for more than 180 minutes.

High arterial oxygen (PO$_2$ greater than 100) was common in both IQ groups for durations up to 500 minutes, reflecting the resuscitation efforts in their behalf, and 5 of the 38 normal infants sustained this high oxygen level from 1000 to 3000 minutes; 2 of the low-IQ infants had durations in excess of 3000 minutes. Both were born in the early days of neonatal care and have been followed on an annual basis. One is blind and severely retarded, but the other had a normal IQ (92) at 2 years, earned a Binet IQ of 122 at 4 years, and has had a normal course of development since then. The relation of the duration of low and high arterial oxygen levels to outcome is not clear.

To allow exploration of the possibility that sensitivity to damage from sustained exposure to high or low levels of arterial oxygen is related to the degree of prematurity, the relations between birth weight and PO_2 values are presented in Table VIII.

No definite tendency for birth weight and duration to interact in relation to IQ group is apparent for either the high or the low PO_2 measure. The evidence from Table VIII suggests that the larger infants had less difficulty establishing normal physiological limits as neonates and a better outcome at 12 months. Few normal infants in the intermediate weight group (1000–1250 grams) and none in the lowest weight group (at or below 1000 grams) had prolonged exposure to low PO_2. When only the low-IQ group is considered, the duration of PO_2 insult does not appear to be an important factor in any category of birth weight.

The interaction between certain of the physiological variables is presented in Figures 1 and 2. Figure 1 presents the bivariate plots for infants who had values above zero for minutes of both pH below 7.2 and PCO_2 above 80. Of the 13 infants in this combined category, 6 are in the low-IQ group. These physiological variables appear to be correlated, and combined high values predominate in infants from the low-IQ group.

TABLE VIII

Incidence of Preterm Infants with PO_2 < 40 for > or < 60 Minutes and PO_2 > 100 for > or < 500 Minutes by IQ Group and Birth Weight Group

	Normal (IQ > 90)		Low (IQ ≤ 90)	
PO_2 < 40	> 60 min	≤ 60 min	> 60 min	≤ 60 min
Birthweight:				
1251–1500 g	7	16	0	2
1001–1250	2	8	3	4
≤ 1000	0	5	1	4
PO_2 > 100	> 500 min	≤ 500 min	> 500 min	≤ 500 min
Birthweight:				
1251–1500 g	5	18	2	0
1001–1250	6	4	3	4
≤ 1000	1	4	3	2

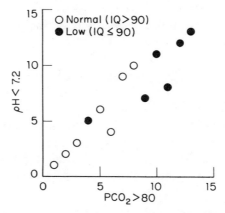

FIG. 1. Bivariate plots for 13 infants with some minutes at both $pH < 7.2$ and $PCO_2 > 80$.

Figure 2 presents the bivariate plots for 15 infants with some min-utes at both PCO_2 above 80 and PO_2 above 100. In this case, the two values are not correlated and there seems to be some indication that duration of exposure to high PO_2 is less related to low IQ than is the duration of exposure to the high level of PCO_2, at least for these infants, who had both insults.

Trends in infant mental development have also been examined in a preliminary manner for the group of preterm infants. As was noted in

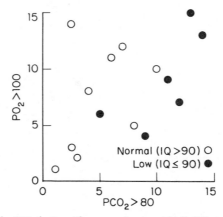

FIG. 2. Bivariate plots for 15 infants with some minutes at both $PO_2 > 100$ and $PCO_2 > 80$.

Table IX

*Patterns of IQ Performance from 6 Months
to 12/24 Months for 39 Preterm Infants*

IQ, 6 months		IQ, 12/24 months	
Normal (IQ > 90)	26	Normal	16
		Low	10
Low (IQ ≤ 90)	13	Low	8
		Normal	5

Table II, mental test scores at 6 months are positively correlated with later tests, but less so and less significantly than with the Apgar score at 5 minutes. Testing patterns of the 39 infants tested at 6 months who had tests at either 12 or 24 months, or both, are shown in Table IX.

The three groups with some abnormal scores (consistent, moving up, and moving down) are not distinguishable by GA, SES, RDS, or sdBW/GA. Males are more numerous (six of eight) in the consistently low group.

Of the entire group of 23 infants who are not consistently normal, a disproportionate number are more than two standard deviations below the expected weight for gestational age. In this category are 10 of these 23 infants, but only 2 of the 16 consistently normal infants. Another way of stating this relation is that 10 of 12 infants with low sdBW/GA have one or more low IQ scores at 6, 12, or 24 months. The "moving up" group has 3 of these infants, perhaps because GA is overestimated, i.e., the infants may actually be more premature than supposed. If so, the 6-months scores are undercorrected and low. In the "moving down" group are 4 (of 10) small-for-date infants. This IQ effect cannot be related to GA effects. In the consistently low group there are 3 (of 8) small-for-date infants. (Note that *small-for-date* is used here to denote those more than two standard deviations below normal, rather than the conventional measure of three standard deviations below normal.)

The 10 infants in the "moving down" group appear to be a mixed group, with 3 low SES; 2 with delayed language at 24 months, attributed to more than one language in the home; and so forth. The "moving down" group shows the biggest drop in IQ between 6 and 12 months, and for the 7 infants in this group tested at all three ages, the mean IQs are 108.7 (6 months), 93.9 (12 months), and 86.1 (24 months).

The consistently normal group tested at all three ages ($N = 7$) has means of 115.3, 112.4, and 99.8, respectively.

In summary, the measured IQs at 6, 12, and 24 months for this group of small preterm infants are correlated with each other and with a number of variables related to the intensive care received during the neonatal period. The relative success of the early minutes of resuscitation is related to development at 6 months, and the physiological status of the neonate appears to be related in complex ways to development at 12 months. The measures of absolute values of neonatal physiological insult (i.e., highest or lowest abnormal value reached) are not predictive of slow development in infancy. The long duration of some abnormal physiological states, and particularly of pH below 7.1 and PCO_2 above 80, seems to occur more frequently among infants who subsequently show developmental delays in infancy. Further exploration of combined effects seems justified by these exploratory data, as does further analysis of the IQ instability factors beyond 6 months of age.

Discussion

The overview of the literature reveals a large and growing body of psychological, physiological, and medical research that is moving in the direction of delineating relationships between perinatal environmental insults and measured infant intelligence. The increasing awareness of a need for an interdisciplinary approach is evident from many of the illustrative studies cited. Many of the longitudinal studies have not focused on infant development, but where it is examined, the influence of perinatal insults on infant outcome is often noted. There is evidence that infant development may be a more sensitive indicator of some perinatal events than is later development, perhaps because of the larger effects of environment beyond infancy on measures of childhood intelligence. However, these transient effects in infancy remain largely unexplained.

The three methods of sample selection discussed have individual merits and seem to be complementary methods of approaching the problem. Large prospective studies of normal populations give a perspective on incidence of insult and abnormal outcome that is often lost in more discrete studies. They delineate the cultural practices and environmental manipulations of a society, put them in perspective with relation to each other, and examine their influence on outcome for the entire population. The wealth of data available in these studies suggest that additional hypotheses can be investigated as they are put forward. Discrete studies of specific insult and outcome are extremely difficult to define and control in research on human infants. Some of the problems have been presented and confronted in the studies reviewed. Groups of specific insult variables, clearly defined, seem to be related to general effects on development as measured by infant intelligence tests. Delayed development in infancy is clearly not a specific outcome; discrete insults may be related to discrete, rather than general, effects. Research using high-risk populations, with their varied range of insults and outcomes, seems a valid method of exploring the relations between perinatal events and infant status. Small sample size makes some analyses difficult, as exemplified by data presented for the small preterm infant from our own studies. Pooling of data on high-risk infant groups is an appealing possibility if the data can be made sufficiently comparable among investigators.

Many of the environmental insults that are of greatest concern to society are extremely complex and difficult to analyze with precision. Illustrative are the interrelated variables attendant upon poverty that may be relevant to infant development. The research methods reviewed here are, in combination, being used to approach and analyze these complex questions of environmental effects.

The level of sophistication now available in both physiological and behavioral research is, perhaps, the real challenge to the interdisciplinary investigation. Apparently lacking is "crossover" in the generation of hypotheses and in the design of studies to take full advantage of current knowledge and techniques in human research. Perhaps it is inevitable that interdisciplinary studies lag behind those in specific disciplines. The precise definition of physiological variables is not likely to be totally productive if the outcome measure is limited to IQ. Even in infancy a more discrete or analytical approach to measures of intelligence may be rewarding. Conversely, a detailed investigation of intellectual abilities may not be revealing if perinatal insults are defined in a global manner that fails to take account of the known associations between insult variables and specific neurological consequences.

References

Alden, E. R., Mandelkorn, T., Woodrum, D. E., Wennberg, R. P., Parks, C. R., and Hodson, W. A., 1972, Morbidity and mortality of infants weighing less than 1,000 grams in an intensive care nursery, *Pediatrics, 50*:40.

Allen, M. G., Pollin, W., and Hoffer, A., 1971, Parental, birth, and infancy factors in infant twin development, *The American Journal of Psychiatry, 127*:1597.

Amiel-Tison, C., 1969, Cerebral damage in full-term newborn: Aetiological factors, neonatal status and long-term follow-up, *Biologia Neonatorum, 14*:234.

Anderson, R. B., and Rosenblith, J. F., 1964, Light sensitivity in the neonate: A preliminary report, *Biologia Neonatorum, 7*:83.

Apgar, V., 1953, A proposal for a new method of evaluation of the newborn infant, *Current Research in Anesthesia and Analgesia, 32*:260.

Apgar, V., 1964, Drugs in pregnancy, *Journal of the American Medical Association, 190*:840.

Apgar, V., Girdany, B. R., McIntosh, R., and Taylor, H. C., 1955, Neonatal anoxia, I: A study of the relation of oxygenation at birth to intellectual development, *Pediatrics, 15*:653.

Bailey, C. J., 1968, Interrelationship of asphyxia neonatorum, cerebral palsy and mental retardation: present status of the problem, *in* "Neurological and Psychological Deficits of Asphyxia Neonatorum," W. F. Windle (ed.), Thomas, Springfield, Illinois.

Bayley, N., 1969, "Manual, Bayley Scales of Infant Development," Psychological Corporation, New York.

Berendes, H. W., 1964, Obstetrical complications and mental deficiency, *in* "Proceedings of the International Copenhagen Congress on the Scientific Study of Mental Retardation," J. Oster (ed.), National Association for Retarded Children, Inc., New York.

Bert, P., 1943, "Researches in Experimental Physiology," M. A. Hitchcock and F. A. Hitchcock (trans.), College Book Co., Columbus, Ohio.

Bowes, W. A., Brackbill, Y., Conway, E., and Steinschneider, A., 1970, The effects of obstetrical medication on fetus and infant, *Monographs of the Society for Research in Child Development, 35*:4.

Brackbill, Y., Kane, J., Manniello, R. L., and Abramson, D., 1974, Obstetric premedication and infant outcome, *American Journal of Obstetrics and Gynecology, 118*:377.

Braine, M. D. S., Heimer, C. B., Wortis, H., and Freedman, A. M., 1966, Factors associated with impairment of the early development of prematures, *Monographs of the Society for Research in Child Development, 31*:4.

Brazelton, T. B., 1973, Neonatal behavioral assessment scale, *Clinics in Developmental Medicine,* No. 50, Spastics International Medical Publications, J. B. Lippincott Co., Philadelphia.

Broman, S. H., Nichols, P. L., and Kennedy, W. A., 1975, "Preschool IQ: Prenatal and Early Development Correlates," Lawrence Erlbaum Associates (publisher), Halsted Press Division, Wiley, New York (distributor).

Brown, J. K., Purvis, R. J., Forfar, J. O., and Cockburn, F., 1974, Neurological aspects of perinatal asphyxia, *Developmental Medicine and Child Neurology, 16*:567.

Calame, A., and Prod'hom, L. S., 1972, Survival rate and quality of survival of 165 premature babies born between 1966 and 1968 with birth weight of 1500 grams or less, *Pediatrics Digest,* October 1972:16.

Caldeyro-Barcia, R., Casacuberta, C., Bustos, R., Giussi, G., Gulin, L., Escarcena, L., and Mendez-Bauer, C., 1968, Correlation of intrapartum changes in fetal heart rate with fetal oxygen and acid–base state, *in* "Diagnosis and Treatment of Fetal Disorders," K. Adamsons (ed.), Springer-Verlag, New York Inc., New York.

Caputo, D. V., and Mandell, W., 1970, Consequences of low birth weight, *Developmental Psychology*, 3:363.

Cattell, P., 1940, "The Intelligence of Infants," The Science Press Printing Co., Lancaster, Pennsylvania.

Churchill, J. A., and Berendes, H. W., 1969, Intelligence of children whose mothers had acetenuria during pregnancy, *in* "Perinatal Factors Affecting Human Development," *Proceedings*, Pan American Health Organization, Scientific Publication No. 185.

Conway, E., and Brackbill, Y., 1970, Delivery medication and infant outcome: An empirical study, *in* "The Effects of Obstetrical Medication on Fetus and Infant," W. A. Bowes, Jr., Y. Brackbill, E. Conway, and A. Steinschneider (eds.), *Monographs of the Society for Research in Child Development*, 35:4, 24–34.

Corah, N. L., Anthony, E. J., Painter, P., Stern, J. A., and Thurston, D. L., 1965, Effects of perinatal anoxia after seven years, *Psychological Monographs*, 79:3.

Drage, J. S., Berendes, H. W., and Fisher, P. D., 1969, The Apgar scores and four-year psychological examination performance, *in* "Perinatal Factors Affecting Human Development," *Proceedings*, Pan American Health Organization, Scientific Publication No. 185.

Drillien, C. M., 1961, Longitudinal study of growth and development of prematurely and maturely born children, VII: Mental development 2–5 years, *Archives of Diseases of Children*, 36:233.

Drillien, C. M., 1964, "The Growth and Development of the Prematurely Born Infant," Williams & Wilkins, Baltimore.

Drillien, C. M., 1972, Aetiology and outcome in low-birthweight infants, *Developmental Medicine and Child Neurology*, 14:563.

Dweck, H. S., Saxon, S. A., Benton, J. W., and Cassady, G., 1973, Early development of the tiny premature infant, *American Journal of Diseases of Children*, 28:126.

Escalona, S. K., 1968, "The Roots of Individuality," Aldine, Chicago.

Escalona, S. K., 1974, The present state of knowledge and available techniques in the area of cognition, *in* "Methodological Approaches to the Study of Brain Maturation and Its Abnormalities," D. P. Purpura and G. P. Reaser (eds.), University Park Press, Baltimore.

Ferreria, A. J., 1969, "Prenatal Environment," Charles C Thomas, Springfield, Illinois.

Fitzhardinge, P. M., and Ramsay, M., 1973, The improving outlook for the small prematurely born infant, *Developmental Medicine and Child Neurology*, 15:447.

French, F. E., Howe, L. P., Bierman, J. M., Connor, A., and Kemp, D. H., 1958, Community-wide pregnancy reporting in Kauai, Hawaii, *Public Health Reports*, 73 61.

Gesell, A., and Amatruda, C. S., 1947, "Developmental Diagnosis" (2nd ed.), Paul B. Hoeber, Inc., New York.

Gottfried, A. W., 1973, Intellectual consequences of perinatal anoxia, *Psychological Bulletin*, 80:231.

Graham, F. K., 1956, Behavioral differences between normal and traumatized newborns, I: The test procedures, *Psychological Monographs*, 70:20.

Graham, F. K., Ernhart, C. B., Thurston, D., and Craft, M., 1962, Development three years after perinatal anoxia and other potentially damaging newborn experience, *Psychological Monographs*, 76:3.

Holden, R. H., 1972, Prediction of mental retardation in infancy, *Mental Retardation*, 10:28.

Holley, W. L., and Churchill, J. A., 1969, Physical and mental deficits of twinning, *in* "Perinatal Factors Affecting Human Development," *Proceedings*, Pan American Health Organization, Scientific Publication No. 185.

Holley, W. L., Rosenbaum, A. L., and Churchill, J. A., 1969, Effect of rapid succession of pregnancy, in "Perinatal Factors Affecting Human Development," Proceedings, Pan American Health Organization, Scientific Publication No. 185.

Honzik, M. P., Hutchings, J. J., and Burnip, S. R., 1965, Birth record assessments and test performance at eight months, American Journal of Diseases of Children, 109:416.

Hunt, J. V., Harvin, D., Kennedy, D., and Tooley, W. H., 1974, Mental development of children with birthweights ≤ 1500 grams, Clinical Research, 22:240-A (abstract).

James, L. S., 1969, Problems of neonatal intensive care units, in "Report of 59th Ross Conference on Pediatric Research," Stowe, Vermont.

Jordan, T. E., 1969, Extension and validation of the ad hoc child development scale, EDAP Tech. Note No. 3.2, Central Midwestern Regional Educational Laboratory, St. Louis, Missouri.

Jordan, T. E., 1971, Early developmental adversity and the first two years of life, Multivariate Behavioral Research Monographs, 6:1.

Jordan, T. E., and Spaner, S. D., 1970, Biological and ecological influences on development at twelve months of age, Human Development, 13:178.

Jordan, T. E., and Spaner, S. D., 1972, Biological and ecological influences on development at twenty-four and thirty-six months of age, Psychological Reports, 31:319.

Kelsey, F. O., 1973, Drugs in pregnancy and their effects on pre- and postnatal development, in "Biological and Environmental Determinants of Early Development," J. I. Nurnberger (ed.), Williams & Wilkins, Baltimore.

Knobloch, H., and Pasamanick, B., 1963, Predicting intellectual potential in infancy, American Journal of Diseases of Children, 106:43.

Kraemer, H. C., Korner, A. F., and Thoman, E. B., 1972, Methodological considerations in evaluating the influence of drugs used during labor and delivery on the behavior of the newborn, Developmental Psychology, 6:128.

Lubchenco, L. O., Bard, H., Goldman, A. L., Coyer, W. E., McIntyre, C., and Smith, D. M., 1974, Newborn intensive care and long-term prognosis, Developmental Medicine and Child Neurology, 16:421.

Lubchenco, L. O., Horner, F., Reed, H., Hix, I., Jr., Metcalf, D., Cohig, R., Elliott, H., and Bourg, M., 1963, Sequelae of premature birth: Evaluation of premature infants of low birth weights at ten years of age, American Journal of Diseases of Children, 106:101.

McKeown, T., and Record, R. G., 1971, Early environmental influences on the development of intelligence, British Medical Bulletin, 27:48.

McKhann, G. M., Coyle, P. K., and Benjamin, J. A., 1973, Nutrition and brain development, in "Biological and Environmental Determinants of Early Development," J. I. Nurnberger (ed.), Williams & Wilkins, Baltimore.

Mendelson, M. A., 1967, Interdisciplinary approach to the study of the exceptional infant: A large scale research project, in "Exceptional Infant," Vol. 1, J. Hellmuth (ed.), Brunner/Mazel, New York.

Montague, A., 1971, Sociogenic brain damage, Developmental Medicine and Child Neurology, 13:597.

Moreau, T., and Birch, H. G., 1974, Relationship between obstetrical general anesthesia and rate of neonatal habituation to repeated stimulation, Developmental Medicine and Child Neurology, 16:612.

Myers, R. E., 1969, Fetal asphyxia and perinatal brain damage, in "Perinatal Factors Affecting Human Development," Proceedings, Pan American Health Organization, Scientific Publication No. 185.

Outerbridge, E. W., Ramsay, M., and Stern, L., 1974, Developmental follow-up of survivors of neonatal respiratory failure, Critical Care Medicine, 2:23.

PARMALEE, A. H., JR., AND SCHULTE, F. J., 1970, Developmental testing of preterm and small-for-date infants, *Pediatrics*, 45:21.

QUIMBY, K. L., ASCHKENASE, L. J., AND BOWMAN, R. E., 1974, Enduring learning deficits and cerebral synaptic malformation from exposure to 10 parts of halothane per million, *Science*, 185:625.

RAWLINGS, G., REYNOLDS, E. O. R., STEWART, A., AND STRANG, L. B., 1971, Changing prognosis for infants of very low birth weight, *Lancet*, 1:516.

RECORD, R. G., McKEOWN, T., AND EDWARDS, J. H., 1970, An investigation of the difference in measured intelligence between twins and single births, *Annals of Human Genetics*, 34:11.

ROSENBLITH, J. F., 1961, The modified Graham Behavior test for neonates: Test–Retest reliability, normative data and hypotheses for future work, *Biologica Neonatorum*, 3:174.

ROSENBLITH, J. F., 1973, Prognostic value of neonatal behavioral tests, *Early Child Development and Care*, 3:31.

ROSENBLITH, J. F., 1974, Relations between neonatal behaviors and those at eight months, *Developmental Psychology*, 10:779.

ROSENBLITH, J. F., AND ANDERSON, R. B., 1968, Prognostic significance of discrepancies in muscle tonus, *Developmental Medicine and Child Neurology*, 10:322.

ROSENZWEIG, M. R., 1971, Effects of environment on development of brain and behavior, *in* "Biopsychology of Development," E. Tobach, L. R. Aronson, and E. Shaw (eds.), Academic Press, New York.

SAMEROFF, A. J., AND CHANDLER, M. J., 1975, Reproductive risk and the continuum of caretaking casualty, *in* "Review of Child Development Research," Vol. 4, University of Chicago Press, Chicago.

SCARR, S., AND WILLIAMS, M., 1971, The assessment of neonatal and later status in low birth weight infants, paper presented at the biennial meeting of the Society for Research in Child Development, Minneapolis.

SCARR-SALAPATEK, S., AND WILLIAMS, M. L., 1973, The effects of early stimulation on low-birth-weight infants, *Child Development*, 44:94.

SCHACTER, F. F., AND APGAR, V., 1959, Perinatal asphyxia and psychological signs of brain damage in childhood, *Pediatrics*, 24:1016.

SECHZER, J. A., FARO, M. D., BARKER, J. J., BARSKY, D., GUTIERREZ, S., AND WINDLE, W. F., 1971, Developmental behaviors: Delayed appearance in monkeys asphyxiated at birth, *Science*, 171:1173.

SILVERMAN, W. A., 1969, What is the present status of retrolental fibroplasia? *in* "Problems of Neontal Intensive Care Units," 59th Ross Conference on Pediatric Research, Ross Laboratories, Columbus, Ohio.

SOULE, B., STANDLEY, K., COPANS, S., AND DAVIS, M., 1973, Clinical implications of the Brazelton Scale, Paper presented at the annual meeting of the Society for Research in Child Development held in Philadelphia.

STAHLMAN, M. T., 1969, What evidence exists that intensive care has changed the incidence of intact survival? *in* "Problems of Neonatal Intensive Care Units," 59th Ross Conference on Pediatric Research, Ross Laboratories, Columbus, Ohio.

STAHLMAN, M. T., HEDVALL, G., DOLANSKI, E., FAXELIUS, G., BURKO, H., AND KIRK, V., 1973, A six-year follow-up of clinical hyaline membrane disease, *Pediatric Clinics of North America*, 20:433.

SUMI, S. M., LEECH, R. W., ALVORD, E. C., JR., ENG, M., AND UELAND, K., 1973, Sudanophilic lipids in the unmyelinated primate cerebral white matter after intrauterine hypoxia and acidosis, *in* "Biological and Environmental Determinants of Early Development," J. I. Nurnberger (ed.), Williams & Wilkins, Baltimore.

THOMAS, A., CHESS, S., AND BIRCH, H., 1968, "Temperament and Behavior Disorders in Children," New York University, New York.

USHER, R., AND MCLEAN, F., 1969, Interuterine growth of live-born Caucasian infants at sea level: Standards obtained from measurements in 7 dimensions of infants born from 24 and 44 weeks of gestation, *Journal of Pediatrics*, 74(6):901–910.

WERNER, E. E., BIERMAN, J. M., AND FRENCH, F. E., 1971, "The Children of Kauai," University of Hawaii Press, Honolulu.

WERNER, E. E., HONZIK, M. P., AND SMITH, R. S., 1968, Prediction of intelligence and achievement at ten years from twenty months pediatric and psychological examinations, *Child Development*, 39:1063.

WILLERMAN, L., BROMAN, S. H., AND FIEDLER, M., 1970, Infant development, preschool IQ, and social class, *Child Development*, 41:69.

WINDLE, W. F., 1969, Asphyxial brain damage at birth, with reference to the minimally affected child, *in* "Perinatal Factors Affecting Human Development," *Proceedings*, Pan American Health Organization, Scientific Publication No. 185.

YERUSHALMY, J., BIERMAN, J. M., KEMP, D. H., CONNOR, A., AND FRENCH, F. E., 1956, Longitudinal studies of pregnancy on the island of Kauai, Territory of Hawaii, I: Analysis of previous reproductive history, *American Journal of Obstetrics and Gynecology*, 71:80.

9 Understanding "Why": Its Significance in Early Intelligence

MARION BLANK
AND DORIS A. ALLEN

INTRODUCTION

The past decade of developmental research has led to a heightened respect for the intellectual functioning of the very young child. Following the direction set by Piaget many years ago, several investigators have suggested that from the earliest months the child categorizes and interprets the world that confronts him (Kagan, 1972; Eimas, in press; Haith *et al.*, 1969). According to this view, the child develops a large repertoire of concepts that define the objects, people, places, and events with which he has contact. The processes through which the categories are defined differ according to the age of the child and the type of information involved. For example, neonates have been found to give preferential attention to moving objects and to light and dark contrasts, indicating that these perceptions may be present in the visual system at birth (Kagan, 1972). Also at a very early age infants appear to recognize and even to prefer the human face and voice over other shapes and sounds, a preference that some investigators have interpreted as suggesting that the human child has a perceptual set for attending to these human attributes (Fantz, 1961; Eimas *et al.*, 1971). Other kinds of information processing appear to be dependent upon the child's maturation

MARION BLANK·Rutgers Medical School.
DORIS A. ALLEN·Albert Einstein College of Medicine.

and/or his experience with the external world. Gibson (1969) has suggested that the young child's early attention to single features gradually gives way to perception of bundles of features, which are perceived at a later developmental stage as distinctive features that the child uses in deriving higher-level categories. It is difficult to say at what point in the child's development his early percepts become organized as concepts. What is important to our purposes is that the child is no longer being viewed as a passive recipient of external stimulation; rather, he is seen as an active processor of information from a very early age (see Kessen, 1965). Investigators generally agree not only that the child's early learning is extensive and complex but that it is also accomplished nonverbally.

This view, which increases our respect for the young child's nonverbal functioning, has had a curious dual effect on the study of language development. On the one hand it has stimulated research on language, for with the new interest in the complexity of preverbal intelligence, investigators have become eager to use the child's early language as a mirror for reflecting his prelinguistic knowledge of the world (e.g., the earliest words show what is uppermost in the child's mind). On the other hand the enhanced respect accorded nonverbal intelligence has led to a downplaying of the role of language in the child's cognitive development. For many years there was a strong tendency to view language as a major force in promoting the child's intellectual growth (see Nelson, 1974, for a review of this work). Now, however, language is seen by a number of theorists as subordinate—rather than requisite—to concept development (Bloom, 1970, 1973; Brown, 1973a and b; R. Clark, 1974; Nelson, 1973a and b, 1974; Sinclair, 1971; Slobin, 1973). According to these theorists, acquiring language is a matter of mapping linguistic structures on previously acquired averbal cognitive concepts. This view is mirrored in McNamara's statement (1972) that "infants learn their language by first determining, independent of language, the meaning which a speaker intends to convey to them and by then working out the relationship between the meaning and the language. To put it another way, the infant uses meaning, that is, nonverbal meaning acquired through his perceptual motor systems, as a clue to language, rather than language as a clue to meaning" (pp. 1–2). That is, the concepts the child has attained on the sensorimotor level serve as the basis for the first words that he uses. These include not only names of familiar objects and persons, such as "table," "bottle," "ball," "Mommy," and "Daddy," but also relational terms, such as "more," "all gone," and "up."

Eve Clark (1973, 1974) has pointed out, however, that the task of matching word with concept is more difficult than may be readily apparent. Citing Gibson's model, Clark hypothesizes that in the early stages of language acquisition the child will have meanings that are quite at variance with adult meanings for the same word because he evolves semantic categories by means of processes that are the same as those he uses in forming perceptual categories. That is, rather than attending to a whole object when it is named by the adult, he attends first to single perceptual features and then to progressively more complex distinctive features. He categorizes on the basis of these features, overextends these categories, and progressively refines the semantic criteria for the object named until his use of a term matches that of the adults in his world. For example, Clark (1974) suggested that learning the name of a given object involves the child forming the initial hypothesis: "A word refers to some identifiable (perceptually salient) characteristic of the object pointed to." The child's subsequent use of words involves the following strategy:

> Pick out whatever seems to be the most salient characteristic(s) perceptually, and assume (until given counter-evidence) that that is what the word refers to. Act on this assumption whenever you want to name, request, or call attention to something. (p. 116)

In her near-classic example of the possible procedures used by the child in acquiring the word *dog*, Clark observed that there are a number of features of real-world dogs to which the child might attend when he hears the word in the presence of the animal. That is, the four-leggedness or the hairy coat or the size of the dog (or a combination of these) might be more salient to the child than the total dog-ness.

There are other views of how the child acquires meanings. The examples given above are merely intended to represent some of the ways in which the language and cognitive–perceptual interrelationships are currently being viewed. Despite some differences, almost all of the current approaches to this problem share the basic idea that in some way language mirrors, and does not determine, cognition. They also share the feature that the words or phrases they have chosen to analyze deal with terms that represent objects, relations, or events that are perceivable in a sensorimotor way. McNeill (1970*b*) used the term *portrayable correlate* (p. 1069) to refer to these constructs. Language, however, contains many terms that have no immediately perceivable correlates. Once the child becomes aware of the existence of such terms, we believe the language-learning task inevitably becomes more complex. As we hope to show, it seems likely that such terms are learned by the child as language words and not as codings of pre-established concepts. In addition, we believe that the mastery of such terms lead the child to adopt a dramatically different mode of functioning that requires him to go beyond the sensorimotor based coding and decoding of meanings. In other words we are suggesting that the linguistic mastery of terms that lack portrayable correlates ultimately gives the child access to types of information and informing processing that are inaccessible through sensorimotor learning.

The terms to which we are referring might best be exemplified by the question words referring to cause (i.e., *why*) manner (i.e., *how*), and time (i.e., *when*).* Our selection of these question words from the total set of *"wh"* words in the language stands in contrast to the traditional practice of treating *how, why,* and *when* as belonging to a single class that includes *what, who, where,* and *which.* Investigators who have worked with children's question words (Brown, 1968; Ervin-Tripp, 1970; Klima and Bellugi, 1966) have reported that *why, how,* and *when* are acquired later than *who, what,* and *where.* Nevertheless, since investigators categorize these words within a single congeneric group, the later acquisition of *why* and *how* has seemed to represent only a quantitative difference in the development of a single category. Our own experience in working with young children, however, indicates that these words are acquired in a different manner and function in a different way. For a number of reasons, which we hope will become clear in the course of this chapter, the major focus here will be limited to the development of the child's use of—and understanding of—the *wh* word *why.*

* When we think about words that lack perceivable correlates, the category that might first come to mind is the entire functor class. This category goes much beyond *why* and includes such terms as *is, of,* and *about.* Brown (1973*a*) has an extended discussion on this topic. In general, as he points out, many of these words can be mastered through the child's attending to the context in which they occur and then incorporating them into his growing set of combinations and ultimately into his syntactic and morphological rule system. As a result these words may be used appropriately by the child even though he does not understand, nor need to understand, their "meaning." Since we are concerned with the child's search for meaning, we are not going to focus in this chapter on the development of these other functors, although we believe them to be of great importance in the child's developing language system.

INVESTIGATING WHY

Our thoughts on the meaning of *why* first evolved as a result of our experience in a teaching program for preschool children (Blank, 1973; Blank and Solomon, 1968, 1969). We found that in contrast to the relative ease with which the youngsters in the program dealt with questions introduced by *what, who,* and *where,* questions of the *why* and *how* types seemed to pose great difficulties.

In an effort to understand such difficulties we reviewed the literature that dealt with the acquisition of these terms. Several investigators have reported the appearance of *why* by 2 years of age, but the child's use of the word at this age has rarely been analyzed (see Brown, 1968; Fahey, 1942; Weir, 1962). This neglect of *why* may stem from the fact that the word seems to be used in ways that adults perceive as meaningless. It is not until the child is close to 3 years old that the term begins to be used "meaningfully" in the sense that his use of *why* more closely matches the adult's use of it (e.g., in a question such as "Why Daddy sleeping?"). Most of the reports on the child's use of *why* are confined to this post-3-year-old period (Brown, 1973b; Isaacs, 1930; Lewis, 1951; Piaget, 1952a).

Although there are few such reports and those that are available tend to be brief, the literature contains some intriguing facts that support our belief that the word *why* occupies a rather unique position in the child's repertoire. First, the child seems to produce it before he understands it. This pattern of development contrasts to the almost universal sequence in child language wherein comprehension precedes production. Second, its meaningful use is greatly delayed in comparison to other *wh* question words, such as *what, where, who,* and *which.* Third, although children ask *why* questions of adults, they almost never ask them of other children (Piaget, 1952a). This suggests that the child perceives *why* as serving a different role from that of his other question words.

These facts, along with our clinical observations of the difficulties that many children experience with *why,* led us to investigate the child's acquisition of this word. We chose to avoid artificial, testlike situations in which the child's use of *why* would be demanded by an adult. Because the child's earliest use of *why* had been reported to be meaningless, it was clear that any test situation would only show the child's lack of comprehension. Instead we felt it essential to use a naturalistic situation in which the child might spontaneously produce or respond to this question in a normal interchange with an adult. Accordingly we chose to analyze only data collected under such conditions.

The data are part of a longitudinal study of the language development of one child, a white upper-middle-class child named Dusty (see Allen, 1973). These data were obtained from audiotaped play sessions conducted bimonthly in Dusty's own room when she was between the ages of 18 and 31 months. In each session the major participants were Dusty and the adult "playmate." Each session averaged about one hour, yielding a total corpus of 27 hours of adult–child interaction. Because our goals involved understanding the child's comprehension and production of *why*, we examined all interchanges in which this term occurred. These included the child's use of the term and the adult's response, as well as the adult's use of the term and the child's response. In all instances the accompanying nonlinguistic behavior was noted so that the use of *why* could be examined in context.*

The analysis of *why* can be seen with greater clarity if it is set within the framework in which the other *wh* question words were used. The establishment of such a framework is not difficult, for in a typical session the overwhelmingly predominant form of interchange used by the adult with the child was the question form. Questions such as "Shall we play ball?", "Where did the airplane go?", "What is this?", and "What are you going to make?" abound. In fact, in every session during the period in which Dusty was between the one- and three-word stages, over 50% of the adult verbalizations were in the question form. Such frequent use of questions is probably not confined to the dialogues studied here. An examination of many reported dialogues between adults and children reveals a comparable prominence of questions (see especially Baldwin and Baldwin, 1970).

Both our data and the reports of other investigators show that adults, when talking to young children, seldom use the question in its traditional role of information seeking. When adults ask the names of objects (e.g., "What this?") or ask about events and locations (e.g., "Where's your nose?"), they know the answers. In such situations

---

* We recognize the potential hazards of making generalizations about linguistic phenomena on the basis of one case. However, at many points our findings agree with the reported, albeit scattered, observations that exist in the literature on the young child's use of *why*.

adults seem to rely upon questions as one means of initiating and sustaining interaction with verbally limited partners.

This mode of behavior may be relevant to the commonly cited phenomenon that children frequently ask questions to which *they* already know the answers (Chrelashviti, 1972; Lewis, 1951). For example, the following interchange is quite typical:

> Child (pointing to a toy horse): "What's that?"
> Adult: "What *is* that?"
> Child: "Horsie."

This type of interchange has been interpreted as showing that the child uses questions in a peculiarly immature way: since he already knows the answer, he is obviously not using the question to gain information. Instead, it has been suggested, the child uses such questions to gain attention. But in fact the data on adult–child interchange cited here suggest that the child is modeling himself, and accurately modeling himself, after the adult pattern to which he has been exposed. If adults who are all-knowing and all-powerful ask questions to which they clearly know the answers, children have every reason to believe that this is a legitimate, and perhaps even major, use of questions.

Although questions are extensively asked by adults, only a limited number of question forms is used when they speak to young children. Specifically, aside from yes–no questions, the major *wh* question words used by the adult are *what, who,* and *where.* As is clear from developmental studies (Brown, 1968; Ervin-Tripp, 1970; Klima and Bellugi, 1966), these question words are the ones mastered earliest by the child. It seems likely that the adult recognizes that these forms are easiest for the youngster to comprehend, and therefore he relies on them extensively. (See Snow, 1972, and Gleason, 1973, for comparable illustrations of the way adults modify their speech to young children.)

The adult's reliance on *what, who,* and *where* is not difficult to explain, nor upon reflection is it in any way unexpected. A sufficient response to *where* (e.g., "Where's the ball?") is usually a pointing gesture, while a response to *what* and *who* (e.g., "What's this?") is usually a single nominal label. Appropriate responses to these questions therefore demand little beyond the child's sensorimotor repertoire; they refer to immediately available objects that he clearly perceives, require actions that he can easily perform, or demand single-word responses that he can readily produce. Thus the adult who uses these questions capitalizes on the child's already-developed skills to begin to engage him in a dialogue.

The "strategy" adopted by adults seems extremely productive, for it leads children to become active participants in the exchange even when they are still limited to single-word utterances. When Dusty was only 18 months old, she responded to most of the questions posed to her. For example, with a single word (e.g., "cookie") she was able to meet the demands of a whole range of questions, such as, "What's that?" "What do you want?" and "More what?" At times, given her limited verbal repertoire, her answers were not quite "appropriate" by adult standards. For example, if while eating a cookie she was asked, "What are you doing?" her response might be, "Cookie." Since she had no verbs in her repertoire at the time, her answer was the closest she could come to an adequate response. Therefore, although this type of answer is not truly sufficient from an adult perspective, the adult generally sees it as meaningful and readily accepts it from the child.

Following these early stages, Dusty proceeded to make rapid progress. By the time she was 20 months old, she was able to produce multiword responses to questions. For example, when asked, "What do you want me to do with the teddy bear?" she replied, "Get down teddy bear." Dusty's production of question words also showed rapid progress. Once she could produce multiword utterances, she began to ask such questions as, "What's that?" "Who's that?" and "Where baby go?" Dusty's acquisition of the *wh* question words *what, who, where,* and *which* followed a regular progression from comprehension (manifested first by pointing, and then by nominal response, and eventually by more complex predicative strings) to production of her own simple *wh* questions.

The pattern of question asking and answering outlined above is compatible with the reports in the literature on the development of *wh* questions in young children. The one question word that did not follow this pattern was *why*. It occurred during this period but in ways totally different from any other form of question. First, it was produced by the child, and produced regularly and repeatedly, without any apparent comprehension. A similar reversal in the comprehension–production sequence is reported by Brown (1968) in his analysis of one child's acquisition of this term. Second, to attain even preliminary mastery, Dusty took a period of nine months from the time she first used *why* to the time she used it in any way meaningful to an adult. This interval represents an unusually long period, particularly when contrasted with the rapid understanding she displayed of almost any other term she employed. Third, in contrast to *what, who,* and *where, why* questions were rarely asked by the adult. The first use of *why* by the adult in our corpus occurred in the session when Dusty was 20 months old. At that time the adult asked one *why* question, while *what, where,* and *how many* formed the basis of 131 other questions.

Despite the infrequent use of *why* by the adult, Dusty used this term herself even at the first taping session, when she was 18 months old. Her use of this word was not frequent, but it was consistent. It occurred in every session but one, and it was always used more extensively by the child than by the adult.

STRATEGIES FOR WHY

Although Dusty used the term *why* in ways not consonant with the adult use, analysis of her production and comprehension indicated clear and changing patterns over time. These patterns seem to reflect a set of three basic strategies that Dusty adopted in mastering this elusive term. Not only are the strategies indicative of the enormous perseverance that she was willing to use in coping with unknown material, but they also seem to reflect a level of functioning that was different from that found in her other linguistic behavior.

Strategy I

This strategy, like those that followed, was marked by a cleavage between Dusty's production of *why* and her response when *why* questions were asked of her. At this first stage one might be somewhat hard-pressed to consider her responses to *why* questions representative of a true strategy. When asked *why,* as in, "Why is the dolly going to sleep?" she almost invariably ignored the *why* (e.g., gave no response at all, tentatively touched the object named, or else changed the subject (e.g., she moved away to another toy). Ervin-Tripp (1970) has noted similar behavior on the part of young children when *why* questions are put to them. In effect children seem either to ignore the question or to try out techniques from their sensorimotor repertoire that have previously been found to be successful. For example, if asked, "Why is the boy wearing boots?" a child might reach and touch the boots. This sensorimotor type of response is appropriate and effective with other questions or commands (e.g., "Where are your shoes?" and "Show me your shoes"). It is, however, ineffective, in the case of *why*. In the absence of further information the only major avenue open to the child at this point is to ignore the *why* in the question that has been asked, and this is the tack that Dusty selected most often. This behavior contrasted strongly to the nearly universal and nearly always appropriate answers she gave to *what* and *where* questions and questions that required an answer of yes or no.

In spite of the fact that Dusty appeared unable to respond to adult-asked *why*'s, she did seem to have a production strategy for this term. As stated earlier, she was able to ask *why* questions at this age. One exchange in which *why* occurred involved a toy cat that had, in the course of its existence, lost its head. The exchange went as follows:

> Adult: "The cat has a body but no head."
> Dusty: "Why?"
> Adult: "Why? I don't know why. Did someone break it?"
> (Dusty turned away and walked over to the toy box.)

This exchange exemplified the major qualities that were to characterize the child's strategy in producing *why* questions over the next six months. First, it occurred only in response to an adult statement, never as a means of initiating dialogue with the adult. Thus Dusty might approach the adult and as an initiating question ask, "Where ball?" She would never do this with *why*. Instead, she would use this term only after the adult had verbally expressed an observation or a request. From the beginning, then, as Brown (1968) has also suggested, *why* was tied to linguistic context, not to perceptually based material. This suggests that unlike words that were related to portrayable correlates, *why* was derived not from physical reality but from linguistic dialogue. Second, *why* always occurred when the adult's utterance contained a negative, such as *no* or *not*. The sentence type used by the adult seemed not to have any bearing on this pattern. Dusty used *why* in response to commands, assertions, and questions alike. *In all cases, however, the preceding utterance contained a negative term.* It appears that she sensed some semantic connection between *why* and negation. This may have derived from a number of sources. For example:

1. In the few times young children are asked *why*, it is generally a

rhetorical question in reaction to some undesirable behavior by the child (e.g., spilling milk provokes "Why did you do that?"). The quality of reprimand may then be translated into the semantic equivalent of undesirability (*no* or *not*). As a result, when the child hears a statement containing a negative, she tries out "Why?" in response, since this has been the term paired with negation.

2. Adults, when wanting to be polite, frequently phrase requests in the form of negative *why* questions (e.g., "Why don't you sit down here?"). Again, the child may hear this and connect *why* and negation.

3. Adults themselves frequently ask, "Why?" when they hear a negative statement (e.g., when someone says "I don't want to—" a common response is "Why?" or "Why not?" Thus a variety of sources seem to coalesce to lead the child to pair the components of *why* and negation.

The occurrence of this type of pairing suggests that Dusty recognized some of the contextual features accompanying the use of some kinds of *why*s even when she had not mastered their finer meanings. Bloom (1970) reported a similar sort of context-sensitive phenomenon in which words were used "appropriately" by the child even though they were semantically anomalous. In Bloom's data this occurred with temporal adverbs (e.g., "next Monday" and "last night"). As in the case of *why* these terms lack portrayable correlates, and as in the case of *why* the child seems to rely upon features of the linguistic context as cues for producing them.

Dusty's regular and systematic use of *why* might lead an observer to claim that the child had a different concept for the term to which the adult mind is not privy. Even within her own frame of reference, however, Dusty appeared to be uncertain as to what the word might mean. Some evidence for this claim lies in the fact that her use of *why* at this period was limited to the single-word question even when she was regularly producing her other question words (*who, what,* and *where*) in sentences of three to four words in length. It appears that Dusty was unclear as to how to expand the *why* utterance even when she had found a means for doing so with her other question words.

The child also was not helped in any clear way by the adult at this point. Most of the *why* questions that Dusty asked were nonsensical from an adult viewpoint. Largely because the word was semantically anomalous, the response offered by the adult to the child's *why*s generally reflected faltering confusion (as in the cat example above). Typically the adult might say something like, "I don't know why," or "Because it's just like that," or "Why do you think it is?" None of these answers seems to yield any clear pattern that might give the child a sense of when it would be acceptable and appropriate to use this term. In fact, of the first 19 *whys* that Dusty asked, only 5 received replies that might suggest to her that a meaningful response to her question was possible. (For example, while playing with a sharp toy Dusty was told, "Don't put that in your mouth." She asked, "Why?" and the adult answered, "Because that would hurt you.")

Given this confusing situation, one may wonder why Dusty, and other children, bother to produce the number of *whys* that they do. No clear answer is possible. We believe, however, that a central factor is the power of the question form in human communication. The asking of a question almost begs for an answer. It is probably for this reason that *why* attracts children's attention and leads them to search for its meaning. However, as shown above, they appear to be unable to derive the meaning of the word through comprehension of the adult's usage or through discerning key contextual (nonlinguistic) features that could give *why* some meaning. As illustrated above, production alone is insufficient to give children the information they need to understand and use the term appropriately. It is probably for this reason that Dusty embarked on a second type of strategy.

Strategy II

The pattern of production and comprehension outlined above was essentially maintained until Dusty was 25 months old. Then, for a one-month period, no instances of *why* occurred. The absence of *why* may have been due to chance factors (that is, Dusty may have produced them at other times during the month but not in the two sessions that were recorded). On the other hand, the cessation may have reflected a major point of reorganization. In any event, when *why* reappeared one month later, a new pattern emerged. Dusty's production shifted from single-word utterances to the use of *why* with strings of words. For example, the following exchange occurred at about this time:

> Dusty (referring to the garage door on a toy garage): "Pull up the shade."
> Adult: "All right, but that's not a shade.
>   That's the garage door."

Dusty: "Why the garage door? Why?"
Adult: "Hmm?"
Dusty: "Why the garage door?"
Adult: "What?"
Dusty: "Why the garage door?"

This dialogue captures several of the qualities that were present in Dusty's second strategy. First, she no longer used *why* only as an isolated term. Instead, similar to the strategy for *where* (e.g., "Where garage door?") she seemed to formulate *why* questions by placing a nominal or adjectival word or phrase after the question word. Second, the word or words placed after the *why* were almost always partial repetitions of what the adult had just said (see Clark, 1974, for a similar observation). Third, as illustrated in the dialogue above, Dusty continued to receive puzzling feedback from the adult because her use of *why* was still inappropriate. Her response to the adult's feedback at this stage, however, was quite different from the response she showed in Strategy I. She repeatedly pursued the interchange, almost as if she were intent upon getting some meaningful answer. Thus, while her previous strategy was tied into salient semantic features of the preceding adult utterances (e.g., the use of the negative), the present strategy involved expansion of the adult's nominal or adjectival construction— thereby extending her *wh* category to include an unknown term.

The changes in Dusty's production of *why* were paralleled by changes in her response to *why*s asked by adults. In place of the avoidance that Dusty previously demonstrated when asked *why*, at this stage she now answered, "I don't know." This latter phrase had been in her repertoire since 21 months of age and had been used freely in answer to other *wh* questions. It was not until 26 months, however, that she ever used it in reponse to *why*.

The reason for this sudden shift in Dusty's comprehension and production strategy can only be speculated upon. What seems significant is that *it occurred along with a major spurt in the production of more syntactically complex utterances*. The latter included the use of coordinating conjunctions (e.g., *and*), auxiliaries in questions (e.g., *can I*) and sentence adverbials (e.g., *now, first,* and *maybe*). It is of interest that all of these terms are functors that have no portrayable correlates and that all reflect a greater sensitivity to the more subtle intricacies of connected discourse.

Regardless of the factors responsible for the change, the new uses of *why* marked the beginning of a rapid acceleration in Dusty's mastery of this word. In the next month she produced 26 *why* questions in one hour in contrast to the average of three to four such questions in each hour during the preceding eight months. As inevitably happens in children's language development, Dusty continued to use the more primitive types of *why* along with the more elaborated types. For example, she still used *why* as a single-word question, and more often than not her *why*s functioned primarily as responses to adult's utterances rather than as a means of initiating dialogue about an event. It was not until the third strategy emerged that there was a marked decline in her more primitive uses of *why*.

Strategy III

The next major step in Dusty's acquisition of why occurred in the 28th month. At that time, she began to take an affirmative, not a negative, statement by the adult and repeat it, prefacing it with *why*. This is illustrated in the following dialogue:

> Dusty: "Where's Bobby?"
> Adult: "He's home reading a book."
> Dusty: "Why he reading a book?"

This new use of *why* reflects an interesting development. Dusty no longer followed *why* with a noun or an adjective alone (as in, "Why garage door?" or "Why green?"). Instead, she took the whole of a relatively long adult utterance, preceded it with *why*, and repeated it with question intonation. Significantly mastery of the adult meaning for *why* seems to demand this achievement. *Why* almost always refers to either predicates or whole sentences. Thus *what*, *where*, and *who* can be meaningfully used when the focus is solely on the nominal phrase (e.g., "Where ball?"). By contrast, *why* with a nominal phrase is usually meaningless (e.g., "Why ball?"). It takes on meaning only when it goes beyond the single object focused on in the nominal and encompasses an entire event. It would seem valuable to determine whether the need to attend to the entire sentence in formulating *why*s has benefits that extend beyond the use of *why* itself. For example, it may lead to increased skill in coping with longer strings of words, or it may refocus the child's attention from the salient nouns and adjectives to less salient features embedded in the predicate.

In Strategy III another use of *why* appeared. Dusty no longer used *why* only as a response to a statement by the adult. Instead she used it to initiate discourse about observable changes in the environment. For example, at one point the adult folded up a piece of paper and placed it in her pocket, and Dusty said, "Why you put this in your pocket?" With this we can see that Dusty was truly beginning, and only then just beginning, to tap the traditionally accepted role of *why* "to secure an explanation by which the formulation of one event may be fitted together with the formulation of others" (Lewis, 1951, p. 259). Although Dusty's use of *why* in this manner was less common than the "why the garage door" type, it was ultimately much more productive for her. Almost always the adult interpreted this type of question as meaningful and comfortably gave a relevant answer.

Although these *whys* can be and frequently are interpreted as meaningful by the adult listener, we believe that a child's use of the term does not necessarily mean that he has a total grasp of the concept. Our reason for this conclusion is that even at 30 months Dusty was as likely to ask meaningless *whys* as to ask meaningful ones. For example, at one point the adult said, "That's the lake," and Dusty replied "Oh why?" At another time, the adult said, "You're stepping on the washcloth," and Dusty replied, "Why?"

Strategy III was also marked by changes in Dusty's response to the adult's *why* questions. In contrast to her earlier avoidance of the term and her later use of "I don't know," Dusty now began to maintain the exchange after the question was posed. For example, one exchange at 23 months went as follows:

> Adult: "Leave the cups there."
> Dusty: "No."
> Adult: "Why?"
> Dusty: "Let's put on the counter."

Another exchange, at 29 months, proceeded in this way:

> Adult: "Why are you putting tissue in the closet?"
> Dusty: "So be cool, be cool."

It seems clear that Dusty was beginning to grasp the idea that some feature associated with the event or situation should be cited in answer to a *why* question (e.g., the placing of the tissues in the closet will result in a change of state). It seems equally clear, however, that as Piaget (1952a) has demonstrated, she had no real understanding of the causal or logical relationships that might be involved. For example, she was as likely to make a response that was inappropriate to the situation as she was to offer an appropriate response. One exchange went as follows:

> Dusty (referring to a blanket): "I can't wash this."
> Adult: "Why not?"
> Dusty: "In here."

Responses of this sort are the ones that have led investigators to suggest that the young child at first processes *why* questions as *what* and *where* questions (Ervin-Tripp, 1970). Such an interpretation would explain the locative answer given by Dusty in the example above. Our data, however, suggest that rather than being an initial strategy, this type of response represents a rather late development. From a faltering beginning in which *why* questions asked by adults were avoided, Dusty had become able not only to respond to *why* questions but also to recognize that some feature of the situation should be used in the response (as in the "so be cool" example given earlier). At certain times no feature may have been clearly evident to the child; nevertheless she still felt compelled to respond. In these cases, lacking any other cues she might then treat the adult *why* as a *what* or *where* question.

It is evident from these examples that Dusty's task of understanding *why* was far from finished at 31 months. She had still not determined which of several possible attributes should be selected for an appropriate response, nor had she determined how different features may relate to different *why*s (e.g., internal states to *why*s of motivation and physical attributes to *why*s of cause). Even though true causal or logical thinking was not present at this early age, Dusty's preliminary acquisition of *why* still represents a major achievement. Over a period of months she steadfastly pursued the meaning of this elusive term through employing a course of hypothesis testing. Each successive strategy led her closer to the adult's meaning of the term, so that ultimately she was able to use the word in sustained interchanges with the adult.

The Relationships between Concepts and Language

The picture we have constructed of the child's active search for the meaning of *why* is compatible in many respects with recent models of early intelligence. As stated in the introduction, these models emphasize the child's ability to function in accord with relatively complex strategies (see Eimas, 1975; Fantz, 1965; Nelson, 1973a; Sinclair, 1971) rather than to function, as had been long maintained, as a passive recipient of stimulation. There is, however, a difference between the view put forth here and other recent formulations of the child's early intellectual functioning. The difference lies in the relationship that is posited between the linguistic and the conceptual domains. One current model is based on a "concept-matching" scheme (Nelson, 1973a,b). In this view, the child learns to match the word he hears with the objects and relations he has long since understood on a nonverbal level. This approach seems essentially valid for a wide range of words and word groupings that the young child learns. These include, in addition to individual lexical items, such semantic relations as the possessive ("Daddy chair"), disappearance ("all-gone ball"), recurrence ("more milk"), and spatial relationships ("ball table").

This concept matching stands in contrast to the long-standing "concept-formation" approach in which the child is believed to learn a word and then search for its referent (see Brown, 1958). This view, which has been developed most fully by the Russian theorists, claims that the child's learning of words is central to his concept development. This idea is typified in the statement that "by naming objects, and so defining their connections and relations, the adult creates new forms of reflection of reality in the child, incomparably deeper and more complex than those which he could have formed through individual experience" (Luria and Yudovich, 1959, p. 11). Nelson (1973a) maintains the position that this view is not tenable because "the word alone can have little salience or attraction compared to the nonlinguistic events to which it refers." Concept formation, according to this argument, "puts an enormous strain on memory and cognitive processing ability in that the child must hold in memory not only all the instances of Word but all of the relevant attributes of these instances, until he has extracted the invariance common to all. Although there are common strategies for solving this problem, their use implies a sophistication in and capacity for the use of problem-solving skills that have never been attributed to the infant" (Nelson, 1973a, p. 100). Despite the logic of this argument, our analysis in this chapter suggests that this concept-formation approach may be the one that a young child adopts in mastering the word *why*. In addition it is likely that a similar process is followed, at least in part, in his learning of other terms that lack portrayable correlates, such as *when, how, yesterday,* and *before.* This is not to say that the concept-formation approach is correct and the concept-matching approach incorrect. Each is valid, but for a different domain. When the child is trying to label perceived entities and relationships, the concept-matching model seems valid. When the child is faced with linguistic terms for which there is no perceptually available referent, however, the concept-formation view seems to offer a better interpretation of the child's functioning.

Our discussion has not touched upon the question of whether the young child does, or does not, have a grasp of the nonverbal concepts underlying *why* prior to learning their linguistic representations. We tend to agree with Clark that "just as the acquisition of linguistic structure is affected by psychological processes, so is the efficiency of these processes affected in its turn by the child's growing linguistic knowledge" (R. Clark, 1974, p. 1). It may well be that at certain points in the child's development it is easier for him to focus on the linguistic functioning of *why* than it is to determine the conceptual content of such a complex term.

By attending to the adult–child dialogues in which Dusty produced and responded to *why* questions, we found it possible to describe a succession of strategies that she seemed to have employed in attempting to master the term. We assumed that Dusty's use of *why* was never "meaningless"—but rather that her assumptions about the appropriate use of *why* did not always match those of the adult. Dusty's patterns of comprehending and producing *why* questions are surely not the only ones possible for a child. Nevertheless the patterns she exhibited are dramatic examples of the types of strategies that young children are capable of when they are ready and willing to move beyond the realm of concrete, physical reality in order to gain access to the realm of linguistic and conceptual meanings.

References

Allen, D., 1973, The development of predication in child language, unpublished doctoral dissertation, Teachers College, Columbia University.
Baldwin, A., and Baldwin, C., 1970, "Cognitive Content of Mother–Child Interaction," OE Project Report, Cornell University, Ithaca, New York.
Barten, S. S., and Blank, M., 1972, Soviet research on speech and language: An American perspective, *Early Child Development and Care*, 1:3.
Bever, T., 1970, The cognitive basis for linguistic structures, *in* "Cognition and the Development of Language," J. R. Hayes (ed.), Wiley, New York.

BLANK, M., 1973, "Teaching Learning in the Preschool: A Dialogue Approach," Charles E. Merrill, Columbus, Ohio.

BLANK, M., 1974, Cognitive functions of language in the preschool years, *Developmental Psychology*, 10:299.

BLANK, M., AND SOLOMON, F., 1968, A tutorial language program to develop abstract thinking in socially disadvantaged preschool children, *Child Development*, 39:379.

BLANK, M., AND SOLOMON, F., 1969, How shall the disadvantaged child be taught? *Child Development*, 40:47.

BLOOM, L., 1970, "Language Development: Form and Function in Emerging Grammars," MIT Research Monograph No. 59, Cambridge, Massachusetts.

BLOOM, L., 1973, "One Word at a Time: The Use of Single Word Utterances Before Syntax," Mouton, The Hague.

BRAINE, M. D. S., 1974, Beginning grammar, *Science*, 184:1275.

BROWN, R., 1958, "Words and Things," Free Press, Glencoe, Illinois.

BROWN, R., 1968, The development of WH questions in child speech, *Journal of Verbal Learning and Behavior*, 7:279.

BROWN, R., 1973a, "A First Language: The Early Stages," Harvard University Press, Cambridge, Massachusetts.

BROWN, R., 1973b, Development of the first language in the human species, *American Psychologist*, 28:97.

BROWN, R., AND BELLUGI, U., 1964, Three processes in the child's acquisition of syntax, *Harvard Educational Review*, 34:133.

CHRELASHVITI, N. V., 1972, On a critical moment in the child's mental (speech) development, *Early Child Development and Care*, 1:197.

CLARK, E. V., 1973, What's in a word? On the child's acquisition of semantics in his first language, *in* "Cognitive Development and the Acquisition of Language," T. E. Moore (ed.), Academic Press, New York.

CLARK, E. V., 1974, Some aspects of the conceptual bases for first language acquisition, *in* "Language Perspectives—Acquisition, Retardation, and Intervention," R. L. Schietelbusch and L. L. Lloyd (eds.), University Park Press, Baltimore.

CLARK, R., 1974, Performing without competence, *Journal of Child Language*, 1:1.

EIMAS, P. D., 1975, Speech perception in early infancy, *in* "Infant Perception," L. B. Cohen and P. Salapatek (eds.), Academic Press, New York.

EIMAS, P. D., SIQUELAND, E. R., JUSCYK, P., AND VIGORITO, J., 1971, Speech perception in infants, *Science*, 171:303.

ERVIN-TRIPP, S., 1970, Discourse agreement: How children answer questions, *in* "Cognition and the Development of Language," J. R. Hayes (ed.), Wiley, New York.

FAHEY, G. L., 1942, The questioning activity of children, *Journal of Genetic Psychology*, 60:337.

FANTZ, R. L., 1961, The origin of form perception, *Scientific American*, May:66.

FANTZ, R. L., 1965, Usual perception from birth as shown by pattern selectivity, *Annals of the New York Academy of Sciences*, 118:793.

GIBSON, E. J., 1969, "Principles of Perceptual Learning and Development," Appleton, New York.

GLEASON, J. B., 1973, Code switching in children's language, *in* "Cognitive Development and the Acquisition of Language," T. E. Moore (ed.), Academic Press, New York.

HAITH, M., KESSEN, R., AND COLLINS, D., 1969, Response of the human infant to level of complexity of intermittent visual movement, *Journal of Experimental Child Psychology*, 7:52.

Isaacs, S., 1930, "Intellectual Growth in Young Children with an Appendix on Children's 'Why' Questions by Nathan Isaacs," Harcourt, Brace, New York.

Kagan, J., 1972, Do infants think? *Scientific American,* 226:74.

Kessen, W., 1965, "The Child," Wiley, New York.

Klima, E. S., and Bellugi, U., 1966, Syntactic regularities in the speech of children, *in* "Cognition and the Development of Language," J. Lyons and R. J. Wales (eds.), Edinburgh University Press, Edinburgh.

Kuenne, M. R., 1946, Experimental investigation of the relation of language to transposition behavior in young children, *Journal of Experimental Psychology,* 36:471.

Lenneberg, E., 1967, "The Biological Foundations of Language," Wiley, New York.

Lewis, M. M., 1951, "Infant Speech" (2nd ed.), Routledge and Kegan Paul, London.

Lewis, M. M., 1963, "Language, Thought and Personality in Infancy and Childhood," Harrap, London.

Luria, A. R., 1961, "The Role of Speech in the Regulation of Normal and Abnormal Behavior," Liveright, New York.

Luria, A. R., and Yudovich, F., 1959, "Speech and the Development of Mental Processes in the Child," Staples Press, London.

McNamara, J., 1972, Cognitive basis of language learning in infants, *Psychological Review,* 79:1.

McNeill, D., 1970a, "The Acquisition of Language: The Study of Developmental Psycholinguistics," Harper & Row, New York.

McNeill, D., 1970b, The development of language, *in* "Carmichael's Manual of Child Psychology," P. H. Mussen (ed.), Wiley, New York.

Nelson, K., 1973a, Structure and strategy in learning to talk, *Monographs of the Society for Research in Child Development,* Vol. 38.

Nelson, K., 1973b, Some evidence for the cognitive primary of categorization and its functional basis, *Merrill–Palmer Quarterly of Behavior and Development,* 19:21.

Nelson, K., 1974, Concept, word, and sentence: Interrelations in acquisition and development, *Psychological Review,* 81:267.

Piaget, J., 1952a, "The Language and Thought of the Child," Routledge and Kegan Paul, London.

Piaget, J., 1952b, "The Origins of Intelligence in Children," International Universities Press, New York.

Rosch, E. H., 1973, Natural categories, *Cognitive Psychology,* 4:328.

Schlesinger, I. M., 1971, Production of utterances and language acquisition, *in* "The Ontogenesis of Grammar," D. K. Slobin (ed.), Academic Press, New York.

Sinclair, H., 1971, Sensori-motor action patterns as a condition for the acquisition of syntax, *in* "Language Acquisition: Models and Methods," R. Huxley and E. Ingram (eds.), Academic Press, New York.

Slobin, D. I., 1973, Cognitive prerequisites for the development of grammar, *in* "Studies of Child Language Development," C. A. Ferguson and D. I. Slobin (eds.), Holt, Rinehart and Winston, New York.

Snow, C. E., 1972, Mothers' speech to children learning language, *Child Development,* 43:549.

Stern, W., 1930, "Psychology of Early Childhood," Holt, New York.

Vygotsky, L., 1962, "Thought and Language," MIT Press, Cambridge, Massachusetts.

Wier, R., 1962, "Language in the Crib," Mouton, New York.

10 Cross-Cultural Studies of Infant Intelligence*

FREDA REBELSKY
AND PATRICIA A. DANIEL

It is no longer fashionable to talk of *primitive* tribes. Yet we can, and do, talk about whole groups of people as being disadvantaged, deprived, and with restricted word codes, ad nauseum. This review of cross-cultural studies of infant intelligence starts from a specific developmental bias: "People are different in important ways around the world; different societies need different types of children and adults; societies differ from each other. . . . We are impoverished, as human beings, even within our own culture, when we call differences in development 'worse' " (Rebelsky, 1972, p. 130). This chapter first elaborates on this bias and then discusses the concept of intelligence in general and its application to cross-cultural research. Then we explore some specific issues and speculations in the field of cross-cultural infant intelligence.

Cross-cultural research is useful in that it can help us open our eyes to the differences and commonalities in development. (Excellent reviews of the value of cross-cultural research may be found in Whiting and Whiting [1959], Munroe and Munroe [1975], and LeVine [1970].) The differences, if seen as adaptive, enlarge our perspective and our understanding of what is normal. Cross-cultural research should enable us to see what all members of the human species have in common and what are the limits of plasticity of organism and culture. When similarities and differences among cultures are found, the question of causality arises. It is tempting to use the concept of culture to *explain* differences, but we

---

* John Thomas and Gail Gutman reviewed the literature and made helpful comments in preparation for this chapter.

FREDA REBELSKY AND PATRICIA A. DANIEL · Boston University.

find it more useful to think of culture as a "carrier variable," as a medium in which different processes are taking place (Lewis and Wilson, 1972). In other words, it is not enough to talk about the differences in behaviors in different cultures; we must ask what is causing these differences—what is being done in these cultures that leads to these differences.

We want to explore not only what it is that is done in different cultures to produce different behaviors, but why. All humans live in a society and must become adequate members of their own society. There are wide differences in what cultures ask of their members, and we can ask why it is that certain behaviors are sufficient in that culture or family. Individuals are raised to behave appropriately—we are all "products" of our culture, and what we do "pays off" in our culture. In the sense that people are raised to behave adaptively, given their particular cultural framework, we might say that all humans are intelligent. Cole *et al.* (1971) draw a similar conclusion from their cross-cultural work:

> If there is a general principle to be gleaned from the method upon which our work is based, it derives from our belief that the people we are working with always behave reasonably. When their behavior appears unreasonable, it is to ourselves, our procedures, and our experimental tasks that we turn for an explanation. (p. xv)

In a great many cultures of the world, there is "full employment," that is, every member of the group functions and is necessary for the functioning of the group. Some nations need all of their people to work, and the expectation, for example, in the kibbutz is that all members will work their best at whatever they do. There are no better or worse jobs, no better or worse people.

A reality is that this chapter will be read largely by a United States audience, and such readers, as members of that culture, find it very difficult to believe that all people are smart, adaptive, and reasonable. And in this culture, since we believe the opposite to be true, it is true. This attitude is in sharp contrast to what we are beginning to learn about the Chinese culture, where all persons are considered worthwhile and important to society (Kagan, 1974). The United States culture has a difficult time equating the problem-solving abilities needed by a doctor and by a plumber, or even equating the social importance of both tasks. We live in a society of elites, which significantly does not need whole groups of people who are labeled *different* or *worse*. We attempt to change many of these groups, the extremes on our scales of anything. We are a competitive society, with "haves" and "have-nots" and, therefore, must be uncomfortable with the idea that "all men are created equal."

As the reader proceeds through this chapter he may find that his own cultural biases color his perceptions and expectations so that he is willing to believe certain data and not other data or is critical of certain practices of other cultures. Aware of the stumbling blocks of these ethnocentric tendencies, Goldberg (1973) wrote, "My conviction, that cross-cultural research is necessary, is tempered by the concern that it may be methodologically, ethically, and politically impossible" (p. 1). It may be close to impossible to carry out this type of research, but at least we can be cautioned and aware that we may be "locked into" our culture. This awareness may lead us to approach the data on cross-cultural infant intelligence with as much openness as possible.

WHAT IS "INTELLIGENCE"?

It is within Western society that intelligence testing and, specifically, infant intelligence testing began. Use of the term *intelligence* at any age, and particularly in dealing with other cultures, is fraught with difficulties. One problem in measuring intelligence cross-culturally is the initial (conscious or below-awareness) biases of the investigator: "We observe a proliferation of reports which appear to show, by experiments that seem to be carefully controlled, that the experimenter's social group is extremely intelligent, and that alien social groups are unintelligent in proportion to their distance from his own" (Labov, 1973, p. 428). Other evidence of investigator bias comes from a study of the biographical characteristics of United States investigators of black–white intelligence. Sherwood and Nataupsky (1968) found that those whose research was categorized as concluding that blacks are innately inferior intellectually came from the higher socioeconomic backgrounds. (See Chapter 11 by Golden and Birns in this volume for a discussion of social class issues in infant intelligence testing.)

Even if investigators were not prone to judging intelligence as those qualities that are prevalent in their own social group, there would still be the problems of defining the concept of intelligence. Traditionally intelligence has been thought of as a "bundle of cognitive abilities" (Feldman et al., 1974, p. 3) that are present in varying degrees in particular individuals. Largely through the work of Piaget we have come to think of intelligence not in terms of what is demonstrable or "missing" in a child's repertoire of abilities, but rather in terms of what the child is doing and what the processes of his thought are. What we find with this approach is that children are constructing their own worlds through active manipulation and change and that during development there is adaptation to the environment and reorganization of the world. The child constructs his own world and it is real; his construction may be different from that of adults, or it may be different in different populations of children, but in each case it is a legitimate adaptive construction of the world. Given this approach, the questions to be asked are why there are these differences and how they come about.

When it actually comes to measuring intelligence, our choices reveal further what it is that we mean by the concept *intelligence*. The act of measurement imposes structure on an essentially structureless concept (Wesman, 1968, p. 273) and asks that the appropriate behavior exhibit itself in the testing situation. For example, many intelligence tests impose the duality *verbal/motor* on the concept and expect that what is intelligent can be seen in a situation in which the individual is constrained to follow instructions and to use the materials provided in the setting provided. Which skills we sample further specify what "intelligence" is considered to be. For example, developmental psychologists can easily point to infant abilities not measured by any infant test (Freedman, 1971). The infant's ability to differentiate among tastes, textures, and smells is well known, yet not one infant test measures these skills.

Whatever the investigator's choice for the concept of intelligence, applying this notion to another culture has special problems. Cole et al. (1971, p. xii) claimed that the implication of Piagetian theory is "more development means more powerful structures [levels]." When a foreign sample performs poorly on a Piagetian test (such as conservation of volume), the conclusion is that such-and-such a level has not been reached in that sample. The follow-up is that the culture studied is not as developed or is more "primitive." But the real issue lies in the value of a test formed by Western minds to a people not of that "mind." Cross-cultural investigators have often fallen victim to the misconception that if a particular test measures something that is an important skill or experience in their own culture, then that same test can be used in another culture and those same important experiences or skills will be found. Interestingly, when these are found, it is in groups who come close to sharing the investigator's structure of the world and his concept of intelligence. For example, in testing Senegalese children on Piaget's task of conservation of continuous quantity, Greenfield and Bruner (1969) found that only those who had been to Western schools developed this ability.

The warning here is that in making tests for samples of different backgrounds, we must be sure we are testing the appropriate skills before we draw any hasty conclusions about intelligence. Kagan and Klein (1973) raised the important distinction between natural cognitive skills and culture-specific skills. Intelligence tests are used to tap natural cognitive skills (underlying potential) by measuring culture-specific ones (acquired ability). The Kpelle children of north central Liberia provide an example of the relationship between culture-specific skills and natural cognitive skills, while at the same time providing an object lesson in cross-cultural methodology. Cole et al. (1971) found that in this rice-farming culture children were good at estimating amounts of rice but inaccurate when dealing with length measurements. The culture afforded many opportunities to deal with quantities of rice, but other measurements were not as consistent—length measurements varied by the item being measured. (European culture once had different linear metrics, too. Horses were measured by "hands," land was measured by "rods," cloth was measured by "feet.") If Kpelle children were tested only on length measurements, the investigators would mistakenly infer that they had inferior measurement skills.

The necessity of adapting tests to different cultures is apparent. Cross-cultural testing may not be methodologically impossible, as Goldberg stated, but it is an increasingly difficult task as we learn more about the difference between what the test was designed to measure and what the test items do indeed show in that culture. An example is "the game" that Watson (1972) sees as indicative of mother–infant interaction. The smiling and cooing exchanges that are so prevalent among mothers and babies in this culture are absent among the Dutch (Rebelsky, unpublished data), but does that mean that in Holland there is no mother–infant interaction? We may agree on what capabilities are appropriate to test in the organism, but the items we use may not enable us to discover those capabilities.

WHAT IS "INTELLIGENCE" TO THE NATIVE CULTURE?

At some point the cross-cultural investigator will be satisfied with some concept of intelligence and with test items and techniques that tap skills that are available in the culture. But a further question arises: Does the native culture view intelligence in the same way as the investigator? This question exemplifies the issues surrounding the emic–etic distinction as discussed by Price-Williams (1974): "The emic approach describes a phenomenon in terms of its own units. The etic approach imposes a measurement that is external to the phenomenon" (p. 96). In the case of intelligence testing, an investigator who uses the emic approach would judge intelligence in terms of what skills the culture itself considers indicate intelligence. The etic approach is represented by the investigator who takes Western intelligence tests and imposes them on non-Western cultures, assuming that the units of intelligence are the same.

Wober (1972), in two studies in Uganda, demonstrated how overlooking such a simple concern could lead to problems. His research showed that "various groups of Ugandans tend to associate their concept of intelligence with slowness, but not with quickness" (p. 327). In the first study villagers linked the term *intelligence* (*obugezi* in their vernacular) with "slowness." Village primary teachers and Baganda elite (with some Western education) were noncommittal in equating intelligence with slowness or quickness. But Baganda medical students, asked in English, did equate intelligence with quickness. What are the implications of this research? Simply this: If the majority of a culture rates intelligence as slowness, how fair is an alien test that rewards fast responses and thereby rates intelligence as a function of quickness? What is the validity of even testing such a population if the nature of testing is as foreign and useless to them as are the field researchers who are giving the test? Can the issue be resolved if we make a culture-fair test, or are we perhaps measuring something in the other culture that they don't even consider to be intelligence? Our use of "speed" as a measure of intelligence is indeed old; Porteus (1931) noted this, too, when he declared: "The aborigine in his natural state has all the time there is and probably has never heard the injunction to hurry in his life" (p. 308).

INFANT INTELLIGENCE CROSS-CULTURALLY

In the measuring of infant intelligence some of the problems stated above seem to be removed. The infant (0–3 years) has very little experience with the culture compared to adults of that culture. Thus it is theoretically possible to test something approaching "constitutional" intellectual capacity in the infant, relatively free as he seems to be from cultural influences. But we shall see, through many studies in different cultures, that the infant may be influenced by his cultural surroundings from the first hour of his life (Brazelton, 1972), and even perhaps prenatally.

If we survey the infant testing work done in Western and non-Western societies using Western tests and norms, it is reasonable to conclude (as did Werner, 1972, and Munroe and Munroe, 1975) that the "results are clear-cut: infants from Europe and the United States are usually at the very bottom. Thus, since developmental tests have been standardized around a mean of 100, almost all non-Western groups have an average above 100" (Munroe and Munroe, 1975).

These advanced developments have been found most strongly in African traditional societies (for a contrasting view, see Warren, 1972), with Asian and South American samples also advanced but less so, and tend to be most dramatic in the first year of life. Some authors claim that the development is largely psychomotor (Werner, 1972, and Dasen, 1973), but advances in social and language development have also been demonstrated (Ainsworth, 1967; Brazelton, 1973; Dasen, 1974; Kilbride and Kilbride, 1970).

Examples of the types of data that have been collected can be found in Brazelton *et al.* (1971) and Goldberg (1972). Both of these investigators worked in Zambia (formerly known as Northern Rhodesia), using measures that had been standardized on Western (United States) infants. Zambia is a sparsely populated country of about 4 million people living in an area roughly the size of Texas, Georgia, and Louisiana. It is characteristic in the traditional care of Zambia's 72 tribes and contemporary infant care in the major city of Lusaka that the nursing infant spends most of his time carried in a cloth sling (usually facing the mother's back), is nursed on demand, sleeps with his mother at night, and is vigorously (to a Westerner, even roughly) handled. For example, a Zambian mother will position the infant on her back by gripping him around one elbow or under one armpit and swinging him over her shoulder. Brazelton *et al.* (1971), using the Brazelton Newborn Assessment Scale, reported that on the first day of life hospitalized Zambian babies were less active and responsive than United States infants but were more alert and responsive by the fifth day and were very advanced over American norms by the tenth day. Goldberg (1972) used the Bayley motor scale and found a mean of 125.7, 1.5 standard deviations above Bayley's United States mean (Bayley, 1969).

Descriptions of the advanced development of African babies stress in particular their earlier achievements in sitting, walking, and talking. In movies and photos African babies look "older" than they are, since they are performing behaviors United States observers attach to later months. On the other hand, some of the United States hand–eye coordination seems "too early" for Dutch observers, for there such behaviors tend to occur later (Rebelsky, 1972).

In these African cultures, in general, there is a decline in scores, as compared with Western norms, between the first and second years, and usually by the second year non-Western infants begin to score lower than do Western groups—or restated, somewhere in the second year Western groups begin to score higher in the infant intelligence test items.

The few studies that show differences between infants of the same cultural group who have been reared in a traditional fashion compared to a more westernized manner find lower scores for Westernization and urbanization (Geber, 1957; Ainsworth, 1967; Leiderman and Leiderman, 1973). This suggests at least that the precocity of infants in traditional societies cannot be accounted for by genetic origin (unless one believes that certain genes lead one to Westernization!).

How can we account for these differences in infant performance cross-culturally? Again it is not sufficient to attribute causality to the culture without questioning further what it is about the culture that is related to these differences. At this point we do not have enough data to point to clear explanations for these phenomena, but cross-cultural research does supply us with a fertile source of hypotheses and suggestions for future work. Most of the following explanations and speculations are based on only a few studies, and even on nonpublished statements, and therefore are meant to be provocative rather than complete.

Prenatal Factors Affecting Infant Intelligence

Prenatal activity of the mother may be an important variable in determining cultural differences in infant behavior. Women in many Western societies do less physical activity than do traditional women, and this may in some way affect prenatal development (perhaps through a general adaptation syndrome to greater stimulation, perhaps even to a different internal physical environment when a pregnant mother is active). The placidity of the Chinese baby at birth (Freedman and Freedman, 1969) may be at least partly a response to the gait and movement patterns of Oriental women. Margaret Mead's movie *Four Families* (1959) shows these gait differences with surprising clarity.

Nutritional intake is supposedly better in Western societies, but the findings of the recent National Institutes of Neurological Diseases and Blindness Collaborative Study suggests that, even within the affluent United States doctors have been prescribing small weight gains and perhaps less than optimal diets in pregnancy. In addition the differences in the United States between the infant mortality rates of our wealthy and poor suggest that prenatal care may be one factor in infant survival, and we can speculate that it is also related to infant intelligence (U.S. Department of Health, Education and Welfare, 1970). A Western society like Holland or Denmark, with very adequate prenatal feeding for mothers of all social classes, has a lower infant mortality rate than does even our wealthy class in the United States. Interestingly Leiderman and Leiderman (1973) reported that when Zambians moved from their villages to towns, pregnant women ate less well. In the tribal villages special foods were the rule for pregnant women (usually a higher protein and calcium intake), and these foods were missing in the city food purchases. The traditional society may have found a more healthful diet for pregnancy than could be available, for a variety of reasons (cost, knowledge, etc.) in the big city.

Birth and Care of the Neonate

Postnatally there are many differences in infant care in traditional and Western societies. For example, differences have been found in delivery and early postnatal care across cultures. Brazelton *et al.* (1969, 1972) have described in detail the relatively nontraumatic delivery in Mayan Indians (Zinacantecan) in Mexico, where infants are born quiet yet alert. In observing deliveries, Brazelton noted the very different reactions of these babies to the outside world than we would expect from American hospital-delivered infants: "Their limb movements were free and smooth, and they lay quietly on the blanket, looking around the room with alert faces for the entire hour after delivery. In addition to quiet motor activity, they demonstrated a striking sensory alertness" (Brazelton, 1972, p. 97). Gunders and Whiting (1968) demonstrated hospital delivery as a stressor in one Israeli study. And Brazelton (1973) reported that Zambian infants born in city hospitals often looked flaccid and wizened and had poor motor control, scoring very low on Apgar and Brazelton tests, and yet within a week at home the babies were alert, with excellent muscle tone and control, and scored higher on the Brazelton than did Boston babies.

A recent study by Warren and Parkin (1974) argues that there are no differences among Western infants, lower-class Uganda infants, and upper-class Uganda infants on measures taken from several infant tests. However, all of the babies in this study were hospital-born, sedation of the mother was not reported, and testing was done in the first five days of life. The usual African precocity is noted more in traditional care and after the first five days of life. Hospital birth and maternal sedation, as well as the early testing, can easily explain the lack of differences found. In fact, the reader will recall the description of the Zambian procedure for placing the infant in the sling. Given these conditions, head control for the infant must develop rapidly, and remarkable head control was noted also by Geber and Dean (1957) and by Brazelton (1973). Yet Warren and Parkin found no remarkable head control. It would be strange if they had found it, with standard hospital care in handling newborns.

Early Infant-Rearing Differences

Other rearing differences can be seen in the early months in Western and traditional societies (e.g., Munroe and Munroe, 1971). If we believe that babies are actively trying to organize their worlds, then stimulation based on their behaviors (i.e., contingent stimulation) may be seen as an inducement to development. Lewis and Goldberg (1969), Friedlander and Wisdom (1971), and Watson (1972) have demonstrated the enlivened development of infants who can make the world happen for themselves. In a real sense that type of contingency occurs earlier when one can walk or sit alone and provide the stimulation to oneself without being carried about (as Held and Hein, 1963, demonstrated years ago in cats' development). The culture may encourage this kind of stimulation and feedback by putting the child in appropriate situations:

> The Ganda baby is held sitting face outward on his mother's lap as she pauses to visit with family or guests; this brings him from the beginning into the midst of the social group and gives him much stimulation . . . he is given complete freedom to move about. I have no doubt that this absence of confinement interacts with social stimulation to account for his very precocious locomotor development. (Ainsworth, 1967, p. 429)

Contrast this with one Western society, the Dutch (Rebelsky, 1967), in which babies are fed for ten minutes at a prescribed time that is adhered to (the mothers in the sample varied no more than five minutes from a feeding schedule set before the infant's birth). For large parts of the day the infant is on its back, alone, tightly blanketed in a crib with a canopy, in its own room, within a culture that will not interact with the baby except at scheduled intervals. Under these circumstances the Dutch baby has fewer opportunities to try out motor or social skills and receive feedback from the environment than does the Ganda infant.

Apart from differences in opportunities for contingent stimulation there may be developmental implications in the differences in absolute amount of stimulation available to infants who are near others all day and night compared with Western infants who are, at least for a part of each day, isolated in their own beds in their own rooms.

In some Western societies the type of maternal attentiveness cited by Rubenstein (1967) is related to "exploratory behavior" in a 6-month-old infant. But once again how we define *attentiveness* and *exploration* is linked to our cultural views. Exploration in that study was based on 6-month-old infants' interactions with new toys and their willingness to leave them for other new toys (reminiscent of United States infants' "tiring" of their mobiles and liking to look at new ones at age 3 months). Rebelsky's Dutch colleagues, to whom she presented the Rubenstein data, felt that those babies rated high by Rubenstein were unable to be exploratory in the Dutch sense, because the babies left the items instead of remaining to puzzle over them. (Then, too, that's how Rebelsky and her colleagues seemed to each other. Rebelsky ran around doing several studies in a few years, while the Dutch puzzled long and deep over a single study in the same time period.)

Another example of the effects of differences in mother–infant interaction comes from Japan. The Japanese mother is in greater bodily contact with her infant and attempts a soothing stimulation "toward physical quiescence and passivity with regard to his environment" (Caudill and Weinstein, 1969). Thus in Japan "contingency" and "stimulation" may be related to a quieter, less distractible, less "curious" infant. The point should be clear by now: our ideas about what is stimulating to an infant and what a stimulated infant will do are very much products of our own cultural ideas. These cultural views may be in the form of the positive virtues of activity, independence and exploration and may inhibit us from understanding the complex, subtle interactions between caretakers and infants.

Clarke-Stewart (1973) has reviewed the many, largely Western, studies that report interactions between mothers and their infants. These studies are yet another reminder of the large number of behaviors that are contained in the word *stimulation*, even within our own culture. Talking to an infant, playing with him, expressing affection—all are types of maternal caretaking that have been considered in the United States to be related to infant competence. Yet physical proximity, caressing, amount of feeding time, number of baths—all are ignored as potentially related. Clarke-Stewart also noted that mothers and children in the United States become increasingly concerned with material objects and that in the United States "the child's cognitive development and the complexity of his play with objects was apparently influenced by the amount of time mother spent with him playing with materials" (Clarke-Stewart, 1973, p. 93). In Zambia, on the other hand, Goldberg (1972) reported that interaction is more interpersonal and less related to material objects. Does this mean fewer interactions, or worse interactions, or just different interactions between mother and infant?

At 6, 9, and 12 months Goldberg (1972) administered the Albert Einstein Scales of Sensorimotor Development to Zambian infants. On some scales (e.g., the space scale) the African babies were advanced, while on the object scales, the Zambian infants were less advanced by the ninth month than the American validation sample (Corman and Escalona, 1969). Goldberg commented on the passivity and lack of responsivity of the Zambian babies at the older age. Removing objects is a practice in administering this particular scale, and Goldberg speculated that removing objects is interpreted by the infants to mean "don't play with that" and that they have learned to obey such prohibitions. Such "good" behavior leads to "bad" performance!

The Dutch babies provide another example of the role of stimulation. In Holland infants usually move from the relatively quiet atmosphere of the crib to the playpen at 6 months. The mean 6-months developmental quotient (DQ) on the Cattell test of infant development of Dutch infants who were placed in a playpen at 6 months was 83.4 ($N = 7$); those who had not yet had playpen stimulation had DQs of 69.0 ($N = 3$) (very small Ns—as usual for most of the studies reported) (Rebelsky, 1972).

Second-Year Shifts in Performance across Cultures

The second-year score decline in non-Western groups has been reported frequently (Werner, 1972). Almost all of the factors proposed for this "involve the idea of *discontinuity* between near-optimal developmental conditions and later changes so contrastive as to be traumatic for the infant" (Munroe and Munroe, 1975). For example, if mother's milk has been the major food in the first year, it is a less adequate food for an older infant (Kaplan, 1972; Pollitt and Granoff, 1967), and other supplements may be needed. If a sibling has been born, mother's milk may be used for the new child, lessening the amount for the older child. In addition, if other foods begin to be given, they may (under present acculturation patterns) be inadequate nutritionally, too.

So too for the issue of stimulation: if the infant had a year of souped-up, contingent stimulation and is replaced by a new sibling, he may be receiving less intense interaction in his second year. The types of stimulation needed in later years also may be more varied than in prior years, and then the influence of the relative freedom allowed the Western child to be a "tireless explorer" (Fraiberg, 1959) in a world of toys, people, and so forth may increase the Western second-year scores, while the lack of these stimuli may begin to depress the scores of traditional society 2-year-olds.

And finally, it is after the first- and second-year test items that all the notions of what constitutes intelligence begin to differentiate along the lines mentioned at the start of this review. The early items on the infant intelligence tests may be passed very easily by some groups. In the later test items there is a gradual shift toward items that are more "normed" for Western infants, and that therefore may become more difficult for non-Western infants. Additionally there may be, in the second year, a falloff due to wariness of the experimenter and the demands of a testing situation. The Munroes (1975) suggested that

> the second-year falloff mirrors some actual decline in relative capabilities, then the pattern of infant development in most traditional societies may be summarized as follows: either favorable pre-natal conditions or a high level of early stimulation apparently results in first-year psychomotor developmental precocity, which, in the second year, erodes and dissolves as the stimulation level is reduced, as the social expectations change, and as the nutritional situation deteriorates. The upshot is a developmental quotient on Western-based tests somewhat below the norm for Western two-year-olds. In contrast, among Western groups and in modernizing sectors of traditional societies, infants may experience different pre-natal conditions or may receive a lower level of early stimulation that remains more or less stable throughout the infancy period and that appears to eventuate in a steady and unfluctuating development.

Again perhaps a comment should be added. It is unlikely that a culture will provide so little stimulation to an infant that it will not survive as an adequate adult in that society. The Dutch begin playpen freedom and increased toys at about 6 months. The Albanians, who reportedly bound their males on cradle boards and propped them in corners covered with a black cloth to keep them hidden from the "evil eye," also did this only for the first 6 months.

The Dennis (1973) research on the crèche in Lebanon and Skeels's (1965, 1966) important work on institutionalized infants in Iowa also suggest that there can be significant reversals through stimulation at other life times than had previously been supposed. The human organism is remarkably plastic and can undergo various kinds of deprivations without significant loss and with the possibility of "catching up" later. Our cultural notion is that early experiences provide a framework, and perhaps even a limiting factor, for all future development. Yet we have never systematically explored the results of a major shift in environmental stimulation (social, nutritional, or any other sort) at later stages of development. The work of Tanner (1963) on size and the follow-up studies of Dutch children malnourished during World War II (Stein *et al.*, 1972) strongly suggest that there are mechanisms for "catch-up" throughout life. Perhaps we should begin to focus less on the limitations and negatives inherent in some early developmental interactions and focus more on what we might do to provide more optimally for individual growth and development at any stage of life. In a real sense we all can be more "intelligent" than we are now!

CONCLUSION

This chapter has provided, of necessity, a general overview of a complicated topic. We can state with clarity that Western infant tests are differentially responded to by different cultural groups and that different cultures rear their children differently. Yet, given the presently available data, it is impossible to ascertain what particular factors, within and across cultures, influence the development we see. Further research is needed to clarify our limited findings, but these writers hope that we will use these findings to provide a better way for the world's peoples to live with and understand differences, without trying to obliterate them.

REFERENCES

AINSWORTH, M., 1967, "Infancy in Uganda," Johns Hopkins University Press, Baltimore.

AKIM, B., MCFIE, J., AND SEBIGAJJU, E., 1956, Developmental level and nutrition: A study of young children in Yganda, *Journal of Tropical Pediatrics*, 2:159.

AMES, E. W., April 1971, Family structure and childrearing in India, paper presented at Society for Research in Child Development, Minneapolis.

ARAI, S., ISHIKAWA, J., AND TOSHIMA, K., 1958, Développement psychomoteur des enfants Japonais, *Revue de Neuro-psychiatrie Infantile et d'Hygiène Mentale de l'Enfance*, 5–6:1.

BARDET, C., MASSE, G., MOREIGNE, F., AND SENECAL, M. J., 1960, Application due test de Brunét–Lézine à une groupe d'enfants Oulofs de 6 mois a 24 mois, *Bulletin Société Médicine d'Afrique Noire*, 5:334.

BAYLEY, N., 1969, "Manual for the Bayley Scales of Infant Development," Psychological Corp., New York.

BIESHEUVEL, S., 1943, "African Intelligence," Morija Printing Works, South Africa.

BRAZELTON, T. B., 1972, Implications of infant development among the Mayan Indians of Mexico, *Human Development*, 15:90.

BRAZELTON, T. B., 1973, Presentation to the American Academy of Pediatrics, New York.

BRAZELTON, T. B., KOSLOWSKY, B., AND TRONEK, E., 1971, Neonatal evaluation of urbanizing blacks in Lusaka, paper presented at Society for Research in Child Development, Minneapolis.

BRAZELTON, T. B., ROBEY, J. S., AND COLLIER, G., 1969, Infant development in the Zinacanteco Indians of Southern Mexico, *Pediatrics*, 44:274.

Calhoun, J. B., 1972, Plight of the Ik and Kaiadilt is seen as a chilling possible end for man, *Smithsonian*, November:27.

Caudill, W., and Frost, L., 1972, A comparison of maternal care and infant behavior in Japanese-American, American and Japanese families, in "Influences on Human Development," U. Bronfenbrenner (ed.), Dryden Press, Hinsdale, Illinois, p. 329.

Caudill, W., and Weinstein, H., 1969, Maternal care and infant behavior in Japan and America, *Psychiatry*, 32(1):12.

Cesa-Bianchi, M., Chierici, G., Mallardi, A., Damascelli, A. R., Bregani, P., and Della Porta, V., 1972, Intellectual development and stimulation in early childhood: An investigation of the irreversibility of the learning process, in "Determinants of Behavioral Development,"F. J. Monks, W. W. Hartup, and J. de Witt (eds.), Academic Press, New York and London, p. 387.

Clarke-Stewart, A. K., 1973, Interactions between mothers and their young children: Characteristics and consequences, *Monographs of the Society for Research in Child Development*, 38(6–7).

Cole, M., Gay, J., Glick, J. A., and Sharp, D. W., 1971, "The Cultural Context of Learning and Thinking," Basic Books, New York.

Corman, H. H., and Escalona, S. K., 1969, Stages of sensorimotor development: A replication study, *Merrill–Palmer Quarterly*, 15:351.

Cravioto, J., 1967, Motor and adaptive development of premature infants from a preindustrial setting during the first year of life, *Biologia Neonatorum*, 11:151.

Cravioto, J., Birch, H., DeLicardie, E., Rosales, L., and Vega, L., 1969, The ecology of growth and development in a Mexican preindustrial community, Report I: Method and findings from birth to one month of age, *Monographs of the Society for Research in Child Development*, Ser. No. 128.

Cravioto, J., and Robles, B., 1965, Evolution of adaptive and motor behavior during rehabilitation from kwashiorkor, *American Journal of Orthopsychiatry*, 35:449.

Dasen, P. R., 1973, Preliminary study of sensorimotor development in Baoulé children, *Early Child Development and Care*, 2:345.

Dasen, P. R., 1974, Le développement psychologique de jeune enfant Africain, *Archives de Psychologie*, 41:341.

Dennis, W., 1973, "Children of the Crèche," Appleton-Century-Crofts, New York.

Falade, S., 1955, "Le Développement Psycho-moteur du Jeune Africain Originaire du Sénégal au Cours de Sa Première Année," Foulon, Paris.

Falade, S., 1960, Le développement psycho-moteur de l'enfant Africiane du Sénégal, *Concours Medical*, 82:1005.

Feldman, C. F., Lee, B., Dickson, M., Dickson, J., Pillemer, D. B., and Murray, J. R., 1974, "The Development of Adaptive Intelligence," Jossey-Bass, San Francisco.

Fraiberg, S. H., 1959, "The Magic Years," Scribner's, New York.

Francis, S. H., Middleton, M. R., Penney, R. E. C., and Thompson, C. A., in prep. Social factors related to aboriginal infant health, *Report to the Minister of Interior, Commonwealth of Australia*, from the Department of Psychology, Australian National University, Canberra.

Freedman, D. G., 1971, Behavioral assessment in infancy, in "Normal and Abnormal Development of Behavior," G. B. A. Stoelinga and J. J. Vander Werff Ten Bosch (eds.), Leiden University Press, Leiden, The Netherlands.

Freedman, D. G., and Freedman, N. C., 1969, Behavioral differences between Chinese-American and European-American newborns, *Nature*, 224:1227.

Friedlander, B. Z., and Wisdom, S. S., April 1971, Pre-verbal infants: Selective operant responses for different levels of auditory complexity and language redundancy, paper presented at Eastern Psychological Association, New York.

GEBER, M., AND DEAN, R. F. A., 1957, Gesell tests on African children, *Pediatrics*, 20:1055.

GEBER, M., 1958, The psychomotor development of African children in their first year and the influence of mother behavior, *Journal of Social Psychology*, 47:185.

GOLDBERG, S., 1972, Infant care and growth in urban Zambia, *Human Development*, 15:77.

GOLDBERG, S., June 1973, On issues and problems in cross cultural research, paper prepared for Burg Wartenstein Symposium No. 57: Cultural and Social Influences in Infancy and Early Childhood.

GOLDBERG, S., 1975, Infant development and mother–infant interaction in urban Zambia, *in* "Cultural and Social Influences in Infancy and Early Childhood," S. R. Tulkin and P. H. Leiderman (eds.), Stanford University Press, Stanford, California.

GORDON, H., 1970, The intelligence of English canal boat children, *in* "Cross-cultural Studies of Behavior," I. Al-Issa and W. Dennis (eds.), Holt, Rinehart, and Winston, New York, p. 111.

GRANTHAN-McGREGOR, S. M., AND BACK, E. H., 1971, Gross motor development in Jamaican infants, *Developmental Medicine and Child Neurology*, 13:79.

GREENFIELD, P. M., AND BRUNER, J. S., 1969, Culture and cognitive growth, *in* "Handbook of Socialization Theory and Research," D. A. Goslin (ed.), Rand McNally, Chicago. p. 633.

GUNDERS, S. M., AND WHITING, J. W. M., 1968, Mother–infant separation and physical growth, *Ethnology*, 7:196.

HELD, R., AND HEIN, A., 1963, Movement-produced stimulation in the development of visually guided behavior, *Journal of Comparative and Physiological Psychology*, 56:872.

HINDLEY, C. B., 1968, Growing up in five countries: A comparison of data on weaning, elimination training, age of walking and IQ in relation to social class from five European longitudinal studies, *Developmental Medicine and Child Neurology*, 10:715

JELLIFFE, D. B., 1962, Culture, social change and infant feeding: Current trends in tropical regions. *American Journal of Clinical Nutrition*, 10:19.

KAGAN, J., November 1974, Child rearing in China, talk at New England Psychological Association, Boston.

KAGAN, J., AND KLEIN, R. E., 1973, Cross-cultural perspectives on early development, *American Psychologist*, 28:947.

KAPLAN, B. J., 1972, Malnutrition and mental deficiency, *Psychological Bulletin*, 78:321.

KHATRI, A. A., Orphanage environment and specific abilities: A study of differences in performance of family-reared and orphanage-reared female children on sub-tests of intelligence, first draft (not for publication).

KILBRIDE, J. E., ROBBINS, M. C., AND KILBRIDE, P. L., 1970, The comparative motor development of Baganda, American white, and American black infants, *American Anthropologist*, 72:1422.

KITANO, H., 1961, Different child-rearing attitudes between first and second generation Japanese in the United States, *Journal of Social Psychology*, 53:13.

KOHEN-RAZ, R., 1968, Mental and motor development of kibbutz, institutionalized, and home-reared infants in Israel, *Child Development*, 39:189.

KONNER, M. J., 1972, Aspects of the developmental ethology of a foraging people, *in* "Ethological Studies in Child Behavior," N. Blurton-Jones (ed.), Cambridge University Press, London.

KRIPPNER, S., 1974, Foundlings, environment, and IQ, *Psychology Today*, February:12.

LABOV, W., 1973, A clear demonstration, review of M. Cole, J. Gay, J. A. Glick, and D. W. Sharp, "Cultural Context of Learning and Thinking," *Contemporary Psychology*, 18:428.

LEIDERMAN, P. H., AND LEIDERMAN, G. I., June 1973, Familial influences on infant development in an East African agricultural community, paper prepared for Burg Wartenstein Symposium No. 57: Cultural and Social Influences in Infancy and Early Childhood.

LEVINE, R. A., 1970, Cross-cultural study in child psychology, in "Carmichael's Manual of Child Psychology" (3rd ed.), P. H. Mussen (ed.), Wiley, New York.

LEWIS, M., AND BAN, P., June 1973, Variance and invariance in the mother–infant interaction: A cross-cultural study, paper prepared for Burg Wartenstein Symposium No. 57: Cultural and Social Influences in Infancy and Early Childhood.

LEWIS, M., AND GOLDBERG, S., 1969, Perceptual–cognitive development in infancy: A generalized expectancy model as a function of the mother–infant interaction, Merrill–Palmer Quarterly, 15:81.

LEWIS, M., AND WILSON, C. D., 1972, Infant development in lower-class American families, Human Development, 15:112.

LUSK, D., AND LEWIS, M., 1972, Mother–infant interaction and infant development among the Wolof of Senegal, Human Development, 15:58.

MEAD, M., 1959, "Four Families," McGraw-Hill Text Films, New York.

MOYLES, E. W., AND WOLINS, M., 1971, Group care and intellectual development, Developmental Psychology, 4:370.

MUNROE, R. H., AND MUNROE, R. L., 1971, Household density and infant care in an East African Society, Journal of Social Psychology, 83:3.

MUNROE, R. L., AND MUNROE, R., 1975, "Cross-cultural Human Development," Brooks-Cole, Monterey, California.

PHATAK, P., 1970, Motor growth patterns of Indian babies and some related factors, Indian Pediatrics, 7:619.

POLLITT, E., AND GRANOFF, D., 1967, Mental and motor development of Peruvian children treated for severe malnutrition, Revista Interamericana de Psicologica, 1:93.

PORTEUS, S. D., 1931, "Psychology of a Primitive People: A Study of the Australian Aborigines," Books for Libraries Press, Freeport, New York (1972 reprint of 1931 edition).

PRICE-WILLIAMS, D., 1974, Psychological experiment and anthropology: The problem of categories, Ethos, 2:95.

RABIN, A. I., 1958, Behavior research in collective settlements in Israel: Infants and children under conditions of "intermittent" mothering in the Kibbutz, American Journal of Orthopsychiatry, 28:577.

RAMAROSA, Z., 1959, Psychomotor development in early childhood in the Tananarive region, working paper, meeting on the Basic Psychology of African and Madagascan Populations, C. S. A. Publications No. 51, Tananarive.

REBELSKY, F. G., 1967, Infancy in two cultures, Nederlands Tijdschrift voor de Psychologie, 22:379.

REBELSKY, F. G., 1972, First discussant's comments: Cross-cultural studies of mother–infant interaction—description and consequence, Human Development, 15:128.

REBELSKY, F. G., AND ABELES, G., 1971, Infancy in Holland and the United States, paper presented at Society for Research in Child Development, Santa Monica, California.

RUBENSTEIN, J., 1967, Maternal attentiveness and subsequent exploratory behavior in the infant, Child Development, 38:1089.

SHERWOOD, J. J., AND NATAUPSKY, M., 1968, Predicting the conclusions of Negro–White intelligence research from biographical characteristics of the investigator, Journal of Personality and Social Psychology, 8:53.

SKEELS, H. M., 1965, Effects of adoption on children from institutions, Children, 12:33.

SKEELS, H. M., 1966, Adult status of children with contrasting early life experiences: A follow-up study, *Monographs of the Society for Research in Child Development, 31*(Ser. #105).

STEIN, Z., SUSSER, M., SAENGER, G., AND MAROLLA, F., 1972, Nutrition and mental performance, *Science, 178:*708.

TANNER, J. M., 1963, The regulation of human growth, *Child Development, 34:*817.

TULKIN, S. R., 1972, An analysis of the concept of cultural deprivation, *Developmental Psychology, 6:*326.

U. S. Department of Health, Education, and Welfare, 1970, "The Health of Children," Washington, D.C.

VOUILLOUX, P., 1959, Étude de la psycho-motricite l'enfants africains au Cameroun: Test de Gesell et reflexes archaiques, *Journal de la Société d'Africanistes, 29:*11.

WARREN, N., 1972, African infant precocity, *Psychological Bulletin, 78:*353.

WARREN, N., AND PARKIN, J. M., 1974, A neurological and behavioral comparison of African and European newborns in Uganda, *Child Development, 45:*966.

WATSON, J. S., 1972, Smiling, cooing and "the game," *Merrill–Palmer Quarterly, 18:*323.

WERNER, E., 1972, Infants around the world: Cross-cultural studies of psychomotor development from birth to two years, *Journal of Cross-Cultural Psychology, 3:*111.

WERNER, E., BIERMAN, J., AND FRENCH, F., 1971, "The Children of Kauai: A Longitudinal Study from the Prenatal Period to Age Ten," University of Hawaii Press, Honolulu.

WESMAN, A. G., 1968, Intelligent testing, *American Psychologist, 23:*267.

WHITING, J. W. M., AND WHITING, B. B., 1959, Contributions of anthropology to methods of studying child rearing, *in* "Handbook of Research Methods in Child Development," P. H. Mussen (ed.), Wiley, New York.

WOBER, M., 1972, Culture and the concept of intelligence: A case in Uganda, *Journal of Cross-Cultural Psychology, 3:*327.

YOUNG, H. B., TAGIURI, R., TESI, G., AND MONTEMAGNI, G., 1962, Influence of town and country upon children's intelligence, *British Journal of Educational Psychology, 32:*151.

11 Social Class and Infant Intelligence

MARK GOLDEN
AND BEVERLY BIRNS

INTRODUCTION

There is generally widespread agreement that social class differences in intellectual development are present in older preschool children, as reflected in their performance on standard intelligence tests beginning during the third year of life, and later in their academic achievement in school. However, there is disagreement about whether such differences are present in infancy. There has also been a great deal of controversy about how social class differences in intellectual development can best be explained or interpreted, as well as strong disagreement about what can or should be done about such differences.

Before we explore these issues further, some discussion of what is meant by such terms as *social class* and *infant intelligence* may be useful. While there have been many definitions of social class, they seem to reduce to a relatively small number of factors. Studies of social class usually use the following indices of socioeconomic status (SES), either individually or combined: the education and occupation of the head of the household, income, source of income (wages or public assistance), residential area, and quality of housing. Hollingshead's (1957) Two-Factor Index of Social Position, for example, which is widely used, is based on the education and occupation of the head of the household. On the basis of such indices individuals or families are classified into two or more social classes, ranging from upper class to lower class. Recent investigators, particularly those who have been involved in providing social services to poor families, have pointed out that such

MARK GOLDEN AND BEVERLY BIRNS · State University of New York at Stony Brook.

categories as *lower class* are too broad and do not adequately reflect great differences in levels of functioning between poor, stable, working families and socially disorganized, multiproblem families (Miller, 1964; Geismar and La Sorte, 1964; Pavenstedt, 1965).

It is important to distinguish *socioeconomic status* (SES), in which people are merely classified into various groups on the basis of the foregoing indices, from class-related *process variables,* such as nutrition, patterns of mother–child interaction, language experience, etc., which tend to be associated with social class and may have a more direct effect on children's development. If we could identify such process variables during infancy, perhaps we could discard the social class concept in our research. At the present time, however, social class indices, such as parents' education and occupation, predict the later intellectual development of children better than any other measure we now have available during the infant period, including the child's own infant test scores (McCall *et al.,* 1972).

It is essential to distinguish between social class and race or ethnicity, since these factors are often confounded with social class. When making comparisons among different racial or ethnic groups, even if they are equated on certain SES indices such as the number of years of schooling, we cannot assume that their educational experience has been the same, since we know that the quality of education has not been the same for all ethnic and racial groups in this country. In reports of results on social class the particular racial or ethnic groups involved should be identified, since the presence or magnitude of SES differences found on a particular measure may depend on the population studied.

It is also necessary to keep in mind that there may be an interaction between social class and sex on some cognitive and personality measures (Birns and Golden, 1973). For example, there may be social class differences for one sex and not the other, or sex differences for one social class and not another. Making social class comparisons on only one sex precludes the possibility of studying such social class by sex interactions. In reports of social class differences results on males and females should be reported separately.

What about the term *infant intelligence?* Perhaps a definition of the term *infant* may be a good starting point, since the word has many meanings. According to Webster's unabridged dictionary, the term derives from the Latin word *infans,* which roughly translated means "one who cannot speak." By this definition, since most children usually say their first words by about 12 months of age, the infant period would be limited to the first year of life in humans. We would opt for a somewhat broader definition of infancy to include what Piaget refers to as the *sensorimotor period,* approximately the first 18–24 months of life. Intelligence has been defined in many ways, including the ability to learn, to remember, to solve problems, to reason, to adapt to one's environment, etc., but there is no generally agreed-upon definition. When we speak of infant intelligence, we are referring to *sensorimotor intelligence.* Although children can understand and use language to a limited extent during the sensorimotor period, according to Piaget (1952) sensorimotor intelligence operates predominantly on a presymbolic and preverbal level. While we have defined the infant period as roughly the first 2 years of life, since SES differences on some intellectual measures first manifest themselves during the third year, we will review social class research on children up to 3 years of age.

Are there social class differences in sensorimotor intelligence? This question is inseparably enmeshed with problems of measurement, with the particular intellectual measures used in SES comparisons, with the validity of these measures, and with the age of the infants being studied. Until recently, attempts to measure infant intelligence, and hence studies of SES differences, were largely based on standard infant tests or developmental scales, such as the Gesell, the Cattell, and the Bayley. These tests were initially conceived to be downward extensions of the standard intelligence tests for older children, such as the Stanford–Binet, and were expected to correlate with later measures of intelligence and with academic achievement. While intelligence tests for older preschool children are highly correlated with social class and with later school performance, during the first 18 months of life the infant test scores of normal babies do not seem to be related to later measures of intelligence, success in school, or social class. The validity of infant tests has been questioned on a number of grounds (Lewis and McGurk, 1973). Do infant tests fail to detect social class differences because there are no SES differences in sensorimotor intelligence or because the tests are not valid?

During the 1960s, stimulated to a great extent by the "rediscovery" of Piaget, developmental psychologists began to question the value of standard infant tests, and particularly the usefulness of such global measures as DQ or IQ scores, in understanding intellectual processes in babies. Using a variety of new cognitive measures, which dealt with more discrete unidimensional aspects of behavior and which did not rely so much on children's motor ability, psychologists began to take a "new look" at infant intelligence. The new measures included scales of cognitive development derived from Piaget's observations on the sensorimotor period; measures of attention to visual and auditory stimuli, which are assumed to reflect central information processes; instrumental learning and problem solving; and exploratory and play behavior. Do these new cognitive measures correlate more highly with social class and later intelligence than standard infant tests? We will review studies of social class comparisons of children's behavior in which these new measures were used.

It is also possible that there may be social class differences in children's experience during the sensorimotor period—for example, in their language experience—that may not be reflected in their intellectual development until later. Basil Bernstein (1960), a British sociolinguist, has hypothesized that there are social class differences in the extent to which parents from different social classes use different linguistic codes or styles of communication with their children. He has described two different linguistic codes, *elaborated* and *restricted*, which are assumed to be characteristic of middle-class and lower-class speech patterns, respectively. Bernstein believes that the two linguistic codes arise out of fundamental differences in life styles and outlook and that these different linguistic codes are reflected in social class differences in cognitive style and intellectual development.

On the basis of Bernstein's ideas Hess and Shipman (1965) have hypothesized that there may also be social class differences in patterns of mother–child interaction, in the teacher–pupil aspect of their relationship, which may subsequently be reflected in the children's performance on standard intelligence tests and in school. Middle-class children may be more successful in these situations because they have learned to assume the roles expected of them through earlier interactions with their mothers. Hess and Shipman found SES differences in patterns of interaction between black mothers and their 4-year-old boys on various learning tasks, and these patterns were related to the children's intellectual performance. How early can such social class differences in patterns of mother-child interaction be observed? While there has been a great deal of speculation about the nature of SES differences in mother–child interaction during infancy, recently a few investigators have begun to make direct naturalistic observations of the interactions between mothers and infants from different social classes, with particular emphasis on those aspects of behavior assumed to be related to children's cognitive and language development. Are there SES differences in patterns of mother–child interaction during the sensorimotor period? And are the differences that may be present related to children's later cognitive and language development? We will review studies of social class comparisons of mother–child interaction in order to attempt to answer these questions.

Throughout the relatively brief history of the intelligence testing movement, there has been a continuing controversy about what intelligence tests such as the Stanford–Binet actually measure. While there are reliable individual and group differences in performance on such tests, how do we explain these differences? Finally, what can or should be done about such differences? Historically the major controversy has revolved around the heredity–environment issue. Recently a new controversy has emerged among social scientists who have taken an environmentalist position. Can social class differences (e.g., in intellectual performance, personality functioning, and maternal behavior) that seem to favor the middle class, judged by middle-class standards, be construed as deficits in the lower class or as merely cultural variations or differences?

First we will discuss the heredity–environment issue and then deal with the deficit–difference question. Binet, who developed the first successful prototype for most standard intelligence tests now in use, did not set out to measure intelligence. He developed his mental scale, which was not called an intelligence test, to identify children who were likely to do poorly in school, so that they could be given special educational treatment. Where Galton had previously failed to develop a useful measure of intellectual functioning, which he had planned to use for eugenic purposes, Binet succeeded admirably, since his scale correlated highly with academic achievement. While Binet (1909) did not assume that his scale measured innate intelligence, such an assumption was made by subsequent users and adaptors of his scale in the United States (Terman, 1916; Goddard, 1920; Yerkes and Foster, 1923), who were followers of Galton. They assumed that individual differences and social class, ethnic, cultural, and racial differences in performance on such tests were largely due to heredity. As Kamin (1974) pointed out in a recent devastating critique of the intelligence testing movement in this country, the leaders of this movement expressed these views long before there were any research data to support their ideas, i.e., before the heritability studies were actually carried out. While the heritability studies later reported in the literature may provide evidence for a significant genetic contribution to individual differences in performance on such tests, they do not provide *direct* evidence that group differences can be explained on the same basis. The genetic point of view has certain educational implications. If one assumes that intelligence is fixed at birth and that intellectual development is predetermined, there is very little that can be done to increase a person's level of intellectual functioning through environmental enrichment or education.

In 1961 Hunt published *Intelligence and Experience,* a seminal work that has had a major impact on developmental psychology and early childhood education. Hunt presented evidence contrary to many of the assumptions of the hereditary view, particularly the belief in fixed intelligence and predetermined intellectual development. While Hunt proposed an *interaction* point of view (i.e., intellectual development is a function of the interaction of heredity and environment), the thrust of his ideas seemed to shift the pendulum to an environmental position. He presented data from animal research and studies of institutionalized babies showing that a restricted environment and lack of intellectual stimulation during infancy may have permanent, irreversible, detrimental effects on intellectual and problem-solving ability. Hunt's belief in the importance of early experience is also based on an epigenetic view of cognitive development, which assumes that later stages of intelligence are based upon and are hierarchically related to early stages. He also assumes that as children grow older their behavior patterns tend to become fixed and more difficult to modify. Therefore the impact of early experience is likely to be greater on children's intellectual development. In a paper that appeared at about the same time, Fowler (1962) presented evidence that infants and young children are capable of much more cognitive learning than has been expected of them. He argued that there should be greater emphasis on accelerating cognitive development as early as possible, so that children can achieve their full intellectual potential.

During the 1960s, as part of the War on Poverty, psychologists and educators became concerned with the educational problems of poor children in this country. The academic achievement of poor children has been considerably less than that of middle-class children. They seem to be behind middle-class children in intellectual development when they first enter school, as reflected in their relatively lower performance cn standard intelligence tests. They get farther and farther behind their middle-class peers in school as they grow older, which has been explained on the basis of a "cumulative deficit hypothesis" (Ausubel, 1964; Deutsch, 1964). Poor children drop out of school earlier and in greater numbers, and fewer of them go on to college. As a result they are forced to take low-paying, menial, dead-end jobs or remain chronically unemployed. Helping poor children succeed academically was seen as a way of helping them break out of poverty.

Operation Head Start was established in 1965 on a national scale. Initially the goals of Head Start were fairly modest. Four- and five-year-old children from poverty areas were provided with a summer nursery school program. One of the major goals of such a program was to help poor children make a better transition from home to school by helping them to develop greater self-confidence, positive attitudes toward learning, and an expectation of success in school. The summer program had very little impact on their subsequent academic achievement in schoo.. The programs were expanded and changed in a number of importart respects. Children were enrolled in Head Start programs throughout the school year. The programs were extended downward to include younger children, with an increasing emphasis on stimulating cognitive and language development and pushing academic skills. The programs were also being evaluated on a more stringent basis, in terms of measurable increases in children's intelligence test scores and later academic achievement in school.

In general, the evaluation studies of Head Start and similar programs have been disappointing. Even in programs that were judged to be excellent, a familiar pattern emerged:

1. In comparison to similar children who are not in the program, children in the program often show dramatic IQ increases after a relatively brief period of time, which Zigler and Butterfield (1968) attributed at least in part to changes in motivation.
2. These IQ increases tend to level off while the children are still in the program, generally below the performance of middle-class children.
3. Children's IQ scores often drop to their original level after they leave the program, with some exceptions to be described later.
4. While children who had been in a preschool program often show initial superiority in their functioning in school over children without such experience, the differences seem to wash out by the end of the first or second grade.

These results have led to different conclusions and recommendations. Jensen (1969) concluded that compensatory education has failed because SES differences in intellectual development are genetically determined. He recommended that children from different social classes be given different kinds of education in line with their innate abilities. On the other hand, some proponents of compensatory education concluded that the programs did not begin early enough or continue long enough. On the basis of the similar disappointing results of his own intervention study with children between 15 and 36 months of age, Schaeffer (1970) recommended that on the one hand the child's education should begin from birth at home, directly involving the mother in the educational process from the beginning, and that on the other hand the child should be provided with educational enrichment throughout the school years. Hunt (1969) and others (Denenberg, 1970) have also argued for preventive (rather than compensatory) intervention programs beginning in early infancy. Are such infant intervention programs necessary for lower-class children during the sensorimotor period? Are intervention programs that begin early in life, particularly during the first 2 years, more effective than those that begin later, in terms of both their immediate and their long-term effects on children's intellectual development? We will review intervention studies with children under 3 years of age in order to attempt to answer these questions.

At about the time the heredity–environment issue flared up again with the publication of Jensen's (1969) explosive article in the *Harvard Educational Review,* the deficit–difference controversy emerged among environmentalists. While the environmental-deficit point of view has been fairly prevalent among proponents of early intervention for poor children, its most articulate spokesman has been Hunt, whose ideas appeared in a collection of articles entitled *The Challenge of Incompetence and Poverty* (1969). The basic assumptions of the environmental-deficit view seem to be as follows. The relatively lower intellectual performance and school failure of poor children is no longer attributed to a genetic deficit but is explained on the basis of various environmentally produced psychological deficits—e.g., in language and cognitive ability—as well as aspects of personality and motivation assumed to be related to learning and achievement. Hunt, for example, believes that this problem is particularly acute in a highly technological society, where the need for unskilled labor is diminishing. Many poor children may not develop the kinds of intellectual skills required to function in such a society. In this sense they may be functionally incompetent and doomed to a life of poverty unless something is done to prevent it early in life. Since these intellectual deficits seem to be present long before these children enter school, as reflected in lower performance on standard intelligence tests, it is assumed that they are due to deficiencies in the children's home environment.

While less value-laden terms have been used, poor children have often been referred to as "culturally deprived." Oscar Lewis (1966) explained cultural deprivation on the basis of the "culture of poverty." Lewis believes that in most industrial capitalist societies there exists a culture (or subculture) of poverty that has certain common characteristics. While most poor people do not have these characteristics, according to Lewis, the members of this subculture, who represent the most economically impoverished and socially disorganized segment of society, may perpetuate their own poverty as a result of self-defeating attitudes, values, and behavior patterns. These are socially transmitted from one generation to the next and prevent the children in these families from taking full advantage of educational and other opportunities to break out of poverty. For such children "equal opportunity" may be an empty phrase.

Soon after Lewis published his ideas, they were strongly criticized by many social scientists. A volume edited by Leacock, *The Culture of Poverty: A Critique* (1971), contains a number of excellent articles critical of Lewis's views. From the point of view of a developmental psychologist, Tulkin (1972) questioned the validity of the assumption that social class differences in intellectual performance on standard intelligence tests and differences in maternal behavior that seem to favor the middle class, judged by middle-class standards, can legitimately be considered as deficits in the lower class. He pointed out that while anthropologists no longer view cultural differences from an ethnocentric point of view (reflected, for example, in such terms as *primitive societies*), psychologists who interpret social class differences in terms of deficits may still be operating on an ethnocentric basis. Tulkin also presented evidence that standard intelligence tests are culturally biased and tap a relatively narrow range of intellectual competence, specifically the range related to academic success in a middle-class–oriented school system. This does not mean that such tests may not be useful for some purposes. But if people who are not middle class in our society or who are from a different culture obtain lower scores on these tests, this does not mean that they are intellectually inferior, as a result of either a genetic or an environmental deficit. Tulkin argued for a relativistic approach, similar to the one taken by cultural anthropologists, in the explanation and understanding of social class differences in our society. He also believes it may be more fruitful, in terms of finding solutions to social problems such as poverty, to consider the possibility that the deficits may be in the educational system and in society rather than in poor children and their families. The position one takes on this issue is more than a semantic argument among academicians, and it may have profoundly different implications for dealing with educational and social problems in this country.

SOCIAL CLASS COMPARISONS OF CHILDREN'S BEHAVIOR

First we will review studies of social class comparisons of infants' behavior during the first year of life and then report similar research on children during the second and third years. Tulkin (1973) and Tulkin and Kagan (1972) compared the behavior of 56 ten-month-old girls and mothers from white middle-class and working-class families. The children were studied in various situations. They were observed at home under naturalistic conditions. Middle-class infants spent more time crawling and playing with objects than working-class babies, possibly because the middle-class children spent less time confined in a playpen and were given more toys to play with by their mothers. There were no SES differences in the amount of spontaneous vocalizing by the infants when they were not interacting with their mothers.

The children were also studied under laboratory conditions. In one situation they were presented with two types of tape-recorded speech passages. The first type involved meaningful and nonmeaningful speech. There were no social class differences in the children's responses to the passages themselves, in terms of differences in attention or vocal behavior to meaningful and nonmeaningful speech. However, the middle-class infants tended to look more than the working-class babies at the female coder, who was seated behind them, following the meaningful passages, as if looking for the speech source. This is similar to a finding by Kagan (1971) that upper-middle-class 8-month-old babies looked longer at the speaker baffle, when there was no coder in the room, following meaningful speech passages. The children in Tulkin's (1973) study were also presented with tape-recorded passages of a fairy tale read by their own mothers and by a stranger. The middle-class infants showed greater differential responding to the two voices than the working-class babies. The middle-class children quieted more than the lower-class infants when they heard their mothers' voice ($p < 0.05$), and vocalized more when their mothers stopped speaking ($p < 0.10$). They also tended to look more at their mothers after hearing the mothers' voice ($p < 0.06$) and looked more at the coder after hearing the stranger's voice ($p < 0.03$).

The children were also observed in a standard laboratory play situation. The only significant SES difference in the infants' play behavior involved an experimentally elicited "conflict." After the babies had a chance to play with a few toys, a familiar and a new toy were presented to them. The middle-class infants seemed to be more "reflective" in making a choice. Before choosing a toy, they shifted their gaze more from one toy to another, as if trying to decide which one to play with. Once they had made a choice, the middle-class infants tended to play with the toy they had chosen longer and looked less at the rejected toy than the working-class babies.

In a similar standard laboratory play situation, Messer and Lewis (1972) found few social class differences in the play behavior of 1-year-old children. The sample included 99 boys and girls from two different SES groups. There were no social class differences in the children's play style, reflected in how frequently they shifted from one toy to another and how long they played with a single toy. There were significant SES differences in only two aspects of the children's behavior. Higher SES babies tended to use more floor space and vocalized more than lower SES infants.

Lewis (1969) has studied changes in children's attention as a function of age, social class, and intelligence. The procedure involves presenting children with the same visual stimulus for a number of trials and then introducing a new stimulus. An important measure of attention is fixation time, i.e., how long the child looks at the stimulus. In general, children show a response decrement (i.e., shorter fixation time) as the same stimulus is repeated and an increase in fixation time when a novel stimulus is introduced. Older children show more rapid response decrement and recovery than younger children, which suggests that this response pattern reflects more mature behavior. Lewis believes that response decrement and recovery in attention reflect central information processes, with more rapid decrement and recovery indicating a higher level of cognitive functioning. How does this measure of attention relate to other intellectual measures and to social class? In a study of 32 three-month-old infants from five different social classes, lower SES babies showed greater response decrement than higher SES infants (Lewis and Wilson, 1972). Thus on this measure lower-class infants manifested a higher level of cognitive functioning than middle-class babies, at least at 3 months of age. In a study of 64 children at 1 year of age, Lewis (personal communication) did not find social class differences in a similar measure of attention.

In a follow-up study (Lewis, 1969) 40 of these children were tested on the Stanford–Binet at 44 months of age. There was a significant positive correlation between rate of response decrement at 1 year of age and IQ at 44 months ($r = 0.46$ and 0.50 for girls and boys, respectively; $p < 0.05$). These results support Lewis's contention that rate of response decrement in attention may be related to intelligence. At 12 months it predicts intellectual performance at 3½ years better than any other measure we now have available for normal babies of this age, including standard infant tests. In terms of social class Lewis's research on attention indicated that middle-class infants do not show superior information-processing skills to lower-class babies on the sensorimotor level on a measure that has been shown to be related to later intelligence.

Wachs *et al.* (1971) did a cross-sectional comparative study of 102 infants between 7 and 22 months of age from two different social classes. Most of the low SES babies were black. The high SES infants were from white middle-class families; they were matched with the poor children on the basis of age and sex. Children from the two SES groups were compared on Uzgiris and Hunt's Infant Psychological Development Scales (1966), which were based on Piaget's observations of infants during the sensorimotor period. There were essentially no SES differences on "The Development of Object Permanence Scale" or on "The Development of Schemas for Relating to Objects Scale." There were social class differences starting at 7 months of age on "The Development of Means Scale," which assesses infants' ability to use tools to obtain desirable objects that are out of reach. At 7 months of age, for example, middle-class infants were superior to lower-class babies in the use of a support to obtain a distant object. The children were also presented with

"Learning and Foresight Tasks," which were designed to assess their ability to anticipate the consequences of their actions. No children were able to master any of the tasks before 15 months. Starting at 15 months of age there were consistent SES differences at all ages on one of these tasks, a stacking toy that involves placing rings on a pole. The children were presented with two sets of rings, one with a hole and one that was solid. The lower SES babies attempted to place the solid rings on the pole more often than the higher SES infants. Starting at 15 months there were also SES differences on a measure of "Vocal Imitation," which assesses both the number of appropriate words children spontaneously use for objects and the number of words that can be elicited through imitation. The middle-class children were superior to the lower-class babies on both language indices.

White (1975) did a longitudinal study of 40 children between 1 and 3 years of age from five different SES groups (Hollingshead's Classes I through V). At 12 months of age there was no relationship between social class and social competence, as measured by White's Index of Social Competence, or between social class and intellectual competence, assessed by various measures, including the Bayley mental scale. At 3 years of age, however, social class correlated significantly with intellectual competence, as measured by the Stanford–Binet ($r = 0.65$, $p < 0.001$), but not with social competence ($r = 0.04$).

A research team at the Albert Einstein College of Medicine, which included the present authors, has carried out a series of studies to discover how early social class differences in cognitive development are present and which factors contribute to these differences. We knew that earlier studies had failed to find SES differences during the first few years of life (Pasamanick and Knobloch, 1961; Hindley, 1962; Bayley. 1965), but we questioned the results on two grounds. First, they were based on standard infant tests, whose validity has been challenged because they correlated so poorly with later measures of intelligence Infant tests can detect gross developmental problems resulting from serious organic impairment or the kind of severe deprivation experienced by institutionalized babies, but such global measures may be relatively insensitive to social class influences during the sensorimotor period. We assumed that the new scales of sensorimotor intelligence based on Piaget's observations (Uzgiris and Hunt, 1966; Corman and Escalona, 1969) might be more related to later cognitive development and hence might detect social class differences earlier than standard infant tests. Second, previous studies had compared children from middle- and lower-class families without differentiating between children from poor, stable, working families and those from socially disorganized, welfare families. Pavenstedt (1965) and Malone (1963) reported marked differences in patterns of child rearing as well as in the intellectual and personality functioning of 3-year-old children from these two types of poor families. We assumed that if more infants from impoverished, socially disorganized families were studied, SES differences in cognitive development might be manifested earlier.

We did a cross-sectional study (Golden and Birns, 1968) in which 192 black children at 12, 18, and 24 months of age, ranging from fatherless welfare families to intact middle-class families, were compared on the Cattell Infant Intelligence Scale and the Piaget Object Scale. We hypothesized that there would be no social class differences on the Cattell but that there would be SES differences on the Object Scale.

The Object Scale seemed like an ideal alternative to standard infant tests such as the Cattell. The child's instrumental response on the Object Scale remains the same from the easiest to the most difficult item; he is required to search for hidden objects under a cloth under increasingly complex conditions. Whereas tests such as the Cattell are largely concerned with increments in children's perceptual–motor skills, the Object Scale seems to assess their increasing knowledge about objects and their laws of displacement. The development of object permanence also seemed to be an important precursor of later cognitive development.

There were no significant differences in either the Cattell or the Object Scale scores between black children from fatherless welfare families and those from intact middle-class families during the first 2 years of life. We did a longitudinal follow-up study (Golden et al., 1971) in which we retested as many of the children in the 18- and 24-month cross-sectional samples as we could on the Stanford–Binet at 3 years of age. Whereas at 2 years there was a nonsignificant 6-point mean IQ difference (96 versus 102) between children in our lowest and highest SES groups, a year later at 3 years of age there was a significant 21-point mean IQ difference (94 versus 115) between the two extreme SES groups. The children in the 18-month follow-up sample showed the same pattern of IQ differences at 3 years (see Table I). The fact that we obtained similar results in two independent samples increased our confidence in the findings. Furthermore the range in mean IQ scores for

TABLE I

Mean IQ Scores of Black and White Children from Different Social Classes in Two Longitudinal Studies

Class race age sample	$(N)^a$	18	24	30	36
		Age in months			
A. Black welfare					
1. 18-month sample	(10)	110^b			94
2. 24-month sample	(11)		96		93
B. Black middle class					
1. 18-month sample	(5)	106			115
2. 24-month sample	(11)		102		115
C. White low education	(30)		92	103	
D. White high education	(30)		113	126	

[a] This represents only the two extreme SES groups in the follow-up sample in the study of black children. The total follow-up sample included 89 children. For purposes of data analysis, at 3 years of age the IQ scores of the children in the 18- and 24-month cross-sectional samples ($n = 89$) were combined.

[b] At 18 and 24 months of age the Cattell Infant Intelligence Scale was used with the black children. At 24 months the Bayley Mental Scale was used with the white children. At 30 and 36 months of age the Stanford–Binet was used with both groups.

our sample of black children was almost identical to that reported by Terman and Merrill (93 to 116) in their 1937 Stanford–Binet standardization sample of 837 white children between 2½ and 5 years of age. Finally, the Object Scale did not prove to be more related to later intellectual development than the Cattell. At 18 months neither the Object Scale nor the Cattell correlated with the Stanford–Binet at 3 years of age. At 24 months the correlations between the Binet and the Object Scale and the Cattell were 0.24 ($p < 0.05$) and 0.60 ($p < 0.005$), respectively.

In the original cross-sectional study children were also rated on seven behavior rating scales while they were being tested on the Cattell and the Object Scale. These included such behaviors as delay capacity, attention, persistence, cooperation, and pleasure in task. While there were no SES differences on any of these measures at 18 or 24 months of age, most of them correlated with the Cattell, and a few correlated significantly with the Stanford–Binet at 3 years of age (Birns and Golden, 1972). A particularly interested finding was that the "pleasure in task" rating at 18 months was the only measure at this age that correlated significantly with the Stanford–Binet ($r = 0.29$, $p < 0.05$). That is, at 18 months of age the extent to which the child enjoyed doing sensorimotor tasks was more predictive of his later intelligence than was his success on the tasks themselves. The correlation between "pleasure in task" at 24 months and the Binet was even higher ($r = 0.43$, $p < 0.005$), with the correlation between the Cattell and the Binet ($r = 0.60$) partialled out. This finding suggests that while there may be discontinuity between sensorimotor intelligence and later verbal measures of intelligence, there may be continuity in terms of certain aspects of personality or cognitive style that can be observed in infants and that may be related to later intelligence. However, these behaviors were not related to social class.

Since we did not find social class differences in intellectual development or cognitive style during the first 2 years of life but did find significant SES differences in intellectual performance at 3 years of age, we focused our research on children between 2 and 3 years of age to see if we could discover factors that might explain why social class differences emerge at this time.

We did a longitudinal study* of 60 white males between 24 and 30 months of age from two different SES groups. Comparisons on a number of measures were made between 30 boys whose mothers had completed college and 30 boys whose mothers had not gone beyond high school (whom we will refer to as the high-education and the low-education groups). The measures included: (1) *standard intelligence tests* (Bayley mental scale at 24 months and Stanford–Binet at 30 months); (2) *verbal inventory*, which assesses verbal comprehension and production in a standard test situation; (3) *verbal and nonverbal learning*, in which children were presented with identical perceptual-discrimination learning tasks under verbal and nonverbal conditions; (4) *delay capacity, persistence, and embedded-figures tasks;* and (5) *mother–child interaction*, assessed by means of videotaped samples of mothers reading stories to their children. In addition, the Wechsler Vocabulary Scale was administered to the mothers.

On the basis of our previous research we did not expect to find

* This research was presented at a symposium on Social Class and Cognitive Development at the Biennial Meeting of the Society for Research in Child Development, Philadelphia, March 1973. It was reported by various members of the research team, which, in addition to the present authors, included Wagner Bridger, Albert Montare, Ellen Rossman, and Abigail Moss.

social class differences in IQ at 2 years of age, but we expected SES differences on some of our other measures. We had selected measures that we believed might detect social class differences earlier than standard intelligence tests and might correlate with later intelligence.

Contrary to our expectations, there was a large significant mean IQ difference between our two SES groups at 2 years of age, as well as social class differences on some of the other measures. In this paper we will focus on the procedures and results at 2 years of age.

Whereas in our earlier study (Golden *et al.*, 1971) there was only a 6-point (96 versus 102) nonsignificant IQ difference between the two extreme SES groups at 2 years of age, in the subsequent study there was a significant 21-point IQ difference (92 versus 113) between the children in the high- and the low-education groups ($p < 0.01$). However, the two studies differed in several important respects. In the first study the children were black, the study included both boys and girls, and the Cattell Infant Intelligence Scale was used. In the subsequent study the children were white, only boys were included, and the Bayley mental scale was employed. While these factors may have contributed to the differences, we believe that the difference in results was largely due to a difference in the socioeconomic composition of the families in the two studies, which we will briefly summarize.

1. *Black welfare families:* The families were drawn from Hollingshead's Class V and were all on public assistance. Of these families, 93% did not have a father living in the home.

2. *Black middle-class families:* These were selected from Hollingshead's Classes I, II, and III. All of the families included both parents. While in all of these families one or both parents had some schooling beyond high school, only 8% of the mothers had graduated from college.

3. *White low-education families:* The criteria for selecting children for this group was that the mother had not gone beyond high school and the father had not graduated from college. Most of the fathers were skilled blue- or white-collar workers or semiprofessionals, including sanitation workers, electricians, carpenters, policemen, and firemen.

4. *White high-education families:* The criterion for selecting children for this group was that the mother had graduated from college, whether the father had graduated from college or not. However, 90% of the fathers were college graduates, and most of them were professional, business, or managerial people.

The IQ scores of the children in these four groups between 2 and 3 years of age are presented in Table I, where we also included the data on the 18-month follow-up sample of black children.

An examination of these data indicates that the difference in results of the two studies at 2 years of age is largely due to the fact that the children in the high-education group in the present study obtained substantially higher IQ scores than those from the black middle-class families in the previous study. We attribute this difference to differences in the parents' education. While 100% of the white high-education mothers completed college, only 8% of the black middle-class mothers in the earlier study finished college. However, even if the educational levels of the parents in the two studies were similar in terms of amount of formal schooling, we could not assume that their educational experience had been the same, since we know that the quality of education for blacks and whites in this country has not been the same.

Before we report some of the other data on the children in the present study, a social class comparison of the mothers' Wechsler vocabulary scores may be of some interest. The mean score for the high-education mothers was 70 (with 80 as the maximum possible score), whereas the low-education mothers obtained a mean score of 44, with very little overlap in the vocabulary scores of these two groups of mothers. The difference was significant at the $p < 0.001$ level. While this is not surprising, it indicates that the mothers of the children in our two SES groups differed greatly, not only in terms of amount of formal schooling but also in their language competence.

Since we assumed that language plays a major role in explaining why social class differences in intellectual performance first manifest themselves during the third year of life and not earlier, we wanted to assess the children's verbal ability. We felt that standard intelligence tests were inadequate for this purpose for several reasons. They include both verbal and nonverbal items. There is no clear-cut distinction between verbal production and comprehension. What is particularly lacking is an adequate measure of verbal comprehension of infants and young children. Since there were no language tests available for 2-year-old children, we developed a verbal inventory that we believed might detect SES differences earlier than standard intelligence tests, particularly in language comprehension.

The inventory consists of two subscales: (1) *comprehension*, in which the child is required to give a *nonverbal response* to a verbal statement by the examiner; and (2) *production,* in which the child is required to give a *verbal response* to a verbal statement by the examiner. Prior to use in the present study a reliability and validation study was carried out on 96 white children at 2½ and 3 years of age, equally divided by age, sex, and social class. There were highly significant SES and age differences, but no overall sex differences. The total verbal inventory was highly correlated with the Stanford–Binet at 2½ ($r = 0.82$) and 3 ($r = 0.84$) years of age. While the inventory contains a few verbal reasoning items, most of the items are concerned with the child's knowledge of verbal concepts, so that for the most part the inventory measures verbal knowledge rather than reasoning or problem-solving ability. The fact that the inventory correlates so highly with the Binet indicates that at least at this age the Stanford–Binet may largely be a test of verbal knowledge rather than a measure of reasoning or problem-solving ability.

In the present study the children in the high-education group obtained significantly higher scores than the low-education group on the total inventory (verbal comprehension and verbal production) at both 2 and 2½ years of age. While the comprehension scores were higher than the production scores at 24 months, SES differences were present in both, and the correlations with the Bayley for comprehension ($r = 0.66$, $p < 0.01$) and production ($r = 0.61$, $p < 0.01$) were about the same. The correlation between the total inventory and the Bayley was somewhat higher ($r = 0.70$, $p < 0.01$), and its correlation with the Binet at 30 months was even higher ($r = 0.86$, $p < 0.01$). Verbal comprehension does not appear to be more sensitive in detecting social class differences at 2 years of age than verbal production or the Bayley mental scale. It is possible that with children under 2 years of age, measures of verbal comprehension may pick up SES differences earlier and correlate more with later measures of verbal intelligence than standard infant tests.

Several investigators have shown that language can facilitate perceptual discrimination learning as early as the first year of life (Koltsova, 1960; Katz, 1963), but there have been no published studies on whether there are social class differences in this respect. In the present study (Golden *et al.*, 1974) the children were presented with identical perceptual learning tasks under verbal and nonverbal conditions. The essential difference between the two conditions was that under the verbal condition the children were provided with verbal labels for the objects to be discriminated, whereas under the nonverbal condition they were not. Since there do not appear to be social class differences in sensorimotor intelligence, but there are SES differences in verbal intelligence, we hypothesized that there would be social class differences under the verbal condition but not under the nonverbal condition. The results confirmed our hypothesis. While there were no social class differences under the nonverbal condition, the children in the high-education group did significantly better than the low-education group under the verbal condition ($p < 0.01$). Furthermore, whereas nonverbal learning did not correlate with IQ, verbal learning at 24 months correlated with the Bayley at 2 years ($r = 0.37$, $p < 0.01$) and correlated even more highly with the Stanford–Binet at 2½ ($r = 0.48$, $p < 0.01$).

Koltsova (1960) reported that providing a verbal label can facilitate perceptual discrimination learning in children as young as 12 months of age, but to our knowledge this finding has not been replicated in this country. This should, of course, be done. But in addition it would be of interest to see how early there are social class differences in children's ability to use verbal information to facilitate learning, and whether such a measure in children under 2 years of age can predict later intelligence better than standard infant tests.

In the present study *delay capacity* was assessed by means of the following "waiting games."

1. A *hiding game,* in which a reward (cookie) was hidden under one of three boxes and the child was asked to wait until a signal was given (the examiner blew a whistle) before he searched for the cookie. The children were not prevented from responding prematurely and were allowed to have the cookie whether they waited or not. Some children immediately searched for the cookie and eagerly gobbled it up before the signal was given. Other children seemed to enjoy the waiting game itself, anticipating the signal with mounting excitement, playfully pretending to reach for the cookie before the signal was given, and just as eagerly returning the uneaten cookie to the examiner to be hidden again.

2. A *train game,* in which the child was allowed to activate a miniature train set by means of a starting switch that he held in his hand. Again the child was told to wait until the signal was given before he started the train. On both tasks the children were given a number of practice trials until they demonstrated that they understood the instructions. There were 10 delay trials given for each task, ranging from a 5- to

a 50-second delay, randomly presented. The delay scores consisted of the number of trials on which children waited until the signal was given before responding.

There were significant social class ($p < 0.01$) and age ($p < 0.01$) differences in delay capacity. The children in the high-education group demonstrated greater delay capacity than those in the low-education group, and at 2½ the children showed greater delay capacity than they did at 2 years of age. At 24 months of age the delay scores on the two tasks were highly correlated ($r = 0.75$, $p < 0.01$), which indicates that there was a relatively high degree of consistency in this trait, at least on these tasks and at this age. Delay capacity also correlated with the Bayley at 2 years of age ($r = 0.43$, $p < 0.01$). While the ability to delay was an important aspect in these tasks, other factors may have been involved. To some extent there may have been an element of compliance, but this did not appear to be essential.

The *persistence* tasks used in the present study also involved compliance, but the children's performance on these tasks was not at all correlated with social class, IQ, or age. Language also played a role, to the extent that through verbal instructions the examiner was able to get the children to inhibit a response to a very desirable goal object and respond when a signal was given later. Luria (1961) expressed the view that when children's behavior can be controlled or regulated by language they have reached a higher level of mental functioning. But more was involved than the verbal regulation of behavior or simply the ability to wait. Many of the children obviously derived a great deal of pleasure from the waiting game itself, from postponing gratification, which in Freudian terms also reflects a higher level of ego functioning.

Finally, the children's performance on the *embedded-figures* tasks in the present study were not related to social class or IQ. The *mother–child interaction* data will be presented later in this paper, with similar research by other investigators.

In reviewing studies of social class comparisons of cognitive development during the first few years of life, we have focused on recent research using newer measures since SES differences have not been demonstrated on standard infant tests. It is important to keep in mind, however, that there are very few such studies reported in the literature. The research evidence indicates that, in general, behaviors that involve language or children's responses to language are related to both social

class and later intelligence, whereas with only a few exceptions measures of nonverbal behavior that do not involve language do not relate
either to SES or to later intelligence.

The sensorimotor measures that relate either to social class or to
later intelligence can be summarized briefly. In Tulkin's study (1973)
middle-class 10-month-old girls seemed more "reflective" than lower-
class girls in making a choice between a familiar and a new toy. In the
study by Wachs *et al.* (1971), starting as early as 7 months of age, middle-
class infants were more advanced than lower-class babies on the "development of means scale," a Piagetian-based measure that assesses children's ability to use tools to obtain distant objects, and middle-class
babies were also superior to lower-class infants in one "learning and
foresight task" starting at 15 months. We do not know how these
measures relate to later intelligence. Lewis (1969) found that a measure
of response decrement at 12 months of age, which he believes reflects
information-processing ability, was significantly correlated with IQ at
3½ years of age, but there were no SES differences on this measure at 1
year of age (Lewis, personal communication). At 3 months of age there
was an inverse relationship between rate of response decrement in
attention and social class, with lower-class babies showing superior
"information-processing" skills than middle-class infants.

The most consistent finding is that cognitive measures that involve
language are related to social class as early as the first year of life, and
that starting at 2 years of age such verbal measures are highly correlated
with children's performance on standard intelligence tests, such as the
Bayley mental scale or the Stanford–Binet. The relationship between
infants' early vocal behavior or their response to language and later
intelligence should be studied. In these early precursors to language we
may find the roots of social class differences, as well as individual
differences, in later intelligence. Such behaviors in early infancy seem to
manifest themselves most clearly in the infant's interactions with other
people, and especially his mother. For this reason social class comparisons of mother–child interaction, which we will review in the next
section of this chapter, seem like a particularly fruitful area of research.

SOCIAL CLASS COMPARISONS OF MOTHER–CHILD INTERACTION

Research concerning the relationship between an infant's growth
and development and the behavior of its primary caretaker is as elusive

as it is compelling. How can we best select among all the events, actions, and nonactions that help shape the life of a growing human being—the smiles, words, and caresses, the responding and nonresponding to signals of distress or pleasure? We will begin this review with some history and theory. Then we will describe the very meager but critical area of research that attempts specifically to relate patterns of mother–infant interaction to SES and to the child's cognitive development during this period and later.

In 1951 John Bowlby published an influential monograph, *Maternal Care and Mental Health,* which attempted to document the devastating and apparently permanent effects on children of being separated from their mothers in infancy, which has been referred to as *maternal deprivation.* The research he reviewed was primarily based on institutionalized infants, who showed not only serious emotional problems but serious intellectual impairment as well. Babies reared in such institutions, deprived of both sensory and social stimulation, had difficulty relating to people, obtained low IQ scores, and did poorly in school during childhood and adolescence.

Bowlby's work had a strong impact. Wherever possible orphanages have been replaced by early adoption, foster-home placement, or reforms in institutional care. A further positive effect was to stimulate research on the effects of the child-rearing environment, and in particular the mother's role, on the child's development. While earlier studies focused on the mother's behavior, more recent research has been concerned with the mother–child interaction itself, and how it relates to the child's intellectual and personality development.

Unfortunately Bowlby and others have drawn certain questionable inferences from research on institutionalized infants:

1. Until recently it was generally assumed in this country, without any direct evidence, that group day care for infants would have the same negative effects on children as residential institutional care. On the basis of this assumption group day care for infants was prohibited by law in most places in the United States until a few years ago.
2. It was also assumed by many people, without any direct evidence, that infants from impoverished families experience a maternal deprivation, though perhaps less severe, similar to the deprivation of institutionalized children.
3. A further assumption was that impoverished infants, who were believed to experience such early social deprivation, would demonstrate the same permanent, irreversible intellectual impairment often found in institutionalized children, although there is very little evidence that poor infants show intellectual deficits or emotional problems in comparison to middle-class babies during *infancy.*

On the basis of such assumptions intervention programs, which may not be necessary, have been recommended for infants from impoverished families. However, Yarrow (1961) has pointed out that it is not possible to make generalizations about institutional care or its effects on children, since institutions vary greatly in terms of the quality of care provided and not all children are affected in the same way. Therefore it is even less valid to generalize from studies of institutionalized infants to the experience of poor home-reared babies or those in group day-care centers.

While there has been a great deal of speculation about the nature of social class differences in the ways mothers interact with their infants, it is only recently that a few investigators have begun to make direct naturalistic observations of the patterns of interaction between mothers and babies from different social classes.

Lewis and Wilson (1972) described differences in mothers and infants from five social classes (Hollingshead's two-factor index). Thirty-two 12-week-old infants and their mothers were observed for a two-hour period and behaviors of both were coded. Differences in infant behavior demonstrated that lower SES infants vocalized twice as much as middle SES infants, smiled twice as much, and fretted and cried about half as much as their middle-class peers. Lower SES mothers touched and held their infants more than middle-class mothers. There were no SES differences in amount of maternal vocalization, but there were differences in the occasions that elicited maternal vocalization. The middle-class mothers were much more likely to vocalize responsively when their infants vocalized. They also touched and held their babies when they cried and more often watched them while they played. Lower SES mothers, on the other hand, were more likely to touch their infants when they vocalized and vocalized when they fretted. It is possible that the middle-class mother's vocal response to her infant may be a precursor to later responding when he speaks and to answering the child's questions. A child whose questions are answered not only learns more about the world from the answers but also is encouraged to ask further questions.

Lewis and Freedle (1973) studied the patterns of vocal interactions between 3-month-old infants and their mothers. The authors pointed out that the phonetic aspect of babbling in infants, in terms of how advanced the child may be in this respect, does not seem to be related to later verbal ability. They hypothesized that perhaps the semantic or communication aspects of infants' vocal interactions with their mothers may be a precursor or anlage of later language development. Infants who are more advanced in these early prelinguistic patterns of interpersonal communication may show greater language competence later. The sample consisted of 80 mother–child dyads, including male and female, black and white infants distributed across Hollingshead's five social classes. Naturalistic observations were made of the mother–child interaction at home. While there were no SES differences in how much the mothers spoke to their children, there were social class differences in how much the infants vocalized. Lower-class infants vocalized more than middle-class babies. The social class differences in the patterns of the infants' vocal responses to their mothers' vocalizations were of particular interest. Whereas the lower-class infants were more likely to respond vocally when their mothers were speaking, the middle-class babies were more likely to stop vocalizing and listen. Early social class differences in the extent to which babies listen when their mothers are speaking may be related to later SES differences in children's ability to use verbal information for learning (Golden et al., 1974).

Lewis and Freedle (1973) also compared children in terms of whether they responded differently when their mothers were speaking to them and to another person. Middle-class infants vocalized more when their mothers were speaking to them, whereas lower-class babies did not make this distinction. Lewis and Freedle hypothesized that such differentiated vocal responding reflects more advanced communication skill at this age. There is some support for this assumption in a preliminary report of the follow-up data on three subjects at 2 years of age. The linguistic competence of the children at age 2 was assessed on various measures, including their spontaneous use of language in a play situation, their performance on a verbal comprehension task, and the Peabody Picture Vocabulary Test. In general, the communication skills of the three children at 12 weeks were related to their language ability at 2 years of age. There was also a perfect ordering of linguistic competence among the children at 2 years of age and the degree to which they responded differently when their mothers spoke to them and to another person. While these results tend to support the authors' assumption that the communication skills of infants may be precursors of later language ability, the follow-up data must be replicated on a larger number of children before we can have confidence in these important findings.

Tulkin and Kagan (1972) reported a study of 30 white middle-class and 26 white working-class mothers with their 10-month-old daughters. The results of this study showed that in the working-class homes the babies experienced more noise, greater crowding, more interaction with many adults, and more time in front of the TV. Lower-class girls had less opportunity to explore and manipulate objects, they were more restricted, and they had fewer toys than their middle-class peers.

As in previous studies SES differences were not found in the amount of affection or discipline demonstrated. However, significant SES differences were present in the mothers' attempts to keep the babies "busy" and in their verbal behavior. Every verbal behavior coded was more frequent among the middle-class mothers than among the lower SES mothers. Tulkin suggested that it was not that the two SES groups in his study differed so greatly in this respect, but rather that within the middle-class group there was a small subgroup of unusually verbal mothers. In addition, the middle-class mothers also responded more often and faster to their babies' frets.

A study of 106 two- and three-year-old white children and their mothers was completed at our laboratory (Rossman et al., 1973) that investigated the ways that mothers of two different social classes read to their children. In addition to videotaping the mother–child interaction in the laboratory, we administered a questionnaire to the mother about her reading practices at home. The questionnaire data supported previous findings that middle-class mothers have more books in their homes and read more frequently to their children than do working-class mothers.

In the laboratory the mothers were instructed to "go through the book as you would at home." The results revealed social class differences in several dimensions of behavior. The middle-class mothers and their children were more affectionate and seemed to enjoy the reading situation more than the lower SES pairs. However, the SES differences in verbal behavior were most striking. The middle-class mother was more verbally explicit, used more complex language, and gave more spontaneous explanations. She also expected more from her child, asked more questions, and was more likely to respond to her child's questions. Furthermore, most of the middle-class mothers finished reading the story at least once before discussing it, whereas very few of the working-class mothers finished reading the story. In discussing the pictures, the middle-class mothers tended to relate the pictures to the stories, while the working-class mothers did not. The data on the children also demonstrated clear-cut SES differences, the most pro-nounced being that the middle-class children were more verbally ex-plicit than the working-class children. These SES differences in lan-guage patterns in the mother–child interaction in general support Bernstein's ideas, as well as the research findings by Hess and Shipman (1965) and Bee et al. (1969) described earlier.

Arising out of a concern about the effects of the home environment of poor infants on their intellectual development, recently there have been a number of studies on mother–child interaction among poor families. These studies have shown that there are great differences in the child-rearing environment, and in particular in patterns of mother–child interaction, among poor families, which are related to the chil-dren's cognitive development. In an intervention study with black males between 15 and 36 months of age, Schaefer (1970) found that hostility in the mother correlated with hostility in the child and that these measures of hostility in turn correlated with low task orientation and low mental test scores in the children. In a study of 36 poor mothers and their first-born children between the ages of 9 and 18 months, Clarke-Stewart (1973) demonstrated that there was a strong relationship between the infants' intellectual, language, and social competence at 18 months and earlier maternal behaviors. These included such behaviors as verbal stimulation, provision of toys, affection, and the appropriateness of the mother's response to the baby. Such studies indicate that there are great differences in the ways poor mothers interact with their infants, and therefore it is not possible to make generalizations about the maternal behavior of poor mothers with infants.

The most consistent finding in the few studies of social class com-parisons of mother–child interaction during the infant period is that there appear to be SES differences as early as the first year of life in the area of language, but clear-cut consistent social class differences have not been found in other aspects of behavior. We are not saying that the mother's nonverbal behavior during infancy is not important in terms of the child's development. Most studies of mother–infant interaction have not been concerned with social class. These studies show that babies whose mothers are attentive, warm, stimulating, responsive, and en-couraging develop better than infants whose mothers are inattentive, cold, hostile, rejecting, restrictive, and less sensitive to their babies' needs (Blank, 1964; Yarrow et al., 1973; White, 1975).

On the basis of such studies perhaps we can learn from "successful" mothers from every social class the specific maternal behaviors that foster cognitive, language, social, and emotional development in infants.

Early Intervention Studies

On the basis of research on animals and institutionalized babies that suggests that early environmental deprivation during infancy may have permanent irreversible adverse effects on later intellectual and problem-solving ability, some people (Hunt, 1969) have recommended that in order to prevent later intellectual deficits in lower-class children, intervention should begin in infancy. The "failure of Head Start" has been explained on the basis that compensatory programs that begin at 3 years of age may be too late and that preventive programs that begin in infancy may be more effective (Schaefer, 1970). In reviewing early intervention studies, we will focus on programs that include children under 3 years of age in order to see whether early intervention is better than later intervention, in terms of both immediate and long-term effects on children's intellectual development. In particular we are interested in seeing whether intervention programs that begin in infancy (i.e., during the first two years of life) are more effective than programs that start later.

In 1967 the Parent and Child Center (PCC) programs were established as a downward extension of Head Start. The programs were designed to serve low-income children from birth to 3 years of age and their families. Thirty-six federally-funded (OEO), community-controlled Parent and Child Centers (PCCs) were established in various parts of the United States. The PCCs were designed to provide comprehensive child development, health care, and social services to poor families with children under 3 years of age. Each PCC developed its own child development program. Approximately half the centers provided both center-based and home-visiting programs; 11 provided only center programs, in which the emphasis was on working directly with the infants; and 6 PCCs provided only home-visiting programs, which emphasized facilitating the babies' development through education of the parents.

While the programs were primarily service-oriented, there was a plan to evaluate the effects of the various types of programs on children and their families. Thus far a report on only the first year of operation has been published (Costello, 1970). There is a great deal of descriptive information about the programs and the population served, which included 2,585 children during the first year of operation. However, quantitative data on the impact of the program on the children's development are limited. The children in six centers were given the Bayley Scales of Infant Development twice over a 10-month period, with 79 children pre- and posttested. There was no control group. The experimental children's development during this period was evaluated by a comparison of their pre- and posttest scores, as well as a comparison of the performance of the PCC children with the national norms provided by Bayley's standardization sample. On the pretest, when the children were about 1 year old, they obtained a mean Bayley mental score of 77.4, well below the national average. One the posttest, after 10 months in the program, they obtained a mean of 87.7, a 10.3 gain. One the motor scale the children showed a 7.3 increment, from 91.1 to 98.4. There was no clearcut indication that one type of child development program was more effective than any other. The greatest seemed to occur in PCCs with well-organized programs in which the goals and methods were clear to the staff and the outside observers. Several of the PCCs have been carrying out more extensive evaluations of their own programs. When the results of these studies are published, they will provide more information about the impact of these programs on the children's development.

One of the most successful early intervention studies has been carried out by Heber et al. (1972). They pointed out that approximately four-fifths of the mentally retarded population in the United States fall within the 50–75 IQ range, that they show no evidence of organic impairment, and that a disproportionately large percentage are poor and members of a minority group. Heber referred to this type of retardation as "socio-cultural mental retardation," which he believes may be environmentally determined. Heber's aim was to see whether it is possible to prevent this kind of retardation through early environmental intervention beginning in infancy.

Prior to undertaking the intervention program he did an epidemiological study of the residential area of Milwaukee having the lowest median income in the city. This area contained only 2½% of the city's population but one-third of its educable retarded schoolchildren. All families living in this area with a newborn infant and another child of at least 6 years of age were included in the epidemiological study. IQ tests (the Peabody Picture Vocabulary Test) were given to the mothers, the fathers, and the older siblings. While all of these were poverty families, they seemed to fall into two categories in terms of the risk or probability of producing a retarded child. Families in which the mothers had IQ scores of less than 80, which included less than half the study sample, accounted for four-fifths of the children with IQs of less than 80. Furthermore, only the children whose mothers had IQ scores of less than 80 showed a decline in intelligence as they grew older, while impoverished children whose mothers had IQs above 80 did not show a decline at 6 years of age. Heber assumed that a mentally retarded mother living in a slum creates a very different social environment for her children than a poor mother of normal intelligence living in the same neighborhood.

Heber selected 40 black "high-risk" families for his intervention study. The selection criterion was that the mother had a newborn infant and her full Wechsler Adult Intelligence Scale IQ score was under 80. The 40 families were randomly assigned to the experimental and the control groups, with 20 families in each. While the experimental (E) and control (C) families were not matched beforehand, they did not differ in socioeconomic or family status or number of children, nor did the infants differ in terms of height, weight, or birth complications. The program began when the children were 3 months old and continued until they were 6 years of age. There were two major aspects of the program: (1) family intervention, and (2) infant intervention. The family intervention program consisted of vocational training for the mothers, as well as helping them to improve their reading, homemaking, and child-rearing skills. The infant intervention program involved placing the babies in a day-care center, which they attended all day, 5 days a week, 12 months a year, from the age of 3 months to 6 years of age. The intervention program was divided into two periods: (1) the infant period (up to 24 months), and (2) the early childhood period (from 24 to 72 months). During the infant period the program stressed facilitating perceptual–motor and cognitive–language development, with a one-to-one teacher–child ratio maintained until 12–15 months of age. During the early childhood period the children participated in more structured organized group classroom instruction, with emphasis on three aspects of learning: language, reading, and math/problem-solving.

The data show that at 66 months the E group had a mean IQ of 124 and the C group a mean of 94, a most impressive difference of 30 points! This difference is comparable to that between lower- and middle-class children at this age. At what age do the two groups diverge? Heber reported that the Gesell scores at 6, 10, and 14 months were comparable for the two groups. At 18 months the E group exceeded the C group by a few months, but the C group was still close to the norm. By 22 months the E group exceeded the C group, which was still close to the norm, by four to six months, and the gap between the two groups steadily increased from this point on. Heber also compared the IQ scores of the children in the experimental group with the scores of older siblings who were not in the program and younger siblings who entered the program later as part of the E group. The comparisons were made of the average IQ scores the children obtained between 36 and 66 months of age. Whereas the scores of the older and younger siblings in the E group were comparable, the IQ scores of the oldest siblings who were not in the program were 39 points lower! The IQ scores of the control children were also higher than those of their siblings who were not tested as regularly, which indicates that repeated testing alone may increase children's performance on standard intelligence tests.

What impact did the program have on other aspects of the children's development? The nutrition and medical care provided to the experimental children were greatly superior to what was available to the control children. Consequently the health and the physical development of the E children were expected to be superior to those of the C children, which may have been responsible for the difference in their intellectual development, rather than the educational aspects of the program. Independent medical evaluations of the children revealed no significant differences between the two groups in height, weight, or blood analyses. After 2 years of age the children were evaluated on a more comprehensive battery of measures, which included: (1) standard intelligence tests; (2) performance on learning and problem-solving tasks; (3) various language measures; and (4) several measures of personality and social development, one of which involved an assessment of the mother–child interaction in a series of learning situations similar to those used by Hess and Shipman (1967). The E children showed marked superiority to the C children on most of these measures. A particularly interesting finding in the mother–child interaction situation was that whereas the mothers in the two groups did not differ in teaching or verbal ability, the children in the experimental group substantially increased the level of verbal communication and exchange of information with their mothers (e.g., by asking more questions), which in turn resulted in faster and more successful learning. Heber's intervention program has achieved a great deal more than raising IQ scores. He has apparently succeeded in increasing the intellectual and language competence of high-risk children in a variety of situations, so that their performance appears comparable to that of middle-class children of this age. The real test of the program, of course, is how well the experimental children succeed in school. Heber plans to have the children in the two groups independently evaluated at the end of the first grade, a year after the E children have left the program, to see whether they sustain their gains and how well they do in school.

Heber considered the intervention during infancy to be essential. During the first 18 months the difference in intellectual performance between the E and the C children was slight. However, by 24 months of age there was a 25-point mean IQ difference between the two groups, which increased to 30 points at 66 months of age. Clearly the most visible impact of the program on the children's intellectual performance, as measured by standard tests, occurred between 18 and 24 months of age, a period of rapid language growth. On the basis of similar intervention studies with older children, continued intervention during the early childhood period (from 24 to 72 months) was probably essential if the experimental children in Heber's study were to maintain their gains. However, the design of Heber's study does not allow us to determine how early it was necessary to begin the infant intervention program in order to achieve these results.

A well-designed intervention study by Gordon (1973) was concerned with the effects of the age the child first enters the program and length of time in the program. Gordon's approach stressed parent education as a way of stimulating cognitive development in poor infants during the first two years of the child's life. The sample of mothers and children consisted of 258 poor families. The program consisted of two phases: (1) the home-based parent education program (for children between 3 and 24 months of age); and (2) the home-learning center program (for children between 2 and 3 years of age). Gordon trained a group of women who were of the same SES and ethnic group as the study families to function as parent educators. During the first phase of the program the parent educators made weekly visits to the homes of the study families and spent one hour demonstrating a carefully designed Piagetian-based "curriculum" to the mothers. It involved teaching the babies various sensorimotor skills, such as searching for hidden objects. The mothers were also encouraged to label objects and actions for their babies. During the second phase of the program, when they were between 2 and 3 years of age, the children spent two hours twice a week in a home learning center. The center was simply the home of one of the study mothers, where five or six children were involved in small-group instruction and activities under the guidance of a home learning center director who had previously served as parent educator. The mother in whose home the center operated served as an assistant to the director. The center director also made weekly visits to the homes of the children in her program to demonstrate to the mothers the instructional materials used at the center. Eleven such home learning centers were operating at the same time.

To determine the effects of age of entry and length of time in the program, Gordon used the following eight treatment groups: intervention (1) from 3 to 36 months; (2) from 3 to 24 months; (3) from 12 to 36 months; (4) from 3 to 12 months and 24 to 36 months (with no intervention between 12 and 24 months); (5) from 3 to 12 months; (6) from 12 to 24 months; (7) from 24 to 36 months; and (8) a control group who were not provided with any intervention at all. Gordon hypothesized that (1) the intervention program would have the greatest impact on the children who received the most intervention; and (2) given the same amount of intervention, the children who entered the program earlier would benefit more than those who began later.

Up to 24 months of age the children were evaluated on the Griffiths scales and the sensorimotor tasks used in the training program. At 3 years of age the Stanford–Binet, the Peabody Picture Vocabulary Test, and the Leiter international scale were administered to all of the children. The Binet scores were factor-analyzed and yielded three factors: language, memory, and perceptual–motor ability. The children's scores on each factor were analyzed separately. The results were fairly consistent across all measures: (1) the more training the children had the better their performance, with the greatest difference being between children with two or three years and those with only one year or no training; and

(2) given equivalent periods of training, the age at which the children entered the program did not significantly affect their performance on any of these measures. In Gordon's study the critical factor did not seem to be when the children entered the program but how long they were in it.

Painter (1969) was concerned with the question of what the most strategic age is for educational intervention for socially disadvantaged children. The subjects in her intervention study were the younger siblings of 4-year-old children attending a compensatory nursery school. She selected children between 8 and 24 months of age and provided them with a highly structured home-tutoring program that stressed language and concept development. Painter chose to work with children of this age to see whether it is possible to prevent the intellectual "deficit" in low SES children that seems to emerge between 15 months and 3 years of age. On the basis of early results of compensatory studies with older preschool children, programs with a highly structured curriculum that emphasized cognitive and language development seemed to be the most effective in increasing the level of the children's intellectual functioning. Painter wanted to see whether such a structured curriculum could be devised for infants between 8 and 24 months and to determine how effective such a curriculum would be with children of this age.

There were 20 children in the study, including male and female, black and white infants. Painter randomly assigned 10 of the children to the experimental group and 10 to the control group. The E babies were tutored in their homes for one hour a day five days a week for a period of one year by female college graduates. The mothers were not directly involved in the tutoring sessions. The children in both groups were tested before and after the intervention program on a number of intellectual measures. The pretest scores of the E and the C groups on the Cattell Infant Intelligence Scale were similar: 98.8 and 98.4, respectively. On the posttest on the Standard–Binet the experimental group obtained a mean of 108.1 and the control group a mean of 98.8, a significant 9.3 IQ difference ($p < 0.05$). On the basis of these results Painter concluded that a home-tutoring program with a highly structured curriculum that emphasizes language and concept development can be effective in increasing the intellectual performance of socially disadvantaged infants of this age.

In order to determine whether early or later intervention is more effective in the long run, Painter plans to compare the intellectual performance of the children in this study at 4 years of age with that of their older siblings' pre-nursery-school performance on standard intelligence tests, and later with their academic achievement in school. If comparative studies during the later preschool and elementary school period indicate that these children do better than their older siblings, it would demonstrate that early intervention was more effective than later intervention. On the other hand, if the older siblings do as well or better, it would suggest that infant training may not be necessary.

Karnes et al. (1970) carried out an intervention program to facilitate intellectual development in low SES infants by working only with their mothers. There was no direct intervention with the children. In this respect the study is unique. Karnes believed that if feelings of dignity and self-respect were fostered in the mothers and if they were taught ways to facilitate their children's intellectual development, the cognitive and language skills of the children might be enhanced. The program for the mothers began when the infants were between 12 and 24 months of age. Karnes worked with a group of 15 mothers, who attended two-hour weekly group sessions for a period of about 15 months. The training sessions included both mother-oriented and child-oriented topics. The child-centered aspect of the training program included demonstrations of how the mothers could use educational play materials with their children to stimulate their intellectual and language growth. The importance of establishing a positive relationship between mother and child was also emphasized. During the parent-centered discussions the mothers were encouraged to become politically active, which many of them did, to reduce the feelings of powerlessness so often expressed by the poor.

At the end of the training period the mean IQ scores of the children in the experimental and a matched control group at about 3 years of age were 106 and 91 respectively, a significant 15-point difference. An even more striking finding was based on a comparison of the IQ scores of six children in the experimental group with the scores obtained by their older siblings prior to the time their mothers were enrolled in the program. Whereas the mean IQ of the six children in the E group was 127 at age 3, the mean score for their siblings was 89, an impressive, significant 38-point difference! This is comparable to the 39-point mean IQ difference Heber et al. (1972) found at about the same age between children in his experimental group and their untreated older siblings.

While the number of subjects was small, the results of this comparison between siblings before and after their mothers were enrolled in the program demonstrate that the program had a strong impact in terms of changing the ways the mothers interacted with their younger children. What is even more impressive is that these results were accomplished through work with the mothers, without direct intervention with the children.

Schaefer (1970) carried out a home-tutoring program for low SES black males, starting at 15 months and continuing until the children were 3 years of age. Schaefer's rationale for selecting this particular age period for his intervention program stemmed from research evidence that indicates that early sensorimotor development does not predict later intelligence and that social class differences emerge during the second and third years of life, a period of rapid language growth. Since intellectual performance in older children and adults is highly correlated with language ability, Schaefer's intervention program stressed the facilitation of language skills. At the same time personality characteristics (e.g., cooperation, curiosity, and perseverence) that might help the child succeed in school were reinforced. An attempt was also made to enhance the children's self-esteem and feelings of competence.

The tutors were college graduates who were trained to work directly with the children to facilitate their language skills. The tutors visited each child's home five times a week for approximately one hour. The parents were encouraged, but not required, to participate. There were approximately 60 children in the study, about half in the experimental group and about half in the control group. The children were not randomly assigned to the two treatment groups. The E and C children were selected from different poverty neighborhoods in Washington, D.C. The neighborhoods were comparable in terms of reading readiness scores at school entrance. The E and C families were also comparable in terms of family income (under $5,000), the mother's education (under 12 years), and the mother's occupation (unskilled or semiskilled if she was employed).

Intelligence tests were administered at a center by experienced psychologists to both experimental and control infants at 14, 21, 27, and 36 months of age. The Bayley mental scale was administered up to 27 months, and the Stanford–Binet was given at 3 years. Whereas the two groups did not differ in IQ at 14 months, before the intervention program began (105 versus 108 for the E and C groups, respectively), there was a significant 17-point difference favoring the experimental children (106 versus 89) at 3 years of age, when the program terminated. At 36 months the children in the E and the C groups also differed significantly on other intellectual and verbal measures (the Johns Hopkins Perceptual Test, a nonverbal measure of intelligence, and the Peabody Picture Vocabulary Test). Children in the two groups also differed in measures of task orientation (derived from the Bayley Infant Behavior Profile). A finding of particular interest in this study was that the ratings of maternal hostility were significantly correlated with the ratings of the child's hostility at 36 months, and both were significantly correlated with the child's task orientation and IQ at 3 years of age. In subsequent follow-up testing (Bronfenbrenner, 1974) after the program had terminated, the differences between the E and the C groups progressively diminished, and by the end of the first grade their IQ scores did not differ significantly (101 versus 97), nor did they differ in their academic achievement. On the basis of the "disappointing" follow-up data, Schaefer (1970) concluded that intervention should begin at birth, involving the mother in her infant's education as early as possible, and that the enrichment program should continue throughout the school period.

Levenstein's (in press) mother–child home program is considered by the American Institute for Research in the Behavioral Sciences (Wargo et al., 1961) to be one of the 10 most successful early intervention programs in the United States. The program has been successfully replicated throughout the country. Levenstein believes that one of the most important factors leading to intellectual and educational deficits in disadvantaged children stems from the patterns of verbal interaction between poorly educated mothers and their children during the early preschool years. She attempted to change the mother–child verbal interaction pattern from what Bernstein (1960) called a "restricted code" to an "elaborated code," the dominant linguistic patterns of lower- and middle-class people, respectively. Levenstein also strongly emphasized the importance of fostering a positive emotional relationship between mothers and their children. The program was designed to facilitate children's intellectual, verbal, and psychosocial development. Levenstein works directly with the mother–child dyad in changing their patterns of verbal and social interaction.

While the program has evolved since its inception in 1967, currently the basic program consists of 46 semiweekly visits by toy demonstrators in each of two school calendar years, starting when the children are 2 years of age continuing until they are 4. Levenstein considers this to be an optimal age for such a program because of the rapid growth of language during this time and because children are still quite emotionally involved with their mothers. The experience of interacting in a positive way with their mothers in a learning situation and on a one-to-one basis prepares children to learn in a group later. The toy demonstrators show the mothers how to stimulate their children's cognitive and language growth through the use of carefully selected age-appropriate play materials and books (referred to as "verbal interaction stimulus materials" or VISM). The toy demonstrators, who follow detailed curriculum guidelines, encourage the mothers or other family members to interact with the children during the training sessions as early and as much as possible. Once the mother comfortably interacts with the child, the toy demonstrator fades into the background. The VISM are permanently left in the home, so that they can be used between visits. Initially the toy demonstrators were female social work graduates with master's degrees. Currently many of them are paid former mother–participants with a high school education or less. The low SES toy demonstrators seem to be as effective as the more highly educated women, as reflected in the fact that the children whose mothers they have trained show comparable intellectual gains. The mother–child home program has served more than 200 low-income children and their families, most of whom are black.

Longitudinal data have been reported (Madden *et al.*, in press) on 44 children in two treatment groups (T-68 and T-69). These children were in the program for two full years, between 2 and 4 years of age, and were in the first grade at the time of the last follow-up. Twenty-one of the children (T-68) who entered the program in 1968 showed the following pattern of intellectual gains: (1) at 2 years of age, before they started the program, they obtained a mean Cattell infant intelligence score of 90.4; (2) by the end of the second year of the program they obtained a mean Binet score of 108.9, a significant gain of 17.4 points; (3) in the first grade they obtained a mean IQ of 105.4, essentially maintaining their intellectual gains three years after they had left the program. The other treatment group (T-69), consisting of 23 children who entered the program in 1969, showed a very similar pattern: (1) at 2 years of age they obtained a mean IQ of 88.8; (2) by the end of the second year of the program they obtained a mean IQ of 108.2, a significant gain of 19.4

points; and (3) in the first grade they obtained an average IQ of 105.8. By contrast, 25 control children obtained a mean IQ of about 91 when they were first tested between 2 and 4 years of age and an average IQ of approximately 96 in the first grade, showing very little change in their intellectual performance. Whereas the children in the treatment and the control groups were functioning at about the same intellectual level during the early preschool period, by the first grade there was about a 15-point IQ difference between them. Of particular importance is the fact that the children in Levenstein's intervention program maintained their intellectual gains three years after they left the program, which is in sharp contrast with the usual decrement in intellectual performance of children in other preschool programs after they have left the program.

The mother–home child program has been replicated in more than 21 other agencies in the United States, with comparable though some-what smaller intellectual gains. Levenstein has attributed the success of her program to the fact that she worked directly with the mother–child dyad, changing their patterns of verbal and social interaction at a critical time in the child's intellectual development. These changes in the patterns of mother–child interaction may be permanent and may continue to have a favorable effect on the child's intellectual development long after he has left the program.

One of the first model infant day-care centers in the United States was Caldwell's Children's Center at Syracuse University. Children are enrolled in the center as early as 6 months of age and remain until they enter school. They spend as much as nine hours a day, five days a week at the center. The program strongly emphasizes cognitive and language development. Teacher training is intensive and continuous. The teachers are encouraged to verbalize frequently to the children, to label objects and actions, and to read to babies as early as the first year of life. Caldwell (1970) compared the intellectual gains of children who entered the program before and after 3 years of age. A relatively large group of children ($N = 86$) who entered the program prior to 3 years of age showed an average IQ gain of 14 points after approximately two years in the program. Most of these children started between 12 and 24 months of age. Another group of children ($N = 22$) who entered the program at about 3½ years of age showed an average IQ gain of 18 points after approximately 1½ years in the program. The two groups did not differ in their intellectual performance during the later preschool period, although the children with infant day-care experience had begun several years earlier and had been in the program more than twice as long as those who entered the program after 3 years of age. Caldwell's research demonstrates that children can benefit from a group day-care experience during the first three years of life, but in terms of later intellectual development children who begin this experience early do not have an advantage over children who start much later.

An intervention study by Palmer (1972) at the Harlem Research Center provides data on the question of whether early intervention is better than later intervention. On the basis of animal research demonstrating the importance of early experience to development, Palmer assumed that intervention designed to change intellectual, affective, or social development in children should begin as early in life as possible. In order to determine the effects of age on the success of intervention, Palmer provided children with eight months of intervention beginning at 2 and 3 years of age.

The sample consisted of 310 black males: 240 of the children served as experimental subjects and 70 as controls; 120 of the experimental children were randomly assigned to the two-year intervention sample and 120 to the three-year sample. The experimental subjects at each age were randomly further subdivided into two treatment groups: (1) concept training, and (2) discovery. Children in the concept-training group were taught age-appropriate concepts, such as big/little, open/closed, and same/different. The children were provided with individual instruction for two one-hour sessions a week over a period of eight months. The discovery group was not taught these concepts but spent the same amount of time with instructors who played with the children with the same materials.

The children were assessed on a battery of tests, including the concept familiarity index (CFI), which tested the child's knowledge of the concepts taught in the training sessions, and the Stanford–Binet, as well as a number of other measures. All the experimental children were evaluated immediately at the end of training and one year after treatment. The children in the two-year sample were also evaluated two years later. The children in the control group were assessed on the same measures at the same ages. Immediately after training the two experimental groups performed significantly better on the concept familiarity index than the controls, and the concept-training group outperformed the discovery group. This was true for both the two- and the three-year samples. In the one-year follow-up for the two-year sample, the concept-training group did not perform significantly better on the CFI than the controls, whereas, surprisingly, the discovery group did. Two years after the training ended, neither of the experimental groups performed significantly better on the CFI than the controls. Thus, while concept training had a short-term effect on the two-year sample, one or two years later the effects of such training at 2 years of age seemed to wash out. On the other hand, in the one-year follow-up for the three-year sample, the results obtained immediately after training were sustained a year later. The long-term effects of the intervention program were greater for the children who started later.

How did the intervention program generalize to other measures, such as the Stanford–Binet? Immediately after training, the experimental children in the two-year sample obtained significantly higher Binet scores than the controls (96 versus 93), although the difference was quite small. A year after treatment the IQ scores of the experimental and the control groups did not differ significantly (94 versus 92). Immediately after training, the experimental children in the three-year sample performed significantly better on the Binet than did the controls (99 versus 93). A year later the concept-training group maintained a significant superiority over the controls on the Binet (100 versus 92), whereas the discovery group did not (97 versus 92).

On the basis of the research reviewed here—with the exception of Heber *et al.* (1972), which differs from the others in many important respects—it would be difficult to conclude that, in general, early intervention is better than later intervention or that programs that begin in infancy are more effective than those that start later. With the exception of Heber's program, which we will discuss later, the short-term immediate effects of intervention on children's intellectual performance ranged in gain approximately 10–19 IQ points. There appears to be no relationship between the amount of intellectual gain children showed at the end of a program and the age of the children when they entered it. In terms of the long-term effects of intervention on children's later intellectual development after they have left a program, we have data on only a few studies that involved children under 3 years of age. The only study in which children maintained their intellectual gains several years after they had left the program is Levenstein's (Madden *et al.*, in press) mother–child home program. However, these results may have been due more to the nature of her program than to the age of the children.

We also have follow-up data on Schaefer's (1970) home-tutoring program, which was comparable to Levenstein's in many important respects. Schaefer's program began earlier than Levenstein's but continued for approximately the same length of time. In Schaefer's program the children experienced more than twice the number of contacts as those in Levenstein's program. Whereas the immediate gains in both programs were similar, the children in Levenstein's program maintained their gains in relation to the controls several years after they had left the program, while those in Schaefer's program did not. The major difference between the two programs is that Schaefer's tutors worked primarily with the children, whereas Levenstein's toy demonstrators worked with the mother–child dyad. Levenstein's results support Schaefer's conclusion that intervention programs that directly involve mothers in the education of their children are likely to have more lasting effects than those that involve only the children. Levenstein assumes that the period from 2 to 4 years of age is the optimal time for intervention. She may be right, but her study does not permit us to draw this conclusion because she did not provide the same two-year program to children who started at different ages. This brings us to a discussion of a serious problem in the comparison of intervention programs that are directed at children of different ages: it is very difficult to determine the effect of age when the programs differ in so many other respects.

The program of Heber *et al.* (1972), for example, differs from the others reviewed here in so many ways that it is difficult to make comparisons. Undoubtedly this is one of the most effective early intervention programs for high-risk, very low SES children reported in the literature. It is also probably one of the most intensive, most extensive, and perhaps most costly (per capita) programs of its kind, which may make it impractical on a large scale. But Heber's intervention study may also differ from the others in terms of its purpose. Heber wanted to determine whether sociocultural familial retardation (which comprises four-fifths of the retarded population of the United States and is prevalent among impoverished minority groups in this country) was genetically or socially transmitted from one generation to the next. He wanted to see whether it was possible to prevent this kind of retardation through an educational program for children from high-risk families beginning in early infancy and continuing until 7 years of age. Heber succeeded admirably. He worked with children whose mothers and older siblings had very low IQ scores (below 80), and by 2 years of age these children were functioning on a middle-class level intellectually. At

24 months they obtained a mean IQ of approximately 124, 25 points higher than the score of the control group and 39 IQ points higher than the scores of older siblings who were not in the program. At 5½ years of age, at the time of the last reported follow-up, the children in the experimental group were still functioning on the same high level intellectually, although, of course, they were still in the intervention program.

What is particularly impressive about Heber's study is that the intellectual differences between the E and the C children were manifested not only in large IQ differences but in similar differences in functioning on a wide variety of measures and in a wide variety of situations. The ultimate test of the impact of the program, according to Heber, is how the children do in school after they have left the program. Of course, their performance may also depend on the school they attend.

While Heber's intervention study answers a number of important questions, it does not permit us to conclude that in order to achieve his results it was necessary to begin as early as he did, when the children were 3 months of age. During the first 18 months the children in the experimental and the control groups differed very little in their intellectual performance. By 24 months of age there was a 25-point IQ difference between them, which increased relatively little after this age. These data suggest that the 18–24 months period is critical in terms of social class differentiation in intellectual development, perhaps because of the rapid growth of language during this period.

In contrast to most other intervention programs, Heber's succeeded in raising the intellectual level of high-risk, low-income children to that of middle-class children, almost 20 points higher than the scores obtained by the experimental children in Levenstein's highly successful program. Could Heber have achieved these results if he had started when the children were 12 or 18 months of age or even older? Engelmann (1970) reported the results of a two-year intervention study on low SES black children, beginning when the children were 4 years old and using the Bereiter–Engelmann method. This approach stresses a highly structured, academically oriented language, reading, and mathematics program, in which children are drilled in these skills in small groups. Whereas at the start of the program the children's mean IQ was 95, at the end of two years in the program it increased to 121, a significant 26-point gain. The most dramatic effect of the program was shown by two children who started the program with IQs in the 80s and by the end of kindergarten were reading at the third-grade level! This result suggests that the program may have succeeded in doing more than increase the children's IQ scores; it seems also to have had a strong impact on their academic achievement. This intervention program, which began when the children were 4 years of age, produced intellectual gains as large as any reported in the literature, including those in Heber's study. This indicates that it may not be necessary to begin in infancy in order to achieve these results.

The intervention programs we have reviewed vary in a number of important dimensions, including the age of the child when intervention begins. They differ in such respects as: (1) whether the program was carried out in a center or in the child's home; (2) whether it was directed only to the child, only to the mother, or to the mother–child dyad; (3) the frequency and intensity of contacts, ranging from one or two hours a week to all-day, five-day-a-week programs; (4) the duration of the programs, which ranged from one to six years; (5) the content and methods employed; and (6) the population studied. All of these variables may interact with age and confound any interpretations that may be drawn of the specific effects on their subsequent development of the age of the children when intervention begins.

If a comparison is made between children in the same program who begin at different ages but who are in the program for the same period of time, the effect of other contaminating variables can be eliminated. In the few studies reviewed here in which this experimental design was employed, earlier intervention was not more effective than later intervention (Caldwell, 1970; Palmer, 1972; Gordon, 1973). In comparing programs, we have primarily looked at their effects on the children's performance on standard intelligence tests, which may not always be the most appropriate or most sensitive measure of the effects of a program. While there may be little difference between early and later intervention programs in terms of IQ scores, it is possible that programs that begin earlier in life may have more pervasive and enduring effects on aspects of the children's personality or cognitive style that may be important for learning and academic success. Unfortunately standard measures of personality and social and emotional functioning, which could be used to compare the effects of different intervention programs on these important aspects of development, are not available at the present time.

Standard intelligence tests are useful in this respect. However, such tests can be construed only as intermediate criterion measures; they are useful only because they correlate with academic achievement, which must be viewed as the ultimate criterion of the success of an early intervention program. Intervention programs that succeed in increasing children's scores on standard tests but do not have a measurable impact on their school achievement may be doing little more than improving children's skills in performing on such tests. While early intervention programs must be judged by how well they prepare children to succeed in school, it must be remembered that how well children do in school depends not only on the quality of their preschool experience but also on the quality of the education provided to them once they enter school.

CONCLUSIONS

On the basis of the data available to us at the present time we would have to conclude that, in general, social class differences in infant or sensorimotor intelligence probably do not exist. This conclusion is based both on the results of earlier SES comparisons using standard infant tests and on more recent research in which newer cognitive measures were employed. While there may be SES differences on a few specific aspects of sensorimotor behavior, the relationship between these behaviors and later intelligence has not been demonstrated as yet. Clear-cut, consistent, pervasive social class differences in intellectual performance on a variety of measures emerge somewhere between 18 and 24 months of age. Since SES differences in cognitive development first manifest themselves during a period of rapid language growth, it is reasonable to assume that these differences may be due to language.

There may be a discontinuity between the sensorimotor and the verbal periods in terms of individual differences both in children's intellectual competence and in the environmental conditions that facilitate cognitive development on these two qualitatively different levels of intelligence. This discontinuity could explain the absence of a correlation between measures of sensorimotor and of verbal intelligence. While sensorimotor intelligence may be the foundation for later intelligence, as Piaget believes, there is no reason to assume that the rate of cognitive development or intellectual competence of normal children should be the same on the sensorimotor and the verbal levels.

Environmental conditions that facilitate intellectual development during the sensorimotor and the verbal periods may also differ. While children can understand and use language to a limited extent during the sensorimotor period, their knowledge about the world is acquired primarily through their own direct explorations of their immediate environment. Given an average expectable environment with an opportunity to explore and manipulate objects and a sufficient amount of attention and affection by care-giving adults, children reared under a variety of social conditions can acquire on their own the kinds of perceptual–motor skills and knowledge measured by infant tests and Piaget-type scales. On the sensorimotor level the child's construction of reality, in terms of the basic dimensions described by Piaget (such as object permanence and spatial, causal, and temporal relations), does not appear to be socially transmitted but seems to be largely acquired through the child's own direct experience, and therefore such knowledge may be universal. After 18 months of age, as children become increasingly capable of learning about the world through language, social class and culture begin to have a much greater impact in terms of shaping children's cognitive development. That is, social class and cultural diversity in cognitive development may largely be mediated by language.

While social class differences do not seem to be present in sensorimotor intelligence, there is some evidence that SES differences in the presymbolic vocal interactions between infants and their mothers may be present as early as the first year of life (Lewis and Freedle, 1973; Tulkin, 1973; Tulkin and Kagan, 1972). These differences in vocal interaction may be the early precursors of later social class differences in language and cognitive development. SES differences in language experience may begin very early in life without having much impact on children's intellectual development until later. Through such vocal interactions middle-class children may be primed to be more responsive and to pay greater attention and listen more when their parents speak to them than lower-class infants. In this respect middle-class children may be better prepared to acquire knowledge through language, once they become capable of doing so, first from their parents and later in school from teachers.

In order to narrow the intellectual gap between children from different social classes, which emerges between 18 and 24 months of age, how early must we begin intervention? Heber *et al.* (1972) have demonstrated that through an intensive intervention program beginning at 3 months of age it is possible to raise the intellectual performance of very low SES, high-risk infants (whose mothers and older siblings obtain IQ scores below 80) to the level of middle-class children by 2 years of age. In order to achieve such results, how early must we begin? The design of Heber's study does not permit us to answer this question. Engelmann (1970) reported similar results for low SES children in a two-year intervention program starting at 4 years of age. One of the most effective and practical intervention programs reported in the literature, Levenstein's mother–child home program, is directed to children between 2 and 4 years of age. In the few intervention studies in which children in the same program began at different ages, there is no evidence that earlier intervention is more effective than later intervention (Caldwell, 1970; Gordon, 1973; Palmer, 1972). While infant experience may be extremely important, the impact of later experience on cognitive development may be underestimated. Studies reported by Skeels (1966), Dennis (1973), and Kagan and Klein (1973) indicate that even gross, environmentally produced intellectual retardation is not necessarily irreversible. In these studies children showed significant intellectual retardation and apathy during infancy while they were in a very restricted, unstimulating environment. However, when they were shifted to a more stimulating environment later, they seemed to catch up intellectually and appeared to function normally in other respects. While severe environmental deprivation in infancy may result in permanent irreversible deficits in learning and problem-solving ability in animals, this may not be the case for humans. Unlike other animals, human beings may be much more plastic, may be more responsive to later environmental changes, and may retain greater flexibility and capability of changing their behavior throughout life.

We mention these studies only to show that even gross, environmentally produced intellectual retardation in infancy can be reversed later. Lower-class children in our society do not differ greatly from middle-class children in cognitive and personality development in infancy, nor is there evidence that the social environment of lower-class children is less favorable in terms of fostering these aspects of development during the sensorimotor period. While there may be SES differences in early language experience, it is possible that such differences may be made up at a later age. Although it may be possible to accelerate aspects of sensorimotor development through early environmental intervention, there would appear to be little point in doing so since the rate of sensorimotor development does not seem to be related to later intelligence for normal children. For these reasons infant intervention for normal, home-reared children would seem to be unnecessary.

What must be done to improve the academic skills of lower class children in our society? Whether one perceives social class differences as deficits in lower-class children and their families, judged by middle-class standards, or as cultural variations or differences may make a great difference in terms of educational goals and methods.

From a deficit point of view, one of the implicit goals of early childhood education seems to be to make lower-class children as much like middle-class children as possible, not only in terms of intellectual and language competence but also in certain important aspects of their character makeup and personality. Such a goal may be questionable from several standpoints.

First, is it possible to achieve such a goal through education alone, even if the child's parents are included in the educational process? Bernstein (1960) believes that social class differences in linguistic and cognitive style stem from and reflect fundamental differences in life style and outlook. If this is true, is it possible to produce basic changes in the linguistic and cognitive style of poor children and their parents only through education, without materially changing their lives economically, socially, and politically?

And second, even if this were possible, would it be completely desirable? Early intervention programs for low SES children, to the extent that such programs are successful, may profoundly change the ways in which the children experience life, a change that in some ways may be undesirable. An essential ingredient in the rearing of middle-class children seems to be designed to develop distance from their immediate experience. This may be achieved in several ways. More of their experience, feelings, and impulses may be filtered through language and expressed verbally. Middle-class parents often place greater value on abstract than practical knowledge, although there may also be ethnic differences in this respect. Middle-class children are trained from a very early age to postpone gratification and to develop a future orientation. All of these aspects of middle-class character development have adaptive and positive features. However, there may be some negative side effects. For example, to the extent that experience and feelings are filtered through language, their intensity may be diminished and diluted. To the extent that a person places greater value on abstract knowledge, he may be highly competent in academic situations but incompetent in dealing with practical problems. To the extent that an individual becomes future-oriented, which may be society's way of keeping our noses to the grindstone, he may find it difficult to live in the present and to enjoy each moment.

Implicit in the deficit point of view is an assumption that lower-class children and their families are inferior in certain respects. While middle-class educators may attempt to cloak these beliefs in scientific terminology and to conceal them, perhaps even from themselves, poor children and their families may sense and resent these negative attitudes toward them. In their resentment children may resist all efforts to "educate" them, and at the same time they may fulfill the teachers' underlying expectations of failure. This may be at least one of the reasons why our educational efforts with poor children in this country have on the whole been so spectacularly unsuccessful, despite the expenditure of large sums of money.

If educators could develop the belief, and this may require a great deal of self-examination, that poor children are not inferior to middle-class children but merely different as a result of very different life experiences, the educational process might take on a very different quality. It would require a recognition on the part of the middle-class educator of poor children that they have a common task—the child's education—and a mutual problem. There is a vast cultural and experiential gap between middle-class teachers and poor children, which becomes even greater if they also differ racially and ethnically. They hardly speak a common language. This gap must be narrowed if anything of educational value is to occur between them. From this point of view the child would not have to do all of the accommodating, to use Piaget's term. Both middle-class educators and lower-class children have to accommodate to each other, to develop mutual respect, and to find a common meeting ground to carry out their joint educational task.

Under the best of circumstances education may have a modest impact on the problem of poverty, but it is not a panacea, as some proponents of compensatory education originally had hoped. Poverty is basically an economic problem which probably can be eliminated only through the political process.

References

Ausubel, D. P., 1964, How reversible are the cognitive and motivational effects of cultural deprivation? *Urban Education*, Summer:16.

Bayley, N., 1965, Comparisons of mental and motor test scores for ages 1–15 months by sex, birth order, race, geographic location, and education of parents, *Child Development*, 36:379.

Bee, H. L., Van Egeren, L. F., Streissguth, A. P., Nyman, B. A., and Leckie, M. S., 1969, Social class differences in maternal teaching strategies and speech patterns, *Developmental Psychology*, 1:726.

Bernstein, B., 1960, Language and social class, *British Journal of Sociology*, 11:271.

Binet, A., 1909, "Les idées modernes sur les enfants," Ernest Flammarion, Paris.

Birns, B., and Golden, M., 1972, Prediction of intellectual performance at three years on the basis of infant tests and personality measures, *Merrill–Palmer Quarterly*, 18:53.

Birns, B., and Golden, M., March 1973, The interaction of social class and sex on intelligence, language, personality, and the mother–child relationship, paper presented at the Biennial Meeting of the Society for Research in Child Development, Philadelphia.

Blank, M., 1964, Some maternal influences on infants' rates of sensorimotor development, *Journal of Child Psychiatry*, 3:668.

Bowlby, J., 1951, "Maternal Care and Mental Health," World Health Organization, Geneva.

Bronfenbrenner, U., 1974, "A Report on Longitudinal Evaluations of Preschool Programs," Vol. 2, "Is Early Intervention Effective?" Department of Health, Education, and Welfare Publications No. (OHD), 74–25.

Caldwell, B. M., 1970, The rationale for early intervention, *Exceptional Children*, 36:717.

Clarke-Stewart, K. A., 1973, Interactions between mothers and their young children: Characteristics and consequences, *Monographs of the Society for Research in Child Development*, 38:(Serial No. 153).

Corman, H., and Escalona, S. K., 1969, Stages of sensorimotor development: A replication study, *Merrill–Palmer Quarterly*, 15:351.

Costello, J., August 1970, Review and summary of "A National Survey of the Parent–Child Center Program," prepared for the Office of Child Development, U.S. Department of Health, Education, and Welfare.

Denenberg, V. H. (ed.), 1970, "Education of the Infant and Young Child," Academic Press, New York and London.

Dennis, W., 1973, "Children of the Creche," Appleton-Century-Crofts, New York.

Deutsch, M., 1964, Facilitating development in the preschool child: Social and psychological perspectives, *Merrill–Palmer Quarterly*, 10:249.

Engelmann, S., 1970, The effectiveness of direct instruction on IQ performance and achievement in reading and arithmetic, *in* "Disadvantaged Child," Vol. 3, J. Hellmuth (ed.), Brunner/Mazel, New York.

Fowler, W., 1962, Cognitive learning in infancy and early childhood, *Psychological Bulletin*, 59:116.

Geismar, L. L., and La Sorte, M. A., 1964, "Understanding the Multi-Problem Family," Association Press, New York.

Goddard, H. H., 1920, "Human Efficiency and Levels of Intelligence," Princeton University Press, Princeton, New Jersey.

Golden, M., and Birns, B., 1968, Social class and cognitive development in infancy, *Merrill–Palmer Quarterly*, 14:139.

Golden, M., Birns, B., Bridger, W. H., and Moss, A., 1971, Social class differentiation in cognitive development among black preschool children, *Child Development*, 42:37.

Golden, M., Bridger, W. H., and Montare, A., 1974, Social class differences in the ability of young children to use verbal information to facilitate learning, *American Journal of Orthopsychiatry*, 44:86.

Gordon, I. J., 1973, A home learning center approach to early stimulation, in "Revisiting Early Childhood Education," J. L. Frost (ed.), Holt, Rinehart, and Winston, New York.

Heber, R., Garber, H., Harrington, C. H., and Falender, C., 1972, Rehabilitation of families at risk for mental retardation, Progress Report.

Hess, R. D., and Shipman, V., 1965, Early experience and the socialization of cognitive modes in children, *Child Development*, 36:869.

Hess, R. D., and Shipman, V. C., 1967, Cognitive elements in maternal behavior, in "Minnesota Symposia on Child Psychology," J. P. Hill (ed.), University of Minnesota Press, 1:58.

Hindley, C. B., 1962, Social class influences on the development of ability in the first five years, in "Child and Education: Proceedings of the XIV International Congress of Applied Psychology," Munksgaard, Copenhagen, 3:29.

Hollingshead, A. B., 1957, "Two-Factor Index of Social Position," published by the author, New Haven, Connecticut.

Hunt, J. McV., 1961, "Intelligence and Experience," Ronald Press, New York.

Hunt, J. McV., 1969, "The Challenge of Incompetence and Poverty," University of Illinois Press, Urbana.

Jensen, A. R., 1969, How much can we boost IQ and scholastic achievement? *Harvard Educational Review*, 39:1.

Kagan, J., 1971, "Change and Continuity in Infancy," Wiley, New York.

Kagan, J., and Klein, R. E., 1973, Cross-cultural perspectives on early development, *American Psychologist*, 28:947.

Kamin, L. J., 1974, "The Science and Politics of I.Q.," Wiley, New York.

Karnes, M. B., Teska, J. A., Hodgins, A. S., and Badger, E. D., 1970, Educational intervention at home by mothers of disadvantaged infants, *Child Development*, 41:925.

Katz, P. A., 1963, Effects of labels on children's perception and discrimination learning, *Journal of Experimental Psychology*, 66:423.

Koltsova, M. M., 1960, "The Formation of Higher Nervous Activity of the Child," Veb Verland, Volk und Gesundheit, Berlin.

Leacock, E. B. (ed.), 1971, "The Culture of Poverty: A Critique," Simon and Schuster, New York.

Levenstein, P., in press, The mother–child home program, in "The Preschool in Action," R. K. Parker (ed.) (2nd ed.), Allyn and Bacon, Boston.

Lewis, M., 1969, A developmental study of information processing within the first three years of life: Response decrement to a redundant signal, *Monographs of the Society for Research in Child Development*, 34:(Serial No. 133).

Lewis, M., and Freedle, R., 1973, The mother–infant dyad, in "Communication and Affect: Language and Thought," P. Pliner, L. Kranes, and T. Alloway (eds.), Academic Press, New York.

Lewis, M., and McGurk, H., 1973, Infant intelligence scores . . . True or False? in "Annual Progress in Child Psychiatry and Child Development," S. Chess and A. Thomas (eds.), Brunner/Mazel, New York.

Lewis, M., and Wilson, C. D., 1972, Infant development in lower-class American families, *Human Development*, 15, 112.

Lewis, O., 1966, The culture of poverty, *Scientific American*, 215:19.

Luria, A. R., 1961, "The Role of Speech in the Regulation of Normal and Abnormal Behavior," Liveright, New York.

Madden, J., Levenstein, P., and Levenstein, S., in press, Longitudinal IQ outcomes of the mother–child home program, 1967–1973, *Child Development*.

Malone, C. A., 1963, Some observations on children of disorganized families and problems of acting out, *Journal of the American Academy of Child Psychiatry*, 2:22.

McCall, R. B., Hogarty, P. S., and Hurlburt, N., 1972, Transistors in infant sensorimotor development and the prediction of childhood IQ, *American Psychologist*, 27:728.

McCall, R. B., Appelbaum, M. I., and Hogarty, P. S., 1973, *Monographs of the Society for Research in Child Development*, 38:(Serial No. 150).

Messer, S. G., and Lewis, M., 1972, Social class and sex differences in the attachment and play behavior of the year old infant, *Merrill–Palmer Quarterly*, 18:295.

Miller, S. M., 1964, The American lower classes: A typological approach, *in* "Mental Health of the Poor," F. Riessman, J. Cohen, and A. Pearl (eds.), Free Press, New York.

Painter, G., 1969, The effect of a structured tutorial program on the cognitive and language development of culturally disadvantaged infants, *Merrill–Palmer Quarterly*, 15:279.

Palmer, F. H., 1972, Minimal intervention at age two and three and subsequent intellective changes, *in* "The Preschool in Action," R. K. Parker (ed.), Allyn and Bacon, Boston.

Pasamanick, B., and Knobloch, H., 1961, Epidemiological studies on the complications of pregnancy and the birth process, *in* "Prevention of Mental Disorders in Children," G. Caplan (ed.), Basic Books, New York.

Pavenstedt, E., 1965, A comparison of the child-rearing environment of the upper-lower and very low-lower class families, *American Journal of Orthopsychiatry*, 35:89.

Piaget, J., 1952, "The Origins of Intelligence in Children," Margaret Cook (trans.), International University Press, New York.

Rossman, E., Golden, M., Birns, B., Moss, A., and Montare, A., March 1973, Mother–child interaction, IQ, and social class, paper presented at the Biennial Meeting of the Society for Research in Child Development, Philadelphia.

Schaefer, E. S., 1970, Need for early and continuing education, *in* "Education of the Infant and Young Child," V. H. Denenberg (ed.), Academic Press, New York and London.

Schaefer, E. S., and Aaronson, M., 1972, Infant education research project: Implementation and implication of the home-tutoring program, *in* "The Preschool in Action," R. K. Parker (ed.), Allyn and Bacon, Boston.

Skeels, H. M., 1966, Adult status of children with contrasting early life experiences, *Monographs of the Society for Research in Child Development*, 31:(Serial No. 105).

Terman, L. M., 1916, "The Measurement of Intelligence," Houghton-Mifflin, Boston.

Terman, L. M., and Merrill, M. A., 1937, "Measuring Intelligence," Houghton-Mifflin, Boston.

Tulkin, S. R., 1972, An analysis of the concept of cultural deprivation, *Developmental Psychology*, 6:326.

Tulkin, S. R., 1973, Social class differences in infants' reactions to mother's and stranger's voices, *Developmental Psychology*, 8:137.

Tulkin, S. R., and Kagan, J., 1972, Mother–child interaction in the first year of life, *Child Development*, 43:31.

UZGIRIS, I. C., AND HUNT, J. McV., 1966, An instrument for assessing infant psychological development, Unpublished manuscript, University of Illinois.

WACHS, T. D., UZGIRIS, I. C., AND HUNT, J. McV., 1971, Cognitive development in infants of different age levels and from different environmental backgrounds: An exploratory investigation, *Merrill–Palmer Quarterly, 17*:283.

WARGO, M. J., CAMPEAU, P. L., TALLMADGE, G. K., 1961, "Further Examination of Exemplary Programs for Educationally Disadvantaged Children," American Institute for Research in Behavioral Sciences, Palo Alto, California.

WHITE, B., 1975, Critical influences on the development of competence, *Merrill–Palmer Quarterly.*

YARROW, L., 1961, Maternal deprivation: Toward an empirical and conceptual re-evaluation, *Psychological Bulletin, 58*;459.

YARROW, L. J., RUBENSTEIN, J. L., PEDERSEN, F. A., AND JANKOWSKI, J. J., 1973, Dimensions of early stimulation and their differential effects on infant development, *in* "Annual Progress in Child Psychiatry and Child Development," S. Chess and A. Thomas (eds.), Brunner/Mazel, New York.

YERKES, R. M., AND FOSTER, J. C., 1923, "A Point Scale for Measuring Mental Ability," Warwick and York, Baltimore.

ZIGLER, E., AND BUTTERFIELD, E. C., 1968, Motivational aspects of changes in IQ test performance of culturally deprived nursery school children, *Child Development, 39*:1.

12   Looking Smart: The Relationship between Affect and Intelligence in Infancy

JEANNETTE HAVILAND

INTRODUCTION

Without being wholly conscious of it, parents, pediatricians, and particularly psychologists have used facial expression to infer the existence and development of intelligence. We use facial expression or "affect" to denote consciousness, interest, surprise, intention, fear, or frustration; then we use these states of emotions to determine motivation, knowledge, and ability. This may surprise some readers, since we claim to be looking at behavior to determine motivation, knowledge, and ability. By *behavior* we usually mean actions accomplished—"grasped the block," "looked under the pillow," "turned away." Awareness of these actions accomplished seems to block awareness of the affect accompanying, preceding, substituting for, or following the action, even though we use affect to interpret the action.

This blockage of psychological awareness has had serious consequences for the direction of research in this century. Those who test infant intelligence and observe infant behavior use affect continuously to infer intelligence and knowledge, but they do not acknowledge it. Hence in research we use as primary variables the behaviors that the testers and observers believe to be crucial; these behaviors actually form only a portion of their unacknowledged system for assessing knowledge.

JEANNETTE HAVILAND · Educational Testing Service.

The present research view of intelligence is much like that of a television picture with strong interference, so that random points are missing, making the picture lose its form. The impact of coherent theories of cognitive development that emphasize sensorimotor development has been so great that less and less attention has been given to other portions of the infant's behavior that influence his interactions with the social world, including the influential aspect of looking smart.

It is time for us to examine ourselves and our methods of assessing intelligence and intelligent behavior. Just to be objective and honest, we must admit that almost never do we assess an infant's intelligence solely by observing his actions or by observing his sensorimotor behaviors. We infer the infant's awareness, understanding, and knowledge by an intuitive, unstructured, unsystematic method that takes into account affect, environment, interpersonal relationships, and sensorimotor behaviors. Isolating a single variable invariably results in questions about the validity of the assessment and the predictive quality of the assessment. Furthermore isolating sensorimotor behaviors results in assessments that give minimal information about the infant's social interactions, which largely determine his cognitive environment.

In this chapter we will show that in practice no one really assesses infant intelligence by assessing motor or sensorimotor behaviors, not on tests such as the Bayley Scales of Infant Development and not on assessments of intellectual growth and change such as Piaget's. However, no one has systematically studied the use made of affect in assessment.

We will show from a brief review of studies of affect that it is possible to study affect and that it has a meaningful place in our interpretation of infant behaviors. Further, we will show that infants can be strikingly different in facial expression—even twins show strong, measurable individual differences from the second week of life.

Last we will show how the study and assessment of affect may lead to new or renewed understanding of infant cognitive–affective disorders. In the case of autism cognitive development is so clearly involved with social and emotional development that study of these afflicted children may lead to a new interpretation of infant cognition and cognitive development as an interactive development.

If we would determine and understand infant intelligence, we must study how the infant reveals his intelligence and how the adult community responds to the infant's looking smart.

Using Affect on Measures of Infant Intelligence

At one time or another we all use a shorthand method of assessing intelligence. We say, in effect, "He looks smart." What do we ordinarily mean by this? Usually we use this shorthand method when we are unable to observe a person's problem-solving abilities systematically, or we may use it in spite of these observations in a case in which a person acts stupid, but we keep giving him another chance because we cannot quite believe that a person who looks that smart could act so dumb. Why do we persist? In part it is because we have a fairly reliable system of inferring intelligent behavior from intelligent affect. If a student sits in class and gazes attentively at the lecturer, the blackboard, and other relevant objects; laughs appropriately; looks puzzled during confused explanations; and is somewhat excited during animated discussions, we expect him to do well in the course. The student who lacks affect, who gazes into space, looks sleepy, or reacts inappropriately, we do not expect to do well. We have been wrong, particularly in the latter case, because lectures are the sorts of events that inspire stupid affect. However, the affect system is commonly useful for shortcut assessments. None of these observations is particularly startling, but they all gain in importance when we systematically review psychological tests of intellectual behavior and problem solving and find that a significant variable in the determination of infant cognitive ability is infant affect, not alone "manual–tactile" ability, as Piaget, among others, has claimed and as most developers of tests, such as Bayley and Gesell, emphasize.

A clear example of this is contained in the commonly used Bayley Scales of Infant Development: "The Bayley Scales of Infant Development (BSID) are designed to provide a tripartite basis for the evaluation of a child's developmental status in the first two and one-half years of life. The three parts are considered complementary, each making a distinctive contribution to clinical evaluation" (Bayley, 1969, pp. 3–4). The Mental Scale assesses sensory–perceptual abilities and other bases of abstract thinking. The Motor Scale measures control of the body, coordination, and locomotion. The Infant Behavior Record assesses the "child's social and objective orientations toward his environment" Even the briefest of reviews reveals that affect plays a major role in enabling the examiner to determine the infant's abilities. The scale titled the "Infant Behavior Record" is most conspicuous in this regard. Let us take each category of the Behavior Record and observe how affect is used to assess intelligent behavior.

In the first category of the Infant Behavior Record, "Social Orientation," the examiner must discover whether the infant behaves differentially toward objects, mother, and examiner. The first indication is "interest," as in our student in the lecture above, but then more specifically the examiner notes "freezing, frowns, wariness, brightening, smiling, laughing, vocalization, fussing" (p. 1). These are commonly called affects. From the occurrence of these affects and presumably their appearance in what seems to the examiner to be an appropriate sequence, although that is not specifically mentioned, the examiner infers that the infant can discriminate objects from persons and his mother from a stranger. Presumably one could set up a conditioned learning situation in which it is proved that the infant can reliably make such a discrimination, but in all probability the inference is correct and takes considerably less time than devising a situation in which affect is not used. It is our unacknowledged "shorthand."

The next items—"Cooperativeness" and "Fearfulness"—involve a stronger dichotomy between positive and negative affect than the first category. The first primarily involves an assessment of "enjoyment" in the tasks at hand or "resistance" to them. One should point out that this is not a trivial measure of intellectual competence. If an infant "enjoys" the testing situation, he probably enjoys many activities that will relate to academic achievement and possibly language, specifically; that is, he enjoys working with puzzles, making discoveries, and interacting with new people in goal-oriented tasks.

Fearfulness is used as an indication of many things during infancy. If it is very strong, it is cause for concern about development, because it interferes with normal exposure to the environment. If fear is not apparent at all, the examiner looks for its interaction with age and situational variables. The child could be reckless or unaware of danger, or he might not show affect in general and not show fear in particular, or any one of several possibilities. Of course, fear of strangers is expected and part of the developmental norm for infants between 8 and 12 months. In any case, fearfulness can serve as an indicator of recognition of difference, although it is not the sole indicator and probably not even the predominant one.

The next area examined on the Bayley scale is "Tension." This covers tension in the whole body and may be part of affect. An inert, flaccid infant lacks affect and would inspire the examiner to rely heavily on manual–tactile indications of cognition. The extreme lack of tension greatly inhibits ability to predict intelligence, except as it predicts lack of intelligence. On the other hand, "tautness," "startle," "quiver," and "trembling" (Bayley, 1969, p. 2) are indications of extreme affect, although they do not determine the particular affect. Only when combined with other affects and behavior sequences do they gain meaning. For example, an infant who startles easily and is tense may also be fearful or he may be excited. Facial expression and determination of approach or avoidance would tell the examiner which was more likely. These affects in combination with manual–tactile abilities are determined differently. A 2-month-old infant who startles at noises in the testing room but does not cry, who tenses when he reaches for the red ring, and who stiffens when being picked up by the examiner may be designated as a tense infant, but his tenseness is in each instance a response to something and an indication of awareness. On the other hand, an infant who is taut and quivering and does not react easily and intensely with testing stimuli is thought of in a different category. In each instance the categorization produces a part of the assessment of intelligence.

The next category is wholly affective and is called "General Emotional Tone." This assesses distress or contentedness during the testing procedure. This no doubt is highly related to "cooperativeness," although one describes a general state and the other relates more directly to interaction with the examiner. It is clear, though, that a distressed infant will not be a cooperative one. The infant may be happy and noncooperative or cooperative and only moderately content, and various changes may occur during which he is in one or the other of these conditions. Again the relevant behavior includes affects—crying, fussing, and whining, or smiling, laughing, crowing, and animation (Bayley, 1969, p. 3).

We could go on indefinitely, but it is apparent that affect is the primary determinant in the assessment of infant development from the Infant Behavior Record. Every single item on this test relies on an assessment of infant affect and an inference about which affect it is and whether or not it is appropriate. It is not possible to rate an infant without affect on this scale. However, the reader must be reminded that this assessment, a conspicuous phenomenon, occurs in the absence of systematic knowledge of what is being assessed.

Let us turn to the other scales, which rely more heavily on motor behaviors or language and problem solving. Here the examination of the use of affect becomes more complex. Part of the problem in describing the use of affect to determine development and intelligence from these two scales is that the use of affect by the examiner changes rapidly as the range of the child's abilities widens. During the first three months 40%* of the items cannot be assessed in the absence of appropriate affect, 58% might be so assessed but probably are not, and 2% (one item—"head turns") could be assessed without affect. From 3 to 8 months 25% of the items need affect to be assessed, 17% probably need affect, and 57% could be assessed even if the examiner could not recognize affect. From 8 to 18 months, only one item ("jabbers expressively") requires affect, another 33% probably need affect, and 75% can be assessed without affect. Obviously the best cue to early infant development is affect. When the infant can manipulate his environment by turning his head, picking up blocks, and removing pellets from bottles, then we can begin to look at behavior without assessing affect. Even then it is an unusual and uneconomical thing to do.

Our assessment of affect usage in these scales is dependent upon our definition of *affect*. Some items are difficult to bisect into affect or sensorimotor and would not be dissected in a real testing situation. Categories that begin with "regards" as in "regards person," "regards cube," and so on, are especially difficult. In some sense the object itself may draw the gaze and the child may have no conscious volition and no affect; on the other hand, "regards" may include "shows interest." "Prolonged regard" has this quality. As soon as the child's interest is inferred, we have an affect state. Therefore, in practice, the infant could usually be described as having interest, and a glance without interest or without affect would be very strange (a cold glance or a glance that appears to go "through" an object). "Responds" also has this quality. Occasionally, one may mean "responds" in the sense of a reflex response, such as the orienting reflex. The relationship between the orienting reflex, the orienting response, and interest is not known. It is probably not a direct or one-to-one relationship but involves considerable cognitive awareness and discrimination during the process of responding, attending, and showing interest. On the other hand, interest may be only the conscious prolonging of the orienting reflex, which ontologically becomes separate but is not separate in the infant. Can an infant orient without having an adult infer interest or other affect? It

---

* Two testers who regularly use the Bayley in research evaluation of infants categorized the items with 100% agreement.

seems improbable, and if it does occur, it would require unusual circumstances that do not pertain to the present testing situation. Therefore all items that begin "regards" or "responds" have been classified as indicating affect. The justification for this becomes easier to understand later when we examine Piaget's use of "regards" in denoting the infant's awareness. In any case the percentages are clearly boosted by the inclusion of "responds" and "regards" in the category of affective behaviors.

Most other categories are clearly affectual or not. These include "smile" (item 18), "anticipatory excitement" (item 22), "play" (item 36), and expression of "attitudes" (e.g., item 42). Items that do not require affect to score include "picks up cube," "turns head," "eye–hand coordination," and so forth. However, a child who performed these behaviors correctly but had no affect or even affect unrelated to the behavior would give cause for grave concern (Bayley, 1969).

In every instance affect is either necessary to or is the common method for the determination of awareness, interest, recognition, cooperation, anticipation, and change of state. All of these words reflect cognitive states in the infant that cannot be determined or inferred from any other source than affect.

The motor scale has no affect items on it, although again the infant who performs tasks without affect would be very strange indeed. Also one should note that the motor scale is the least good predictor of later development and in particular of later cognitive development. Although it is correlated to some degree with the mental development scale, much of that correlation is of a noncausative nature. There is some relationship between the ability to move oneself and to bring objects to the self that is reflected in correlation of motor and mental scales in infant scores, but this is incidental to the present discussion.

Which scale is the best predictor of later mental or cognitive development? Birns and Golden (1972) have suggested, after many examinations of infant intelligence test items, that one of the best predictors of later intelligence test scores is positive affect during testing. To generalize this suggestion, one would predict that an infant who is interested in problems (the interest would be determined from affect, primarily) at the first testing is more likely to have mastered solutions to these problems at a later date than an infant who shows no interest at the first testing.

Thus, to summarize the importance of affect in infant intelligence testing, it seems as though a very good predictor of later intelligence may be affect, but even if it is not a good predictor, it is the main index of intelligence in infancy. It probably is at any time, but we systematically ignore it in testing situations.

PIAGETIAN USES OF AFFECT TO INFER COGNITION

No one maintains that infant intelligence tests tell us much about how the infant learns to behave intelligently in his world. For this we turn to the cognitive epistemologist Jean Piaget, who has described the development of logical thinking and the structure of knowledge in young children (e.g., Piaget, 1971). Even in Piaget's assessment of cognitive structure one finds unacknowledged but extensive use of affect to infer knowledge.

Although Piaget certainly never intended that one should go through his observations of infant behavior and pull out descriptions of affect, it is possible to give a sketch of how Piaget uses affect to determine mental states and sometimes even uses affect sequences from his diary observations to resolve theoretical positions.

To illustrate the impact of affect on observation of cognition, we have reexamined Piaget's *The Construction of Reality* (1971), noting each affect and its use. The reader must keep in mind that these observations cannot be used directly to develop a developmental scale of affect or even to "prove" that the child has an awareness of the affect described. They indicate only that we, the observers, are using affect to describe cognition, and they show to some extent how we do it even when we are not aware of so doing. Presumably we could use affect to determine intelligence more effectively if the usefulness of affect was apparent and systematically examined.

In his observations of the very young infants (2–4 months) Piaget relies primarily on interest, recognition pleasure, and crying to determine the infant's beliefs about the world. For example, Lucienne sees Piaget at the extreme left of her visual field and smiles vaguely; she then looks away but constantly returns to the place in which she sees him and dwells on it. If the infant had merely turned her head with a vacant gaze and no facial mobility, Piaget probably would have found it difficult to say that she recognized him or was "bringing to himself [sic] the image of his desires" (p. 12). There is something in the smooth turn of the head accompanied by a searching gaze, the stopping of the head, the fastening of the gaze on the "desired" object, and the looking with *interest* and even *pleasure* that arouses in the heart of the trained genetic epistemologist a belief that the child has desires and recognizes a particular object and also, though this is more complex, that the child does not disassociate these objects from himself.

The notion that the child does not disassociate objects from his own behavior is illustrated by "crying at random or by looking at the place where it [the desired object] disappeared or where it was last seen" (p. 12). Piaget illustrates the idea that the object has no motion of its own but is associated with the child; he infers this from the child's *astonishment* when the object disappears without any activity on the part of the child. When Jacqueline is watching Piaget's watch, he drops it; it falls too fast for Jacqueline to follow the trajectory, or so Piaget suggests, so that she does not follow the movement and then she "looks at my [his] empty hand with *surprise*" (p. 16, italics mine). Here, it is the surprise that indicates to Piaget that the child thought she had control over the watch and was surprised when it disappeared without any behavior change on her part. Without the affect of surprise Piaget would not have been able to come to the conclusion that the child had any such expectation—there was no reported change in reaching, head direction, or any other nonaffectual behavior.

Disappointment is also a cue to Piaget that the child has expected an occurrence and has no ready explanation for its not occurring. More precisely though, the disappointment itself is not as important as the sequence of affects. At 0;7 (5) Laurent loses a cigarette box that he has just grasped and swung to and fro. Unintentionally he drops it outside the visual field (it is not clear how Piaget determined that the dropping was unintentional, but he could have done so by assessing affect). He then immediately brings his hand before his eyes and looks at it for a long time with an expression of "*surprise, disappointment,* something like an impression of its disappearance" (p. 25, italics mine). After a short time Laurent again swings his hand and "looks intently at it." Piaget interprets this to mean that Laurent either wishes that the box will reappear or that he believes that it might if he repeats box-swinging behaviors. The box does not appear, of course, and Laurent stops searching altogether. How Piaget knew that Laurent had stopped searching is a good question. Again it may have been affect; he may have shown interest in another activity, or there may have been practically no affect. We will return to the meaning of "no affect" shortly.

Here we have an excellent example of the interaction of affect and motor behavior that enables the observer to reach reasonable explanations of the infant's cognitive process. To emphasize the importance of affect, consider the sequence without affect. Laurent swings a box to and fro but shows no interest or excitement in this activity. The box falls from his hand, but he continues to gaze in the direction of his hand with no change in affect, resumes swinging the empty hand, and after a while stops. In this case, one would wonder whether he had realized that the box had dropped; the continued arm swinging might be self-stimulatory as in the case of infants who rock themselves. It would be very difficult to distinguish between the possibilities (1) that the object did not matter to the swinging behavior; (2) that the child was not aware that the object was missing, which is simply another version of the first possibility; or (3) that the child was wishing that the object would return. As soon as one adds that he was interested in swinging the box, was surprised at its disappearance and then disappointed, began swinging the arm with an air of attentive expectation, then Piaget's explanation seems reasonable, if not obvious. So it is with much intelligent, problem-solving behavior: the affect is necessary to interpretation.

This interaction between affect and behavior is used many times. The affect "curiosity" is frequently used in this way. Laurent shows "curiosity when he is first shown a whole pencil which is then lowered partly behind a screen." Piaget writes that "he looks at this extremity with curiosity, without seeming to understand" (p. 30). The curiosity expression occurs only when Laurent can see less than three centimeters of the pencil. If he can see more than that, he grasps the pencil. Here the interaction is between *curiosity* to indicate misunderstanding and *grasping* to indicate understanding of the wholeness and continuity of the object. There must have been some affect other than curiosity expressed when the child grasped and reached for the pencil, but it probably seemed too obvious to report at the time.

Crying and anger seem to be related in several instances of cry, no cry, and cry again—followed by "rage." For example, at 0;6 (19) Laurent begins to cry from hunger and impatience upon seeing his bottle. He often frets before the appearance of the bottle but cries only when it appears. But when the bottle disappears, he stops crying. Piaget writes, "I repeat the experiment four more times; the result is constant until poor Laurent, beginning to think the joke bad, becomes violently *angry*" (p. 33, italics mine). Once again Piaget's interpretation of this behavior sequence is determined in part, if not primarily, by affect. First there is a whimper of hunger, denoting a motivational state prior to the appearance of the bottle; then crying and fretting when the bottle appears, denoting recognition of the bottle and desire for the bottle; returning to the hunger state without crying when the bottle disappears, denoting belief in the nonexistence of the bottle. And finally there is rage after several presentations and disappearances of the bottle, denoting belief that the bottle can be commanded to "remake" itself. It is not clear in this instance that the rage signifies belief in the ability to command its appearance. That possibility exists from other examples Piaget gives, including the one concerned with shaking the hand as if it were shaking a box. But the rage could be a reaction to the sequence of affects, a reaction to internal events, or a reaction to inability to control the bottle, rather than an affect-laden demand for the bottle. Note that "manual–tactile" events play no part in this observation. Piaget claims that the child did not even reach for, much less grasp, the bottle since he was not accustomed to holding it himself.

The particular affect that accompanies the disappearance of an object seems to vary. Laurent cried at the appearance of his bottle and quieted at its disappearance; he looked surprised and then disappointed when he dropped the cigarette box; Jacqueline kicked in anger and impatience when Piaget hid her bottle; Lucienne laughed at the disappearance of her stork; Jacqueline "whimpered" once when her doll was hidden but laughed when her stork was hidden. The affect seems to occur as the object is in the process of disappearing. This example seems to verify the idea: Laurent is on a diet and screams when the bottle disappears, but calms when it is gone. During stage III the child may forget that the object exists when it is not apparent. During later stages Piaget presents evidence that memory is not the primary factor in the discovery of displaced objects. It seems to be the act of disappearing and not the disappearance itself that is of interest, but it is difficult to determine from Piaget's reports since the mode of disappearance varies. Sometimes it disappears without the child's being able to determine the procedure (it drops more rapidly than the infant can perceive), or it may disappear gradually behind a screen or hand or be placed under a cloth while the child is watching. The sudden disappearance seems to be the one most likely to produce surprise, the deliberate and observed disappearance more likely to produce pleasure, especially if the object continues to reappear as it often did in the games Piaget was playing with his children. The rage reaction to the disappearance of the bottle was a reaction both to the object that disappeared repeatedly and to unfulfilled expectation.

Affect is also used to determine when an infant expects an activity to occur, a cause and effect relationship. Between the eighth and the ninth months Jacqueline uses arching herself to attempt to induce a reoccurrence of some activity. Piaget knows that she intends that "arching" to cause an event because she shows pleasure when she "produces" the activity and she shows "surprise" or "constant surprise" when she is unable to do so.

"No affect" is one of the more interesting events that Piaget describes. It is difficult to decide when he means that the child did not reach or grasp or when the child actually registered no reaction at all, including no affect. The exceptions to this are few and I may have misinterpreted some. But it seems as though Piaget means that the child is not aware or does not remember an event or object when "nothing" happens or there is "no reaction." For example, Piaget hides the watch from his 8-month-old daughter. He hides it behind his hand, behind the quilt, etc. She does not react and forgets everything immediately. Several times Piaget states that there was "nothing" and the child did not understand or was forgetful. This use of no affect may be the strongest indication that we are using affect to determine an aware and understanding state in the child (or the older person for that matter). I think that this signifies that at all other times we use affect to determine whether the child is attending and dealing cognitively with events as the case below illustrates.

THE CONSEQUENCES OF "NO AFFECT"

The observations of Shirley illustrate the interaction of affect and intelligence in yet another way. Shirley exhibited very little affect. The reaction of caretakers and observers was that she was not very intelligent. She performed almost the same sensorimotor behaviors as Piaget's children with no affect. She was not testable on the Bayley, nor could we use the Gesell developmental scales to describe her behavior. This had a profound effect on her intellectual environment.

Shirley was brought by her mother, who was a high school student, to our day-care center in a local high school when she was 8 months old.

She stayed with us during school hours five days a week from January until June. When she first arrived at the center, she appeared to be a plump, large, not unattractive baby. The well-baby clinicians had stated that she was in good health and had no abnormalities. Her mother described her as an "easy" baby. She never cried or fretted, even if it was considerably past her mealtime or if she were left alone and awake in her crib for a long period of time. On the other hand, she never smiled, cooed, or looked intently at anything but was always extremely relaxed and passive.

Shirley was almost untestable on the developmental scales we commonly used for demonstration in the center. Her responsiveness to persons was almost indiscernible—she would look longer at her mother and move her torso slightly. She was neither cooperative nor uncooperative or fearful or reckless—she was nonresponsive. Her body was either inert or relaxed. Her constant emotional tone was "nonexpressive." She was not blind; she would follow her bottle from the caretaker's hands to her own. She was not deaf; her body would give a startle response if there were a loud noise, although her facial expression would not change, nor would she ever cry. She could be persuaded to grasp a cube in one hand if it were directly over her, but not if it were on the side; she could bring objects to her mouth and held her own bottle routinely both in the center and at home. She could sit with support sometimes, but more frequently she would "melt" back into a prone position.

This behavior, or rather lack of behavior, had a profound effect on her caretakers. We shortly noticed that Shirley was being ignored, if not avoided. It was extremely difficult to play with her or to care for her because she never signaled her desires; nor, in a different frame, did she reinforce her caretakers for their care. Systematic observations revealed that Shirley, although called a "good" baby, was becoming more and more isolated. She was fed, bathed, changed, and placed. She was not talked to, walked, rocked, sung to, placed on the exercise mats with other infants, or even approached unless someone had a task with her or was instructed to talk or play with her.

We could find nothing "wrong" with her, nor could her pediatrician, except lack of affect. She had an extremely low developmental profile, but this was primarily owing to our inability to assess motor or cognitive behavior because we could not assess affect nor could we "motivate" her to participate.

Through a systematic but humanistically oriented behavior modifi-cation program, we intervened and changed Shirley's affect-communi-cation patterns. When she left us at the end of the school year, four months later, she was a somewhat depressed but normal 1-year-old. Still placid except for rare intervals when she would tear around the nursery in a walker with a small smile on her face and her legs churning, she seemed more interesting to strangers in the nursery, who no longer avoided her. Her mother said she had learned to be "smart." Returning student caretakers said she "looked a whole lot smarter and more lovable," and on our developmental tests she was now "testable."

We cannot know, but I suspect from my reading of the literature on autistic children, that we intervened in the development of an autistic child. Reports from mothers on the infancy of autistic children include descriptions that are similar to our description of Shirley. " 'I never could reach my baby.' 'He never smiled at me.' 'He never greeted me when I entered, he never cried or even noticed when I left the room.' 'She never made any personal appeal for help at any time' " (Mahler, 1968, p. 67).

Shirley was very definitely separating herself from the human world. Although she was not so "difficult" as many autistic children are remembered by their parents to have been, still she did not communi-cate with her mother or caretakers in a lovable way; she seemed "strange." Her mother has married and moved away beyond our knowledge of her, so we do not know the long-term effects of our intervention, but we suspect that she is still relatively normal because her mother felt that she was lovable and smart and not just "easy" and easy to ignore.

The consequences of Shirley's lack of affect and general inactivity, combined with mothering that reinforced her pattern of inactivity, led to the development of a child whose abilities were difficult to assess and whose demands, if she made any, were difficult, if not impossible, to interpret at 8 months. From our point of view the main problem was one of affect. Her inactivity, if it were combined with smiling and intense gazing, would not have led to the same concern or the same lack of interaction as did inactivity combined with lack of affectivity. Indeed, our first demand from her was affect—interest as revealed in eye-to-eye contact. Intuitively we knew that was more important than rolling over or grasping a block without aid. Indeed we even suspected, or at least hoped, that she could do both those things if she wanted to, but we could not assess wants, nor did we seem to have any effect on her wants. Here, as always, motivation and awareness had to be measured in affect.

Without intervention we suspect that Shirley would have become more and more isolated from social events. Unlike some autistic children, she showed no motoric precocity, and most likely she would have been categorized as severely retarded in another year or so because her abilities would not have been assessable at all if she were completely withdrawn.

This case illustrates familiar issues in the history of intelligence measures. What is measured by the intelligence tests? How does the measurer know whether he observed the right behaviors or organization of behaviors? How does the child determine his interactive environment, and what are the consequences of his particular environment for his development? This case and this chapter argue that these are all part of the same question: What is the nature and meaning of the infant's interaction with his social environment?

The Nature and Meaning of Infant Affect

Psychologists have not been very concerned with examining the nature and meaning of the affects they use to infer intelligence. There are no published systematic lists, studies, analyses, or ethograms of infant facial expressions. Bridges (1932) described the appearance of emotions in infancy, by which she seemed to mean "meaningful" expression in appropriate situations. Exactly what cues she used to determine the emotion is not clear; those cues were most likely a composite.

Although several researchers (Ekman et al., 1971; Thompson, 1941) have suggested that the face be studied by regions of the face and examples of such studies are found in the animal literature (e.g., Chevalier-Skolnikoff, 1973; Hooff, 1967) and the elements and their relationships have been delineated by Young and Décarie (unpublished), no one has studied the development of facial expression in infancy, from which we derive so much information.

Affect-Related Studies

Psychological studies of affect focus on the smile reflex (as a measure of enjoyment), crying (as a measure of distress–anguish), startle (as both startle and fear), and "state" (as a possible measure of interest–excitement).

It is generally supposed that the smiling response is universal (e.g., Darwin, 1872), and it is known that it appears very early in the human repertoire of facial expressions (Ambrose, 1961; Wolff, 1963). Just when it can be shown to be a reaction to social stimulation is controversial (Sroufe & Waters, 1975). There is also possibility that it occurs infrequently during the neonatal period without social stimulation. Numerous studies have investigated the extent to which the smiling response is under social control (Dennis, 1935), easily conditioned (Brossard and Décarie, 1968), or extinguishable (Brackbill, 1958). Only recently has the "smiling response" been studied as a clew to meaningful behavior in either the infant or the parent.

Distress in infants seems to be nearly universal and can be produced by many stimuli or situations. Naturally enough most research on infantile distress has been directed toward its attenuation rather than its production (e.g., Gordon and Foss, 1966). The longitudinal development of reactions to distressful stimuli or situations seems not to have been studied. The meaning of the cry has received attention (Wolff, 1969) and different cries have been distinguished for hunger and pain.

Fear has not been studied in early infancy except perhaps as undistinguishable from startle. In later infancy there are studies of the conditionability of fear (e.g., Watson and Raynor, 1920), and there are catalogs of older children's fears (e.g., Jersild and Holmes, 1935). The learning of fears in the natural environment is a controversial issue; no one disputes that they can be learned, but the conditions for learning are unclear (see Valentine, 1930). More recently Lewis and Brooks (1974), among others, have been studying infants' reactions to strangers, which might be called fear, or it might be distress, if these are distinguishable in the infant.

The expression of excitement might be said to have been studied in the examinations of individual differences in reactivity to stimulation (e.g., Lipton and Steinschneider, 1964). These measures of reactivity are very sensitive to pre- or postnatal complications (Korner and Brobstein, 1967). Using attentiveness as an indication of excitement, Lewis *et al.*

(1967) found that Apgar scores taken at birth are related to visual attentiveness throughout the first year of life. This would suggest that physiological measures might be good indicators of other affects and might be used to gauge "inner feeling" in some cases.

As for rage, Watson (1928) reported "rage" as a reaction to the prevention of movement of the child's limbs, but there seem to be no further references. Discounting for the moment reactions to obnoxious odors by neonates (e.g., Engen *et al.*, 1963), there is no mention to our knowledge of shame or disgust in early infancy.

As a contrast to these studies, one should mention the only attempt at a cohesive, longitudinal study of emotional reactions during the first year of life. Bridges (1930, 1932) suggested that the infant begins life with an undifferentiated emotion that she called excitement. With increasing age (experience and learning) the infant differentiates first pain and delight and later other affects, including many we have not mentioned here. It is important to note that Bridges's description of the infant relies on assessing "meaningful" emotions, not on looking at what the infant can express *per se*.

This brief review of the science of affect only serves to show how primitive our knowledge is. One also notes immediately that emotions tend to be studied in a vacuum, as if they were unrelated to cognitive or personality development.

Recent Observations of Affect Development: A Beginning

I have been systematically observing and videotaping my own fraternal twins, a boy and a girl, for two years—from 2 weeks of age until now.

The videotapes have aided immeasurably in the development of an ethogram of infant affect. Affect, like all communication systems, requires time and movement for analysis. Still photographs yield unreliable and often meaningless data, whereas videotapes or films are easily coded. The differences in affect between the twins can be seen easily from an examination of the ethograms.

Even the briefest examinations of the tapes show that the twins are quite different in the portrayal of affect. These differences are reliable and stable from the second week after birth to the second year. An

TABLE I

Eyebrow Positions: Percentages of Frequently Occurring Eyebrow Positions for Two Infants Aged 2 Weeks to 6 Months[a]

Alex		Lizbeth	
1. Relaxed	43%	1. Relaxed	45%
2. Raised	29%	2. Raised	30%
3. Weak frown	12%	3. Weak frown	16%
4. Contraction	12%	4. Contraction	8%
5. Strong frown	2%	5. Strong frown	2%

[a] The descriptions of facial positions are adapted from Blurton-Jones (1971).

examination of each area of the face indicates the nature of these differences most clearly.

As shown in Table I, brow positions are nearly identical. The most common position is the relaxed or normal position. The next most common position is the slightly raised brow. Slightly raised brows give the face a quizzical, or curious look and combined with widely opened eyes indicate interest to the observer. Although the twins do not differ on brow position, I have films of other young children who are quite different. In particular a series of films taken in Chiapas, Mexico, of Zinacanteco Indian children shows that a weak frown was extremely common and that the raised or slightly raised brow was never seen.

TABLE II

Eye Openness: Percentages of Frequently Occurring Degrees of Eye Openness for Two Infants Aged 2 Weeks to 6 Months

Alex		Lizbeth	
1. Normal	33%	1. Bit wide	36%
2. Bit narrow	18%	2. Normal	21%
3. Very narrow	14%	3. Bit narrow	15%
4. Bit wide	14%	4. Wide	8%
5. Upper lid down	3%	5. Upper lid down	2%
6. Wide	2%	6. Very narrow	2%
7. Other (closed)	17%	7. Other (closed)	16%

Eye openness is a feature that distinguishes the twins (see Table II). Lizbeth's eyes are most frequently a bit wide, whereas Alex's eyes are either normal or a bit narrow. In the case of eye openness Alex is more variable with more even distribution across all categories than Lizbeth.

The direction of glancing is also quite different (see Table III). Of course, both babies most frequently look straight ahead, but the second most frequent directions for Lizbeth are "side" and "up," and the second most frequent directions for Alex are "down" or "down and to the side."

The fourth table shows that mouth positions are more variable for Lizbeth than Alex. Alex either has a relaxed mouth or his upper lip is slightly square. The slightly squared upper lip may also be a relaxed position for infants. Lizbeth's mouth movements are fairly evenly distributed over all possible positions. This is also true of lip positions. Alex's lips are almost always in the relaxed position (75% of the time), whereas Lizbeth's movements are more variable. Tongue positions are nearly identical for both infants, with the positions appearing in this order: tongue invisible, visible, pushed forward, out of mouth.

To a mouth-oriented observer it would appear that Lizbeth is the more active infant; her movements are more variable and the mouth area of the face is seldom seen at rest. Her interest and responses are easily determined. On the other hand, Alex's mouth is commonly still and relaxed. Little information about his interest, motives, and response comes from the mouth area of the face. This relaxation gives rise to several reactions from observers. The first impression one has is that Alex is a relatively calm and passive infant. However, this is contrasted

TABLE III

Eye Direction: Percentages of Frequently Occurring Eye Directions for Two Infants Aged 2 Weeks to 6 Months

Alex		Lizbeth	
1. Ahead	34%	1. Ahead	34%
2. Down-side	28%	2. Side	19%
3. Down	19%	3. Up	14%
4. Side	14%	4. Down	7%
5. Up	5%	5. Down-side	23%
6. Other	3%	6. Other	23%

Table IV

Mouth Expressions: Percentages of Frequently Occurring Expressions for Two Infants Aged 2 Weeks to 6 Months

Alex		Lizbeth	
Mouth Positions			
1. Relaxed	37%	1. Relaxed	28%
2. Squared upper lip	27%	2. Squared upper lip	17%
3. Squared lower lip	10%	3. Corners raised	15%
4. Corners lowered	10%	4. Corners lowered	10%
5. Corners raised	8%	5. Lips retracted	8%
6. Lips retracted	1%	6. Squared lower lip	7%
7. Other	7%	7. Other	15%
Lip Positions			
1. Relaxed, slight separation	65%	1. Relaxed, slight separation	36%
2. Contraction	8%	2. Lips pressed together	25%
3. Lips pressed together	5%	3. Contraction	16%
4. Lengthening upper lip	3%	4. Lengthening upper lip	8%
5. Two-lip pout	3%	5. Lips rolled in	4%
6. Lower-lip pout	1%	6. Lower lip bit	3%
7. Lower lip bit	0%	7. Lower-lip pout	1%
8. Lips rolled in	0%	8. Two-lip pout	0%

with the fact that mouth movements appear to be very dramatic on Alex's face and command an unusual amount of attention. Consequently his reactions are sometimes seen as more extreme than Lizbeth's.

To the eye-oriented observer Alex appears to be more active and variable; he may also appear to avoid eye contact because he looks down and to the side so frequently. On the other hand, Lizbeth, with eyes directed ahead or up and opened a bit wide, is very appealing and often seems to be asking for interaction in the traditional supplicant manner with eyes raised.

Differences in areas of the face used to express interest and awareness, curiosity and understanding do not seem to be significant indicators of intellectual differences in infants. They reflect a style of responding more than a quantitative difference in responsiveness. The attentive observer can "read" affect from partial cues of either mouth or eye. But the "still" examples of the most frequent expressions only begin to describe the differences. Another aspect of facial communication is the relationship of "figure to ground." This involves both descriptions of "figure" and "ground" and the relationship between figure and ground. The phenomenon being described is easy to illustrate but difficult to analyze. In the instance of babies Alex and Lizbeth we note that Alex is most frequently "at rest" or "normal"; that is, his facial expression is most passive; his "ground" is very bland. Lizbeth seems also frequently resting, but the frequency is significantly lower than Alex's. Lizbeth as she grows older is less frequently seen at rest than Alex. This accounts for the description by observers of Alex as more extreme in affect. His change in facial expression occurs less frequently and occurs on a predominantly bland background, giving an observer the impression that his smiles are happier, his frowns unhappier. Lizbeth seems to be more even-tempered because the "ground" expression is more active than Alex's.

It is interesting and invites speculation when the spontaneous descriptions of relatives and passers-by are noted in conjunction with the schema presented above. Lizbeth is called by fanciful, endearing names such as "little Pumpkin," "woozel," "sweetie," and so on; Alex is called "the judge," a "cool customer," and other rather unusual names. It would be rash to suggest that facial expression determines people's view of their intelligence and personality in any sense, but it would be foolish to ignore the possibility that the infant's facial expression has some control over the social responses of his observers and caretakers.

It seems to be the informal consensus that Alex has an interest in moving things and that he is critical and thoughtful about the cause and effect of events. The "evidence" for this comes from his prolonged and calm contemplation of things coupled with his gaze aversion and relative lack of affective responsiveness around people. Relatives predict that he will do well in academic fields in which people are to be either avoided or used, such as physical science or law.

On the other hand Lizbeth is seen as creative and affectionate. Her father and grandfather report that she has musical affinities and abilities. These expectations are formed from observations of her quick and mobile affective responses, both her attentiveness to people and her quick response to them. The prediction about musical affinity possibly originates from her clear affective responses to music and to her own humming and singing.

Although the differences are not significant when scored on the Bayley, Lizbeth has maintained a higher developmental score on the motor scale and, at first, also on the mental scale. After 1 year Alex began to score consistently higher on the mental scale because of his verbal abilities. No one seemed surprised to see Lizbeth sit up, walk, feed herself, and be toilet trained first. Neither was anyone surprised at Alex's relatively large vocabulary and precise grammar. In fact, the differences in affect are nicely paralleled by differences in speaking style. Alex speaks carefully, searching for his words and arranging them correctly. He has never used a word invented by Lizbeth, nor has he ever invented one himself. Lizbeth plays with sounds, likes to rhyme, and thinks mispronounced words are hilarious. Her own speech is difficult to understand because she uses many letters interchangeably (e.g., "teddy bear" becomes "tebby dare"). She recognizes the interchange but does not correct it. She also uses grammatical shortcuts and does not use prepositions or conjunctions yet, although Alex does. It seems as though relatives' predictions, self-fulfilling prophecies or not, are quite accurate so far—more accurate than the Bayley development scale.

Developmental Changes

Developmentally a few changes can already be noted from the preliminary analysis of data. More different kinds of movement are noted as the babies grow older, although the changes are very small. Out of the 41 possibilities that we coded, 30 were seen during the first 72 days, 1 more during the next 50 days, and 2 more during the next 100 days. The 8 not coded but used by Blurton-Jones (1971) may occur only under unusually stressful circumstances. These small differences suggest that the very young infant has a nearly complete repertoire of facial movement, and perhaps a complete repertoire. We need further analysis of the data to discover whether changes in affect production are a result of particular co-occurrences of individual facial movements developing at differing rates, or whether the reported developmental differences are not differences in production but differences in the observer's belief in "appropriate" production. At this point the latter case is equally likely as the first, although the first possibility is the one most frequently cited (Charlesworth and Kreutzer, 1973).

It is extremely difficult to take an unbiased view of affect; so many beliefs and values commonly distort the message. People in Western societies expect infants to be affectless, although parents respond to distress realistically. Pleasurable affects are thought to be "gaseous" until linked to eye contact and possibly the mother's smile. Fearful responses are treated as "startles" or discomfort until they are linked to strangers and unusual occurrences. Rage is expected early but it is supposed to dissipate rapidly.

One should note that these beliefs are not shared by all cultures. For example, the Zinacantecos (mentioned above) believe that neonates are easily frightened and that fright is very harmful to infants. Many of the signs and cues that we would interpret as distress are interpreted as fright. Mothers believe that they can differentiate fear and distress in very young infants.

THE USES OF AFFECT

The production of affect and its meaning or its relationship to intelligence, personality, and the network of the infant's interactions are still obscure. This is true even though we can reliably observe infants' affective expressions and even though we do use affective cues constantly.

To draw a parallel to verbal communication, there are three areas of concern in the study of affect: "*syntactics* (signs and relations between signs), *semantics* (relations between signs and their designata) and *pragmatics* (aspects which involve sign users)" (Cherry, 1971, p. 243). In this chapter we have dealt primarily with syntactics and pragmatics and only partially with semantics. We have documented the facial movements of two infants and noticed differences in production of movements of different sorts. We have noted that particular configurations of these facial positions have been given semantically meaningful names (Tomkins, 1962, 1963; Young and Décarie, unpublished), but we have hesitated to impart meaning in the instances studied. Taking an entirely different set of observations and tools, we argued that regardless of semantics, sign users—parents, caretakers, and psychologists—interpret facial expressions in infants as if they were meaningful indicators of motivation and intellectual involvement, and there is a wealth of common sense to suggest that it is so.

REFERENCES

AMBROSE, J. A., 1961, The development of the smiling response in early infancy, *in* "Determinants of Infant Behavior," Vol. 1, B. M. Foss (ed.), Methuen, London, p. 179.

ARNOLD, M. (ed.), 1970, "Feelings and Emotions," Academic Press, New York.

BAYLEY, N., 1969, "Manual for the Bayley Scales of Infant Development," The Psychological Corporation, New York.

BETTELHEIM, B., 1967, "The Empty Fortress: Infantile Autism and the Birth of the Self," The Free Press, New York.

BIRNS, B., AND GOLDEN, M., 1972, Prediction of intellectual performance at 3 years from infant test and personality measures, *Merrill–Palmer Quarterly*, 18(1):53.

BLATZ, W. E., AND MILLICHAMP, D. A., 1935, The development of emotion in the infant, *University of Toronto Studies, Child Development Series*, No. 4.

BLURTON-JONES, N. G., 1971, Criteria for use in describing facial expressions in children, *Human Biology*, 43(3):365.

BLURTON-JONES, N. G. (ed.), 1972, "Ethological Studies of Child Behavior," Cambridge University Press, Cambridge, England.

BRACKBILL, Y., 1958, Extinction of the smiling response in infants as a function of reinforcement schedule, *Child Development*, 29:115.

BRIDGES, K. B., 1930, A genetic theory of emotions, *Journal of Genetic Psychology*, 37:514.

BRIDGES, K. B., 1932, Emotional development in early infancy, *Child Development*, 3:324.

BROSSARD, L. M., AND DÉCARIE, T. G., 1968, Comparative reinforcing effect of eight stimulations on the smiling response of infants, *Journal of Child Psychology and Psychiatry*, 9:51.

CHARLESWORTH, W. R., AND KREUTZER, M. A., 1973, Facial expressions of infants and children, *in* "Darwin and Facial Expression," P. Ekman (ed.), Academic Press, New York.

CHATFIELD, C., AND LEMON, R. E., 1970, Analyzing sequences of behavioral events, *Journal of Theoretical Biology*, 29:427.

CHERRY, C., 1971, "On Human Communication," MIT Press, Cambridge, Massachusetts.

CHEVALIER-SKOLNIKOFF, S., 1973, Facial expression of emotion in non-human primates, *in* "Darwin and Facial Expression," P. Ekman (ed.), Academic Press, New York, p. 11.

DARWIN, C., 1872, "Expression of the Emotions in Man and Animals," Murray, London.

DENNIS, W., 1935, An experimental test of two theories of social smiling in infants, *Journal of Social Psychology*, 6:214.

EKMAN, P., FREISEN, W., AND TOMKINS, S., 1971, Facial affect scoring technique: A first validity study, *Semiotica*, 3:37.

ENGEN, T., LIPSITT, L. P., AND KAYE, H., 1963, Olfactory responses and adaptation in the human neonate, *Journal of Comparative and Physiological Psychology*, 56:73.

FREEDMAN, D. G., AND FREEDMAN, N. C., 1969, Behavioral differences between Chinese-American and European-American newborns, *Nature*, 224:1227.

GOODENOUGH, F. L., 1931, The expressions of emotions in infancy, *Child Development*, 2:96.

GORDON, T., AND FOSS, B. M., 1966, The role of stimulation in the delay of the onset of crying in the newborn infant, *Quarterly of Experimental Psychology*, 18:79.

HEILIGENBURG, W., 1973, Random processes describing the occurrence of behavioral patterns in a cichlid fish, *Animal Behavior*, 21:169.

HOOFF, J. VAN, 1967, The facial displays of the catarrhine monkeys and apes, *in* "Primate Ethology," D. Morris (ed.), Aldine, Chicago.

JERSILD, A. T., AND HOLMES, F. B., 1935, Children's fears, *Monographs of the Society for Research in Child Development*, 6(20).

KORNER, A. F., AND BROBSTEIN, R., 1967, Individual differences at birth: Implications for mother–infant relationship and later development, *Journal of Child Psychiatry*, 6:676.

LEWIS, M., BARTELS, B., CAMPBELL, H., AND GOLDBERG, S., 1967, Individual differences in attention: The relationship between infants' condition at birth and attention distribution in the first year, *American Journal of Diseases of Children*, 113:461.

LEWIS, M., AND BROOKS, J., 1974, Self, other and fear: Infants' reactions to people, *in* "The Origins of Fear: The Origins of Behavior," Vol. 2, M. Lewis and L. Rosenblum (eds.), Wiley, New York.

LIPTON, E. L., AND STEINSCHNEIDER, A., 1964, Studies on the psychophysiology of infancy, *Merrill–Palmer Quarterly*, 10:102.

LIPTON, E. L., STEINSCHNEIDER, A., AND RICHMOND, J. B., 1966, Autonomic function in the neonate, VII: Maturational changes in cardiac control, *Child Development*, 37:1.

MAHLER, M. S., 1968, "On Human Symbiosis and the Vicissitudes of Individuation, Vol. 1: Infantile Psychosis," International Universities Press, New York.

ODOM, R. D., AND LEMOND, C. M., 1972, Developmental differences in the perception and production of facial expressions, *Child Development*, 43:359.

PIAGET, J., 1971, "The Construction of Reality," Ballantine Books, New York.

SPITZ, R. A., AND WOLFF, R. M., 1946, The smiling response: A contribution to the ontogenesis of social relations, *Genetic Psychology Monographs*, 34:57.

SROUFE, L. A., AND WATERS, E., 1975, Developmental changes in the function of smiling during infancy. Paper presented at Society for Research in Child Development, Denver, Colorado in April.

THOMPSON, J., 1941, Development of facial expression of emotion in blind and seeing children, *Archives of Psychology*, No. 264, p. 47.

TOMKINS, S., 1962, "Affect, Imagery, Consciousness," Vol. 1: "The Positive Affects," Springer Publishing Company, New York.

TOMKINS, S., 1963, "Affect, Imagery, Consciousness," Vol. 2: "The Negative Affects," Springer Publishing Company, New York.

TOMKINS, S., AND IZARD, C., 1965, "Affect, Cognition, and Personality, Empirical Studies," Springer Publishing Company, New York.

VALENTINE, C. W., 1930, The innate bases of fear, *Journal of Genetic Psychology*, 37:394.

WATSON, J. B., 1928, "Psychological Care of Infant and Child," Norton, New York.

WATSON, J. B., AND RAYNOR, R., 1920, Conditioned emotional reactions, *Journal of Experimental Psychology*, 3:1.

WOLFF, P., 1963, Observations on the early development of smiling, *in* "Determinants of Infant Behavior," Vol. 2, B. M. Foss (ed.), Methuen, London, p. 113.

WOLFF, P., 1969, The natural history of crying and other vocalizations in early infancy, *in* "Determinants of Infant Behavior," Vol. 4, B. M. Foss (ed.), Methuen, London, p. 81.

YOUNG, G., AND DÉCARIE, T., to be submitted for publication, An ethology-based catalogue of facial/vocal behaviors in infancy.

13 The Interplay between Cognition and Motivation in Infancy

Leon J. Yarrow
and Frank A. Pedersen

Throughout the history of psychology there has been lively controversy around the concept of intelligence. A recurrent issue has been whether it is meaningful to conceptualize intelligence as a global attribute or whether it is more meaningful conceptually to think of it in terms of its component functions (Burt, 1972; Guilford, 1956; Spearman, 1927; Wechsler, 1950). For some time there has also been unease about the isolation of cognitive abilities from other aspects of functioning (Dember, 1974; Rapaport, 1951; Wechsler, 1950). The basic question is whether cognitive behaviors are a separate domain, an isolated segment of functioning, or whether these abilities are integrally related to other personality and motivational characteristics. Controversy on these issues has been sharpened in recent years as our concepts of motivation have changed and our view of cognitive functioning has become more differentiated.

First, a word about the new perspectives on motivation. In the past decade there have been important shifts in our thinking about motivation. The old drive-reduction model that saw all behavior as impelled by a need to reduce stimulation has been supplanted by a new model. This new model views the infant as an active seeker of stimulation, one who explores his environment and actively processes stimulation. From this perspective, having an impact on and controlling the environment is as

Leon J. Yarrow and Frank A. Pedersen · National Institute of Child Health and Human Development.

compelling a motive as is the need to reduce basic physiological tensions.

Piaget's (1952) great contribution to developmental theory has been called a theory of cognitive development, but Piaget, perhaps more than any other cognitive theorist, has emphasized the goal-oriented character of behavior. Although he does not talk about motivation *per se*, it is clear that even in his earliest writings Piaget did not draw the neat boundaries of the academic psychologist between thinking and motivation. The concept of adaptation that is central in Piagetian theory emphasizes a dynamic process of interaction between the infant and his environment. Piaget also pointed the way to a more differentiated analysis of cognitive processes. His finely detailed descriptions of infant behavior, in sharp contrast to global measures of development, highlight the varied psychological processes in cognition and their interplay with motivational factors.

The single index of intellectual development, the IQ, proved to be a simple device for cataloging children; it helped in adapting educational experiences to children's abilities. The simplicity of the measure was, however, misleading; in concentrating on a single index of ability, we lost sight of the many and varied aspects of cognitive functioning. Fifty years ago Gesell (1925), one of the pioneers of infant testing, pointed out forcefully the limitations of global measures, "A single summative numerical value cannot do justice to the complexity and variability of infant development. Any adaptation of our tests and methods which, for psychometric convenience, would affix IQ's to infants is undesirable, and is inadequate for the scientific study of growth processes." In spite of these admonitions, the global measure of intelligence still dominates thinking about development.

These theoretical concerns led us to attempt what may seem a paradoxical task, to consider the value of analyzing global measures of early development into component functions in order to gain greater understanding of the relations between cognition and motivation. Our awareness of the close intertwining of cognitive and motivational development evolved in the course of a study of early environmental influences on development (Yarrow et al., 1975a). In this study we were interested in examining selective relations between parameters of the environment and infant development. Rather than using general characterizations of the environment, such as nurturing or depriving, we analyzed mother–infant interaction into more discrete components of stimulation and responsiveness. We also distinguished a number of aspects of infant development, using the items of the Bayley scales to develop a series of clusters. In examining the interrelations among these clusters, we found differing degrees of relationship among separate aspects of development; at the same time we were struck by the interdependence of cognitive, motor, and motivational functions.

In this chapter we discuss these clusters and their theoretical meaning in order to provide a framework for discussion of our thinking about cognition and motivation.

Development of Clusters from the Bayley Scales of Infant Development

There were several reasons why we chose to analyze the Bayley Scales. Although the final publication of Bayley's detailed instructions for administration and scoring and the standardization data were not yet available when our study began, it was clear that this instrument was destined to become the most carefully researched test in the infancy period. Its standardization sample of 1262 infants went beyond any other infant test, and the items were carefully chosen on the basis of Bayley's own normative studies as well as upon others' experience with the Gesell and Cattell tests. Furthermore we were encouraged by the work of Kohen-Raz (1967) in differentiating the Bayley Scales, although his factor analysis yielded only four scales applicable to the 5- and 6-month-old infant. Infant scales designed to measure early cognitive development in terms of Piaget's sensorimotor stages were also being developed at this time by Corman and Escalona (1969) and Uzgiris and Hunt (1975). These scales were still being refined at the beginning of our investigation.

Because of these considerations we decided to group items from the Bayley Scales applicable to 6-month-old infants into clusters. We recognize that our small selected sample did not meet the rigorous requirements for good test construction. We are presenting these clusters and their interrelations for their heuristic value, and we want to emphasize that additional data are needed to provide a sound empirical basis for their wider use.

There were a number of steps in our grouping of items from the Bayley Scales. First, we sorted all of the items from 1 to 12 months in terms of the underlying functions or psychological processes. Then we eliminated items that were nondiscriminating in our sample of 70 infants, items that all infants either passed or failed. We deliberately chose a conceptual basis for sorting items in preference to factor or cluster analysis. With the latter procedures conceptualization essentially represents an attempt to find a common meaning in items that have been found to be related empirically. This approach may lead to meaningless combinations of items, sometimes because of sampling errors, often because there may be correlations between achievements that parallel each other but have no psychological relationship. For example, the mastery of postural controls clearly is psychologically unrelated to the discrimination of a stranger from the mother, but because these abilities develop around the same time, the correlation between these two attainments might be sufficiently great to produce similar loadings on the same factor. While we feel that the conceptual ordering of items is psychologically more meaningful, it was not always easy or clear-cut; often there was some arbitrariness in the assignment of an item to a cluster. This was the case especially with items that appeared to have both motivational and skill components. It was often difficult to establish which was more central.

Through this conceptual analysis we initially distinguished 12 groups of items. Some were classified according to the cognitive functions they tapped, e.g., object permanence and secondary circular reactions; others were grouped in terms of more abstract psychological processes, such as goal-directedness. Still others dealt with the more conventional classifications of early developmental functions: gross motor, fine motor, visually directed reaching and grasping, social responsiveness, and vocalization and language.

As an empirical check on our conceptual groupings, part–whole correlations and Spearman-Brown split-half reliabilities were computed; for one cluster with only two items, tetrachoric correlations were obtained. Clusters with split-half reliabilities of 0.70 or higher were accepted with no further question. Clusters with lower split-half reliabilities were examined, and some items either were reassigned to other clusters or were not used. Four clusters—auditory responsiveness, tactile exploration, social discrimination, and imitation—were dropped because they did not reach a satisfactory level of split-half reliability.

The eight remaining clusters had reliabilities ranging from 0.74 to 0.92. Table I presents the items and the split-half reliabilities for each cluster.

TABLE I
Clusters Derived from the Bayley Scales

Cluster name	Split-half reliability		Item No.	Age placement	Description
1. Goal directedness	0.82	Mental scale	60	5.0	Reaches persistently
			71	5.7	Pulls string, secures ring (?purposeful)
			80	7.1	Pulls string to secure ring (purposeful)
			82	7.6	Attempts to secure three cubes
			96	10.5	Unwraps toys
		Motor scale	25	5.6	Attempts to secure pellet
2. Visually directed reaching and grasping	0.92	Mental scale	37	3.1	Reaches for ring
			46	3.8	Closes on dangling ring
			49	4.1	Reaches for cube
			51	4.4	Eye cooperation in reaching
			54	4.6	Picks up cube
			63	5.2	Lifts cup
			64	5.4	Reaches for second cube
			70	5.7	Picks up cube directly and easily
			73	5.8	Lifts cup by handle
3. Secondary circular reactions	0.92	Mental scale	66	5.4	Bangs in play
			72	5.8	Enjoys sound production
4. Object permanence	0.90	Mental scale	31	2.4	Reacts to disappearance of face
			62	5.2	Turns head after dropped object
			75	6.0	Looks for dropped object
			86	8.1	Uncovers toy
			88	9.0	Picks up cup and secures cube
			91	9.5	Looks for contents of box
5. Gross motor	0.90	Motor scale	13	2.3	Sits with slight support
			18	4.2	Head balanced
			19	4.4	Turns from back to side
			20	4.8	Effort to sit
			22	5.3	Pulls to sitting position
			23	5.3	Sits alone momentarily
			27	6.0	Sits alone 30 sec or more

TABLE I—Continued

Cluster name	Split-half reliability		Item No.	Age placement	Description
5. Gross motor (*continued*)			28	6.4	Rolls from back to stomach
			29	6.6	Sits alone steadily
			31	6.9	Sits alone with good coordination
			33	7.1	Prewalking progression
			34	7.4	Early stepping movements
			36	8.1	Pulls to standing
			37	8.3	Raises self to sitting position
			38	8.6	Pulls self to stand
			40	8.8	Stepping movements
			42	9.6	Walks with help
6. Fine motor	0.92	Mental scale	56	4.7	Retains two cubes
			59	4.9	Recovers rattle in crib or playpen
			69	5.5	Transfers object hand to hand
			70	5.7	Picks up cube directly and easily
			77	6.3	Retains two cubes (three offered)
		Motor scale	15	2.7	Hands predominantly open
			16	3.7	Retains cube briefly
			21	4.9	Partial thumb opposition—radial palmâr grasp
			24	5.4	Unilateral reaching
			26	5.7	Rotates wrist
			30	6.8	Secures pellet—radial raking
			32	6.9	Picks up cube—radial–digital grasp
			35	7.4	Secures pellet—inferior pincer grasp
			39	8.6	Brings two objects together at midline
7. Social responsiveness	0.84	Mental scale	26	2.1	Social smile
			27	2.1	Vocalizes to social stimulus

Table I—Continued

Cluster name	Split-half reliability		Item No.	Age placement	Description
7. Social responsiveness (*continued*)			35	2.6	Anticipatory adjustment to lifting
			53	4.4	Approaches mirror image
			61	5.1	Likes frolic play
			65	5.4	Smiles at mirror image
			76	6.2	Playful response to mirror
			81	7.6	Cooperates in games
8. Vocalization and language	0.74	Mental scale	21	1.6	Vocalizes 3–6 times
			30	2.3	Vocalizes 2 syllables
			55	4.6	Vocalizes attitudes
			79	7.0	Vocalizes 4 different syllables
			84	7.9	Responds to name and nickname
			85	7.9	Says "da-da" or equivalent
			89	9.1	Adjusts to words
			101	12.0	Uses expressive jargon

Description of the Clusters

Cognitive–Motivational Variables

There were three clusters that measured cognitive abilities but that had a strong underlying motivational component: visually directed reaching and grasping, secondary circular reactions, and goal-directedness. These clusters were labeled "cognitive–motivational" to emphasize their dual character. The boundaries between the skill and the purposeful use of the skill are not sharp; the distinction is a subtle one. These cognitive–motivational activities index the earliest manifestations of attempts to master and to obtain feedback from the environment. They may well be precursors in infancy of effectance motivation (White, 1959) in later childhood. These functions are closely dependent on the development of perceptual, motor, and cognitive skills; in turn, they influence significantly the development and elaboration of these skills.

TABLE II

Intercorrelations among Bayley Clusters

	General development		Cognitive-motivational				Motor development		Social responsiveness	Vocalization and language
	Mental development	Psychomotor development	Goal directedness	Reaching and grasping	Secondary circular reactions	Object permanence	Gross	Fine		
General development										
Mental development		0.73	0.86	0.77	0.67	0.66	0.59	0.74	0.71	0.48
Psychomotor development			0.76	0.71	0.63	0.47	0.92	0.86	0.29	—[a]
Cognitive-motivational										
Goal directedness				0.76	0.70	0.64	0.68	0.76	0.56	0.39

Reaching and grasping	0.72	0.51	0.65	0.87	0.34	—[a]
Secondary circular reaction		0.46	0.61	0.62	0.52	—[a]
Object permanence			0.47	0.51	0.47	0.29
Motor development						
Gross				0.78	0.22	
Fine					0.30	—[a]
						—[a]
Social responsiveness						0.61
Vocalization and language						

[a] Dashes represent correlations < 0.20.

The three cognitive–motivational variables—goal-directedness, reaching and grasping, and secondary circular reactions—showed strong interrelations with each other: the correlations were within a narrow range, from 0.70 to 0.76 (see Table II).

Goal-Directedness.   The setting of goals and persistence in activities required to attain these goals are core manifestations of motivated behavior. Until very recently there has been a tendency to think of infants as engaging in essentially random transactions with their environment, but we are coming to recognize that infant behavior has both intentionality and direction. Maintaining an orientation to a goal begins very early in infancy; one of the earliest evidences of goal-directedness is the infant's visual orientation to novel objects. This is followed soon by attempts to secure interesting objects and to explore them.

There were six items in the cluster "goal-directedness" that measured the infant's focused and persistent attempts to make contact with a variety of objects under different conditions. They included attempting to obtain a cube out of reach, pulling on a string to secure a ring that was beyond the infant's immediate grasp, attempting to secure a toy by unwrapping the paper around it, reaching for and trying to pick up three cubes, and attempting to grasp a small pellet.

The strikingly high correlation of this cluster with the Bayley Mental Developmental Index ($r = 0.86$) gives convincing evidence of the centrality of motivation in early development. This conclusion is further strengthened by the high relationship between goal-directedness and other clusters, median $r = 0.68$. The only cluster with which its correlation is below 0.50 is vocalization and language. The fact that this group of items was highly correlated with the fine motor cluster, $r = 0.78$ emphasizes the difficulty of sorting out the relative importance of skill and motivation. Mastery of fine motor skills clearly was basic to performance on these tasks, but the distinctive character of the goal-directedness items was striving and persistence in the face of difficulty.

Visually Directed Reaching and Grasping.   The nine items in this cluster measured primarily the coordination of vision and prehension. Here again, although skill in reaching for and grasping objects was required, there were motivational aspects to these activities. Reaching and grasping requires a desire to obtain the object, enduring attention to the object, and an effort to adapt fine motor skills to secure and to manipulate the object. The development of prehensile skills is a necessary first step to exploration of the stimulus properties of objects and is necessary in obtaining feedback.

Reaching and grasping was also highly related to all the other variables except vocalization and language; the greatest overlap was with fine motor ($r = 0.87$), indicating that these functions are highly interdependent.

Secondary Circular Reactions. The behaviors subsumed under this category are activities that are directed toward producing interesting results (stage III in Piaget's sequence of sensorimotor stages). There were only two items on the Bayley Scales at this age that were relevant to this concept: "bangs objects in play" and "enjoys making sounds." These activities were considered motivational because they involve more than random manipulation of objects; they require the intentional repetition of behaviors in order to obtain feedback. As distinguished from reaching and grasping, in which the infant's behavior is oriented to acquiring an object, secondary circular behaviors have as their goal the manipulation of objects and obtaining responses from them, e.g., shaking a bell to make it ring or squeezing a rubber dog to change its shape. Being able to do something to an object and to observe the consequences of this action undoubtedly enhances the child's developing sense of mastery and competence, the development of feelings that he can have an impact on his environment.

This cluster, secondary circular reactions, was also related to all the other clusters except vocalization and language. Perhaps the slightly lower magnitude of interrelationship was due to its having only two items, but it is noteworthy that these two items were correlated in the 0.60s with much longer clusters. It is particularly striking that the infant's interest in producing effects is so highly related to other aspects of development, reaffirming the central importance of the motivational aspects of cognitive development.

Object Permanence. When the infant has learned that an object out of his immediate sensory experience, beyond his view and his touch, still exists, it means in effect that he has some inner representation of the object. This signals the beginning of abstract thinking. The acquisition of the notion of object permanence is probably a gradual process, beginning early in infancy and extending through early childhood. This cognitive function is closely intertwined with the development of the infant's tie to his mother and affects his ability to tolerate brief separations from his mother. Thus this earliest capacity for symbolic thinking is closely related to the infant's affective and social development (Décarie, 1965).

The object permanence cluster was composed of six items, ranging in age placement from 2.5 to 9.5 months. It included the infant's response to the disappearance of the examiner's face, his behavior when an object was dropped out of sight, and his response to the hiding of a toy or a cube under another object.

Reflecting its cognitive character, this item was more highly related to the Mental Developmental Index ($r = 0.66$) than to the Psychomotor Developmental Index ($r = 0.47$). It was more highly related to goal-directedness ($r = 0.64$) than to any of the other clusters, giving additional support to our central thesis of the close relationship between cognition and motivation. A first step in developing awareness of the existence of objects outside of his immediate sensory experience is the infant's establishing boundaries between the self and the external environment. This is a necessary condition for the internal representation of objects. It becomes sharpened through the infant's interactions with objects, especially as he learns that he can produce feedback and can change the environment.

Gross Motor Development. The development of gross motor abilities is important both as an index of the maturation of the central nervous system and because of its psychological meaning as the very first manifestation of the infant's control of his body in relation to the environment.

The gross motor cluster was composed of 17 items involving head and trunk control and the early stages of locomotion. It consisted mainly of items tapping variations in skill in sitting, standing, stepping, and walking. The infant's gradually developing motor abilities—to sit without support, to hold his head upright, to change his position by rolling from back to stomach, or to pull to a standing position—are also the earliest evidences of the infant's attempts to become a self-sufficient, autonomous being. From a psychological perspective these early developments reflect the infant's capacity to counter the forces of gravity, to bring himself into a position where he can see objects from different perspectives, and to control his relationship to objects through standing and walking.

The heavy weighting of gross motor items in the Psychomotor Developmental Index is attested to by the high correlation of the gross motor cluster with the Psychomotor Developmental Index ($r = 0.92$); its correlation with the Mental Developmental Index was much lower ($r = 0.59$). This cluster was also significantly related to the cognitive–motivational clusters: goal-directedness, reaching and grasping, and secondary circular reactions, (rs ranged from 0.61 to 0.68). These findings suggest that motor skills do not simply evolve through a preprogrammed maturation of the central nervous system in isolation from other areas of development; they are influenced by the infant's transactions with the environment, and they in turn are the means by which he expands his environment.

Fine Motor Development. The fine motor cluster was made up of 14 items concerned with prehensile controls, such as picking up and retaining cubes, unilateral reaching, and bringing two objects together.

The emergence of prehensile abilities is basic to the manipulation and the exploration of objects. Complementing his ability to move through space, it opens up the possibility of more precise control of his surroundings. It is the mechanism through which the infant can obtain feedback independently of his caregiver. It enables him to explore his environment and discover the properties of objects and to learn what he can do with different kinds of objects and what kinds of feedback they provide. It is basic to problem solving, to reaching around detours and using one object to obtain another. These skills contribute to the infant's sense of competence and the development of feelings that he can produce effects or can change his environment.

The highest correlation between the fine motor cluster and other clusters was with reaching and grasping ($r = 0.87$). Its relationship with goal-directedness ($r = 0.76$) underscored the interdependence of motivation and early prehensile skills. This cluster was highly correlated with both the Psychomotor Developmental Index ($r = 0.86$) and the Mental Developmental Index ($r = 0.74$), relationships that reflect the fact that fine motor items occur in both the mental and the motor scales. As with gross motor, this cluster was largely independent of social responsiveness ($r = 0.30$) and vocalization and language ($r < 0.20$).

Social Responsiveness. This cluster was composed of eight items measuring the infant's early responses to people. The infant's smiling, vocalizing, making anticipatory adjustments to being picked up, and engaging in simple play represent his first positive approaches to others. These simple behaviors are perhaps the first indications that he is aware of more than his own feelings, that he is beginning to reach out and become involved with other human beings. Like secondary circular reactions it involves obtaining feedback, but the feedback is from people rather than objects. The infant is becoming aware that human beings are responsive to his behaviors and that the variety of responses that people give far exceeds the response possibilities of inanimate objects.

At a theoretical level cognitive and social development are interrelated. The infant's ability to recognize his mother and discriminate her from other people is dependent on his capacity for perceptual discrimination. He must also have rudimentary memory in order to retain the image of the mother and compare her with other people. His differentiation of himself from his mother signals the beginnings of autonomy. Moreover the quality of his responses to other people, the vigor of his smiles and approach movements, influence his mother's and other persons' responses to him. He begins to associate his actions with effects on other people.

The high correlation between social responsiveness and the Mental Developmental Index ($r = 0.71$) probably reflects the common psychological processes in both measures, a reaching out and responding to people and objects. On the whole, this cluster was more independent of other clusters than were the motor or cognitive–motivational ones. Correlations ranged from 0.22 to 0.61, with a median of 0.47.

Vocalization and Language. Many linguists view language as fundamental to cognitive development (e.g., Chomsky, 1959; McNeill, 1974). It is one of the earliest overt indicators of the child's use of symbols to represent concrete objects and experiences. Moreover language, at least for female infants, is one of the few measures that has been found to be predictive of later intellectual development (Bayley, 1955; Cameron *et al.*, 1967; Moore, 1967). Most standard intelligence tests beyond the infancy period are heavily weighted with measures of verbal abilities.

The cluster "vocalization and language" was composed of six items dealing with only rudimentary aspects of language. It included comprehension as reflected in the infant's responding to his name and making appropriate responses or adjustments to words, as well as the simplest expressive aspects of language, such as vocalizing attitudes and vocalizing simple syllables.

This cluster had very low relationships with all other clusters, except social responsiveness ($r = 0.61$), which probably reflects the common social character of these two measures. It had zero order relationships with Psychomotor Developmental Index and the gross and fine motor clusters. It was the cluster with the lowest correlation with the Mental Developmental Index, $r = 0.48$.

The breakdown of the global indexes of development into differentiated components emphasized the variety of behaviors that make up early infant functioning. Some groups of items, especially social responsiveness and language, were relatively independent of the others; other clusters, particularly the cognitive-motivational ones, were highly related to the Mental and Psychomotor Developmental Indexes, as well as to motor development and object permanence. Within the diversity in infant functioning there is an underlying core of psychologically related behaviors.

Interdependence of Cognition and Motivation

Theorists as diverse as David Rapaport (1951), J. McV. Hunt (1965), Peter Wolff (1960), and George Klein (1967) have commented on the interaction and interdependence of motivation and thinking from very different perspectives. However, it was only with an increased understanding of Piaget's formulations on early cognitive development that the interplay between cognition and motivation in infancy came to be recognized. The unifying theme in Piaget's (1952) discussion of infant activities is the intentionality of behavior. Pervading his descriptions of young infants is their active attempts to process stimuli and to have an impact on the environment.

Peter Wolff (1960) has clarified the central role of motivation in Piagetian theory. He pointed out, "The concept of motivation in sensorimotor theory is inextricably tied to its structural conception. . . . The schema, as the basic structural unit, and the need to function, as the motivational concept, are indissolubly linked to sensorimotor theory: all need to function results from disequilibria in structure and there is no motivation which does not refer specifically to a schematic imbalance" (p. 62). Hunt (1965), in elaborating on Piaget's ideas, discussed the notion of motivation inherent in information processing. He noted the motivational character of the infant's first orienting response to stimuli and to changes in stimulation, of his efforts to maintain perceptual contact with familiar objects, and of his shift in interest to exploring novel objects. He concluded that "a basic source of motivation is inherent within the organism's informational interaction with its circumstances" (p. 270).

We shall not attempt to discuss here the special theoretical contributions of Rapaport or Klein or to analyze their diverse and complementary views on motivation and cognition from a psychoanalytic perspective. Rather, we shall limit our discussion to the few studies in addition to ours that have relevance to the cognitive-motivational thesis in infancy.

Empirical support for the cognitive-motivational thesis comes from two factor analytic studies of the Gesell Developmental Examination at 6 months. Both studies were based on data obtained in the Fels longitudinal study. In the first investigation (Richards and Nelson, 1938) there were only 17 items (probably because the intercorrelations had to be arduously computed on a manual calulator). They found that items such as "reaches for dangling ring," "pats table," and "secures cube" had high loadings on the first factor. These items are very similar to items in our goal-directedness, secondary circular, and reaching and grasping clusters. Although Richards and Nelson recognized that the first factor accounted for a substantial proportion of the variance in test performance at this age, they clung to the conceptual biases of their time and labeled the factor "testability" or "halo effect."

Similar findings, reported 34 years later in another factor analysis of the Gesell test based on a larger sample from the Fels study (McCall *et al.*, 1972), were interpreted from a different perspective. Their first factor replicated Richards and Nelson's findings in its essential features, but it included other items of a manipulative and exploratory nature. Over half of the items with higher loadings on the first factor identified by McCall *et al.* are comparable in content to the items in our cognitive–motivational clusters. They noted that many of these items involve perceptual contingencies and speculated on the relationship of these behaviors to the development of internal control. They also pointed to a common factor of "socially uninhibited extroversion," which they believed might have a pervasive influence on the infant's performance on the test.

Further evidence of the interdependence of cognitive and motivational functions in early infancy comes from findings of a study by Matheny *et al.* (1974). These investigators analyzed the relationships between the Mental Developmental Index from the Bayley scales and ratings of behavior during the test on the Bayley Infant Behavior Record.

Several of these ratings assess characteristics similar to those in our cognitive–motivational clusters: goal-directedness, object orientation, attention span, and banging and manipulating. There are significant relationships between these variables and the Mental Developmental Index at 6 months; the range of correlations was from 0.50 to 0.79. Although these relationships were somewhat lower at later ages and were not significant at 12 months, both goal-directedness and object orientation were significantly related to the Mental Developmental Index at 18 and 24 months. The magnitudes of the relationships at 6 months were quite similar to those we found between the cognitive-motivational variables and the Mental Developmental Index. These data seem to support our view of the importance of motivation in infancy, despite the fact that the motivational variables, such as goal-directedness, were grouped in a cluster labeled "primary cognition."

Considering the different strategies employed in our study and the Fel studies—a conceptual compared to an empirical clustering—and the differences in the test items themselves, there is a notable similarity in findings. In our investigation and in the Matheny *et al.* (1974) study, motivational characteristics such as persistence, attentiveness to objects, and the desire to interact with and elicit feedback from objects were highly correlated with the Mental Developmental Index of the Bayley scales. All four investigations showed that there are common motivational components in measures of early infant development.

These findings buttress the new conception of cognition as an active process. Stimuli do not simply impinge on the young infant; he does not perceive stimuli and passively register discrepancies between a familiar and a novel stimulus. When an interesting object is placed within his visual field, he explores it with his eyes and attempts to learn about its properties through touching and manipulating it. When he discovers that an object gives some feedback, that it makes a sound or changes shape when he hits or squeezes it, he repeats the actions that elicited the responses. When he becomes aware of an obstacle in the way of his obtaining a desired object, he actively attempts to circumvent it. All these active efforts to reach out and to have an effect on the environment are indications of motivated, directed behaviors. They require some level of cognitive awareness, a capacity to process stimuli, and even the beginnings of the ability to handle symbols—for example, being able to compare the present stimulus with a stimulus to which he has been exposed a few seconds earlier, the capacity to retain an image of an object at least momentarily; all these cognitive processes are involved. But the need to reconcile discrepancies, to master the environment, and to repeat activities that produce interesting results all involve more than cognition. They require the coordination of intellect with motivation.

IMPLICATIONS FOR PREDICTION OF LATER DEVELOPMENT

Differentiation of infant functioning and recognition of the intertwining of cognition and motivation in early infancy may have implications for understanding and improving the predictive efficacy of infant tests. For a long time psychologists operated on the assumption that measures of an infant's developmental status were predictive of later intellectual functioning. Most studies, however, found low or zero order correlations between test scores in the first year of life and IQ at 5 years and beyond. It is reasonable to suppose that there might be little continuity between a single score based on a variety of early sensorimotor functions in infancy and the verbal and symbolic skills tapped by adult intelligence tests. However, if one looked at the relationship between specific early skills and specific aspects of later intelligence, there might be more meaningful bases for prediction. We might expect that certain aspects of early development would not be related to later intellectual abilities, while other aspects might be essential building blocks for later symbolic capacities.

Bayley (1955) has been explicit in her rejection of infant intelligence as a single global concept. In a review of the findings on the lack of relationship between global measures of early development and later intelligence, she observed, "these findings give little hope of our being able to measure a stable and predictable intellectual factor in the very young, I am inclined to think the major reason for this failure rests in the nature of intelligence itself. I see no reason why we should continue to think of intelligence as an integrated (or simple) entity or capacity which grows throughout childhood by steady accretions" (p. 807).

Motivational differences in infants have long been recognized, but these differences have not been appreciated for their possible predictive significance. We do not believe that these differences are to be understood as simply residing in the infant; rather, motivation represents the infant's relationship with the environment. As we have noted elsewhere in a discussion of the relations between the early environment and later development (Yarrow *et al.* 1975*b*), if the infant interacts actively with people and explores objects, a sequence of interactions may be set in motion that is in some measure self-reinforcing and self-perpetuating. "The infant affects his environment, not simply by selectively filtering stimulation through his individualized sensitivities, but also by reaching out and acting on his environment. He learns about the world through his active manipulation and exploration of inanimate objects, and he elicits stimulation from caregivers and others in his environment by his signals and the quality of his responsiveness to their responsive behavior to him." By his active exploration of objects, his initiative, and his responsiveness to people the infant exerts a powerful effect on his environment and in this sense determines the continuity of his environment. Rather than looking for continuity in isolated infant skills, we believe it is essential to identify the infant characteristics that help maintain environmental continuity.

Conclusions

There are many aspects of infant functioning that can be distinguished. These distinctions are useful in sharpening our theoretical understanding of this early period of development and compel us to appreciate the complexity of infant functioning. They provide a basis for studying selective relations between the early environment and the emergence of specific capacities in infancy. Within this differentiation we find a common core of motivational characteristics. The few studies we have reported are only a small beginning in unraveling the relations between cognition and motivation. The findings of the pervasiveness of motivational functions and their intrinsic relationship with cognitive development strongly indicate the need for a reorientation in our thinking about measurement in infancy. We must conceptualize infant development in terms other than a taxonomy of skills; we must be sensitized to the motivational components of infant abilities. This sensitivity should help in the conceptualizing of infant behavior in more dynamic terms, and ultimately it might lead to more adequate measures of infant functioning.

References

Bayley, N., 1955, On the growth of intelligence, American Psychologist, 10:805.

Bayley, N., 1969, "Bayley Scales of Infant Development: Birth to Two Years," Psychological Corp., New York.

Burt, C., 1972, Inheritance of general intelligence, American Psychologist, 27:175.

Cameron, J., Livson, N., and Bayley, N., 1967, Infant vocalizations and their relationship to mature intelligence, Science, 157:331.

Chomsky, N. A., 1959, Review of B. F. Skinner, "Verbal Behavior," Language, 35:26.

Corman, H. H., and Escalona, S. K., 1969, Stages of sensorimotor development: A replication study, Merrill–Palmer Quarterly, 15:351.

Décarie, T. G., 1965, "Intelligence and Affectivity in Early Childhood," International Universities Press, New York.

Dember, W. N., 1974, Motivation and the cognitive revolution, American Psychologist, 29:161.

Gesell, A., 1925, "The Mental Growth of the Pre-school Child," Macmillan, New York.

Guilford, J. P., 1956, The structure of intellect, Psychological Bulletin, 53:267.

Hunt, J. McV., 1965, Intrinsic motivation and its role in psychological development, in "Nebraska Symposium on Motivation," D. Levine (ed.), University of Nebraska Press, Lincoln.

Klein, G., 1967, Preemptory ideation: Structure and force in motivated ideas, in Motives and thought: Psychoanalytic essays in honor of David Rapaport, Psychological Issues, 5:(No. 18/19).

Kohen-Raz, R., 1967, Scalogram analysis of some developmental sequences of infant behavior as measured by the Bayley Infant Scale of Mental Development, Genetic Psychology Monographs, 76:3.

Matheny, A. P., Dolan, A. B., and Wilson, R. S., 1974, Bayley's Infant Behavior Record: Relations between behaviors and mental test scores, Developmental Psychology, 10:696.

McCall, R. B., Hogarty, P. S., and Hurlburt, N., 1972, Transitions in infant sensori-motor development and the prediction of childhood IQ, American Psychologist, 27:728.

McNeill, D., 1974, The development of language, in "Carmichael's Manual of Child Psychology," Vol. 1 (3rd ed.), P. H. Mussen (ed.), Wiley, New York.

Moore, T., 1967, Language and intelligence: A longitudinal study of the first eight years, Human Development, 10:88.

Piaget, J., 1952, "The Origins of Intelligence in Children," International Universities Press, New York.

Rapaport, D., 1951, Toward a theory of thinking, in "Organization and Pathology of Thought," D. Rapaport (ed.), Columbia University Press, New York.

Richards, T. W., and Nelson, V. L., 1938, Studies of mental development, II: Analysis of abilities tested at the age of six months by the Gesell Schedule, Journal of Genetic Psychology, 52:327.

Spearman, C., 1927, "The Abilities of Man," Macmillan, New York.

Uzgiris, J. C., and Hunt, J. McV., 1975, "Assessment in Infancy: Toward Ordinal Scales of Psychological Development in Infancy," University of Illinois Press, Urbana.

Wechsler, D., 1950, Cognitive, conative and non-intellective intelligence, American Psychologist, 5:78.

White, R. W., 1959, Motivation reconsidered: The concept of competence, Psychological Review, 66:297.

White, R. W., 1963, Ego and reality in psychoanalytic theory, Psychological Issues, 3(No. 11).

Wolff, P. H., 1960, The developmental psychologies of Jean Piaget and psychoanalysis, *Psychological Issues*, 2(No. 5).

Yarrow, L. J., Rubenstein, J. L., and Pedersen, F. A., 1975a, "Infant and Environment: Early Cognitive and Motivational Development," Hemisphere–Wiley, Washington, D.C.

Yarrow, L. J., Klein, R. P., Lomonaco, S., and Morgan, G. A., 1975b, Cognitive and motivational development in early childhood, *in* "Exceptional Infant," Vol. 3, B Z. Friedlander, G. M. Sterritt, and G. E. Kirk (eds.), Brunner/Mazel, New York.

Author Index

Aaronson, M. 350
Abeles, G. 296
Abramson, D. 254
Ainsworth, M. D. 83, 91, 285, 286, 289, 293
Akim, B. 293
Alden, E. R. 241, 254
Allen, D. 264, 276
Allen, L. 93
Allen, M. G. 240, 254
Alpern, G. D. 50, 52
Alvord, E. C., Jr. 257
Amatruda, C. S. 54, 61, 62, 67, 93, 224, 255
Ambrose, J. A. 368, 376
Ames, E. W. 293
Ames, L. B. 48, 52, 93
Amiel-Tison, C. 239, 254
Anastasi, A. 31, 52, 102, 120, 200, 201, 219, 220
Anderson, D. 40, 52
Anderson, M. 57
Anderson, R. B. 240, 254, 257
Anderson, R. M. 51, 52
Anthony, E. J. 255
Apgar, V. 230, 233, 235, 239, 254, 257
Appelbaum, M. I. 121, 196, 350
Arai, S. 293
Armstrong, D. A. 200, 220
Arnold, M. 376
Aschkenase, L. J. 257
Astrachan, M. A. 58
Ausubel, D. P. 305, 348

Back, E. H. 295
Badger, E. D. 349

Bailey, C. J. 235, 254
Baker, C. T. 122
Baker, P. 176, 194
Baldwin, A. L. 84, 91, 200, 216, 220, 264, 276
Baldwin, C. 264, 276
Ball, R. S. 6, 17, 28, 31, 35, 36, 38, 39, 43, 50, 57, 98, 122, 168, 190, 196
Ball, T. J. 50, 52
Ban, P. 296
Banham, K. M. 51, 52
Bard, H. 256
Bardet, C. 293
Barker, J. J. 257
Barlow, F. P. 44, 54
Barsky, D. 257
Bartels, B. 377
Barten, S. S. 276
Bass, L. G. 48, 49, 57
Bayley, N. 6, 14, 16, 29, 33–35, 37, 39, 41, 42, 48, 50, 52, 53, 55, 58, 60, 61, 65, 66, 68–70, 72, 79, 80, 83, 84, 87, 88, 91, 92, 94, 98–100, 103, 110, 120, 121, 190, 192, 194, 200, 202, 203, 220, 224, 254, 286, 293, 311, 348, 355, 357, 359, 376, 381, 392, 396, 398
Bear, R. M. 209, 221
Beckwith, L. 86, 87, 92
Bee, H. L. 348
Beintema, D. 51, 56
Bell, S. M. 51, 52, 133, 145, 161, 167, 194
Bellugi, U. 262, 265, 277, 278
Benjamin, J. A. 256

Benton, J. W. 255
Berendes, H. W. 226, 227, 254, 255
Berliner, D. C. 11, 16
Bernstein, B. 62, 92, 302, 325, 335, 346, 348
Bert, P. 236, 254
Bettelheim, B. 376
Bever, T. 276
Bierman, J. M. 77, 89, 92, 94, 255, 258, 297
Biesheuvel, S. 293
Binet, A. 19, 21, 22, 24, 25, 27, 52, 201, 206, 303, 348
Bing, E. 71, 92
Birch, H. G. 232, 256 258, 294
Birns, B. 51, 55, 143, 144, 147, 161, 281, 300, 312, 313, 348–350, 359, 376
Blank, M. 119, 120, 263, 276, 277, 326, 348
Blatz, W. E. 376
Bloom, L. 260, 269, 277
Blurton-Jones, N. G. 370, 374, 376
Bolton, T. L. 53
Borgman, R. D. 196
Bourg, M. 256
Bovet, M. C. 138, 146, 161
Bowes, W. A. 230, 231, 254
Bowlby, J. 48, 53, 83, 92, 167, 194, 321, 348
Bowman, R. E. 257
Brackbill, Y. 200, 202, 203, 220, 231, 232, 254, 255, 368, 376
Bradway, K. P. 43, 53
Braen, B. B. 46, 53

Braine, M. D. S. 241, 254, 277
Brazelton, T. B. 51, 53, 192, 194, 239, 254, 286, 288, 293
Breese, F. H. 91
Bregani, P. 294
Bridger, W. H. 314, 349
Bridges, K. B. 367, 369, 376
Brill, S. 148, 161
Brobstein, R. 368, 377
Broman, S. H. 74, 75, 81, 92, 94, 95, 104, 105, 107, 108, 121, 187–189, 192, 196, 197, 226, 239, 254, 258
Bronfenbrenner, U. 335, 348
Brooks, J. 5, 8, 17, 368, 377
Brossard, L. M. 368, 376
Brown, J. K. 235, 236, 254
Brown, R. 116, 120, 260, 262, 263, 265, 266, 268, 275, 277
Brownlee, L. 162
Brucefors, A. 64, 68, 70, 88, 92
Bruell, J. 177, 194
Bruner, J. S. 153, 161, 169, 183, 194, 295
Brunet, O. 61, 64, 92
Buhler, C. 23, 29, 30–32, 35, 39, 41, 42, 53
Burko, H. 257
Burnip, S. R. 93, 121, 256
Burt, C. 1, 2, 13, 16, 28, 53, 379, 398
Bustos, R. 254
Butler, B. V. 93
Butterfield, E. C. 305, 351
Bzoch, K. R. 51, 53

Cahen, L. S. 11, 16
Calame, A. 241, 254
Caldeyro-Barcia, R. 236, 254
Caldwell, B. M. 47, 51, 53, 337, 338, 342, 345, 348
Calhoun, J. B. 294
Cameron, J. 50, 53, 72, 88, 92, 102, 121, 392, 398
Camp, B. W. 93
Campbell, F. A. 92, 94

Campbell, H. 377
Campeau, P. L. 351
Caputo, D. V. 240, 255
Carnap, R. 200, 221
Casacuberta, C. 254
Casati, I. 130, 132, 133, 141, 161, 162
Casler, L. 83, 92
Cassady, G. 255
Castner, B. M. 93
Catalano, F. L. 50, 53
Cattell, J. 23, 24, 53
Cattell, P. 35, 41, 42, 44–45, 53, 61, 65, 67–69, 87, 92, 224, 255
Caudill, W. 290, 294
Cavanaugh, M. C. 45, 48, 53
Cesa-Bianchi, M. 294
Chaille, S. E. 27, 53
Chamberlain, M. B. 57
Chandler, M. J. 190, 196, 226, 235, 257
Charlesworth, W. R. 374, 376
Chase, H. P. 83, 92
Chatfield, C. 376
Cherry, C. 375, 376
Chess, S. 258
Chevalier-Skolnikoff, S. 367, 376
Chierici, G. 294
Chomsky, N. A. 392, 398
Chrelashviti, N. V. 265, 277
Churchill, J. A. 227, 229, 255
Clark, E. V. 261, 277
Clark, R. 260, 271, 276, 277
Clarke-Stewart, A. K. 290, 294, 325, 348
Cobos, L. F. 144, 161
Cockburn, F. 254
Cohen, I. 53
Cohen, L. B. 162
Cohig, R. 256
Cole, M. 280, 282, 283, 294
Collier, G. A. 194, 293
Collins, D. 277
Conger, J. J. 37, 221
Connor, A. 92, 255, 258
Conway, E. 231, 254, 255
Copans, S. 257
Corah, N. L. 235, 255

Corman, H. H. 17, 51, 54, 98, 129, 135, 141, 161, 290, 294, 311, 348, 381, 398
Costello, J. 327, 348
Coyer, W. E. 256
Coyle, P. K. 256
Craft, M. 255
Cravioto, J. 82, 83, 92, 294
Crissey, O. L. 43, 53
Cronbach, L. J. 9, 17
Cunningham, B. V. 39, 53

Damascelli, A. R. 294
Darwin, C. 8, 19, 22, 23, 27, 41, 53, 368, 376
Dasen, P. R. 161, 285, 294
Davis, M. 257
Dean, R. F. A. 288, 295
Décarie, T. G. 51, 53, 103, 121, 133, 141, 143, 146, 161, 367, 368, 375–377, 390, 398
De Gouger, M. W. 58
Delicardie, E. 83, 92, 294
Della Porta, V. 294
Dember, W. N. 379, 398
Denenberg, V. H. 306, 348
Dennis, W. 83, 92, 179, 181, 194, 211, 221, 292, 294, 345, 348, 368, 376
De Saix, C. 196
Deutsch, M. 305, 348
Dickson, J. 294
Dickson, M. 294
Dobzhansky, T. 170, 174, 194
Dodds, J. B. 51, 54, 63, 93
Dodgson, M. C. H. 60, 92
Dodwell, P. C. 125, 161
Dolan, A. B. 121, 398
Dolanski, E. 257
Doll, E. A. 51, 53
Drachman, R. H. 47, 51, 53
Drage, J. S. 239, 255
Drillien, C. M. 49, 54, 224, 225, 238–241, 255
Driscoll, G. P. 29, 37, 39, 54
Drummond, W. B. 21
Duncanson, J. P. 202, 221
Dunphy, D. 53
Dweck, H. S. 241, 255

Edwards, J. H. 257
Eichorn, D. H. 106, 114, 121
Eimas, P. D. 259, 275, 277
Ekman, P. 367, 376
Elkind, D. 168, 194
Elliot, H. 256
Emerson, P. E. 211, 222
Eng, M. 257
Engelmann, S. 341, 345, 348
Engen, D. G. 369, 376
Erickson, M. T. 88, 92
Erlenmeyer-Kimling, L. 79, 92
Ernhart, C. B. 255
Ervin-Tripp, S. 262, 265, 267, 274, 277
Escalona, S. K. 17, 45, 49, 51, 54, 70, 88, 93, 98, 129–130, 135, 141, 161, 224, 240, 255, 290, 294, 311, 348, 381, 398
Escarcena, L. 254
Esquirol, J. D. 20, 21, 54

Fahey, G. L. 263, 277
Falade, S. 294
Falconer, D. S. 189, 194
Falender, C. 121, 349
Fantz, R. L. 51, 54, 89, 93, 259, 275, 277
Faro, M. D. 257
Farrand, L. 23, 24, 53
Faxelius, G. 257
Feldman, C. F. 282, 294
Ferreria, A. J. 229, 255
Fiedler, M. 95, 122, 197, 258
Fillmore, E. A. 29, 34, 35, 38, 39, 50, 54
Fisher, P. D. 255
Fitzgerald, H. E. 200, 221
Fitzhardinge, P. M. 241, 255
Flavell, J. 184
Forfar, J. O. 254
Foss, B. M. 368, 376
Foster, J. C. 303, 351
Fowler, W. 213, 221, 304, 348
Fox, R. 178, 194
Fraiberg, S. H. 291, 294
Francis, S. H. 294

Frandsen, A. 44, 54
Frankenburg, W. K. 51, 54, 63, 93
Freedle, R. 322, 323, 344, 349
Freedman, A. M. 254
Freedman, D. G. 80, 89, 93, 104, 121, 165, 179, 188, 191, 192, 195, 282, 287, 294, 376
Freedman, N. C. 192, 195, 287, 294, 376
Freisen, W. 376
French, F. E. 94, 227, 255, 258, 297
Frichtl, C. 51, 54
Friedlander, B. Z. 289, 294
Frost, L. 294
Furfey, P. H. 39, 54
Furth, H. G. 141, 161

Gagné, R. M. 203, 204, 221
Gaiter, J. L. 140, 161
Gallagher, J. J. 45, 49, 54
Galton, F. 22, 54, 303
Garber, H. 121, 221, 349
Gardner, B. T. 183, 195
Gardner, R. A. 183, 195
Garrett, H. E. 202, 221
Garrison, K. C. 202, 221
Gay, J. 294
Geber, M. 192, 195, 286, 288, 295
Geismar, L. L. 300, 348
Gesell, A. 29–33, 39, 41–43, 54, 61–67, 87, 93, 98, 102, 224, 255, 355, 380, 398
Ghiselin, M. 165, 195
Giblin, P. T. 132, 161
Gibson, E. J. 260, 261, 277
Gilbert, J. A. 23, 54
Gilliland, A. R. 44–46, 54, 57
Girdany, B. R. 254
Giussi, G. 254
Gleason, J. B. 265, 277
Glick, J. A. 294
Goddard, H. H. 25–27, 41, 54, 55, 303, 348
Goffeney, B. 74, 93
Goldberg, I. D. 53

Goldberg, S. 281, 283, 285, 286, 289, 290, 295, 296, 377
Golden, M. 51, 55, 143, 144, 147, 161, 281, 300, 312, 313, 315, 317, 323, 348–350, 359, 376
Goldman, A. L. 256
Gooch, B. 92
Goodenough, F. L. 21, 23, 26–29, 43, 55, 168, 376
Goodwin, M. S. 95
Gordon, H. 295
Gordon, I. J. 330–332, 342, 345, 349
Gordon, T. 368, 376
Gottesman, I. I. 175, 177, 195
Gottfried, A. W. 140, 148, 161, 235, 255
Graham, F. K. 231, 235, 239, 255
Granoff, D. 82, 94, 291, 296
Grant, W. W. 58
Granthan-McGregor, S. M. 295
Gravem, H. 93
Greenfield, P. M. 283, 295
Griffiths, R. 35, 41, 42, 44, 46, 47, 55, 61, 63–65, 67, 93
Guilford, J. P. 15, 17, 379, 398
Gulin, L. 254
Gunders, S. M. 288, 295
Gutierrez, S. 257

Haith, M. 259, 277
Hale, G. A. 222
Hall, G. S. 26
Hallowell, D. K. 39, 44, 48, 55
Halverson, H. M. 93
Hamburg, D. A. 182, 183, 195
Harlow, H. F. 83, 93
Harms, I. E. 45, 55
Harpring, E. B. 80, 95, 104, 106, 122, 187, 190, 197
Harrington, S. 121, 221, 349
Harrison, G. A. 176, 195

Harvin, D. 256
Haviland, J. M. 7
Hayes, K. J. 182, 195
Heber, R. D. 110, 121, 211–213, 221, 327–330, 333, 339–342, 344, 345, 349
Hedvall, G. 257
Heider, F. 200, 221
Heiligenburg, W. 376
Heimer, C. B. 254
Hein, A. 289, 295
Held, R. 289, 295
Henderson, N. B. 93
Henri, V. 24, 52
Henry, B. 57
Herring, R. M. 37, 38, 55
Hess, R. D. 209, 221, 302, 325, 329, 349
Heston, L. L. 175, 177, 195
Hetzer, H. 23, 30–32, 39, 53
Hierholzer, H. M. 29, 56
Hill, K. T. 162
Hindley, C. B. 47, 48, 55, 68, 69, 73, 80, 87–90, 93, 295, 311, 349
Hix, I., Jr.256
Hodgins, A. S. 349
Hodson, W. A. 254
Hoffer, A. 254
Hoffman, C. 121, 221
Hogarty, P. S. 17, 56, 94, 121, 162, 195, 221, 350, 398
Holden, R. H. 224, 255
Holley, W. L. 229, 255
Hollingshead, A. B. 299, 349
Holmes, F. B. 368, 377
Honig, A. S. 148, 161
Honzik, M. P. 58, 62, 68, 71, 78–80, 85, 86, 88, 92, 93, 95, 102, 121, 122, 236, 256, 258
Hooff, J. van 367, 376
Horner, F. 256
Horrocks, J. E. 47, 55
Howe, L. P. 255
Hubbell, M. 162
Humphrey, G. 21
Humphrey, M. 21
Hunt, J. 5, 14, 108, 224, 239, 242, 243, 256

Hunt, J. McV. 17, 50, 51, 55, 57, 61, 94, 97, 98, 114, 121, 122, 126, 131, 132, 140, 141, 145, 146, 161–163, 209, 210, 213, 221, 304, 306, 311, 326, 349–351, 381, 393, 398
Hurlburt, N. 17, 56, 94, 121, 221, 162, 350, 398
Husband, R. W. 202, 221
Hutchings, J. J. 93, 121, 256
Hutt, C. 117, 121

Ilg, F. L. 93
Illingworth, R. S. 48, 50, 55, 77, 93
Inhelder, B. 124, 149, 161, 162
Ireton, H. 93
Isaacs, S. 263, 278
Ishikawa, J. 293
Itard, J. G. 21, 55
Izard, C. 377

James, L. S. 246, 256
Jankowski, J. J. 95, 351
Janoff, I. E. 58
Jarvik, L. F. 92
Jastrow, J. 23, 55
Jelliffe, D. B. 295
Jensen, A. R. 105, 106, 121, 306, 349
Jersild, A. T. 368, 377
Johannesson, I. 92
Johnson, N. M. 92
Jones, E. 16
Jordan, T. E. 226, 237, 256
Juscyk, P. 277

Kagan, J. 55, 72, 84, 88, 90, 94, 102, 121, 180, 195, 221, 259, 278, 280, 283, 295, 308, 324, 344, 345, 349, 350
Kalhorn, J. 91
Kamin, L. F. 13, 17, 303, 349
Kane, J. 254
Kaplan, B. J. 291, 295
Karlberg, P. 92
Karnes, M. B. 333, 349
Katz, P. A. 317, 349

Kaye, H. 376
Keller, B. 80, 89, 93, 104, 121, 188, 195
Kelsey, F. O. 230, 256
Kemp, D. H. 255, 258
Kennedy, D. 256
Kennedy, W. A. 92, 254
Kessen, R. 277
Kessen, W. 260, 278
Khatri, A. A. 295
Kilbride, J. E. 285, 295
Kilbride, P. L. 285, 295
King, W. L. 3, 17, 139, 140–142, 147, 161
Kitano, H. 295
Klackenberg-Larsson, I. 64, 68, 69, 73, 92, 94
Klein, G. 393, 394, 398
Klein, R. E. 84, 94, 162, 180, 195, 222, 283, 295, 345, 349
Klein, R. P. 399
Klima, S. 262, 265, 278
Knobloch, H. 48, 49, 55, 76, 94, 192, 195, 225, 256, 311, 350
Kohen-Raz, R. 140, 161, 295, 381, 398
Kohs, S. C. 57
Koltsova, M. M. 200, 202, 203, 220, 317, 318, 349
Konner, M. J. 295
Koontz, C. W. 51, 56
Kopp, C. B. 134, 135, 138, 140, 146, 161, 162, 168, 195
Korner, A. F. 256, 368, 377
Koslowsky, B. 293
Kotelchuck, M. 162
Kraemer, H. C. 231, 256
Kraepelin, E. 23, 56
Kreutzer, M. A. 374, 376
Krippner, S. 295
Kuenne, M. R. 278
Kugel, R. B. 58
Kuhlmann, F. 25–28, 33, 56

LaBarre, W. 171, 172, 195
Labov, W. 281, 295
LaSorte, M. A. 300, 348
Latham, M. C. 161

Laurendeau, M. 125, 162
Leacock, E. B. 307, 349
League, R. 51, 53
Leckie, M. S. 348
Lee, B. 294
Leech, R. W. 257
Lee-Painter, S. 5, 17
Lehrman, D. 170, 195
Leiderman, G. I. 286, 287, 296
Leiderman, P. H. 286, 287, 296
Lemon, R. E. 376
Lemond, C. M. 377
Lennenberg, E. 278
Lester, B. M. 144, 162
Levenstein, P. 335–337, 339–341, 345, 349, 350
Levenstein, S. 350
LeVine, R. A. 279, 296
Lewis, M. 4–6, 8, 17, 52, 56, 89, 90, 94, 99, 110, 121, 141, 142, 147, 162, 190, 195, 205, 221, 280, 289, 296, 309, 310, 320, 322, 323, 344, 349, 350, 368, 377
Lewis, M. M. 263, 265, 273, 278
Lewis, O. 307, 349
Lézine, I. 130–134, 137, 138, 141, 146, 159, 161, 162
Lézine, P. U. F. 61, 64, 92
Lichenstein, H. 92
Linfert, H. E. 29, 56
Lipsitt, L. P. 179, 195, 200, 202, 221, 376
Lipton, E. L. 368, 377
Little, A. 61
Livson, N. 53, 92, 121, 398
Lomonaco, S. 399
Lubchenco, L. O. 239, 241, 256
Luria, A. R. 275, 278, 319, 350
Lusk, D. 296

McCall, R. B. 3, 4, 6, 17, 48, 56, 73, 94, 100–102, 104–108, 110–113, 121, 151, 162, 187–190, 195, 196,

201, 203, 204, 221, 300, 350, 394, 398
McCarthy, D. 50, 53
McClearn, G. E. 168, 196
MacCorquodale, K. 200, 221
MacFarlane, J. W. 48, 56, 93
McFie, J. 293
McGraw, M. B. 44, 56
McGurk, H. 4, 17, 90, 94, 99, 110, 121, 141, 142, 147, 162, 190, 195, 349
McHugh, G. 44, 56
McIntosh, R. 254
McIntyre, C. 256
McKeown, T. 226, 229, 256, 257
McKhann, G. M. 223, 256
McLain, R. E. 162
McLean, F. 258
McNamara, J. 260, 278
McNeill, D. 115, 121, 261, 278, 392, 398
MacRae, J. M. 49, 56, 76, 94
Madden, J. 336, 339, 350
Mahler, M. S. 366, 377
Mallardi, A. 294
Malone, C. A. 312, 350
Mandelkorn, T. 254
Mandell, W. 240, 255
Manheimer, H. 95
Manniello, R. L. 254
Maratos, O. 132, 162
Marcus, M. 92
Marolla, F. 297
Martin, H. P. 83, 92
Masse, G. 293
Matheny, A. P. 52, 99, 103, 121, 394, 395, 398
Mayr, E. 171–174, 195
Mead, M. 287, 296
Mecham, M. J. 51, 56
Meehl, P. E. 200, 221
Mehrabian, A. 133, 162
Mendelson, M. A. 226, 256
Mendez-Bauer, C. 254
Merrill, M. A. 313, 350
Messer, S. G. 309, 350
Metcalf, D. 256
Michalson, L. 52, 56
Middleton, M. R. 294
Miles, M. 52

Miller, D. J. 136, 162
Miller, E. 16
Miller, L. K. 222
Miller, S. M. 300, 350
Millichamp, D. A. 376
Milowe, I. D. 95
Mönckeberg, F. 83, 94
Montague, A. 230, 256
Montare, A. 314, 349, 350
Montemagni, G. 297
Moodie, W. 16
Moore, T. 56, 72, 85, 94, 102, 121, 392, 398
Moreau, T. 232, 256
Moreigne, E. 293
Morgan, G. A. 399
Moriarty, A. 45, 49, 54
Moss, A. 314, 349, 350
Motulsky, A. G. 172, 176, 196
Moyles, E. W. 296
Muehlenbein, J. 39, 54
Munroe, R. H. 279, 285, 288, 291, 292, 296
Munroe, R. L. 279, 285, 288, 291, 292, 296
Munsterberg, H. 23, 56
Murray, J. R. 294
Mussen, P. H. 114, 200, 221
Myers, B. J. 58
Myers, R. E. 234, 256

Najarian, P. 83, 92
Nataupsky, M. 281, 296
Nelson, K. 260, 275, 278
Nelson, V. L. 38–40, 50, 56, 69, 94, 122, 394, 398
Nevis, S. 51, 54, 89, 93
Nichols, P. L. 81, 92, 94, 104, 105, 107, 108, 121, 187–189, 192, 196, 254
Nicholson, J. E. 94
Nissen, C. H. 182, 195
Nyman, B. A. 348

Odom, R. D. 202, 222, 377
Omenn, G. S. 172, 176, 196
Outerbridge, E. W. 239, 256
Overton, W. 8, 17

Painter, G. 332, 333, 350

Painter, P. 255
Palmer, F. H. 338, 342, 345, 350
Paraskevopoulos, J. 140, 141, 145, 146, 161, 162
Parkin, J. M. 288, 297
Parks, C. R. 254
Parmelee, A. H. 161, 162, 242, 257
Pasamanick, B. 48, 49, 55, 76, 94, 192, 195, 225, 256, 311, 350
Pavenstedt, E. 300, 312, 350
Pedersen, F. A. 7, 95, 351, 399
Penney, R. E. C. 294
Peterson, J. 20, 21, 23, 24, 26, 56
Peterson, L. W. 51, 54
Petit, C. 185, 196
Phatak, P. 296
Piaget, J. 7, 8, 51, 61, 98, 113–116, 122–128, 130–134, 136, 137, 149–151, 155, 159, 160, 162, 165, 167, 169, 185, 191, 196, 200, 204, 221, 259, 263, 273, 278, 282, 283, 301, 302, 310, 311, 343, 344, 347, 350, 354, 355, 359, 360–364, 377, 380, 381, 389, 393, 398
Pick, A. D. 191, 196
Pillemer, D. B. 294
Pinard, A. 125, 162
Polansky, N. A. 196
Pollin, W. 254
Pollitt, E. 82, 94, 291, 296
Porges, S. W. 200, 221
Porteus, S. D. 284, 296
Prechtl, H. 51, 56
Premack, D. 168, 196
Preyer, W. 19, 23, 41, 56
Price-Williams, D. 284, 296
Prod'hom, L. S. 241, 254
Purvis, R. J. 254

Quimby, K. L. 224, 257

Rabin, A. I. 296
Ramarosa, Z. 296

Ramey, C. T. 89, 94
Ramsay, M. 241, 255, 256
Rapaport, D. 379, 393, 394, 398
Rawlings, G. 241, 257
Raynor, R. 368, 377
Rebelsky, F. G. 279, 283, 286, 289, 296
Record, R. G. 226, 229, 256, 257
Reed, H. 256
Reynolds, E. O. R. 257
Rheingold, H. L. 84, 94, 211, 221
Rhodes, L. 92
Ricciuti, H. N. 51, 56
Richards, T. W. 38–40, 50, 56, 69, 94, 394, 398
Richmond, J. B. 377
Riess, A. 58
Ringwall, E. A. 51, 53, 56
Robbins, M. C. 295
Roberts, J. A. F. 47, 56
Robey, J. S. 194, 293
Robles, B. 82, 92, 294
Rosales, L. 294
Rosch, E. H. 278
Rosenbaum, A. L. 255
Rosenblith, J. F. 51, 57, 239, 240, 254, 257
Rosenblum, L. 8, 17
Rosenzweig, M. R. 224, 257
Rossman, E. 314, 324, 350
Rovee, C. K. 113, 122
Rovee, D. T. 113, 122
Rubenstein, J. L. 95, 289, 296, 351, 399
Russell, E. C. 58
Ryle, G. 200, 221

Saenger, G. 297
Sameroff, A. J. 190, 196, 200, 204, 221, 226, 235, 257
Saxon, S. A. 255
Sayegh, Y. 211, 221
Scarr-Salapatek, S. 9, 17, 106, 122, 190, 196, 240, 257
Schacter, F. F. 235, 257
Schaefer, E. S. 70, 83, 84, 87, 88, 92, 103, 120, 306,

325, 326, 334, 335, 339, 340, 350
Schaffer, H. R. 200, 211, 222
Schickedanz, D. 161
Schlesinger, I. M. 278
Schulte, F. J. 242, 257
Sebigajju, E. 293
Sechzer, J. A. 224, 257
Sedgley, E. 47, 56
Seegmiller, B. 3, 17, 139, 140–142, 147, 161
Seguin, E. 21, 57
Seligman, M. E. P. 179, 196
Sellers, M. J. 162
Senecal, M. J. 293
Serafica, F. C. 146, 162
Shaperman, J. 168, 195
Sharp, D. W. 294
Sharp, S. E. 24, 57
Sherwood, J. J. 281, 296
Shinn, M. 23, 57
Shipman, V. 302, 325, 329, 349
Shirley, M. 23, 29, 32, 33, 35, 37, 57
Shotwell, A. M. 44, 45, 57
Sigman, M. 161, 162
Silverman, W. A. 236, 257
Silverstein, A. B. 140, 162
Simon, A. J. 48, 49, 57
Simon, T. 19, 21, 22, 25, 52, 57
Simpson, B. R. 43, 57
Simrall, D. 202, 206, 219, 222
Sinclair, H. 260, 275, 278
Siqueland, E. R. 113, 122, 277
Skeels, H. M. 76, 80, 94, 292, 296, 297, 345, 350
Skodak, M. 43, 57, 76, 80, 94
Slobin, D. I. 260, 278
Smith, B. J. 196
Smith, D. M. 256
Smith, R. S. 58, 95, 122, 258
Snow, C. E. 265, 278
Solomon, F. 263, 277
Sontag, L. W. 100, 122
Soule, B. 240, 257
Spaner, S. D. 237, 256
Spearman, C. 379, 398
Spelke, E. 162

Sperry, R. W. 186, 196
Spitz, R. A. 377
Sroufe, L. A. 368, 377
Stahlman, M. T. 239, 257
Stake, R. E. 202, 222
Stambak, M. 162
Standley, K. 257
Stare, F. J. 161
Starr, R. 209, 222
Stein, Z. 292, 297
Steinschneider, A. 254, 368, 377
Stensson, J. 64, 68, 69, 73, 94
Stern, J. A. 255
Stern, L. 256
Stern, W. 23, 57, 278
Stevenson, H. W. 200–202, 220, 222
Stewart, A. 257
Stockbridge, F. P. 28, 57
Stott, L. H. 6, 17, 28, 31, 35, 36, 38, 39, 43, 50, 57, 98, 122, 168, 190, 196
Strang, L. B. 257
Strayer, G. D. 26, 57
Streissguth, A. P. 348
Stutsman, R. 33, 57
Sumi, S. M. 223. 257
Susser, M. 297
Svenberg, I. 92
Symmes, E. 48, 57

Tagiuri, R. 297
Tallmadge, G. K. 351
Tanner, J. M. 292, 297
Taylor, H. C. 254
Terman, L. M. 21, 26, 27, 57, 303, 313, 350
Tesi, G. 297
Teska, J. A. 349
Thoman, E. B. 256
Thomas, A. 240, 258
Thomas, H. 6, 17, 34, 46, 47, 49, 57
Thompson, C. A. 294
Thompson, H. 30, 54, 93
Thompson, J. 367, 377
Thorndike, R. L. 38, 57
Thurston, D. L. 255
Thwing, E. 93
Tompkins, S. 375–377

Tooley, W. H. 223, 256
Toshima, K. 293
Trabue, M. R. 28, 57
Tronek, E. 293
Tuddenham, R. D. 125, 162
Tulkin, S. R. 297, 307–309, 320, 324, 344, 350

Ucko, L. E. 79, 94
Ueland, K. 257
Usher, R. 243, 258
Uzgiris, I. C. 3, 17, 51, 57, 61, 94, 98, 122, 131, 132, 135, 139–142, 146, 150, 151, 159, 161–163, 311, 350, 351, 381, 398

Vaage, M. 92
Vale, C. A. 173, 196
Vale, J. R. 173, 196
Valentine, C. W. 368, 377
Van Egeren, L. F. 348
Van Lawick-Goodall, J. 182, 196
Van Natta, P. A. 93
Vega, L. 294
Vigorito, J. 277
Vouilloux, P. 297
Vygotsky, L. 278

Wachs, T. D. 103, 104, 122, 144–146, 148, 163, 187, 196, 310, 320, 351
Waddington, C. H. 173, 180, 189, 196
Wallin, J. E. W. 33, 57
Wargo, M. J. 335, 351
Warren, N. 191, 197, 285, 288, 297
Waters, E. 368, 377
Watson, J. B. 33, 57, 208–210, 222, 368, 369, 377
Watson, J. S. 113, 122, 206, 208, 222, 283, 289, 297
Watson, R. R. 33, 57
Wechsler, D. 17, 379, 398
Weiner, J. 194
Weinraub, M. 5
Weinstein, H. 290, 294
Weissman, D. 200, 222
Wellman, B. L. 43, 57, 58

Wennberg, R. P. 254
Werner, E. E. 37, 49, 58, 66, 77, 78, 94, 95, 102, 122, 224, 227, 228, 258 285, 291, 297
Wesman, A. G. 282, 297
White, B. L. 181, 197 211–213, 220, 222, 311 326, 351
White, R. W. 117, 122, 385, 398
Whiting, B. B. 279, 297
Whiting, J. W. M. 279, 288, 295, 297
Wier, R. 263, 278
Willerman, L. 75, 95, 122, 190, 197, 225, 258
Williams, M. L. 133, 162, 240, 257
Wilson, C. D. 280, 296, 310, 322
Wilson, R. S. 80, 95, 99, 104, 106, 107, 121, 122, 186–190, 197, 398
Windle, W. F. 233, 236, 257, 258
Winick, M. 59, 95
Wisdom, S. S. 289, 294
Wissler, C. L. 24, 58
Wittenborn, J. R. 36, 43, 58
Wober, M. 284, 297
Wohlwill, J. F. 98, 112, 122
Wolff, P. H. 368, 377, 393, 399
Wolff, R. M. 377
Wolins, M. 296
Woodrum, D. E. 254
Woodward, M. 137, 163
Wortis, H. 254

Yarrow, L. J. 7, 83, 86, 87, 90, 95, 322, 326, 351, 380, 397, 399
Yerkes, R. M. 303, 351
Yerushalmy, J. 227, 258
Young, G. 367, 375, 377
Young, H. B. 297
Yudovich, F. 275

Zachry, W. 138, 159, 163
Zelazo, P. R. 179, 197
Zigler, E. 305, 351

Subject Index

Abbreviated screening tests, use of, 61
Abnormalcy, 48–49, 51, 76–79, 88, 110. *See also* Environmental risk, fetal and neonatal; Retardation, mental
Academic performance, 5–8
Activity level, significance of, 70–71
"Actual ability," 200
Adopted child, the
    screening of, 36, 39, 45–46, 49
    studies of, 76, 80, 86–87, 90, 106
Affect, 353–377. *See also* Personal-social competency
    absence of, 360–364, 375
    development of, 369–375
    nature and meaning of, 367–375
    Piagetian uses of, 360–364, 375
Albert Einstein Scales of Sensorimotor Development, 128–130
Alpern and Ball's Developmental Profile, 50
Ape, development of young, 182–184. *See also* Evolutionary perspective; Primates, similarities among
Apgar scale, 239, 243–246
Aptitude–treatment interaction, 11
Attentiveness, 89–90, 309–310
Autistic child, 366–367

Baby Tests, Buhler, 31–32, 37–40
Bayley, N. (California First-Year Mental Scale), 4, 29, 33–39, 50, 61–62, 65–72, 82, 98, 354–357, 381–393
Bell sensorimotor scales, 51
Berkeley Growth Study, 33–34, 66, 68, 71, 103, 114–115
Biases, learning, 178–180

Binet Scales
    Binet–Simon scale, 28
    Kuhlmann–Binet scale, 28–29, 37–39
    L'Année Psychologique, 24
    1905 scale, 24–27
    1908 scale, 26–27
    1911 scale, 27
    Stanford–Binet scale, 26–27, 38–40, 45, 48, 50
Brain
    environmental risk to, 223–258
    size and growth of, 59–60, 171–172
Brazelton scale, 239–240
Brunet–Lézine test, 61, 64, 68–69, 71–72
Buhler Baby Tests, 29, 31–32, 37–40
Bzoch–League Receptive-Expressive Language Scale, 51

Caldwell's Children's Center (Syracuse University), 337–338
California First-Year Mental Scale (Bayley), 4, 29, 33–39, 50, 61–62, 65–72, 82, 98, 354–357, 381–393
Canalization, 173–194. *See also* Evolutionary perspective
Capacity, latent and manifest, 216–220
Casati–Lézine Scale, 130–131
Child-rearing practices
    cross-cultural studies of, 180–181, 191–193, 285–293
    within social class, 299–351
Chromosomal studies, 79. *See also* Evolutionary perspective; Genetic studies; Heritability
Collaborative Project, 74–75, 226–228, 239–240
Communicative Evaluation Chart from Infancy to Five Years, 51

Composite Developmental Inventory for Infants and Young Children, 51
Compulsory education, 26
Concept-formation approach, 275–276. *See also* Why, use of
Concept-matching, 275–276. *See also* Why, use of
Cord complication, 227. *See also* Environmental risk, fetal and neonatal
Corman and Escalona sensorimotor scales, 4, 51
Creativity, 8, 50
Cross-age correlation. *See* Interage correlation
Cross-cultural studies, 191–193, 279–297
   concept of intelligence as a factor, 281–284
   second-year shifts across cultures, 291–293
   Western and non-Western cultural differences, 285–293
Culture, pressures of, 168, 285–293

Day-care setting, 52, 337–338. *See also* Intervention programs
DDST. *See* Denver Developmental Screening Test
Décarie sensorimotor scales, 51
Delivery. *See also* Environmental risk, fetal and neonatal
   drug risk during, 230–232
   Western and non-Western differences in, 287–288
Denver Developmental Screening Test (DDST), 51, 61, 63
Deprivation effects
   environmental, 180–181, 307–351
   institutional, 83–84, 321–322
   maternal, 83–84
   oxygen, 232–236
Developmental adaptation, 173–194. *See also* Evolutionary perspective
Developmental quotient (DQ), 62–63, 103
Diabetic mother, the, 227. *See also* Environmental risk, fetal and neonatal
Diagnosis, test value in, 36, 61, 67, 89–91
Diet. *See* Nutrition
Drugs, of labor and delivery, 230–232. *See also* Environmental risk, fetal and neonatal

Education. *See also* Intervention programs
   compulsory, 26
   of retarded, 21
   within social classes, 304–351
   special, 21–22, 26
Environmental risk, fetal and neonatal, 223–258, 287
   drugs of labor and delivery, 230–232
   oxygen deprivation, 232–236
   pre-term infant, 240–252
Environmental stimulation, 8–15, 41, 43–44, 70–71, 80–89, 103–110
   cross-cultural differences in, 285–293
   evolutionary perspective of, 165–197
   of sensorimotor intelligence, 143–146
   within social class, 299–351
Epigenetic concept, 97–122. *See also* Sensorimotor intelligence, development of
Ethology, influence of, 8
Evolutionary perspective, 22–23
   canalization, 173–194
   developmental adaptation, 173–194
   group differences, 191–193
   individual level, 186–191
   primates, similarities among, 165–197
   sensorimotor period, 167–169
   species-specific behavior, 176–178
Experience, 11, 14, 82–89. *See also* Environmental risk, fetal and neonatal; Environmental stimulation; Parent-child interaction
   cross-cultural, 285–293
   educational, 9, 12
   home, 9, 70–71, 80
   learning, 199–222

Facial expression. *See* Affect
Fantz–Nevis Visual Preference Test, 51
Father, role of, 71. *See also* Parent-child interaction
Fels Longitudinal Study, 112–120
Fetus
   environmental risk to, 223–258, 287
   in Western and non-Western societies, 287
Fixed intelligence, concept of, 1–4, 13–15, 41, 43–44, 64, 97–98. *See also* Concept of intelligence

Frichtl–Peterson Tool for the Assessment of Motor Skills, 51
Full-term infant, environmental risk to, 223–258

Genetic studies, 79–82, 103–107. *See also* Heritability; Siblings, studies of; Twins, studies of
  genetic myth, 15–16
  genetic pool, 9–10, 15, 165–197
  genetic variability, 165–197
Genevan school, 3
Gesell (Arnold) Developmental Schedules, 3–4, 29–31, 35, 37–41, 43–46, 48, 61–65, 68–69, 71–72, 82, 98, 102–103
g factor, 1–4, 13–15. *See also* Intelligence, concept of Intelligence, fixed
Golden and Birns sensorimotor scales, 51
Graham/Rosenblith Behavioral Examination of Neonates, 51, 239–240
Griffiths (Ruth) Scale of Mental Development, 35, 46–47, 61, 63–64, 68–69, 71–72
Group differences, 191–193. *See also* Cross-cultural studies
Growth
  in brain size, 59–60, 171–172
  somatic, 59–61, 171–172

Harlem Research Center, 338–339
Harvard School of Public Health, 65
Harvard University Center for Research in Child Health and Development, 44–45
Head Start, 305–306, 326. *See also* Intervention programs
Heredity-environment issue, 303–304, 306
Heritability, 9–10, 15, 79–82, 103–110, 165–197, 303–304, 306. *See also* Genetic studies; Siblings, studies of; Twins, studies of
Heritability index, 9–10
Hollingshead's Two-Factor Index of Social Position, 299

Idiocy, 19–20
Individual differences, 186–191. *See also* Evolutionary perspective

Infant tests
  history, of infant testing, 19–58
    early developments in, 19–24
    recent trends and issues in, 47–58
    value of, 59–95, 110–111
Insanity, 19–21
Institutional care, effect of, 83–84, 321–322
Intelligence
  Concept of intelligence, 1–4, 8, 13 15, 27, 281–284, 379. *See also* Fixed intelligence
  Constancy of intelligence. *See* Fixed intelligence
  Sociopolitical question, 1–17
Interage correlation, 68–74, 87–102, 106
Intervention programs, 10–15, 305–306, 326–343
Iowa Tests for Young Children, 34–35, 37–39, 43

Kauai Pregnancy Study, 77–78, 227–228
Koontz Child Development Program, 51
Kuhlmann–Binet scale, 28–29, 37–39
Kuhlmann Tests of Mental Development, 29

Labor. *See* Delivery; Environmental risk, fetal and neonatal
Language development, 4, 20–21, 30–31, 46, 51, 178–180, 392–393. *See also* Vocalization
  concepts and, 274–276
  question words in, 259–278
  sensorimotor behavior and, 115–120
  within social class, 302, 316–325, 344–345
L'Année Psychologique, 24
Latent capacity, 216–220
Learning, 199–222
  biases in, 178–180
  as a determinant of intelligence, 208–213
  intelligence as factor in, 201–208
  predictive value of, 214–220
  question words and, 259–278
Learning ability, "actual" and "potential," 200

Limitations, test, 59–95, 110–111
  Brunét–Lézine test, 64, 68–69, 71–72
  California First-Year Mental Scale (Bayley), 65–66, 68–69, 71–72, 82
  Cattell infant scale, 65, 68–69
  Gessell Developmental Schedules, 62–65, 68–69, 71–72, 82
  Griffiths Scale of Mental Development, 63–64, 68–69, 71–72
Linfert-Hierholzer baby test, 38–40
Louisville Twin Study, 104. See also Twins, studies of

Malnutrition, effect of, 82–83
Manifest capacity, 216–220
Manual skills, 50
Maturation process, belief in, 43–44
Meaning, acquisition of, 259–278
Measurement of Social Competence, 51
Memory, 8, 50, 120
Mentimeter, 28
Merrill–Palmer scale, 39–40, 50
Milwaukee Project (Heber), 110
Minnesota Infant Study, 32–33, 37–38
Mirror response, 141–142
Mother, 170–171
  absence of, 83–84
  behavior of, 70–71, 84–86, 172
  diabetic, 227
  and social class, 320–326
  and son, 70–71, 84–86
  Western and non-Western, 285–293
Motivation, and cognition, 379–399
Multiple regression, 49

Natural selection, 165–197
Nature-of-intelligence controversy, 35–36
Nature–nurture controversy, 8–15
Neonatal Behavioral Assessment Scale, 51
Neonate
  environmental risk to, 223–258, 287
  Western and non-Western, 285, 293
Newborn. See Neonate
Normative ages, 41–42
Northwestern Intelligence Test, 45–46
Nutrition, 9, 12, 82–83, 287

Object permanence capability, 4, 10, 15, 389–390
Oxygen deprivation, 232–236. See also Environmental risk, fetal and neonatal

Parent and Child Centers, 326–327
Parent–child interaction, 103, 107–108, 153
  father in, 71
  mother in, 70–71, 83–86, 170–172, 227, 285–293
  within social class, 299–351
PDI. See Psychomotor development index
Peabody Picture Vocabulary Test, 4, 10
Perceptual–cognitive behavior, 115–120
Personal–social competency, 30–31, 51–52, 103, 391–392. See also Affect
Phenotypic variability, 172–176
Point scales, 33
"Potential ability," 200
Prechtl's Neurological Examination, 51
Prediction, IQ, 4–6, 34–35, 38–40, 45, 48–50, 52, 66–71, 73–76, 87–88, 91, 101–103, 110, 236–238, 396–397
Pre-linguistic Infant Vocalization Analysis, 51
Preterm infant, environmental risk to, 240–252
Primates, similarities among, 165–197
Psychomotor development index (PDI), 63

Question words, use of, 259–278

Racial function, 9, 15, 300
Reflex, 126
Retardation, mental, 19–22, 51, 76–77, 81–83, 105, 107–108, 110, 180–181, 327–330, 345
Riccuti's Object Grouping and Selective Ordering Tasks, 51
Ring and Peg Tests of Behavior Development, 51

School-age children, testing of, 26
School performance, 5–8

Selection, natural, 165–197
Sensation, psychology of, 23
Sensorimotor intelligence, 3–4, 15, 51, 115–120, 123–163.
  age progression in, 141–143
  assessment of, 128–134
  compared to other measures, 146–149
  domains in, 136–140
  environmental influence on, 143–146, 279–297, 299–351
  levels in, 149–158
  nature of, 167–169
Sex differences, 70–75, 87–88, 101–102, 244–245, 300
Shield Speech and Language Developmental Scale, 51
Siblings, studies of, 104–108, 186–190. See also Twins, studies of
Social class, 299–351. See also Environmental Stimulation
  behavior differences within, 308–320
  intervention programs compensating for, 326–343
  mother–child interaction within, 320–326
Social hierarchy, 15–16
Socioeconomic conditions, 5, 8–16, 75–76, 85–86, 102, 107. See also Environmental Stimulation; social class
Somatic growth, 59–60, 171–172
Special education, 21–22, 26. See also Intervention programs
Species-specific behavior, 176–178. See also Evolutionary perspective
Speech, 46. See also Language development; Vocalization
Speech quotient, 72–73
Stanford–Binet scale, 26–27, 38–40, 45, 48, 50
St. Louis Baby Study, 237–238
Stockholm longitudinal study, 64, 68–69
Subject–treatment interaction, 11–12

Syracuse University (Caldwell's Children's Center), 337–338

Thalidomide, effect of, 230. See also Environmental risk, fetal and neonatal
Twins, studies of, 80–82, 104–108, 186–190, 229–230. See also Siblings, studies of
Two-Factor Index of Social Position (Hollingshead), 299

Unitary intelligence. See Fixed intelligence, concept of
Uzgiris and Hunt sensorimotor scales, 3–4, 51, 61, 131–133

Verbal Language Development Scale, 51
Viennese Series, 31–32
Vocabulary, 72. See also Language development
Vocalization, 72–73, 102, 119, 322–323, 344, 392–393. See also Language development

WAIS. See Wechsler Adult Intelligence Scale
War on Poverty, 304–305. See also Intervention programs
Wechsler Adult Intelligence Scale (WAIS), 2–3
Wechsler Intelligence Scale for Children (WISC), 2–3, 45, 74–75
Weight, birth, 227, 230, 244, 245. See also Environmental risk, fetal and neonatal
Why, use of, 259–278
WISC. See Wechsler Intelligence Scale for Children

Yale Clinic of Child Development, 29–31
Yorkes, Bridges, and Hardwick Point Scale, 28